A Jewish Voice from Ottoman Salonica

Stanford Studies in Jewish History and Culture

EDITED BY *Aron Rodrigue and Steven J. Zipperstein*

A Jewish Voice from Ottoman Salonica

The Ladino Memoir of Sa'adi Besalel a-Levi

Edited and with an Introduction

by Aron Rodrigue and Sarah Abrevaya Stein

Translation, Transliteration, and Glossary

by Isaac Jerusalmi

STANFORD UNIVERSITY PRESS

STANFORD, CALIFORNIA

Stanford University Press
Stanford, California

The original *soletreo* text of Sa'adi Besalel a-Levi's memoir is posted in its entirety online: http://www.sup.org/book.cgi?id=18553

Printed in the United States of America on acid-free, archival-quality paper

Library of Congress Cataloging-in-Publication Data

Halevi, Sa'adi ben Betsalel, author.
A Jewish voice from Ottoman Salonica : the Ladino memoir of Sa'adi Besalel a-Levi ; edited and with an introduction by Aron Rodrigue and Sarah Abrevaya Stein ; translation, transliteration, and glossary by Isaac Jerusalmi.
pages cm.–(Stanford studies in Jewish history and culture)
Includes bibliographical references and index.
English with Ladino romanized text and English translation.
ISBN 978-0-8047-7166-5 (cloth : alk. paper)
1. Halevi, Sa'adi ben Betsalel. 2. Jewish publishers–Greece–Thessalonike–Biography. 3. Jewish journalists–Greece–Thessalonike–Biography. 4. Sephardim–Greece–Thessalonike–History–19th century. I. Rodrigue, Aron, editor. II. Stein, Sarah Abrevaya, editor. III. Jerusalmi, Isaac, 1928- translator, transcriber. IV. Title. V. Series: Stanford studies in Jewish history and culture.
DS135.G73H35 2012
305.892'404954–dc23 2011036183

Typeset by Bruce Lundquist in 10.5/14 Galliard

Contents

Editors' Acknowledgments vii
Note on Translation and Transliteration ix
Note on Currencies, Weights, and Measures xi
Note on Sigla Used in the Ladino Romanized Text and English Translation xii
Editors' Introduction xiii

The Memoir of Sa'adi Besalel a-Levi
English Translation 3
Romanized Transliteration 149

Notes 295
Glossary 297
Works Consulted 357
Index 363

Editors' Acknowledgments

Working with a century-old memoir that has iconic stature among scholars of Sephardic history, despite its never having been published in full before this moment, has been a stimulating and poignant experience. The editors have many friends and colleagues who generously donated critical commentary, expertise, and time to this project.

Isaac Jerusalmi gave himself fully to this book for several years. It could not have been realized without his deep knowledge of Ladino and Sephardic culture, extraordinary erudition, and fierce commitment to scholarly inquiry. Nimet Hananel Jerusalmi worked indefatigably together with her husband, Isaac, at all stages of the transliteration and translation as a full partner in this endeavor. Her contribution was truly invaluable.

A number of colleagues were generous enough to read and carefully comment on this manuscript and offer their help. Olga Borovaya offered important insights on Sa'adi's life and career and on the development of Ladino print culture; we are enormously appreciative of her erudition, generosity, and unmatched attention to detail. Matthias Lehmann offered perspicacious suggestions regarding our handling of Sa'adi's conflicts with the rabbinical establishment that influenced the final manuscript in important ways—his many insightful queries were invaluable. Frances Malino pushed us to elaborate on our discussion of women and gender in Sa'adi's account, leading us to reconsider the memoir in fascinating ways. Uğur Zekeriya Peçe was of great assistance in the identification of Ottoman figures and place names. Finally, Devin Naar was relentlessly generous in sharing his fine-grained knowledge of late nineteenth- and early twentieth-century Salonica and Salonican

Jewry. His many questions, suggestions, and insights had a profound influence on this book.

Early on, Esther Benbassa saw the importance of publishing this memoir. Aron Rodrigue is deeply grateful for her precious *compagnonnage de route* now spanning exactly three decades in the development of Sephardic studies.

The Jewish National and University Library of Israel's Manuscripts Department and Institute of Microfilmed Hebrew Manuscripts, which holds the only extant copy of Sa'adi's memoirs, permitted us to publish this transliteration and translation: we are immensely grateful for their stewardship and permission. Crucial financial support came from Stanford University's Sephardic Studies Project, based at the Taube Center and the Mediterranean Studies Forum, and from the Maurice Amado Chair in Sephardic Studies at the University of California, Los Angeles.

We are pleased that this book is appearing as part of Stanford University Press's Studies in Jewish History and Culture series: we offer our appreciation to Steven J. Zipperstein, who, with Aron Rodrigue, edits this series, for his encouragement. Norris Pope has been an astute and munificent editor: we are especially thankful to him, his editorial assistant, Sarah Crane Newman, and the production team at Stanford University Press—especially our copy-editor, Joe Abbott, and our production editor, Mariana Raykov—for their patience with the complex nature of this manuscript.

Our appreciation is also due to Rabbi David E. S. Stein, whose superb work far surpassed an indexer's normal duties, and to Bill Nelson for patiently creating and fine-tuning our maps.

The Levi family of Rio de Janeiro generously provided and permitted us to reproduce the photograph of Sa'adi on the cover of this book. We thank especially Silvio Levi for his help and interest in this project.

We wish that we could convey our appreciation to Sa'adi's great-grandson, Sadi Silvio Levy, who donated his great-grandfather's manuscript to the National Library of Israel in 1977; to Sa'adi's grandson, Leon David Levy, who preserved it; to Sa'adi's son, journalistic collaborator, and relentless champion, Sam Lévy, who likely sent the manuscript from Paris to his nephew, Leon, in Brazil; and, finally, to Sa'adi himself, who had the wisdom to commit to paper the following reflections on his life and the now-lost world of Ottoman and Jewish Salonica.

Note on Translation and Transliteration

It is now customary in scholarly works to transliterate Hebrew words in Ladino texts according to modern standardized Israeli Hebrew. However, this obscures the distinctive Sephardic pronunciations that were common among the Ladino-speaking populations of the Ottoman Empire. For example, the transliteration of the second and third of Sa'adi's names, which would be rendered "Betsalel" and "ha-Levi" according to contemporary rules of Hebrew transliteration, would be alien to Sephardim of Sa'adi's era, who would have pronounced the name "Besalel" and "a-Levi." Similar examples are numerous.

The romanized transliteration of Sa'adi's memoir offers a glimpse into the dizzying multiple linguistic repertoires of Ladino, a cultural universe that is now all but erased. It would be anomalous (and indeed against the spirit of revivifying Sa'adi's voice) to impose a contemporary transliteration system on his writing. This, we believe, would represent a double death of the author, his memoir, and the language he spoke.

Hence, the transliteration of the rich Hebrew vocabulary within Ladino is rendered throughout this book in a way that restitutes the voice of Ladino speakers, as follows:

Punctuation in the original *soletreo* manuscript is irregular. For ease of reading, we have added punctuation and quotation marks to the Ladino transliteration and English translation of Sa'adi's memoir. In all instances except otherwise noted, personal names in transliteration respect the *soletreo* original. Place names have been rendered according to common European usage of the time. Hence, for example, "Salonica" has been used instead of "Saloniko," which Sa'adi, like other Sephardim of the time, employs regularly in the original text.

Transliteration of Ladino and Hebrew Words According to the Sephardic Tradition

א quiescent, not indicated
ג' for both *ch* as in *mucho* and *dj* and is *djudio*
ה quiescent, not indicated
ז' for French *j* as in *juif*
ח soft *h* as in *haham*
ט always simple *t* in Ladino
כ soft *h* as in *haham*
ע glottal stop marked with an ', as in *ta'anith*
צ used as *s* in *sedaka* rather than *ts*
תּ harsh *t* such as in *tefilla*
ת postvocalic, spirantic *th* as in *Ruth*
Dagesh forte for germination such as *battal*

All words that do not derive from Romance languages, including Hebrew or Turkish words, have been italicized throughout this book. The reader should consult the glossary for their translation and analytical explication.

The original Ladino text uses the Hebrew calendar throughout. This has been converted to the Western (Gregorian) calendar in the English translation.

Note on Currencies, Weights, and Measures

Debasements and reforms that occurred in the course of the nineteenth century render it impossible to assign exact values to units of Ottoman currency mentioned in Sa'adi's memoir. Unless one can identify dates of usage, one can only provide approximations. In a major reform in 1844, the Ottoman state introduced the Ottoman *lira*, which equaled one British pound sterling. The *lira* was divisible by one hundred *kurush* (*gurush*, *grosh*), each of which was worth forty *paras*. Another unit of currency was the *medjidiye*, which was worth twenty *kurush*. Coins that existed before 1844 continued to be in circulation for decades afterward. Four such units of currency, discontinued in 1844, are mentioned by Sa'adi: one *metelik* (*metalik*) and one *yüzlük* (*yuzlik*) were worth ten and one hundred *paras* respectively. There existed two types of *beshlik* coins equaling 2.5 and 5 *kurush*. One *altilik* was worth six *kurush*.

An *okke* (*oka*) was equal to 1,283 grams and 400 *dirhems* (*dramas*).

Note on Sigla Used in the Ladino Romanized Text and English Translation

( ) maintained in the Ladino romanized text if used by Sa'adi in his manuscript.

( ) used by the translator to cite biblical references. All biblical quotations rendered in Ladino and added to the Ladino transliterated text are drawn from Avraham Asa's Ladino translation listed in the bibliography.

[ ] used to bracket additions entered into the text by the translator and the editors.

{ } used to indicate *errata* in the original manuscript.

{ } [ ] used to indicate a mistake, usually in Hebrew usage, followed by its corrected form.

[number] used to refer to page number of the original *soletreo* text, which is posted in its entirety online:
http://www.sup.org/book.cgi?id=18553

strikethrough maintained in the Ladino romanized text if used by Sa'adi in his manuscript.

"Ne." and "Rd." in the glossary refer to translations from Joseph Nehama, *Dictionnaire du Judéo-espagnol*; and James William Redhouse, *Redhouse Yeni Türkçe-İngilizce Sözlük*, respectively. See the bibliography.

Editors' Introduction

Autobiographies and memoirs have long captured the attention of students of European Jewish history and culture; in recent years they have been hailed as among the most evocative sources of modern Jewish life, sources whose very production reflected, narrated, and even ushered in modernity. The rich body of memoirs and autobiographies that Jews have penned or translated into English—and, no less, the sophisticated critical scholarship on these sources—have opened entirely new vistas into the Jewish past and into the lives, times, and self-representation of its actors. This diffuse genre of writing, which (with much debate) scholars speak of as "life writing" or "self-narrative," also made its appearance in the Sephardic world. This book—which includes a transcribed and translated edition of the memoir of Sa'adi Besalel a-Levi (1820–1903) from its original *soletreo* (Ladino cursive) form—is the first known memoir in Ladino, the Judeo-Spanish language of the descendants of the Jews expelled from Iberia who settled in Ottoman southeast Europe and Asia Minor beginning in the fifteenth century. Perhaps more important, this memoir paints a vivid portrait of a Jewish cultural tributary (the Sephardic heartland of southeastern Europe) just beginning to tip over the edge of a colossal waterfall of change.

Sa'adi[1] was a resident of the vibrant port city of Salonica (present-day Thessaloniki), an Ottoman, a Jew, an accomplished singer and com-

1. For historical reasons, we choose to refer to "Sa'adi" throughout our introduction. Before the twentieth century when Ottoman successor states determined that surnames of all subjects were required by law, individuals were known by their first names, with some reference to their family ascendance. Accordingly, the most common reference to our author by contemporaries was "Sa'adi the Levite," that

poser, a publisher of Hebrew and Ladino texts religious and secular, a founder of modern Ladino print culture, and a journalist (the editor of *La Epoka*, the first long-lived Ladino newspaper to be published in Salonica). He was also a rebel. More than any other, it is this quality that emerges most powerfully in his memoir. Sa'adi's rebellion pitted him against the Jewish communal leadership of Salonica, which he accused of being corrupt, abusive, and fanatical, and whose leaders, in turn, excommunicated him from the Jewish community. This insurgency, though fierce at the time of its unfolding, can feel thin, even fantastic, at times because the worlds against which Sa'adi agitated no longer exist. The empire he inhabited, still intact at the time he penned this document, would not outlive his children. His home, one of few cities in the world that boasted a majority Jewish population at the beginning of the twentieth century, would, in the decades after Sa'adi composed his memoir, find its Jewish population threatened by wars (1912–13), a major fire (1917), emigration, and a genocide (1943) whose gruesome thoroughness climaxed in this urban center. Even the language in which he wrote, Ladino, mother tongue of the vast majority of the roughly 250,000 Jews in the Ottoman Balkans and Asia Minor, would change dramatically in the ensuing decades. It became transformed by the incursion of dizzying new vocabularies, first Gallicized and eventually pruned of its Hebrew Rashi script[2] and written in the Latin alphabet in republican Turkey and elsewhere. The institution of Ladino print culture that Sa'adi played such an important role in creating blossomed (through the interwar period in Greece) and then rather quickly receded (in the wake of widespread emigration, nationalizing pressures, and the Second World War) as Ladino ceased to serve as a language of popular and intellectual print culture.

At the time Sa'adi composed his memoirs, Salonica in particular and Levantine Jewry more generally had not yet witnessed many of the changes that have come to define Sephardic modernity in historians'

---

is, "Sa'adi a-Levi." The latter became Sa'adi's surname much later; subsequently, Sa'adi's son, Sam, along with other descendants, adopted the surname Levy.

2. Rashi script is a Hebrew font of medieval origins used in the writing of Ladino for some five hundred years.

eyes. The Alliance Israélite Universelle (AIU) had been founded before Sa'adi began this text, but its influence was as yet fledgling. This organization, created in 1860 by the French-Jewish elite, would introduce French Jewish schools across the Levant, offering instruction in French to generations of Sephardic, North African, and Middle Eastern Jews and forever remapping the linguistic and cultural terrain of Jews in these regions. Sa'adi helped Moïse Allatini, a banker and industrialist, establish the first AIU school in Salonica in 1873, a process he describes in the pages that follow; but the tremendous cultural influence this organization would command was yet to be accrued, and Sa'adi's narrative describes an institution struggling to find firm financial footing rather than the towering institution and pedagogic innovator the AIU would become.

Furthermore, crucial aspects of a century-long process of Ottoman governmental reform and centralization effort, known collectively as the Tanzimat, though begun in 1839, were inchoate during much of the period covered by Sa'adi's memoirs. Accordingly, Jews in the empire continued to be beholden to a legal system and power structure that had been in place for centuries but whose dismantling (during the decades that preceded and were to follow the completion of this work) would profoundly alter and arguably erode Jews' and other non-Muslims' traditional place in the Ottoman social fabric. Sa'adi's memoir describes the Ottoman Jewish *millet* (religious community) before these changes became definitive, when its leadership was still able to govern, tax, and legally try its own, when, in short, the Ottoman state granted the rabbinical authorities license to police the religious and social barriers of the Jewish community. These practices, ruthlessly criticized by Sa'adi, would be legislated out of existence in his lifetime and, indeed, were waning even as Sa'adi composed this text.

If Ottoman Jewry was on the cusp of these and other forms of change in the second half of the nineteenth century, it was neither homogenous nor static. Sa'adi himself was aware that he was witnessing a culture in flux. Indeed, as the very first sentence of his preface makes clear ("My purpose in writing this story is to inform future generations how much times have changed within half a century"), he was inspired to reflect on the changes he witnessed precisely because the life he knew appeared

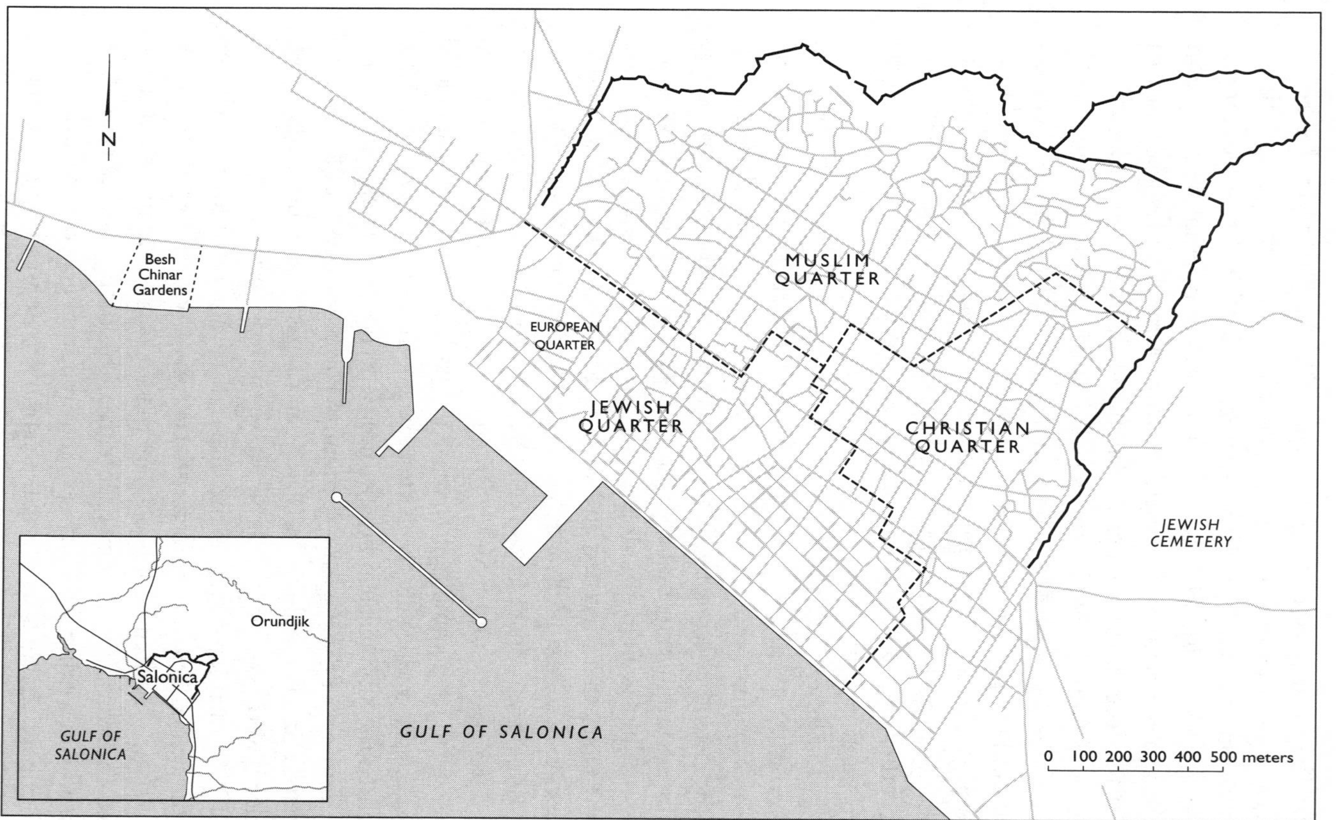

Map 1. The quarters of Ottoman Salonica, c. 1900. The boundaries of the Jewish, Christian, and Muslim quarters are not absolute, with some members of each community living elsewhere.

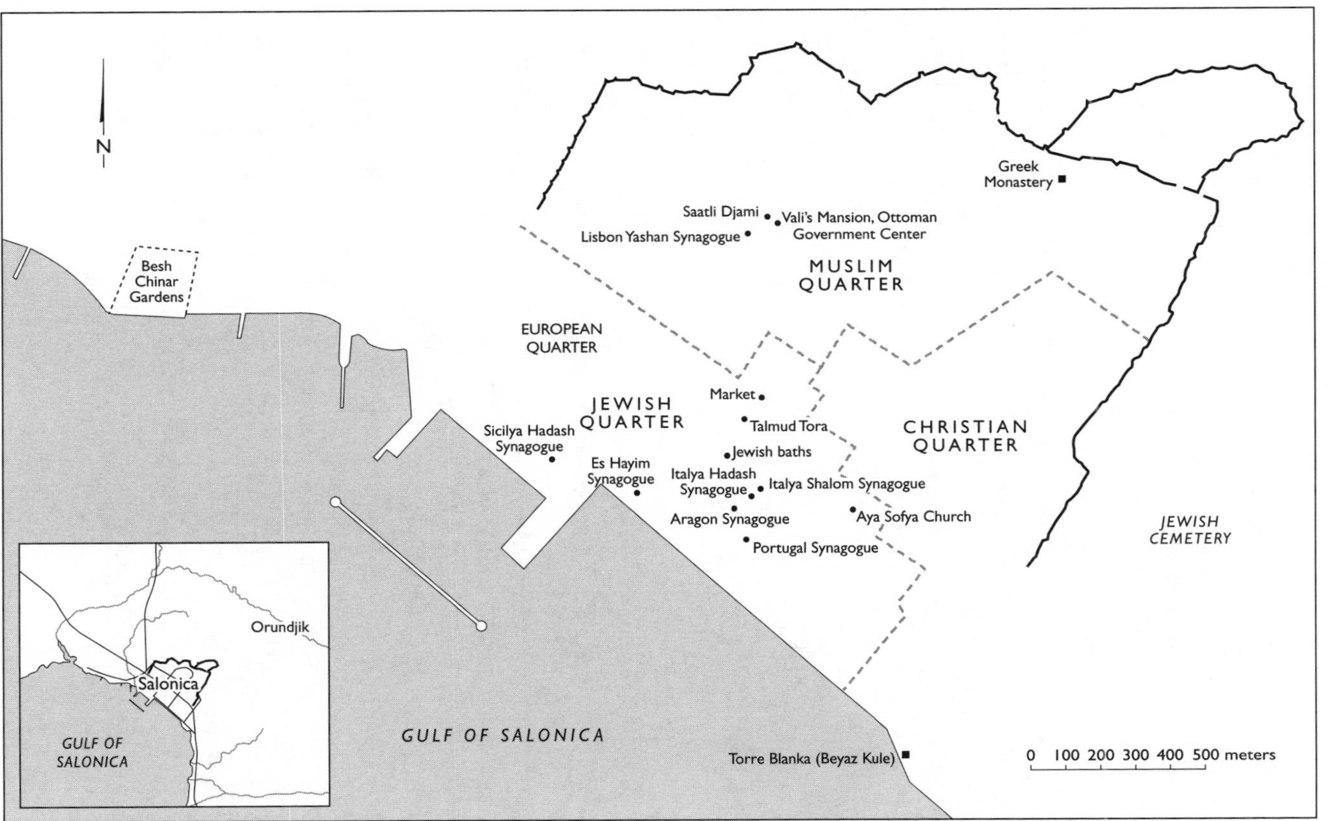

Map 2. Sites in Salonica, including most referenced in Sa'adi's memoir, c. 1900.

Map 3. Salonica in the Ottoman southeastern Europe and Asia Minor, c. 1874, the year of Sa'adi's excommunication by the rabbinical leadership of Salonica.

to be transformed in profound and permanent ways. One might expect this to instill sentimentality, even nostalgia, in an author. But, crucially, Sa'adi's memoirs are in no way nostalgic. On the contrary, this text documents cultural change with something akin to triumph; conversely, when Sa'adi writes ethnographically about traditional mores or norms, he assumes an angry, even intolerant tone. Far from an exercise in nostalgia, these memoirs, begun in 1881, were to document a world its author hoped would become (and indeed helped to make) obsolete.

Anger and intolerance may not make for easy reading, but they are undoubtedly crucial ingredients of a passionate and affecting memoir. As Marcus Moseley has suggested in his masterful study of Jewish autobiography, "bad writing may make good autobiography, and vice versa."[3] What is the source of Sa'adi's biliousness? In Sa'adi's rendition it dates to his traumatic excommunication, in 1874, by a cabal associated with Chief Rabbi Asher Kovo. The causes of this dramatic event were several. Because of his active involvement in attempts to reform communal institutions and create new schools, Sa'adi had become thoroughly unpopular among the traditionalist elite that ran Salonica's Jewish community. He was also among those who challenged the rabbinical taxation system on kosher meat (a familiar point of tension between the rabbinic elite and breakaway factions including, in eastern Europe, the Hasidim) and who questioned communal finances. All this piqued the religious establishment and led to the launching of what Sa'adi describes as a trumped-up accusation that Sa'adi's elder son, Hayyim (Kitapchi Hayyim), had desecrated the Sabbath. Sa'adi's heated defense of Hayyim led to a rabbinical writ of excommunication (*herem*) against father and son alike. The pair were dragged and pursued through the streets by a large crowd, saved from physical harm only by the intervention of the prominent Jewish philanthropist Allatini, who acted to stop the riot. This event would prove the crucial pivot of Sa'adi's life as he presents it, bringing not only emotional distress but severe economic hardship to Sa'adi's family; in addition to being symbolically charged, a *herem* forbade other Jews from visiting the excommunicated or, theo-

3. Marcus Moseley, *Being for Myself Alone: Origins of Jewish Autobiography* (Stanford, CA: Stanford University Press, 2006), 31.

retically, from providing him with work. The accused was not counted as part of the quorum needed for synagogue services. Intended to last thirty-one years, the *herem* was the central trauma of Sa'adi's life, and its memory ripples through nearly every page of his memoirs, occluding any expression of pride, sentimentality, or nostalgia.

And yet, Sa'adi's memoirs indicate that the power of the *herem* in the Ottoman setting had run its course by the mid to late nineteenth century. Thus it was possible for Sa'adi, in defiance of the traditionalist communal leadership and with the help of powerful notables in Salonica and Constantinople, to launch his newspaper, *La Epoka*, soon after his excommunication. Traditional means of social control within the Jewish community, it seems, had by this time been eroded by a reforming Ottoman state, external influences, and shifts in Jewish practices. Indeed, the rabbi whom Sa'adi depicts as abusing the practice of *herem* most egregiously, Shaul Molho, died in 1849, twenty-five years before Sa'adi was excommunicated, leaving open the possibility that Sa'adi's tangle with the traditionalist elite represented the dying gasp of the *herem* as a social policing act. Regardless, for Sa'adi the symbolic power of the *herem* remained strong, producing pain long after the writ was issued against him. As he describes: "My heart aches and my body is crushed, my legs and my arms are paralyzed by this nonsense. As I write this biography that took nine years to finish, I still remember that dark and cursed day; would that the sun had not risen on that day, or at least, I had been sick rather than live through this anguish. I sure pray to God that none of my loved ones live through a similar experience, 'perish the day on which I was born' (Job 3:3)." The emotion of this passage—perhaps the most heated of his narrative—makes clear that it was Sa'adi's battles with the conservative religious leadership (the *rabbanim*, *sinyores hahamim* and *dayyanim*, or rabbis, learned men, and judges) and their lay allies that ignited his passion. Despite the fact that Sa'adi has occasionally some kind words for certain rabbis (notably, Rabbis Gatenyo and Moshe a-Levi), this battle, and Sa'adi's own hostility toward the traditionalist elite as a whole, emerges as the central leitmotif of his memoir; Sa'adi's frequent references to the "fanaticism" produced when unbridled rabbinical power is exercised over an ignorant population, serve as a prelude to the story of his excommunication.

One could say that most of his text is apologia and polemic as much as memoir, the rant of a man shaped by a trauma long since past but still intensely vivid. This book's lack of sentimentality, its vengefulness, its inclusion of what might be called "angry ethnography"—all this takes us into murky territory of the human soul, raising questions about the function and form of "life writing."

Sa'adi's anger at the traditionalist elite not only generated the text we have before us; it also spurred what became his life's work, the publication of newspapers influential among Jewish and non-Jewish readers in turn-of-the-century Salonica: the Ladino *La Epoka* (1875–1911), which was his own creation, and the French *Le Journal de Salonique* (1895–1911), of which he was the director, but which was largely the work of his sons (Sa'adi himself did not know French). These newspapers expressed frequently Sa'adi's (and his son Sam Lévy's) nearly unabiding hostility toward local traditionalist rabbis and lay leaders, whose ways he deemed fanatical, obscurantist, and theocratic. Together with novels and novellas, Ladino periodicals such as these helped create a field of secular cultural production among the Jews of southeastern Europe and the Aegean basin. We will return to these sources, and to the wider landscape of Ladino publishing in the Ottoman lands, later in this introduction.

There are significant reasons why Sa'adi's memoirs provide important perspectives for students of modern Jewish history. Non-Jewish Ottomans of various ethnic and religious origins produced a few such works episodically until the nineteenth century. Those self-narratives by Ottoman Jews we do have access to were produced during or in the aftermath of the watershed events of the early twentieth century (and especially in the interwar period) and tend to emphasize leitmotifs defined by this period, namely the intense transformation of Ottoman Jewry; the importance of AIU-driven educational reform; the rise of regional nationalisms and the wars, nation-states, and population transfers that accompanied them; and, finally, the concordant fraying and collapse of Ottoman society. Sa'adi's memoir suggests that these phenomena, crucial as they were, cannot be understood to have generated or exclusively defined modernity in the Sephardic vein. In fact, before these events unfolded, Ottoman Jewry, like Ottoman society generally, was dynamic, finely textured, and constantly in flux.

The existence and content of Sa'adi's memoir hint at important ways in which the chronologies and typologies of Sephardic Jewish history can be refocused.[4] Sa'adi's memoirs confirm historians' findings that the drift toward that elusive notion of "progress," Sa'adi's bailiwick, began among certain sectors of the Jewish population in southeastern Europe in the 1840s and 1850s. The so-called modern era was not ushered into Ottoman Jewry exclusively from the outside, nor were Levantine Jews like Sa'adi operating within a strict dichotomy of East/West or backward/modern. Instead, "progress" and cultural change (what scholars have called "Westernization") were innovatively reimagined and embraced by individual Jews like Sa'adi. Like all independent thinkers of his time, Sa'adi was inspired by new ideas but translated them into a language all his own. To borrow from the Ladino verb that appeared so often in the feuilletons, belles lettres, and novellas that rolled off the Ladino press in the 1860s and after, Sa'adi learned to *enladinar* (meaning figuratively "to translate," and, literally, "to Ladino-ize"—an act also referred to as *adaptado*, *trezladado*, or as *rezumido* in Ladino belles lettres) "modernity." Sa'adi did not slavishly reproduce the insights of others, but—to borrow an image from his daily reality—he typeset inspirational ideas with his own font. This process was bittersweet, for it encouraged him to chronicle, disparage, and eulogize at the same time, documenting traditional Sephardic customs and simultaneously agitating for the change that would eradicate them forever.

If Sa'adi's reminiscences illuminate the chronology of modern Sephardic history, so, too, do they push us to think carefully about the meaning of "Sephardi" as a cultural category. It will surprise readers to learn that although Sa'adi and his sons were pillars of the world of modern Ladino letters, Sa'adi's paternal family, which moved to Salonica from Holland, was partly Ashkenazi in origin. When his family immigrated to the city (the maternal side from Italy, the paternal side, in 1731, from Amsterdam), Salonica was and would remain for the

4. See the discussion in Matthias Lehmann, *Ladino Rabbinic Literature and Ottoman Sephardic Culture* (Bloomington: Indiana University Press, 2005).

next two hundred years a richly Jewish center whose Jewish population was primarily Sephardi and Ladino-speaking. Into this milieu not only Sa'adi's family but Jewish families of other backgrounds became linguistically and otherwise acculturated. Significantly, Sa'adi's family became Judeo-Spanish while maintaining some of its Ashkenazi markers. Early on in his memoir (Chapter 1) Sa'adi unselfconsciously refers to his family custom of *not* naming children after a living relative, a strictly Ashkenazic practice. In moniker, too, the family preserved a trace of its background: Sa'adi's full name, a piece of which he did not use in his adulthood (or in this memoir), was Sa'adi Besalel Ashkenazi a-Levi. *Ashkenazi/Eskenazi*, a common name among Sephardim in the Balkans and Turkey, could (but did not always) register a non-Sephardic past.

That such a significant figure in the history of Ladino culture was of partly Ashkenazi origin opens up interesting perspectives all but unexplored by scholars of Balkan Jewries. Some tend to think of Sephardiness as a matter of inheritance: something of a hereditary cultural trait. The Sa'adi family story suggests otherwise. The Sephardic cultural world was never insular, rigidly demarcated, or the product of inbred allegiances. On the contrary, its boundaries were porous, and it bled into and was constantly infused by other Jewish and non-Jewish cultures, and vice versa. Ashkenazic Jews had arrived in Ottoman lands since the Middle Ages, both long before and after the expulsions from the Iberian Peninsula, via the Rhineland, Amsterdam, Venice, Hungary, Poland, and Podolia, among numerous other routes. Reverse migrations were undertaken by Sephardic Jews from Ottoman lands, who moved along northern and western trade routes, eventually settling among Ashkenazic communities in eastern Europe and elsewhere.

One might note, by way of further example, the prominent role that Frankos play in Sa'adi's story. Frankos were Jews from Italy, mostly from Livorno and of Iberian origin, who had settled in Ottoman cities such as Salonica since the early eighteenth century. Frequently, but not exclusively, they occupied the upper social echelons of some Levantine Sephardic communities. First French, occasionally Dutch, mostly Tuscan, and, after the unification of Italy, Italian protégés, these merchants were an important part of a trade network of Jews that linked the southern and eastern shores of the Mediterranean littoral with the rest of Europe, mostly through Italy.[5] By the nineteenth century, Franko families such as the Allatini, Fernandez, and Modiano were among the most successful entrepreneurs in Salonica. How apt, then, that when Ottoman officials in Sa'adi's account desire "European-style shirts," they go to a Jewish woman of Italian background, Sa'adi's mother, "a skilled seamstress of *a la franka* (European) style" to have them made (Chapter 3). In part because of their historical class advantage, and in part because of their unique cultural history, most Frankos maintained a sense of distinctiveness from the majority Sephardic population, even though they (like Sa'adi's own maternal Italian ancestors) could be "Judeo-Hispanicized" to the point of taking on Ladino (rather than their native Italian) as a language of the home. To put this another way, many Frankos had been Judeo-Hispanicized by the first half of the nineteenth century, well *before* they became re-Europeanized in the century's second half. At the same time, many others such as Sa'adi's protector Allatini also retained Italian as their language and cultural orientation.

This variety of intra-Jewish acculturation was multifaceted, extending beyond the linguistic realm. An episode from Sa'adi's life suggests it could have an economic dimension. Sa'adi's mother was a descendant of the Morpurgos, a Franko family originating from Italy (but with Ashkenazi origin); unlike many Franko families, hers was poor and (perhaps not coincidentally) integrally embedded into her Sephardic surroundings. From this we learn that the Ottomanization of the Frankos could include downward mobility and the concurrent identification with poorer Sephardic populations of Salonica. Other manifestations of the Frankos' Ottomanization were more ephemeral. During one of his many fracases with Salonican rabbinic authorities, Sa'adi is saved by Franka women who recognize him as the singer much loved for the renditions of Ottoman music he performed at feasts and receptions. Here, an Ottoman cultural form, interpreted through a Jewish lens, served as one of the glues that bound Frankos and local Judeo-Spanish populations together.

Jews and non-Jews took for granted the natural integration of Frankos in the fabric of Ottoman life: cultural cataloguer though he was, Sa'adi

5. For a recent study of this mercantile network, see Francesca Trivellato, *The Familiarity of Strangers: The Sephardic Diaspora, Livorno, and Cross-Cultural Trade in the Early Modern Period* (New Haven, CT: Yale University Press, 2009).

apparently felt no compulsion to explain in detail his many references to this population or, indeed, to account for the lineage (and evident authority) of Allatini, the wealthy and powerful patron so important to the Alliance Israélite Universelle and to Sa'adi personally. At the same time, his description of Allatini and his entourage, as well as other references to Frankos of means, such as the Fernandez and the Modianos, are laden with codes of distinction and class that establish the Frankos at the top of a clear hierarchy in the social stratification of Salonican Jewry.

In sum, one of the profound messages buried in Sa'adi's memoir is that "Sephardic" (like "Mediterranean" and "Ottoman" and "Levantine") was always a flexible category of Jewish culture, never determined by bloodline. *Sephardic* in this context is a historical designation that only crudely refers to an Ottoman Jewish social fabric that was (much like that of surrounding non-Jewish Ottoman populations) far more diverse and subtly divided than the term implies. In this sense Sa'adi's text reveals examples of a larger phenomenon that awaits study: the Eastern Sephardic diaspora included Jews who self-identified as Judeo-Spanish, and who were fully integrated into the Ottoman Sephardic milieu, but whose cultural inheritance and topography stretched through other Jewish diasporas and cultural worlds.

For students of the Ladino language, the current presentation of Sa'adi's memoir in transcription, translation, and (on an associated website)[6] its original, handwritten *soletreo* form is of great significance. Especially for English speakers who may not have access to French or Hebrew sources, there is a woeful shortage of professional Ladino-language learning tools, and the acquisition of reading fluency in *soletreo* is particularly difficult to pursue. It is our hope that this volume, in tandem with the aforementioned website, will help fill this lacuna. Readers interested in the linguistic aspects of Sa'adi's memoir will find particular rewards in the glossary created by Isaac Jerusalmi, which can be found at the back of this volume. In its detailed explication of the dizzyingly multilingual influences on Ladino, this glossary presents a microcosm of a rich linguistic and cultural world that Sa'adi excels in recording and that today is all but vanished.

6. See http://www.sup.org/book.cgi?id=18553

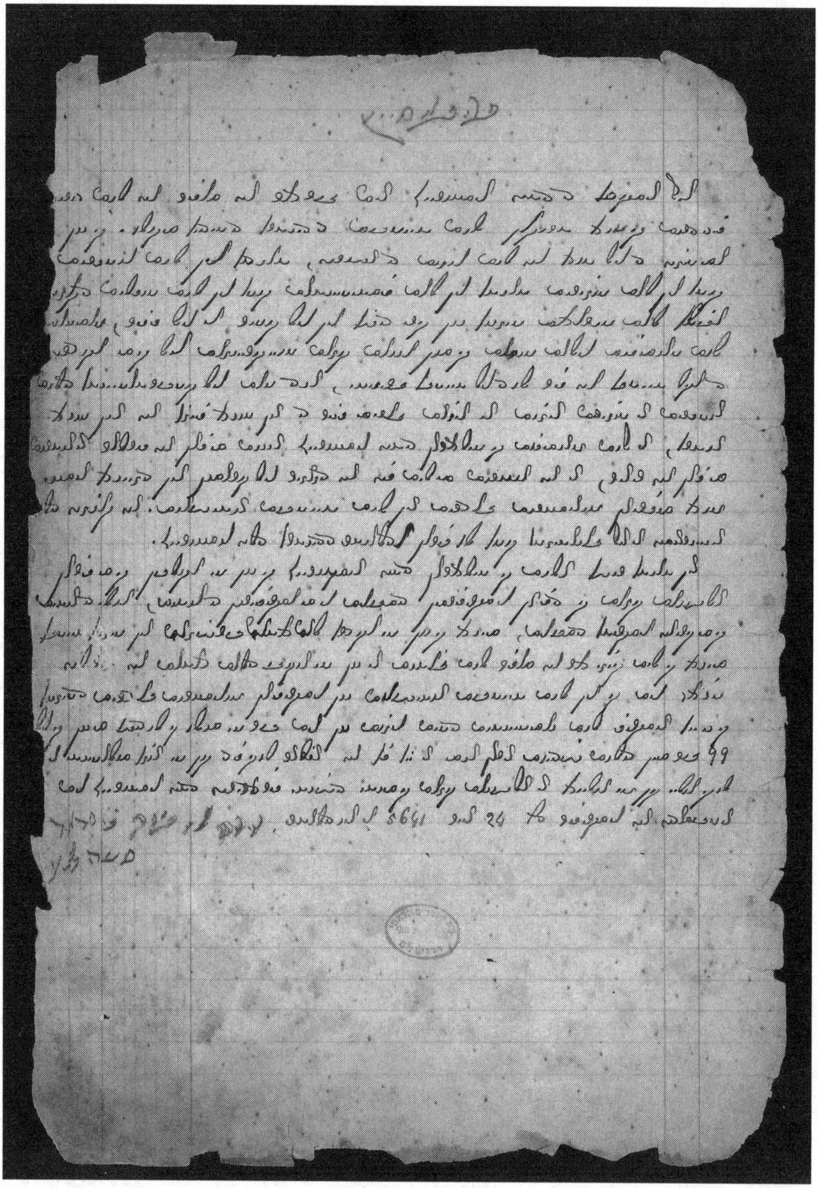

Figure 1. The Preface page of Sa'adi's *soletreo* manuscript. Reprinted with permission of the Manuscripts Department and Institute of Microfilmed Hebrew Manuscripts, National Library of Israel.

In sum, readers will find many themes coursing through Sa'adi's memoir, and it is the task of this introduction to untangle those that appear most vivid to us. As we will suggest, Sa'adi's memoir can be read in many ways: as a meditation on the social landscape of a great Mediterranean city of the late nineteenth century, Salonica; as a narrative by an extraordinary and all but forgotten member of Ottoman society; as a voice of reform; as a chronicle of intra-Jewish communal power struggles; as a landmark memoir that should be considered among a small cadre of crucial self-narratives that illuminate the Jewish past with unusual clarity and intimacy; or, finally, as the personal reminiscences of a preeminent editor of Ladino periodicals, a publisher of Hebrew, Ladino, French, Judeo-Greek, and other language-texts, an Ottoman composer and musician, an amateur ethnographer (if an unselfconscious one), a hot-blooded critic of the injustices he perceived to surround him—the memories, in short, of an extraordinary individual in all his idiosyncrasies. That this memoir functions in all of these registers at once points to its richness and importance for those invested in the Mediterranean, Ottoman, and Jewish literary and lived pasts.

The World of Nineteenth-Century Salonica

When Sa'adi started to commit his reminiscences to paper in 1881, Salonica was on the cusp of becoming a vibrant and cosmopolitan entrepôt, multiethnic and multilingual, constantly crosscut by the movement of bodies, goods, and ideas from western, central, and eastern Europe, the Mediterranean Basin and Middle East. The first regular steamboat line had reached the city in 1840, heralding its transformation into a major port several decades later. By the end of the nineteenth century, Salonica had emerged as the third-largest port in the Ottoman Empire, and the volume of goods passing through it was rising rapidly (doubling, from one to two million tons, between 1880 and 1912 alone). In the 1870s and 1880s a railroad line was constructed that connected the city to Belgrade (via Macedonia) and from there to the larger European rail network. Much of this development was paid for by the Belgian Jewish financier Baron Maurice de Hirsch: he makes a fleeting appearance in Sa'adi's memoir as the supporter of the establishment of an Alliance school in Salonica.

Modern and rapid transportation would lead to increased commerce and trade, transforming Salonica into a boomtown by the end of the nineteenth century. Continuing to export wool and cotton from the surrounding regions, the city developed an industrial infrastructure as well. Many of its small factories supplied Ottoman and Balkan markets with various finished textile products. Tobacco would also become a lucrative crop by the end of the nineteenth century; the main tobacco-growing center of the region was in northern Greece. Salonica eventually emerged as the hub of the tobacco trade and an important center for cigarette manufacture, a business that employed thousands of Jews, especially young women, by the early twentieth century.

A crucial part of this social and economic landscape, Jews—totaling around 50 percent (at its height) to 40 percent of the total population (50,000 out of 90,000 in the 1880s, and 61,439 out of 157,889 according to the first Greek census of 1913, with 39,956 Greeks, 45,867 Muslims, 6,263 Bulgarians, and 4,364 categorized as "others" for the remainder of the population)—constituted the city's largest ethnic group and, broadly speaking, dominated Salonica's urban economy. The old Franko elite, in particular, thrived as Salonica industrialized. The Allatinis (who, together with the Modianos, had once operated in cereal and flour production) became major figures in international trade and banking. They were also active in the tobacco trade, built a modern brick factory, and were instrumental in the establishment of the Bank of Salonica. The Modianos and Fernandeses created the famous Olympos distillery. Hundreds of large and small Jewish enterprises dotted every sector of the Salonican economy, and thousands of Jewish white-collar workers were employed in Jewish and European firms. By the beginning of the twentieth century a significant Jewish middle class had emerged in the city as a result of these socioeconomic forces.

It is striking that Sa'adi's text, largely composed when these extraordinary social and economic transformations were in full swing (that is, between 1881 and the turn of the century), says little about the rapidly changing world around him. Instead, his account is primarily focused on the past, especially on the years between his birth in 1820 and his excommunication in 1874. Of course, Sa'adi's newspaper, *La Epoka*, was chronicling new developments in the period that followed on a regular basis and at the very moment that Sa'adi was writing his memoirs; thus, it is imaginable that Sa'adi drew a distinction between the function of these genres. Yet given that Sa'adi positions himself as a major protagonist in promoting change, the absence of timely reportage of socioeconomic change of any kind in his memoir is striking. In its place, brief mentions of the "modern" are used as foils that associate antiquated ways and quaint mores with malignant ignorance and superstition. Salonica, that teeming city in full transformation around him, provides but a backdrop to Sa'adi's own personal travails and, especially, to the trauma of his excommunication, ever the core of the memoirist's obsessive preoccupation.

Even in times of Salonica's growing prosperity, Jews remained numerous among the city's poor and working class. The majority of Jews in Salonica during this period lived close to poverty and earned income as fishermen, porters, longshoremen, or factory workers in the city's burgeoning industries. Comments in Sa'adi's text about these residents of Salonica are devoid of any sympathy. Instead, these people are referred to as being of the "second" or "third" class and are objects of scorn. The poor are depicted as ignorant, fanatical, and obscurantist masses blindly driven by superstition to obey corrupt communal leaders and malevolent rabbis; some of the most biting sarcasm in Sa'adi's text is reserved for them. The irony of this is that Sa'adi himself was living hand to mouth and greatly feared a descent into poverty; this may have animated his misanthropic tendencies, pushing him to distinguish himself rhetorically from Salonica's poor. It is possible, too, that he blamed his poor neighbors and their "gullible" ways, seeing them as part of a social system that, were it not for the intervention of the noble *cavalliere* Allatini, would have led to his own destruction.

Culturally, Jewish Salonica in the last decades of the nineteenth century was a city in transition. At the time Sa'adi began his memoir, educational options for Jewish children were yet limited: Jewish girls were by and large denied education and boys' training (as was Sa'adi's own) limited to a few years of traditional education in the local *Talmud Tora* schools that were, according to Sa'adi and memoirists of eastern European Jewish culture, cauldrons of neglect and abuse. Emigration had not yet begun to disperse Salonica's Jewries; political and ideological movements had not yet begun to divide them conceptually one from another or from their non-Jewish neighbors. The great majority of Jews in this city (as the great majority of the roughly 250,000 Jews who lived under Ottoman rule in Anatolia and the Balkans) continued to claim Ladino as a mother tongue and maintained only functional oral knowledge of other regional languages. Lest this seem an indication of the isolation of Salonican Jewry, one must remember that with Sephardim a majority or near-majority population in this city, one would be more likely to hear, and be compelled to utilize, Ladino than Turkish, Greek, or Bulgarian on Salonica's streets. Regardless, here, as elsewhere in the empire, the Jewish community was by and large reliant on intra-Jewish institutions for religious, legal, and pedagogic authority. Nearly all Jews, like all other religious groups of the Ottoman Empire, were compelled to be at least outwardly observant and, according to Sa'adi, maintained a firm belief in what might be called folk religion (beliefs that were pan-Mediterranean as much as Jewish): they, like other groups, were inclined to read the future or past through seemingly random events such as the appearance of dogs, boils, or fever; the failure to cover one's windows at home or one's forehead in public; or the ever-present danger of "episodes" and "curses." Perhaps these folk practices provided a measure of psychological protection against very real vulnerabilities: as Sa'adi narrates almost obsessively, catastrophes like fires, earthquakes, and outbreaks of disease were ubiquitous threats to Salonica's urban landscape.

Yet the pace of change was undoubtedly quickening. French, the lingua franca of trade and commerce, was becoming an increasingly desirable commodity, and the Frankos spearheaded pedagogic efforts to spread Jews' knowledge of the language. Franko notables such as Allatini and his brother-in-law, the Tuscan consul Salomon Fernandes, worked in close collaboration with independent Jewish thinkers such as Judah Nehama to open a new Jewish school in Salonica even before the first AIU schools were founded. Allatini was also responsible for sponsoring the *Kupat Hesed 'Olam* (Mutual Welfare Fund), a society that taxed Jewish merchants in order to fund the reform of community institutions. Sa'adi became an important ally of this organization and used his printing press to produce pamphlets that publicized its activities, among them the offering of evening classes in foreign languages and arithmetic at the Great *Talmud Tora*. (This *Talmud Tora*, created in 1520, experienced its heyday in the sixteenth and seventeenth centuries when it attracted Jewish scholars from across Europe and the Eastern Mediterranean.) In 1856 the *Kupat Hesed 'Olam* brought a young rabbi from Strasbourg, Joseph Lippmann, to create a new "modern" school. This effort lasted five years (not three as Sa'adi claims) but ended in failure as a result of rabbinical opposition. Soon after (in 1862) an Italian school was opened in Salonica, also with the support of Franko sponsors. In the same period the Alliance Israélite Universelle contacted Judah Nehama to explore the possibilities of opening schools in the city that would offer Jewish girls and boys instruction in French with Jewish subjects taught according to the dictates of modern Franco-Judaism. It would take nearly a dozen years for this ambition to be realized. Thereafter, the ascendance of the organization was astonishing; by 1908, the director of the Alliance school reported that 2,132 students were being educated in Alliance schools, and an additional 3,250 students were enrolled in private institutions that used the Alliance curriculum. The number of students studying in the city's *Talmud Tora*, meanwhile, had shrunk to 1,849, and the *Talmud Tora* itself had started to transform its curriculum. The Alliance schools would become important factors in the creation of a Francophone Jewish middle and upper-middle class in the city.

How does the world, and how does nineteenth-century Salonica, appear through Sa'adi's eyes? The Jewish topography of the city is ever-present in Sa'adi's text but is never described, suggesting that the author took for granted readers' knowledge of the Jewish geographical template. The vast majority of Jews inhabited the area of Salonica closest to the sea, south of Vardar Street, which cut across much of the city on an east-west axis. This neighborhood did not constitute a Jewish ghetto, the likes of which never existed in the Ottoman Empire. The area was home to the central market of Salonica, source of livelihood for most of the city's Jews. Also located in this area were two Greek *mahalles* (quarters) and a small European quarter inhabited by mostly Frankos and Europeans. Alongside these groups Jews lived in a densely populated, insalubrious area made up of wooden houses and tenements subject to fires and epidemics, such as are repeatedly recounted by Sa'adi. In the mix, too, were the Jewish public buildings that exist as central referents in this text; including the Great *Talmud Tora*, the Es Hayyim Synagogue (founded by Romaniotes, or Greek Jews, long before the arrival of the Sephardim), the Italya Synagogue (founded by Sicilian Jews in 1423, the Italian Jewish communities of the city fissured over time, by the nineteenth century maintaining no less than three synagogues), and the Ashkenazi Synagogue (founded by Jews from Germany and Hungary in 1376). In addition there were numerous synagogues named after the places of origin of Jewish immigrants, including those who fled the Iberian Peninsula in 1492 in the wake of expulsions (e.g., the synagogues Aragon, Katalan, Gerush Sepharad, Mayorka, Kastilya, Portugal, Evora, and Lisbon) and those who immigrated from Italy during the first half of the sixteenth century (e.g., the synagogues Otranto, Pulia, Sicilia, and Kalabria). In the sixteenth and seventeenth centuries these quasi-autonomous congregations governed themselves; by Sa'adi's time they were subject in theory to a single urban Jewish administration and had lost much of their power and influence though still exercising some authority. These sites remained important real and symbolic markers of Salonican Jewish life, and they stand as major signposts in Sa'adi's narrative.

Crucially, Sa'adi's Salonica is a city tied to cities, regions, and countries elsewhere. Sa'adi traces his family roots to Italy and Holland; he travels to Constantinople for reasons related to his publishing and other activities; he acquires (as do competitor printers) fonts of Rashi type from Vienna; and he prints materials in Judeo-Greek for a patron in the city of Ioannina, the last remaining major Romaniot (Greek-speaking) Jewish outpost in the Balkans, in Epirus in western Greece. In maintaining manifold ties outside his home city, he was far from unusual. His memoir references local rabbis' correspondence with colleagues in Smyrna and Alliance advocates in Salonica in constant contact with philanthropists and advisers in Paris; it makes mention of a letter sent to a Jewish journal in London (presumably the *Jewish Chronicle* [Chapter 9]) to report on a local scandal and of a local entrepreneur who obtained a monopoly exporting leeches from Salonica to England, where they were highly valued for medicinal purposes (Chapter 30). Some people mentioned in the pages that follow travel to Europe, conduct business in Thrace (more specifically, in Gumuldjina [Chapter 6]), and vacation in the countryside just outside the city (that is, in Orundjik [Chapter 4]). We witness the arrival of a young Christian woman whom Sa'adi believes comes from Skopje and who wishes to convert to Islam (Chapter 32); of Ashkenazic emissaries from Tiberias (Chapter 25); and of the plague, ostensibly from Egypt (Chapter 13). Women borrow sartorial cues from Aleppo (Chapter 27), and state officials seek military support from Monastir and Skopje (Chapter 32). Last but not least, there are constant official, financial, and personal dealings connecting Salonica to the imperial hub of Constantinople. While Sa'adi was obsessively—at times myopically—engaged with controversies that can feel petty and provincial, his world and city were far from isolated.

Not only is Salonica related to far-flung cities and regions in Sa'adi's account; it is an internally diverse entrepôt. It is home to Muslims, Christians, and Sephardic, Ashkenazic, and Italian Jews. Though never mentioned by Sa'adi, Salonica was also inhabited by *dönmes*, a population of ostensibly Muslim descendants of the followers of the seventeenth-century Jewish self-proclaimed messiah Sabbetai Sevi, who was forcibly converted to Islam by Ottoman authorities. The city is populated with people Sa'adi refers to as Greek, Bulgarian, Turkish, Albanian, European, and "foreign." There are sailors, soldiers, scholars, sultans, businessmen, and bankers, as well as consuls from France, England, Italy, Germany, and Russia. Still, in his obsessive narration of the central traumatic event of his life, his excommunication, and the details that provide the *mise-en-scène* to this drama, Sa'adi recounts little about these people. Turks appear as little more than governors whose henchmen exercise power. Greeks find their way into the text extraordinarily rarely: as victims of fire, as rebels repeatedly crushed by their Ottoman overseers, and, oddly enough, in association with Jews accused of immorality for their frequenting of brothels. European consuls intervene to protect Sa'adi and also as victims of one horrible act of Muslim religious bigotry (a story offered as proof of the ills associated with fanaticism, a central trope in Sa'adi's text). Finally, the sultan appears in his story when Sa'adi describes the leader's visit to the city: about this theme Sa'adi carries on at great length, only to end by pointing out that the communal leadership does not grant him the recognition he believes he deserves for his preparation of a musical tribute to the sultan. (Three panegyric songs and poems in Hebrew and Ladino that Sa'adi composed in honor of this visit appear at the end of this memoir, in keeping with a "last request from my children" that the author appended to his manuscript at an advanced stage in his life.) In no case do these groups have much flesh and blood; Sa'adi's text is resolutely insular in its Jewish and personal preoccupations. Paradoxically, this insularity accompanied the porous coexistence of communities, and, eventually, their cosmopolitan mixture, that were such distinctive features of the Ottoman social landscape.

In spite of all this, Sa'adi's memoir does offer surprising glimpses of daily life in Salonica. The city, in his telling, is palpably dense. As we learn in Chapter 13, a neighbor firing a gun at a stray cat in one domicile could shock a pregnant neighbor into labor. Perhaps this density explains why it was also a city of hidden doors: Sa'adi mentions three (Chapters 13 and 20), including one in his own home. Whether these were built for the protection of those on the inside or for smuggling of contraband goods or people, in Sa'adi's rendering they serve the purpose of creating pathways of communication and transport, and maintaining privacy in the face of a bustling street and public culture. Jewish historians are accustomed to associating Salonica with sites of commerce and cultural encounter—ports, markets, squares, and boulevards, the latter created in the course of modern urbanization schemes begun in the late nineteenth century and noticeably absent from Sa'adi's account. One must remember, however, that homes, courtyards, roofs, and balconies threaded through these sites, not only creating distinctions between places public and private but producing concealed spaces for the kinds of interactions (such as commerce) that could also be seen in the street.

Sa'adi is surprisingly attentive to Salonican sartorial cues, devoting an entire quasi-ethnographic chapter—one that is remarkably nonjudgmental relative to other chapters in which he employs this genre—to the subject "Clothing of Men, Women, and Maidens" (Chapter 27). Clothing and headgear were becoming increasingly nuanced vehicles of expression for Jews and non-Jews in the Ottoman lands (as elsewhere) in the nineteenth century, crucial markers of class, age, social status, even political leaning. Perhaps this slice of cultural life appealed to Sa'adi insofar as it revealed a quotidian practice in which girls, boys, women, and men could seek a modicum of independence from rabbinical oversight. In the realm of clothing choice, women, especially, could push norms without necessarily defying them altogether, thereby perceiving and performing themselves in new ways.

Sa'adi's representations of women also favor his hope that Ottoman Jewry was gradually severing its cord with the rabbinic elite. Multiple references are made to Salonica's "Women's Market," in which girls and women presumably engage in commerce (Chapters 14, 15, 40). Additionally, women reserve particular sway over domestic spaces. Thus, for example, Sa'adi's mother, a seamstress, hosts non-Jewish male clients at her home, and a number of Franka women conceal Sa'adi in their domicile after he flees the punishing grasp of rabbinic henchmen (Chapter 8). At one point a rabbi's wife chides her husband for his ignorance of contemporary trends, identifying for him a violin he had not the secular learning to distinguish. On the other hand, women in the observant milieu receive a portion of Sa'adi's wrath—they are chided for their superstition, their gullibility, their naive ways—and they appear more prominently in his account as victims of rape and disease than as free thinkers or actors. In sum, Sa'adi's sense of the shifting balance of gender norms in nineteenth-century Salonica is ambiguous. He writes of self-confident, even strident, female behavior and appears to have encouraged it in his daughters, who were among the first Jewish girls in Salonica to attend the Alliance school. His daughter Rachel (Carmona) would also have a long and distinguished career as an Alliance teacher. At the same time, women can appear as the markers of stasis in his memoir, at times carrying out rabbinic decrees without question.

Putting aside the question of how and whether Sa'adi judges women, one of the striking features of this memoir is the subtle attention its author pays to aspects of women's physical experiences. He writes, for example, with great specificity of evolutions in female fashion: of sleeves so tight a woman could not wear bracelets under them, of waistlines so narrow they constrict the breath (Chapter 27). He speaks with particular empathy of the pain women underwent on the eve of marriage, when they were subject to rigorous depilation at the hands of a Jewish servant in the Turkish bath: "Facing the bride, [the servant] applied . . . wax to her forehead, her cheeks, even under her eyebrows. When it attached itself to her face, they pulled it off forcefully, tearing it off, while the bride would be screaming with pain. Woe to the bride whose skin was delicate and who would inevitably bleed. Some of them would have swollen cheeks that made them look as if they had chicken pox" (Chapter 28). Innocent of the pleasures that may have been associated with this prenuptial ritual by the women who participated in it, Sa'adi is nonetheless remarkably engaged, here and elsewhere, with the corporeal life of his female peers.

It is possible this engagement was due to the intimacy Sa'adi appears to have felt for his sisters. This intimacy emerges vividly in a story he tells in the thirteenth chapter. Here the author speaks of his older sister coming to live with him to evade contamination from an ill neighbor. Unbeknownst to her, the sister had already been struck with "pestilence," and once in her brother's house, she became convinced (perhaps under the influence of high fever) that "evil spirits" lurked outside her door. To comfort his panicked sister, Sa'adi slept on the floor beside her bed, discovering in the night that the noises she feared were merely generated by feral dogs. Whether it is the sensitivity of a loyal brother of sisters that Sa'adi brought to the story of women's nuptials, one can only guess. Far clearer is the fact that from this text one encounters brilliant details about the lived reality of Ottoman Jewish women. The specificity with which Sa'adi writes about these matters suggests that contemporary accounts may exaggerate the physical and emotional divide that separated men from women in the nineteenth century, in the Ottoman context, and in the larger Jewish world.

As should already be obvious, one gains the feel for various sorts of public and private spaces and practices in this text. Commercial spaces of import include taverns and cafés. Poor and wealthy Jews alike, men as well as women, drink *raki* lustily at such sites (as well as at weddings, picnics, in the face of disease, and in the sickbed), revealing *raki* to be more than an alcoholic drink that carries none of the taboo that vodka ostensibly carried for eastern European Jews of the same generation. Here, *raki* serves as medicine, payment, and celebration, and it is used to extend both honor and hospitality. It brings Jews and non-Jews together in public spaces in which they appear to intermix naturally, even intimately. Coffee, too, is a beverage laden with social cues. It is drunk in various ways by Jews, as well as by non-Jews, to honor and defy, in celebration and disobedience. Coffeehouses thus reveal themselves to be complex social spaces in Sa'adi's Salonica. Disobedient sons of wealthy Jewish families retreat to them to flaunt their indolence; children flee to them in defiance of their teachers; rabbis hire henchmen to scour them for Jews violating prohibitions against smoking and spending money on the Sabbath. One man, so accused, resists arrest by clinging to a coffee sack—suddenly palpable as an icon of secularism, independence, and the extra-Jewish world—only to cause an avalanche of sacks that almost brings about his death (Chapter 6). Sa'adi himself was hardly immune to the battles that raged in Salonica's cafes. The charge of disrespecting the Sabbath was pinned on Sa'adi's son and had a role in plunging Sa'adi into the maelstrom of violence that psychologically prompted the penning of this memoir.

The preceding pages have considered how Salonica appears through Sa'adi's eyes, but one may broaden the frame, pondering how Sa'adi depicts Jewish life in the Ottoman Empire as a whole. Oddly enough, Sa'adi's memoir confirms both of the poles that have bifurcated Ottoman Jewish historiography. On the one hand, this text depicts the flourishing of Jewish culture amid a wider multicultural mosaic and under the rule of an imperial regime indifferent to diversity as long as Islam remained the dominant religion in power, a regime uninterested in micromanaging the cultural affairs of its non-Muslim subjects. On the other hand, Sa'adi's memoir depicts rabbinic despotism—a kind of self-imposed ghettoization—that may have always existed but that had calcified by the Tanzimat era with the approval and enforcement of the Ottoman authorities and in the absence of a well-developed public sphere. Thus Sa'adi the musician partakes in a deeply multi- and intra-ethnic musical world and Sa'adi the poet lionizes Sultan Abdul Medjid *Hân* as "an upright king like no other," urging Jews to whom his Hebrew poem was comprehensible: "with no hesitation let us trust him"

(Epilogue).[7] At the same time, Sa'adi the ethnographer notes that many turn-of-the-century Jews, the religious elite included, do not speak Turkish. (Many of this cohort likely understood some Turkish and were able to make themselves understood within the confines of a limited vocabulary, yet they certainly were not proficient in the language.)

This memoir, then, is at once a barometer of Jewish inclusion and isolation, of symbiosis and marginalization. Sa'adi's text indicates that neither of the opposing interpretations of Ottoman Jewish history stands on its own; neither symbiosis nor separation can capture a complex reality. Rather, individual Jews like Sa'adi lived on multiple registers that historians have come to see as contradictory but that could be experienced concurrently and without apparent illogic. Perhaps this has been unimaginable heretofore because we have not had access to first-person narratives by Ottoman Jews such as the one that follows.

While Sa'adi lived immersed in the intensely Jewish milieu of Salonica, this milieu was inseparable from, and indeed unthinkable outside of, the Ottoman context. The Ottoman social landscape supplied a constant interaction of peoples, combined with the affirmation of difference, factors that were embedded in power hierarchies that spanned religion, class, and gender. None of this is immediately translatable into contemporary vocabularies. It is perhaps best described simply as Ottoman, or in its original Turkish, *Osmanlı*, an extinct social reality that permeates Sa'adi's memoir and, indeed, that memoirs like this are preternaturally equipped to illustrate.

Power, Religion, and Progress

As we have already mentioned, a trauma is at the heart of this text: Sa'adi's dramatic excommunication, as well as the myriad social, economic, and psychological ills that attended this episode of his life. *Herem* (excommunication) in the Sephardic context is a theme little ex-

7. This praise of the sultan followed the time-hallowed tradition of Jewish public affirmations of loyalty to rulers in various contexts. Julia Phillips Cohen, "Fashioning Imperial Citizens: Sephardi Jews and the Ottoman State, 1856–1912" (PhD diss., Stanford University, 2008).

plored by scholars of Ottoman Jewry; on the contrary, scholarship has tended to emphasize vaguely the flexibility of the Sephardic religious elite. Perhaps this appears relative to what one finds in the contemporaneous Ashkenazic world, but to Sa'adi, the rabbis whom he criticized were petty, vituperative, and vengeful, bulwarks opposed to change. In his view they—in alliance with or sometimes under the thumb of unscrupulous merchants and administrators—sapped poor Jews financially by taxing kosher meat, wine, and other foodstuffs (by way of the *gabela* or gabelle tax), by taking advantage of their capacity as legal arbiters, and by levying curses, corporal punishment—including lashes to the feet and a "torture press"—and by extending the threat of what Sa'adi calls "this old weapon, excommunication" to keep Jews at bay from "progress" and to spread fear among their followers, thereby consolidating power.

What did progress mean to Sa'adi or to the conservative elite with whom he battled? As for most Jewish communities of this time, observance of or rebellion against the traditional milieu was marked by practices that can seem banal to the secular eye. In Sa'adi's account, moments of friction between "enlightened" Jews and the traditional establishment crystallized around, among other things, how one structured one's hours, days, weeks, or year, the clothes one wore, the language one spoke, the spaces one frequented, or the music one listened to. In Chapter 11 a musician invited to Salonica to perform at the wedding of the son of a prominent Jewish banker incurs the wrath of a religious leader, *Rav* Shaul, for performing on a violin, an instrument the rabbi had neither heard of by its name nor its sound. (As has already been mentioned, it was the rabbi's wife who identified the offending article: a reminder that women in the Ottoman Jewish milieu were often more likely than men to inhabit the porous boundary between the sacred and the profane, even if they, like this rabbi's wife, were quite pious.) *Rav* Shaul, outraged that a Jewish wedding should feature music in "imitation of the gentiles," ordered the musician to stop and, when the host retorted that the rabbi had no right meddling in a private celebration, excommunicated the visiting musician and all guests who heard him play. To sing Jewish songs in a non-Jewish key, as it were—to engage in musical border crossing and to flirt with the social blurring of boundaries that inevitably accompanied it—was to test the limits of rabbinic flexibility and to push up against traditional religious boundaries. It was also to highlight that many of the boundaries maintained by the conservative elite had been naturalized as "authentically" Jewish with their provenance forgotten. After all, as is suggested in the retort to *Rav* Shaul in Sa'adi's text, the entirety of Sephardic religious musical traditions, which by this time were performed in the synagogue, had in fact been built on the template of Ottoman music that was itself created by Muslim, Christian, and Jewish composers and singers over the centuries.

Sa'adi's obsession with rabbinical abuses sheds an unusually brilliant light on the structure of traditional power relations in nineteenth-century Salonica. Given how enormously complex were the competing systems of power that structured the city's Jewish community, this vivid first-person account is particularly valuable. In the nineteenth century there was no Jewish hierarchy of authority in Salonica, even though the chaos following the arrival of Sephardic Jews after 1492 (when each congregation ran its affairs) had receded. Thus a triumvirate of "chief rabbis" wielded religious authority, while other rabbis maintained considerable influence as well. At the same time, lay notables, the "seven prominent men of the city" (see the text and glossary) or the *gevirim* (powerful lay notables) who may or may not have coincided with the "seven prominent men of the city," appointed the chief rabbis and oversaw the finances of communal institutions such as the *Talmud Tora*, the communal council, and the various welfare associations, sometimes in harmony with the rabbis and sometimes with great conflict. Matters were made even more thorny by the fact that the Ottoman authorities devolved authority to tax the Jewish community to different bodies—sometimes to a chief rabbi and sometimes to a lay notable. The primary "chief rabbi" (the *hahambashi*), which came to be the name given to the rabbi selected by the state as its interlocutor, was not an official position until the nineteenth century. Even then, the community did not necessarily recognize the *hahambashi*'s religious and legal authority, and many Jews followed other more charismatic or powerful rabbinical leaders. As is amply demonstrated in Sa'adi's account, this confused situation of fractured religious and lay communal power could lead to abuses and chaos.

Nor were ambiguities within the Jewish sphere the only ones conditioning the shape of power in Jewish Salonica. As the nineteenth century unfolded and the Ottoman state began to reform itself with the introduction of the Tanzimat Reforms (in 1839), new civil institutions were overlaid atop the traditional, intracommunal authorities responsible for governing non-Muslim communities in the empire. These included civil commercial and penal tribunals, which now claimed jurisdiction over matters hitherto left to the semiautonomous *millets*.[8] Rather than simplifying the execution of power and law, structures such as these complicated further the relationship of individuals, communities, and the state. Many pages in Sa'adi's memoirs reflect faithfully, in all their messy detail, the coexistence of old and new Ottoman realities of governance that were increasingly ubiquitous to the nineteenth century.

This complex social map explains why, in Sa'adi's account, the rabbis relied on a lengthy chain of power relations to ensure their judgments were carried out. Until well into the 1850s the scenario was a predictable one. They call first on the *gevirim* for help in implementing their rulings: the *gevirim* in turn seek assistance from the *Vali* (Ottoman governor of the city), who summons his *kavvases* (armed guards, also called *gendarmes* by Sa'adi) to seize the punished party. The *kavvases* then ferry the subject of rabbinical justice to the mansion or the prison of the *Vali* to be held and/or punished. That the *Vali*'s mansion reappears as a site in which Jewish legal judgments are meted out illustrates quite clearly that the Jewish *millet* was neither an insular nor even a totally autonomous community. Quite the contrary, its authority was juridically extended and maintained by the Ottoman civil administration (despite the fact that leading rabbis, including *Rav* Shaul, of whom Sa'adi often writes, spoke no Turkish and required interpreters when they met with civil authorities). Rabbis could be held in high esteem by (indeed,

8. Ottoman legal changes that affected the internal jurisdiction of the "millet" are illustrated in the Ladino translation of the penal code: see Isaac Jerusalmi, ed., *Kanun Name de Penas: Letras de Muestro Sinyor El Rey, Text of the Ladino Version, Transliteration into Western Characters* (Cincinnati: Sephardic Beth Shalom Congregation and Hebrew Union College, 1975): www.stanford.edu/group/mediterranean/seph_project/library.html.

sometimes even intimidate) Turkish officials—thus Sa'adi reports on a governor who sought to be blessed by *Rav* Shaul.

For all the power the rabbis had accrued, rabbinical writ and punishment were on the whole implemented only by Ottoman state officials, who would carry out rabbinical requests for punishment by imprisoning those accused of malfeasance, and even by implementing the capital punishment decreed (Chapter 9), though this was a rare ruling by rabbis. As this suggests, despite the great sway the rabbis commanded, there had always been limits to their influence. Ottoman authority, in spite of ceding vast autonomy to the *millets*, traditionally maintained the final say. What is more, the imprisoned subject of rabbinical judgment could find his fate reversed as a result of the intervention of a secular Jewish or non-Jewish authority, for the extraterritorial rights that had been granted to European powers beginning with the Capitulations of the sixteenth century (but which became particularly rife and egregious in a weakened, nineteenth-century empire) allowed European consuls to circumvent Ottoman and *millet* jurisdiction. Sa'adi tells of a Jew pronounced guilty by the religious authorities who found his punishment lifted as a result of the intercession of a consul (Chapters 6, 9, and 25), and of a wealthy Jew, possibly a Franko (Chapter 8), who claims immunity from justice as a result of serving as a protégé of the consul. In all cases allies of the charged party lodged successful pleas with the relevant Ottoman authority, who overruled the rabbis and freed the prisoner. Sa'adi himself was rescued in this manner after being accused of offending the chief rabbi. With the intervention of two consuls and "other important figures," the *Vali Pasha* ordered Sa'adi's release in an early escapade, calling him an "independent thinker" and reprimanding the rabbinical authorities that had condemned him. As he did so, the *Vali* cited a new Tanzimat law by which, in Sa'adi's rendition, he claimed that these "Jewish fanatics who have constituted a city council of their own, if they ever come before me, they shall be punished, because the government has its own city council chartered with its laws and privileges to administer its legal functions" (Chapter 25).

The power of the rabbinical elite hence was not unbridled before the Tanzimat and was much diminished after the institution of new reforms. The Jewish religious leadership was compelled to modulate its decisions, to rely on Jewish and non-Jewish power structures, to maintain its own authority and at the same time to deflect and at times reflect pressures generated by the Jewish community, by wealthy (and perhaps especially Franko) pockets of self interest, by the Ottoman political landscape, even by foreign authorities and the international community.

Despite episodes such as this, Sa'adi succeeds (as per his intention) in painting a vivid picture of a Jewish power structure without check or balance within the community. According to his memoir, even in instances in which local secular authorities and international forces collaborated to hedge against rabbinical power, the rabbis and their allies could succeed in remaining more or less omnipotent. An unusual episode along these lines speaks of a controversy sparked after Salonica's rabbis ordered a woman tortured for having sexual relations out of wedlock (Chapter 9). In outrage a British consul initiated a campaign against the rabbis in the international press, and, according to Sa'adi, word of this "despicable act" of religious overreach traveled all the way to the British government, whose representatives submitted a plea for intervention to the Turkish authorities. The *Vali* was ordered to intervene, and he called on members of the Jewish community (in this case the *hahamim*) to identify the responsible parties. The *hahamim*, far from undermining their colleagues, bribed the young woman into refusing to testify against the community or its leaders. Perhaps so coordinated an exertion of outside pressure only strengthened the establishment's resolve: in this instance, rabbinic policing of Salonican Jews' social mores was allowed to persist.

We can conclude that while Sa'adi and like-minded reformers of his generation undoubtedly benefited from alliances built with local Frankos, outside philanthropists, non-Jews, and even governmental officials, there were limits to the efficacy of their labors. Change was not a one-way street, and the flow of power (or its very intensity) could not be reversed overnight. Sa'adi was locked in a heated power struggle whose outcome, the eventual victory of the reformers, though determined by the time of his writing, is only implied in his compulsive retelling of his traumatic excommunication and its aftermath.

Strikingly, despite Sa'adi a-Levi's intense hostility toward the conservative religious establishment, neither in his memoir nor in his periodicals did he ever attempt to articulate a different vision of Judaism. Sa'adi's text, while sharing with proponents of the Jewish Enlightenment (*Haskalah*) critiques of traditional Jewish society (including its educational system, the power it assigned a conservative rabbinate, and the corrupt administration that could rule over it), bears no traces of engagement or familiarity with Enlightenment thought. In this, Sa'adi's memoir differs dramatically from the 1791 autobiography of Solomon Maimon, which provided a corrosive critique of traditional Jewish society and institutions inflected by the discourse of the Enlightenment.[9]

The language and format of Sa'adi's memoir, by comparison, reveals the deep imprint of tradition upon his mental universe. Sa'adi concludes his recollections, for example, by explaining that he survived his many travails because he "obeyed God's will." For a man who described himself as a religious ignoramus because he quit the *Talmud Tora* at a young age, it is striking, further, that practically each page of his memoir is replete with biblical citations—frequently rendered, it must be noted, in a Hebrew of dubious accuracy. However, errors in the written Hebrew words in the *soletreo* text cannot be definitively linked to Sa'adi: they may reflect, at least in part, the limits of the knowledge of the scribe who committed Sa'adi's words to paper after his eyesight failed him. Sa'adi's limited training in Hebrew was likely counterbalanced by his extensive experience in the typesetting of Hebrew texts.

The depth of Sa'adi's religious knowledge aside, his traditional orientation opens a window on an indubitable aspect of the Judeo-Spanish world positioned at the cusp of major change in the nineteenth century. The interspersing of one's speech or writing with biblical references as in the case of other Jewish languages had a broadly cultural (and not always strictly a religious) valence in the popular Judeo-Spanish discursive imagination. Indeed, both Hebrew prayers and biblical sayings, recited orally and frequently by rote on a daily basis, constructed a fundamental template for oral and written expression. Hebrew as a language and the biblical and rabbinical tradition remained central referents of Ladino language and culture. This impulse was to be ruptured

9. See Salomon Maimon, Salomon *Maimon: An Autobiography*, trans. J. Clark Murray (Urbana: University of Illinois Press, 2001).

and displaced in but a generation or two, when French and other cultural influences would provide new and alternative paradigms for modernizing Sephardim. In Sa'adi's lifetime, however, even a man writing outside of (indeed, in contestation with) the conservative religious establishment, exhibited this deeply etched template of Ottoman Judeo-Spanish culture.

At the same time, piety is hardly Sa'adi's inspiration. On the contrary, among the qualities that come through most clearly in the pages that follow are vitriol and no small measure of paranoia. That this is the case reminds us that what is special about this memoir is not its facticity or neutral rendering of events: on the contrary, herein we discover a man in all his passions, meditating on past and present, a personal, even psychological, view of a milieu that is otherwise difficult to see in any way other than highly abstracted. Like all such texts, this deeply personal representation and idiosyncratic fashioning of events past does not make the text less valuable for the historian. On the contrary, together with other sources, it contributes significantly to the weaving of a rich and multicolored historical tapestry.

"My Personal Story Starts Here"

Who, then, was Sa'adi a-Levi: what does his text teach us about his life, and what elements of his own history does it evade? Sa'adi's narrative speaks remarkably little—explicitly, anyway—about its ostensible subject. It takes the author twenty-five chapters, the bulk of his text, to claim: "My personal story starts here" (the title of Chapter 25). The claim is patently false—Sa'adi's predilections and prejudices shape every page of this story and, indeed, are the focus of Chapter 25 no more than any other chapter.

Sa'adi was by profession a printer descended from a long line of printers. At age thirteen he inherited a press—and the *Rashi* type molds along with it—from his father, Besalel a-Levi Ashkenazi, who had inherited it from his own grandfather. At this moment Sa'adi was an orphan in charge of five siblings; the press itself was dilapidated and overseen by three aging printers. Despite these challenges, over the course of sixty-five working years (he retired in 1898) Sa'adi was the printer of a variety of texts: some religious, such as the *Sefer Zohar* (a series of kabbalistic works whose assembly dates to the thirteenth century) and rabbinic *responsa* (including most of the work of Rabbi Hayyim Palachi of Izmir), and others secular, such as his own poems and songs, the first gilded wedding invitations to circulate through Salonica, and the periodicals for which he became famous.

The earliest editors of Ladino periodicals were a relatively small and insular coterie who began to publish in significant numbers in the 1870s. Approximately three hundred Sephardic periodicals appeared between 1845 and 1939: most of these were short-lived and appeared in Salonica (105), Istanbul (45), Sofia (30), and Izmir (23). The vast majority of these appeared in Ladino, though some were published in French and a few others were bilingual. In this context Sa'adi founded *La Epoka* in 1875 and, despite a lack of knowledge of French, *Le Journal de Salonique* in 1895, in all likelihood his sons' creation; the editorship of both papers would pass to his son Sam Lévy in 1898, when Sa'adi retired. All of Sa'adi's sons were involved in their father's printing endeavors: Hayyim, whose alleged actions incurred the wrath of Salonica's rabbinic authorities, initially operated *La Epoka*'s printing press; Besalel contributed articles to *La Epoka* and became its director in 1898; Daout (known as Daout Effendi when he later became a civil servant) assumed direction of *Le Journal de Salonique* in 1900; and Samuel Sa'adi a-Levi, known as Sam Lévy, became the chief editor of both newspapers in 1898.[10] Both of a-Levi's newspapers were instrumental in creating a Jewish newspaper culture in Salonica—*La Epoka* was intended for Salonica's Ladino-speaking population and *Le Journal de Salonique* for the city's multiethnic and French-reading residents. The agenda of these newspapers could be described as Westernizing in a general sense: they introduced readers to current events and developments in science and technology, put them in touch with developments in the wider world, and, as in the case of *La Epoka*, familiarized them

10. For the emergence of modern Ladino print culture, see Olga Borovaya, *Modern Ladino Culture: Press, Belles Lettres, and Theater in the late Ottoman Empire* (Bloomington: Indiana University Press, 2011).

by adapting and translating French novels and stories into Ladino in serialized or feuilleton format.

A publisher by profession, Sa'adi was a musician and a composer by hobby and passion, though he also earned income from these pursuits. Like his grandfather, Rabbi Yeuda a-Levi before him, Sa'adi was a virtuoso of Ottoman Jewish traditional music. A distinct aspect of this musical tradition emerged in the eighteenth century with the *maftirim* choir of Adrianople (Edirne), whose influence spread to other Ottoman cities. Using classical Arabic and Ottoman *makam* (composition rules) and adapted Hebrew prayers, and borrowing from (and performing with) Sufi orders, Muslim and Jewish *maftirim* musicians sang mystical texts to celebrate religious occasions both Jewish and Muslim. In Adrianople the Jewish *maftirim* choir and their paraliturgical singing became a fixture of Sabbath services, and they influenced similar choirs in cities like Salonica. In the memoir that follows, Sa'adi describes becoming a master of Ottoman Turkish music, learning his craft at the feet of an Ottoman music master, Murteza Izzedinoglu, and at the same time absorbing a different and yet parallel liturgical tradition from his Jewish music mentor, Aaron Barzilay. He meets with Muslim singers to rehearse traditional Ottoman and Hebrew songs, creates a choir consisting of both Muslims and Jews, and personally commands a large repertoire of Ottoman Turkish music. It is difficult to identify with certainty whether this is the same musical repertoire and practice that we associate with the *maftirim* choir of Adrianople, though the resemblance is quite striking. Regardless, Sa'adi's musical activities provide yet another illustration of the Jewish place in the Ottoman musical world as it evolved over the centuries.

Sa'adi's son, Sam Lévy, who would become the powerhouse behind his father's journals, lavishly praises his father's singing prowess the first time he mentions the family patriarch in his own memoir: "My father was possessed of an admirable voice with the purity of crystal, a nuanced and captivating sweetness. He inherited it from his grandfather, Rabbi Juda Halévy, who was the most celebrated singer in all the Orient and people of all religions came to consult him about the details of sounds, cadence, harmony, and rhythm."[11] It is in his capacity as a

11. Sam Lévy, *Salonique à la fin du XIXe siècle* (Istanbul: ISIS, 2000), 18.

musician and composer that we see most clearly the *Osmanlı* (that is, quintessentially Ottoman nature of) Sa'adi. Jewish composers were an integral and highly integrated part of the Ottoman musical landscape: they trained (as did Sa'adi) and practiced with non-Jewish masters, and the most distinguished of them in turn trained both Jewish and non-Jewish apprentices.[12] It is all the more interesting that Sa'adi appears most happy when he speaks of music. For someone who lived in the fearful and angry shadow of rabbinic authority, perhaps it was precisely in the extraethnic realm of composition and performance that Sa'adi felt least encumbered. One could postulate that it is here, in the realm of music (and undoubtedly also in the realm of cuisine) that the crisscrossing of multiple traditions that made up such a crucial element of quotidian Ottoman life is most clearly embodied: these were sites of cultural bricolage that nationalist ideologies would eventually condemn as "Levantine," "impure," and "inauthentic." Written a generation before such thinking crystallized, Sa'adi's memoir is situated at the meeting of multiple worlds in mutual interaction that so characterized *Osmanlı* life.

If musical mixing across the boundaries of *millets* was ubiquitous for the musicians involved, it could on occasion raise the hackles of Jewish religious authorities. Such was the case with Sa'adi after he composed a *kaddish* melody in a Turkish style learned during an apprenticeship with the non-Jewish master singer Murteza (Izeddinoglu) and sang this composition at the wedding of a distinguished Salonican Jewish family (Chapter 11). This story is significant, for it signals that as a musician, Sa'adi evinced a deep affinity for—even an intimacy with—this aspect of Ottoman culture.

With his limited educational background Sa'adi was no scholar. He left the *Talmud Tora* after only a few weeks of study, bemoaning the cruel treatment students faced at the hands of despotic and violent instructors. (Sa'adi's disparaging remarks about the *Talmud Tora* echo contemporary Ottoman educational reformers, on the one hand, and, on the other, the remarks of Jewish reformers excoriating the state of traditional Jewish instruction in the *heders* of Eastern Europe.) Though he fancied himself an

12. Maureen Jackson, *Mixing Musics: Turkish Jewry and the Urban Landscape of a Sacred Song* (Stanford, CA: Stanford University Press, forthcoming).

autodidact, it is striking that this memoir offers scant information about the books or journals he read or the intellectual company he kept. While printing rabbinical works well into middle age, Sa'adi devoted the last decade of his life to publishing materials that were designed to educate Jewish readers in modern, secular ways. It may appear surprising to the student of modern Jewish history that Sa'adi never sought to align himself intellectually or politically with the European *Haskalah*, whose ideas and texts he undoubtedly encountered as a modernizer and as a publisher. Was Sa'adi uninterested in or unsympathetic to *maskilim*, the followers of this agenda? Did his passionate antirabbinical polemic simply occlude expression of intellectual or political proclivities? Or was he simply attacking corruption, which he depicted through the prism of old "superstition," thereby aligning himself with proponents of change like the Frankos? That these questions cannot be answered suggests that further attention needs to be paid to understanding the unique quality of "enlightened" thought in the Sephardic milieu or, indeed, the boundaries or nature of Jewish enlightenment as it has been recounted more generally. While some Ottoman Jews of Sa'adi's generation openly aligned themselves with the *Haskalah*, others may have been indifferent to its message while nonetheless supporting the curtailment of conservative rabbinical authority or cultural and communal reform. In the 1880s, while he was writing his memoir, Sa'adi's principal intellectual cohort was an intimate and fiercely divided coterie of Ottoman editors of Ladino journals, such as David Fresco in Istanbul and Aron Hazan in Izmir, who read and criticized one another with equal ferocity. No doubt his memoir was intended for their eyes, as well as for the broader Ladino reading public.

Why did Sa'adi choose to experiment with the genre of memoir? Though we lack concrete evidence—either in this text or in available information about Sa'adi's life—we suspect that Sa'adi became familiar with the genre after reading European biographies and autobiographies published in serialized form in the Ladino press of his time. Sa'adi's lack of an education makes it highly unlikely that he was able to read memoirs in European languages. His familiarity with Ottoman Turkish music notwithstanding, there is no evidence that he had access to Ottoman Turkish texts. This memoir closely follows the structure of the various types of serialized narratives published in the Ladino popular press.

Indeed, as we will explore shortly, it was designed to appear in serialized form in its pages, and portions of it did reach print in this fashion—though only after being copiously edited by Sa'adi's son, Sam Lévy.

We might usefully reflect on what we do not learn about Sa'adi's life. It comes forth in his narrative that he fathered fourteen children, five with his first wife and nine with his second. Yet this text teaches us next to nothing about the Sa'adi family: his parents, siblings, wives, and children are but apparitions. Nor can one, on the basis of this text, reconstruct how Sa'adi spent his time, with whom he was close, where he lived, whence were his intellectual influences, how he evaluated his professional or personal successes and failures, what gave him pleasure. Sa'adi's lapses of consciousness are not only internal. While his memoir paints a rich tableau of nineteenth-century Salonica, it is strikingly tone-deaf to and indeed almost always disparaging of the ample Jewish working class that populated his city. While Sa'adi is contemptuous of people of the "second" or "third class," the only times this population warrants his fleeting sympathetic attention is when it could be used to highlight the abuse of the rabbinical elite, which, in his words, imposed needless taxes "while the poor were crying and languishing in the streets, with no one listening to them" (Chapter 18). It is clear that Sa'adi himself identified and mingled with Salonica's Jewish upper crust though he himself was not from a monied family.

For all of these reasons Sa'adi's turn to the ethnographic (and seemingly farther still from introspection) in Chapters 27, 28, and 29 is particularly riveting. Ethnographic accounts of Ottoman Jewish cultural ways did not abound in the late nineteenth century: one can find a few such sources penned by foreign observers at this time, but it was not until the interwar period that the genre was pursued with intellectual (and sometimes Orientalist) earnest. What does it mean to make ethnography a part of one's memoir? What does it mean to write ethnographically about a living community of which one is a part? A third question raised by Sa'adi's ethnographic dabblings may be more fascinating still: how are we to understand the anger he brings to his ethnographic writings—what does it tell us about Sa'adi or the milieu in which he was situated?

Perhaps the answers to these questions lie in a quasi-autobiographical, quasi-ethnographic tale Sa'adi tells not once but twice in the course of his memoir, depicting a typical wedding night of a young Salonican Jewish couple. The first rendition of this story (Chapter 16) is autobiographical and presents a grotesque version of Sa'adi's first marriage to a young woman he had never met. The bride, startlingly pink from an overly vigorous facial depilation, wearing a bonnet and veil, her cheeks bulging with candies meant to bring good luck, appears "like a mermaid" to her groom, himself swaddled in a turban and layers of robes. Sa'adi witnesses the wedding rituals (the throwing of candy, the kissing of hands, the dancing of women dressed as witches to ward off the evil eye) with a combination of panic and fear, until, en route to the "bridal chamber," carried aloft the shoulders of two men, his head smashes into a hook hanging from the ceiling, producing a painful goose-egg on his brow. Moments later the couple experience their first moments alone together. All does not go well: the pair are "immobilized as if spellbound," mute with fear, and spend their nuptial night "in great discomfort, as if . . . at the peak of a typhoid fever."

Sa'adi's account lacks all sentimentality or nostalgia. On the contrary, his wedding is a site of violence and pain, accompanied by rituals he describes as antiquated by the time of his writing. For this, we learn more about Sa'adi's wedding night than we will about the seven years he would spend together with his first wife. These years are dispatched with in the course of a few sentences; Sa'adi tells us his wife would bear five children, that they would lose two sons to cholera, and that (in the wake of these deaths) his wife would suffer from what sounds like acute postpartum depression; writes Sa'adi, pausing not a moment to mourn, "She did not take care of herself and could not arise from the bed where she gave birth. This disappointment caused her death" (Chapter 16).

Nostalgia is also lacking the second time Sa'adi speaks of wedding nights (Chapter 28), but here personal narrative has morphed into a kind of informal ethnography, with certain leitmotifs persisting—the irritated cheeks of the bride, the mouth swollen with candy, the young groom pompously attired, the rituals of hand kissing, fasting, and *raki* drinking—and Sa'adi himself is removed from the scene. The repetition of motifs is significant, for it suggests that Sa'adi channeled discomfort with (indeed, animosity to) traditional practices through the medium of ethnography. Arguably, though sections of this narrative function as ethnography, history, and chronicle, as a whole the text is apologia, a mechanism for expressing outrage at the ill treatment Sa'adi experienced at the hands of obscurantist rabbis.

All the more, Sa'adi's flirtations with the ethnographer's voice invite hypotheses about the man himself. Perhaps Sa'adi's first marriage was joyless; perhaps he was a hard man; perhaps infant mortality and premature death were so ubiquitous as to render sentimentality an indulgence; or perhaps, in life as in the pages of his memoir, Sa'adi felt removed from the world he inhabited—an observer more than participant, a chronicler even before he put pen to paper, dispositionally suited to notice and record the changes he perceived to be swirling around him such that these changes brought him more pleasure in memory (and on paper) than they did at the time of their unfolding.

It is also possible that one can read in Sa'adi's anger something of the vulnerability of the era. As his memoir unfolds, Salonica experiences earthquakes (Chapter 10), fire (Chapters 15 and 41), war (Chapter 33), revolt (Chapter 42), and disease (Chapter 16). Disease and medicalizing discourse, in particular, pepper this text. Death, to begin, is an omnipresent threat, and it comes quickly. It is believed to be brought on by the ill will of a rabbi and, for women, by the wearing of contaminated furs. Plagues strike often, arriving from as far away as Ethiopia and spreading quickly, unchecked by quarantines. Various ailments remain unchecked or are mistreated. In all of these regards Sa'adi's account prefigures the relentlessly hygienist strictures that were propagated in almost every issue of the Ottoman Ladino press of the late nineteenth and early twentieth centuries. This text depicts a world fragile in the extreme, subject not only to disease but to every other imaginable catastrophe that strikes with dreadful regularity. A nervous energy traverses Sa'adi's memoir: in the language of the time, it could be described as "neurasthenic." And yet Sa'adi was not unrealistic in his descriptions and anxieties. Disease did decimate entire populations of the Ottoman lands. Earthquakes destroyed cities, as in the case of Izmir in the early eighteenth century. As Sa'adi describes, fires burn everything in their path, as they did in 1890, and in the disastrous conflagration that would destroy the traditional Jewish quarters of Salonica in 1917, thereby wiping out the landmarks in this narrative and eerily heralding the end of Jewish Salonica.

Thus it is no surprise that precariousness overhung the residents of the city, non-Jewish as well as Jewish, or that fear should arise again and again in Sa'adi's account. Sa'adi reports that both his mother and father died of fear, that the entire Jewish community of Salonica lived in fear of the curses extended by their rabbis, and that this fear in and of itself could cause misery and even death. Fear, in short, was a free-standing danger: neither symptom nor metaphor, it was itself an agent of change.

Jewish Salonica, a world both deeply rooted and fragile, is an apt metaphor for Sa'adi's memoir. Written to be published in serialized form, bearing the imprint of his journalistic writing, this text had a rich afterlife, appearing in places and forms its author could not have anticipated. To close this introduction, we offer an archaeology of the fate of Sa'adi's memoir: one that takes us through various sedimentary layers of the Sephardic diaspora, along multiple branches of Sa'adi's family tree, and, poignantly and personally, into our own lives.

The Excavation of Sa'adi Besalel a-Levi's Memoir

This text has had a long and checkered history since Sa'adi a-Levi began its composition in 1881. The bulk of this memoir was written over a nine-year period (from 1881–90), most of it in the precise handwriting of a scribe that Sa'adi employed.[13] Sa'adi's vision was deteriorating rapidly in the 1880s, limiting his own writing abilities. Additions to the manuscript were made in the margins over the years by Sa'adi himself. A short epilogue (and possibly other editorial changes) was added later toward the end of the manuscript, as late as 1902, when the author was eighty-two years old and one year from his death. The marginalia suggest that Sa'adi regularly returned to his text to add new information or recollections.

In our view the multiple "fingerprints" left on this manuscript do not call into question its integrity. Instead, they foreshadow the work's re-

13. As reported by his son Besalel in *L'Aksyon*, July 16, 1939. This is also reported in one of the obituaries on Sa'adi published by *Le Journal de Salonique*, Jan. 15, 1903.

markable genealogy. Sa'adi's memoir may be typical of its genre insofar as it was written over time and through the filter of memory. It is, however, unique in one crucial respect. Though not published in full until now, this text has nonetheless exerted a profound influence on the way in which Salonican Jewish history has been remembered and historicized. This was the case because the fragments of Sa'adi's memoir that saw print in 1907 and the 1930s appeared just as the first generation of scholars of Salonican and Ottoman Jewry (especially Joseph Nehama, Michael Molho, and Isaac Emmanuel) were researching and composing works of scholarship that would become the authoritative sources on Salonican Jewry for decades.[14] Without ever being published in full, Sa'adi's memoir became an unacknowledged and unobtainable primary source.

More astonishingly, since its completion the memoir passed through four generations of the a-Levi family, somehow eluding destruction or disappearance despite the dissolution of the Salonican Jewish community and the dispersal of the Sa'adi family over multiple countries and continents—surviving numerous wars, fires, and the genocidal madness of the Second World War, in the course of which Jewish texts and libraries, as well as Jewish bodies, were targeted by the Nazis for annihilation. Subsequently, the only apparent extant copy of Sa'adi's memoir was donated to and then disappeared on the shelves of a modern archive, to be unearthed by accident by one of the scholars who presents it here. By way of conclusion we present the story of this manuscript's journey, partial publication, multiple translations, loss and rediscovery—a story that spans a century and gives voice to chapters of Sephardic history that followed Sa'adi's death.

Fragments of Sa'adi's memoirs first appeared in print in serialized form in 1907, when they were published in *La Epoka* in modified form: some of these publications contained liberal expansions on Sa'adi's original manuscript, perhaps penned by one or more of his sons.[15] In

14. See Devin Naar, "Jewish Salonica and the Making of the 'Jerusalem of the Balkans,' 1890–1943" (PhD diss., Stanford University, 2011).

15. A well-developed description, putatively by Sa'adi, of the founding of *La Epoka* appeared in serialized form in 1907; this version expanded considerably on the history of this newspaper offered in the present translation.

the 1930s additional fragments appeared in installments in the Salonican Ladino newspaper *L'Aksyon* that were prepared for publication by his son Sam Lévy. A complete run of the latter newspaper has not been preserved, so it is impossible to revisit the serialization in full. Roughly contemporaneously (in September 1933), a second version of Sa'adi's reminiscences appeared in the Paris journal *Le Judaïsme Sépharadi*; this was also the doing of Sa'adi's son Sam Lévy, who selected and translated fragments of his father's memoir, publishing them over the course of several years. As we have mentioned, Lévy assumed responsibility for editing his father's journal, *La Epoka*, in 1898: later he would edit *Le Journal de Salonique*, which by the first decades of the twentieth century had become the premier French-language journal of the Judeo-Spanish communities of the Levant, and, on relocating to Paris, *Le Judaïsme Sépharadi* in the 1930s and (as of 1946) *Les Cahiers Séfardis*. Through this work he became known as one of the most important Sephardic journalists of the first half of the twentieth century and last follower of the a-Levi family tradition of printing and journalism. Toward the end of his life Lévy wrote his own fragmentary and episodic recollections in French that have now been published as a book.[16]

In addition to shepherding a portion of his father's memoirs to print, Lévy attempted to guarantee the safety of his father's manuscript. In the first issue of *Les Cahiers Séfardis* (dated Nov. 5, 1946) Lévy indicates that three copies of his father's memoirs existed. One of these, he wrote, he donated to the Bibliothèque Nationale of Paris in 1939. A second copy was entrusted to a "great friend of the family" in California: the last was ostensibly deposited at the "archives" of *Les Cahiers Séfardis*, which meant it remained in Lévy's possession.

Lévy's tantalizing leads resulted in archival dead ends. Numerous searches at the Bibliothèque Nationale in Paris yielded nothing; the other two copies proved equally impossible to locate. Serendipitously, while researching another topic, Aron Rodrigue discovered a copy of Sa'adi's memoirs in the manuscript room at the Jewish National University Library in Jerusalem, quite by happenstance. There is a strong probability, impossible to verify, that this is one of the manuscripts

16. Sam Lévy, *Salonique à la fin du XIXe siècle* (Istanbul: ISIS, 2000).

mentioned by Sam Lévy in 1946. Regardless, the text we have before us undertook a circuitous journey after leaving Sa'adi's hands: a journey involving three generations of a-Levi descendants and a history that reached beyond Salonica, beyond Paris, into the death camp of Auschwitz, through the émigré Sephardic community of Brazil, onto the shelves of a library in Israel, and across the American academy.

The Jewish National Library's copy of the memoirs, written in *soletreo*, has appended to it a (rather imprecise) Spanish-Portuguese romanized transcription. This was composed by Sa'adi's grandson, Leon David Levy, who lived in Rio de Janeiro and likely received the manuscript from his uncle, Sam Lévy, with whom he maintained a correspondence. Leon Levy was the son of Daout (David) Effendi a-Levi, who, before the collapse of the empire, reached a high position in the Ottoman bureaucracy in Salonica. In 1943 and in his very old age, Daout Effendi was deported by the Nazis along with Salonica's Jewish community and killed at Auschwitz. Daout Effendi's grandson (Leon Levy's son and Sa'adi's great-grandson), Sadi Silvio Levy, tells in a foreword to his father's transcription that Sa'adi's original manuscript was donated, along with Leon Levy's version, to the Jewish National and University Library in Jerusalem in 1977. In the same foreword he writes the following: "It is my great hope that this book should be sometime edited, in *Ladino* and *English*, to make it available to the Jewish communities of the world in a *bilingual* edition with some commentaries" (emphasis in original). We regret that Sadi Silvio Levy died but a decade before his wish was realized.

The Ladino manuscript in Jerusalem appears at first sight to be an incomplete text. Missing in this manuscript, for example, are Chapters 34 to 40. However, the page numbering in the accounting-style notebook Sa'adi employed appears continuous, indicating that no pages were removed. It could be that the number "33" of the chapter title was misread as "38" when its author resumed: this does not explain, however, why the subsequent chapter should be numbered "40." Similarly, some of the fragments translated by Sam Lévy in *Le Judaïsme Sépharadi* are nowhere to be found in this text. Other fragments published in *L'Aksyon* in the 1930s diverge from the originals we have before us, bearing Lévy's rather heavy-handed editing full of embellishments and

Gallicisms that marked a later Ladino than that which typifies the bulk of the memoir. Recognizing that we are not dealing with a complete document, we have chosen to present the Jerusalem version—the only extant continuous Ladino *soletreo* manuscript of Sa'adi's memoir—on its own and to transcribe, translate, and annotate it (including its marginalia) without attempting to complement it with other sources, since their integrity cannot be verified. This is in keeping with Sa'adi's own final wish, which was added as a separate freestanding addendum to this manuscript, quite likely late in Sa'adi's life. We have chosen to introduce Sa'adi's memoir with this expression of desire: "My last request from my children is to print this story as soon as possible and by all means, either in our printing press or in Vienna, or in Belgrade, so that not to transgress my request. After you have improved on some sentences and taken care of some difficult words in Turkish and Hebrew, be certain to keep a copy in book form."

Surely Sa'adi could not have anticipated that the first time his memoirs would be published in their fullest possible form, they would appear in transliteration and English translation, let alone in California. Yet in all other respects this publication fulfills both Sa'adi's and his great-grandson's wishes.

The transformation of this first known Ladino language memoir and the collaboration required to produce it also reflect the shifting physical and cultural geography of the Sephardic world as it has been shaped in the generations after Sa'adi's death. For if the transmission of Sa'adi's manuscript to contemporary readers depended on three generations of the Sa'adi family, it has also depended on the work and expertise of three generations of scholars who are committed to the study of (and, to varying degrees, are products and inheritors of) Judeo-Spanish culture.

The translator, Isaac Jerusalmi, grew up in Istanbul, rooted in the Judeo-Spanish culture and milieu of the traditional Jewish quarter of Kuzguncuk, located on the Asian side of the city. Ladino was his mother tongue, Sephardic Jewish culture his daily, lived reality. Jerusalmi studied classical philology at Istanbul University and later, for the rabbinate at the Hebrew Union College in Cincinnati, graduating with a master's degree in Hebrew Letters and with rabbinic ordination. He then specialized in Semitics at the University of Paris-Sorbonne, where he obtained his PhD in Aramaic. In addition to Hebrew, he taught Aramaic and classical Arabic for almost fifty years at the Hebrew Union College in Cincinnati. He is the first Sephardic Jew from Turkey or the former Ottoman lands to be ordained as a Reform rabbi.

Aron Rodrigue, also of Istanbul, belongs to the last generation of Sephardic Jews exposed to Ladino as a language of the home. This was shared with Turkish and French. He experienced the dying vestiges of a multiethnic and multireligious Ottoman Levantine world as they faded away in modern Turkey. He obtained his PhD in Jewish history at Harvard University, specializing in Sephardic history under the mentorship of Yosef Hayim Yerushalmi. He became, together with Esther Benbassa, one of the first contemporary autochthonous historians of the Judeo-Spanish world with academic training and based at a university to start writing the history of Sephardic Jewry anew in the last decades of the twentieth century. He is a professor of Jewish history at Stanford University.

Sarah Abrevaya Stein was raised well outside a Sephardic center, in Eugene, Oregon, as a child of Ashkenazic and Sephardic heritage. Her maternal grandfather, a native Ladino speaker, was born in the Turkish city of Çanakkale, whence, together with his siblings and parents, he migrated via Istanbul and New York to Los Angeles. The first doctoral student of Aron Rodrigue (with the joint mentorship of Steven J. Zipperstein) and one of the only Jewish historians whose work traverses the Sephardic and Ashkenazic worlds, Stein received a PhD in Jewish history at Stanford University. She is professor of history and Maurice Amado Chair in Sephardic Studies at the University of California, Los Angeles.

The members of this trio, spanning several generations, have all been engaged with contemplating, transcribing, registering, and studying what is now the dried Judeo-Spanish tributary of Jewish culture. In publishing these memoirs, we hope to contribute to the understanding of Judeo-Spanish communities at a decisive period in their history through the perspective of a distinctive and colorful local actor. And yet we realize, with poignancy, that this first autobiographical text in Ladino is also one of the last conduits to cultures and topographies now erased, occulted, reshaped, written over by others. Sa'adi a-Levi's rendition of his individual travails, mixed with ethnographic ruminations on the community he was a part of, is hence more than an *apologia pro vita sua*, or defense of his life. It also opens a rare and unique window on the Ottoman Levant in its sunset years, before the transformations and horrors that would forever sweep it out of existence.

It is well known that Sa'adi's language, Ladino, would also all but perish in the course of the twentieth century. Less widely acknowledged is the fact that most contemporary transliterations of Ladino have not done the language justice, Gallicizing, Turkicizing, Hispanicizing, and, most often of all, Hebraizing the language to the extent that it would be hardly recognizable to speakers of Sa'adi's era. Our system of transliteration is described briefly in our Note on Translation and Transliteration, but it is worth stressing here that Isaac Jerusalmi's transliteration of Sa'adi's memoir abides by rules that we consider more appropriately faithful to native speakers of the language. Here we have used Sa'adi's words to resurrect Sephardic pronunciations that have, too often, been erased through distortion in deference to the hegemonic rules of other linguistic systems, most notably Israeli Hebrew. (Another major Jewish language, Yiddish, has been subjected to parallel malformation in current standardized renditions, which eliminate regional and dialectical differences and/or privilege current Israeli pronunciation.) Our method will no doubt surprise even many Ladino specialists, but, crucially, it makes an important point about historical Jewish languages. If Jewish languages are transliterated in a manner that conforms to contemporary predilections over historical, lived practices, they are misunderstood and their histories erased. In this instance faithful transliteration requires a radical approach.

For all the loss it symbolizes, Sa'adi's memoir has also proved a remarkable conduit between the past and the present. In the final stages of readying this book for publication, Sarah Stein located Sa'adi a-Levi's great-great-grandson, Silvio (né Behor Silvio) Levy: the Rio-born grandson of Leon Levy, the son of Silvio Levy, who donated Sa'adi a-Levi's *soletreo* manuscript to the Jewish National Library just over thirty years ago. Extraordinarily, Silvio Levy resides with his wife Sheila Newbury in Berkeley, California, just thirty miles from the press that would publish the memoir of his great-great-grandfather. Like Sa'adi a-Levi, Silvio Levy's son, Andrew, is a musician: like Sa'adi a-Levi's son Daout Effendi, who was a distinguished Salonican public dignitary, Silvio's brother Joaquim (né Eliakim) has served as a prominent minister in Brazil. Neither these nor any other living descendant of Sa'adi were aware of the existence of his memoir.

Aron Rodrigue and Sarah Abrevaya Stein

The Memoir of Sa'adi Besalel a-Levi

Preface

My purpose in writing this story is to inform future generations how much times have changed within half a century. Nothing resembles our present customs! From clothing worn by men and women to home furniture, even to the design of houses and, needless to say, to eating and drinking, everything has undergone a profound change. Some quite curious habits among young men and unmarried girls are also worth mentioning. To anyone with a vivid recollection of the old days, this is like going from a bygone age into a new one, as one observes the behavior of men and women and youngsters of both sexes. On reading this personal story, some young people may joke about it; others will laugh, and still others will be deeply crushed, concluding, "This is how our ancestors suffered in the olden days due to their ignorance and fanaticism." Hopefully, this will be obvious from my narrative as it unfolds!

However, due to my fuzzy recollection of dates, I beg the readers of this story not to chide me for giving precedence to items that should normally come later and *vice versa*. Clearly, as my priority was to describe the facts, I neglected my chronology. In reality, our ancestors, too, rarely wrote down dates. That is why even I failed to keep track of my children's birth dates. This situation does not apply only to me, but to 99 percent of Jews who acted likewise. So, I shall speak only about what I have personally seen with my eyes and what I have heard with my ears, or a few things I heard from real people. I started to write this story on May 23, 1881, and on. It is the pure truth.

Sa'adi a-Levi

Chapter 1

Personal Information

[1a] I, who am mentioned below, am the descendant born in the year 1820 of a certain *sinyor* Besalel a-Levi Ashkenazi. He was a young man dressed according to the Ashkenazi style. As an educated man, he was received as a *shaliah* or traveling fund-raiser, even though he was not needy, neither was he on a fund-raising mission. In those days out-of-town guests were granted hospitality. His host was *sinyor Rav* Modiano,[1] may he rest in paradise. During his stay at the *rav*'s house, he had talks with him and was asked about the reason of his coming to Salonica. He replied, saying that he hadn't come for any fund-raising, but that as an artisan versed in printing, he was looking for a place to establish himself. The *sinyor rav* helped this handsome young man open a printing press where he printed a number of books written by local scholars, among which I still have in my possession one entitled *Meoré Or*, printed by him personally in 1752.[2] It was also the *sinyor rav* who helped him get married in our city. He had two sons, one called Avraam and the other Yeuda a-Levi Ashkenazi. His son Avraam died, leaving no descendants, but my grandfather Yeuda lived to around ninety years old. I was fortunate to know him way beyond my own father who did not get to live to attain half his age. My *sinyor* grandfather had two sons. The oldest was Sa'adi, who died relatively young without any progeny. Therefore my father inherited the printing press. My father, too, died at the age of thirty-six or thirty-seven, leaving his wife with four daughters, with me barely five to six years old. My father lived to marry just one daughter. That same year, he passed away, leaving behind my mother five months pregnant. In time she gave birth to a baby boy whom she named *Chelebon*, who came down with kidney disease. He died at the age of eighteen, three days after surgery. In those days the science of medicine was not as advanced, and there were no qualified

1. In all likelihood Rabbi Yosef Shmuel Modiano (1714–81), some of whose work Sa'adi published.
2. Authored by Jerusalem kabbalist Meir Bakiar, this book was published in 1754, not 1752 as Sa'adi claims.

doctors in our city, except for one Dr. Parsakaki. He did the surgery in his own way, causing his death.

I was named after my father's brother, who died in the pestilence of 1814 and left me as an inheritance his ring with his name engraved on it. My *sinyora* mother placed it on my finger when I was fifteen years old. I have worn it every day since then, even today as I am writing this story. I, too, will leave it as an inheritance after me **[1b]** to one of my sons liable to honor my full name in keeping with our family's custom of not naming a newborn after a living person.[3]

Chapter 2

The Cause of My Father's Death

My father was an observant Jew. In those days all the Jews kept their religious obligations, such as Tora study sessions on the eve of *Shavu'oth*, *Selihoth*, *Osha'na Rabba*, or the Seventh Day of Passover.

One *Shavu'oth* eve, he went after dinner to attend a study session according to the custom of all the Jews when they all went to their synagogues and no one stayed home. That time of the year, nights were shorter, dawn broke early around six thirty, some people would come back home to eat the *enchusa* with some rice pudding, then go to sleep until 1 or 2 p.m. Others went touring the parks, while lower-class people with wicker baskets filled with cheese pies, rice pudding, *raki*, and hard-boiled eggs went with their families to parks on the outskirts of the city to eat, get drunk, and fall asleep on the grass. Most of them returned home sick.

After the prayers, my *sinyor* father and one of his employees from his print shop went to the seashore to get some fresh air. At that time there were neither steamships nor regular mail service.[4] Captains were

3. With this statement Sa'adi indicates his hope that a future grandchild, born to one of his sons, would carry his name after his death. This was in keeping with the tradition of his Ashkenazi ancestors who migrated to Salonica from Amsterdam. Among Sephardim, the opposite custom prevails: to have progeny carry one's name during one's lifetime is considered a divine reward.

4. Regular steamship lines to Salonica were introduced in 1840.

in charge of incoming mail, which they then distributed to the appropriate recipients.

[2a] While on the seashore, my *sinyor* father saw a boat coming from Smyrna, and his printing business dealt mostly with publishing books by scholars from Smyrna. Approaching the deck of the boat, he saw scattered mail addressed to businessmen, and among them was a letter addressed to *sinyor Rav* Gatenyo,[5] who was the contact man and correspondent for scholars in Smyrna. My *sinyor* father picked up that letter for his employee to deliver it, thinking that some urgent matter of interest to him dealing with a book might be involved and that it might not be delivered in time. Because of the holiday, he also thought it appropriate to have a Greek unseal the letter so that the rabbi could read it immediately.[6] He did just that and sent him the letter with his employee, who first went home to have a meal. But as usual, he fell asleep and slept until the evening. When he woke up, he had forgotten all about the letter he had in his pocket. The following night, this employee went to a different study session. In the morning he followed the same routine, ate and slept until the evening. The day after *Shavu'oth*, he came to the print shop to resume his work. My father asked him if he had delivered the letter to its recipient. The employee slapped his forehead saying that he had forgotten all about it. My father told the employee to take it immediately to the rabbi, with apologies, adding that it arrived on *Shavu'oth* and that is why it had been unsealed, to spare him the trouble of finding some gentile to do it on that day.

While this employee went to deliver the letter to the *haham*, my father sat down to have a light lunch. He had a slice of cheese pie left over from *Shavu'oth*, a piece of fresh cheese, a few delicious cookies, and some cherries. Just as he had finished his lunch, the employee came back, but he had not told the *haham* the entire story for fear of assuming blame. The *sinyor haham* asked, "Where did you get this letter?" He answered, "My *sinyor* boss *ham* Besalel gave it to me as is."

5. Possibly Avraam Gatenyo (c. 1791–1880), appointed to the triumvirate of ruling rabbis in 1876. There were other rabbis with the same last name at the same time.
6. To unseal the letter would be considered work forbidden during the religious holiday.

[2b] In his answer the *sinyor haham* said that with this action, he had transgressed the negative command of *ribbi* Yeuda Hasid.[7] When my *sinyor* father, who was meticulous in his religious observance, heard the name of *Ribbi* Yeuda Hasid, he thought that this *Ribbi* Yeuda Hasid was the Angel of Death, who was coming to kill him with a drawn out sword in his hand. On a full stomach and out of great fear, my father became ill; he had to go to bed with shivers, and within nine days he passed away, [on] the night of June 23, 1826.

O poor father! How tragic that you lost your life at its peak because you feared the words of a man who compiled a book of all the negative commandments, such as: No Israelite may marry a *Kohen*; no hen that crows like a rooster may be spared; it must be slaughtered; no young man bearing his future father-in-law's name may marry this man's daughter; no two future father-in-laws bearing identical names can allow the marriage of their children; no goose may be slaughtered in the months of *Teveth* and *Shevat, etc. etc.*

This prohibition on slaughtering geese in *Teveth* and *Shevat*, when geese are fattened, favored the ritual slaughterers who set aside the head, the dewlap, and the neck for themselves, based on the principle that the ritual slaughterer must consume part of the flesh. As of this writing this strange custom has not yet been revoked, simply because ritual slaughterers love to eat those fatty meals.

In conclusion, due to some fearful prohibitions imposed by our ancestors over such shallow matters, people died as victims of the fear created by fanaticism. I will relate many similar cases below.

Chapter 3

Personal Information and My Sinyora Mother's Death

[3a] My *sinyora* mother used to tell me that her family was a descendant from a *sinyor* Morpurgo, who came from Italy and settled

7. A leading rabbi (1140–1217) in classical Ashkenaz in the Rhineland. Sa'adi errs here; it was Gershom ben Judah (d. 1028), also known as Rabbeinu Gershom, who issued the decree banning the reading of others' private correspondence.

in Salonica. He had an only daughter who was married to a certain *sinyor* Avraam Kovo, who had daughters that died, with my mother as the only survivor. He called her Djantil. Yet, because he lost his other daughters and she was the only "cherished" survivor, they called her *Merkada*.[8] By training, she was a skilled seamstress of *a la franka*–style shirts, a trade she inherited from her mother, who in turn learned it from her *sinyora vava*, a trade she had brought from Italy. In an age when there were no sewing machines, all the work was done by hand. All the consulates in Salonica and other high-placed personalities, as well as all the business people, wore her shirts, the outcome of her handiwork. At my father's death I was a five- to six-year-old little boy, our printing house was run by its employees, and revenues were insufficient for the upkeep of five children. It was through sheer hard work, the fruit of her hands, that six souls survived. By herself she managed to marry her three daughters, but I was not lucky enough to get married during my mother's lifetime.

In those days key businessmen and consuls sent their respective *kavases* [bodyguards] to fetch her. The European quarter,[9] however, had none of those fancy stores it has today, but was rather isolated, with their mansions protected by fierce dogs against evildoers. Those dogs were as ferocious as lions; during the day, they had to chain and cage them. One day, the wife of *Musyu* Rika sent for her—he was at the top of the Masonic order[10]—but one of the dogs of her house was not yet restrained, but was roaming around in the courtyard. As she was stepping through the gate, accompanied by the *kavas*, my mother was confronted by this barking dog, **[3b]** was terrified, and started to have shivers that recurred for many months, as if she had malaria. The doctors prescribed that she drink *azarado* wine. This *azarado* wine was old wine fortified

8. Children who survived close encounters with death were renamed *Merkado* or *Merkada*, signaling they were "redeemed" from the clutches of the Angel of Death. Renaming was thought to prevent revisitation by this angel.

9. The *quartier franc*, was the Salonican district that surrounded the Catholic church and was inhabited primarily by Europeans.

10. Freemasonry, which was introduced to Ottomans by Europeans, would have a long and distinguished history in nineteenth-century Salonica, attracting the elite of all communities.

with a dose of iron filings that was exposed to the sun for a few days. She had to drink three cups a day from this wine for forty consecutive days. When this cure was over, this tropical disease recurred. Finally, she, too, died from this disease on September 15, 1837. That is when my brother and I were on our own.

Chapter 4

The Fear of Fanaticism

From my childhood I remember until today the *rabbanim* who have passed away, starting with the death of *Rav* Romano, may he rest in peace, in 1827. Then, the "Seven Honorable Citizens"[11] of the Jewish community appointed as *rabbanim* the *Rav h"r* [Hayyim Shabetai Ben Shabetai] Nehama [d. 1828], the *Rav h"r* Yaakov [bar Avraam] Menashe [d. 1831], and *h"r* Moshe Beraha [d. 1835], head of the ritual slaughterers.[12] When these three[13] passed away, they appointed another three *rabbanim h"r* Avraam Soriano [d. 1836], *h"r* Shaul Molho (1835) [c. 1766–1849], and *h"r* Behor Matalon [d. 1847]. And when these three passed away, they appointed *h"r* Hanania Saporta (1854) [d. 1857] and the *Rav h"r* Asher Kovo [1801–74]. When the latter two died, they appointed the *Rav h"r* Avraam Gatenyo (1876) [c. 1791–1880], *h"r* Mair Nahmias [1804–87], and *h"r* Shemuel Arditi [c. 1811–87]. When these three passed away, they appointed as acting chief rabbi[14] the *Rav h"r* Yakovachi Kovo [c. 1824–1907].[15] However, the most powerful and respected of all these was the *Rav h"r* Shaul

11. *Shiv'a tove a-'ir*, "The Seven Honorable Citizens" (see glossary). In effect this group constituted the secular leadership of Salonica's Jewish community.
12. Here and throughout, *h"r* is used to abbreviate the honorific *haham ribbi* (see glossary).
13. In contrast to other Judeo-Spanish communities Salonica had a triumvirate of rabbis as the communally sanctioned religious leadership of the Jewish community.
14. Ottoman authorities revived the institution of the Chief Rabbinate in Istanbul in 1835 but did not formalize the position of chief rabbi throughout the nineteenth century, appointing acting (*Kaymakam*) chief rabbis instead.
15. Kovo was the last Salonican-born chief rabbi of the Jewish community.

Molho, who was so feared among the people that some believed his curses caused death. By sheer luck, it had already been reported that his curses had caused some cases of death, even before he became a *rav*. **[4a]** Even as a ritual slaughterer, he was already worshipped by second- and third-class folks as if he were one of the prophets.

The first incident that caused a universal fear of him was the quarrel of the *hahamim* against the *gevirim* and the *Rav* Nehama, who was the chief rabbi of the community at a time when this *rav* and the *gevirin*[16] agreed to raise by one *para* the price of a quart of wine over the amount fixed previously.

H"r Shaul was responsible for stirring up all the *hahamim* and a segment of the population. They dispatched the mighty *h"r* Yaakov Djenyo [c. 1769–c.1869/75][17] to drop their idea of raising by one *para* the *gabela* of a quart of wine.[18] The community[19] and the *rav* [Nehama] insisted stubbornly and refused to give in. Again, the other side rejected their answer, threatening the community with strong language. Now, the *gevirim* and the *rav* [Nehama] ordered that *h"r* Yaakov Djenyo be shackled and incarcerated.

Then, *h"r* Shaul and his colleagues became furious and issued a heralded proclamation in the markets and businesses, with the well-known words, "whoever is for the Lord, come to me" (Exodus 32:26). The people closed their stores and gathered at the great *Talmud Tora*; the *hahamim* opened the Holy Ark, kindled some candles, and, having invited *shofar* blowers, pronounced an all-inclusive excommunication.[20]

The *gevirim* were livid! They rushed to the governor, submitting a note for the banishment of three to four *hahamim*, with *h"r* Shaul at their head, along with three of his colleagues. Just about that time, the

16. For the distinction between *gevirim* and *gevirin* see *gevirim* in glossary.

17. Djenyo established a *yeshiva* in Salonica that survived until the annihilation of the community in 1943. Djenyo himself would die in Hebron.

18. This tax on wine, meat, and other foods was the major source of income for the organized Jewish community.

19. Given the context, the *gevirim*.

20. In this passage it is unclear how excommunication is being implemented and who is being excommunicated.

very wealthy banker from Constantinople, *Chilibi* Yeoshua Adjiman,[21] happened to be in Salonica. He had previously befriended *h"r* Shaul by hosting his son, *h"r* Behor Molho, in his house in Istanbul. He advised the *pasha* and the wealthy, saying, "If you persist with your ideas of banishment, I will ask the *pasha* to send to Constantinople three people from among the wealthy, along with the *hahamim* **[4b]** to be judged there to see who is right." When the *gevirim* heard this from *Chilibi* Yeoshua, they changed their minds.

They then went to the *pasha* to request the cancellation of the petition. He answered that he was unable to do so, because he had already informed Constantinople about it, and besides he had in the process incurred many expenses. In an impasse, the *gevirim* had to pay a fine of two hundred thousand *grushes*. They emptied the coffers of the community and had also to borrow Turkish money from the widows at 20 percent interest so that they could withdraw their petition. On top of all this came the unfortunate death of the *Rav h"r* Nehama, who had enjoyed his new rabbinic position for only thirty-one days!

This was the first scary blow to the entire population that resulted from *haham h"r* Shaul Molho's curse.

Then, the community set aside the wine *gabela* to pay the salaries of the *rabbanim* and *dayyanim*, etc. etc.

My readers should not imagine for a moment that *haham h"r* Shaul was a tall and imposing individual. Quite the contrary, he had a lean and short body that barely measured one meter and twenty-five cms. [4'1"], yet his voice, aggressiveness, and determination were those of a twenty-year-old lion that entered the rabbinate without being invited. He was particularly influential with the low-class people whom he adjudicated over as he pleased, and even though he was not a great scholar, he was fair and equitable. He had four sons, all of them *talmide hahamim*, but the oldest, whose name was *h"r* Behor Molho, emanated an impressive authority, superior to that of his *sinyor* father. He was tall as a pine tree and well-built. He looked like an angel in the eyes of

21. One of the major moneylenders and provisioners for the Janissary Corps in Constantinople, Adjiman was killed in 1826 in his home by the orders of the sultan as part of a bloody massacre that disbanded this corps.

all those who approached him, his demeanor commanding respect. He never uttered the word "excommunication," even for the guilty. That is how he endeared himself to everybody.

[5a] In spite of all these fine qualities, he unfortunately died prematurely at the age of forty-four. The cause of his death was the terror he experienced as a witness at the death of *Chilibi* Behor Karmona.[22] That same night, he happened to be a guest at *Chilibi* Karmona's home, when the emissaries of Sultan Mahmud[23] suddenly showed up with a decree in their hands, carrying also a golden noose, which they thrust around his neck and strangled him. Clearly his witnessing this frightening scene affected his heart and made him suffer for a long time. Finally, this caused his death; he was mourned bitterly by the entire population of Salonica.

Second Act of the Fear of Fanaticism

When *Rav* [Shaul] was inaugurated in 1835, sons of the wealthy emerged in a state of ignorance from the *Talmud Tora*[24] since no [modern] schools existed. These well-to-do fathers never trained their sons for a profession. And so, they would spend their time going from coffeehouse to coffeehouse and from picnic to picnic on allowances they received from their parents. All they knew was eating and drinking, playing cards at home during the winter and in picnic areas during the summer. Organized in small groups, they would go for months of merrymaking at summer resorts such as *Orundjik* and *Sedes*.[25] They also agreed to take turns for food to be sent from their homes; breakfast in the morning, lunch at noon, and dinner at night; that is how they spent their time. They slept during the day, woke up around 3–4 p.m., and went hunting. One of these smart alecks observed that they were shooting small birds, grilling them, and then eating them, and could not stand the sight of this

22. Another moneylender for the Janissary Corps.

23. Sultan Mahmud II, who ruled between 1808 and 1839, was the initiator of major Ottoman reforms.

24. Created in 1520, the *Talmud Tora* was the principal Jewish traditional school in Salonica.

25. Urumcuk (Ottoman Turkish version of "Orundjik") is a hillside village located northwest of Salonica. East of Salonica, Sedes is close to the current airport of Salonica.

sin. [5b] He went directly to *Rav h"r* Shaul to tell him all about it. When the *sinyor rav* heard the full story, he took speedy action.

He immediately dispatched his beadle to the marketplace to announce that every adult Jew should come to the Old Sicily (fishermen's) synagogue,[26] had some candles lit inside the synagogue, and with the Holy Ark open, he excommunicated this entire group by blowing the *shofar*. However, there was a young man in this group named Y. F., who, upon learning about this excommunication, went to his consul to clear his name.[27] The consul and this young man's parents went to see the *pasha* for a satisfactory explanation. The *Vali* dispatched two *kavases* to bring *Rav h"r* Shaul. He in turn informed the "Seven Honorable Citizens" and the *gevirim*, who responded immediately. One of the *gevirim* brought an exquisitely adorned horse from his stable. They helped the *sinyor rav* climb onto the horse, all of them holding the *sinyor rav* on both sides for his very first ride on a horse. When the people got wind of this event, they ran immediately to take part in this scene. About two thousand people gathered and accompanied him all the way to the *Vali*'s mansion. The *Vali* took a look from his bay window and saw an approaching horde of Jews. With fewer than twenty *kavases* in his mansion, he became uneasy and inquired about this commotion. At that time they had neither gendarmes nor police. He then looked from his balcony and saw a large crowd of men and a miserable looking person with a robe hanging longer than himself dismounting from a horse. The prominent people of the community held him on both sides and brought him upstairs. The *pasha* came out to welcome him, shook hands with him, took him to the reception room, and seated him in an armchair. The consul, as well as all those who were present there, rose up and reverently greeted the *sinyor rav*, who didn't know one word of

26. *Sicilia Yashan* (*kahal de los peshkadores*) is believed to have been established in 1423 by Jews from Sicily who arrived in Salonica during the period of Venetian rule.
27. Joseph Nehama refers to this incident, identifying the person in question as Yaakov Fernandes, the brother of Salomon Fernandes (see note 71) in his *Histoire des Israélites de Salonique* (Thessaloniki: Communauté Israélite de Thessalonique, 1935–78), 7:720. This family, though obviously local, had foreign citizenship and hence not subject to Ottoman law. For more information about Frankos like the Fernandes family see the introduction to this volume.

Turkish. With his hand he asked someone from the Community to act as an interpreter. They asked the *Vali* why he had summoned the *sinyor rav*. The *Vali* answered that the consul was a plaintiff because one of his subjects had been excommunicated. [6a] The *sinyor rav* responded that he had not excommunicated anyone, except for carrying out the ruling of a previous *rav*. He then pulled out of his bosom a small book composed by the *sinyor* grandfather of said young man who contended that he had excommunicated him. In this book he writes that "any one who eats non-ritually slaughtered fowl deserves excommunication." Therefore [said the *sinyor* rav], "this was not my decision except that I was following what his own *sinyor* grandfather named *R*. Sh. P. had written." When they heard this, the entire audience was dumbfounded. The *Vali* thought it appropriate that *sinyor* Y. F. should get up, kiss the *rav*'s hand, and apologize to him. The consul, too, fully agreed with this idea. All the relatives of *sinyor* Y. F. also kissed his hand. As the *Vali* himself wished to have the *rav* bless him, the *sinyor rav* fulfilled his wish and blessed him. Following this episode, refreshments were served; the *rav* was offered a glass of sour cherry syrup. But thinking that it might be wine, he declined, saying that he doesn't drink anything red.[28] He was then offered a glass of white lemonade. As the delegation was leaving, the Jews, who were impatiently waiting downstairs, heard the news that the *sinyor rav* had been exonerated and broke into a joyous shout, saying, "Long live our Sultan; long live our *Pasha Efendi*." When the *rav* was climbing his horse to return home, they started to sing unanimously, "This is a day of redemption. This is a day of redemption." Now when the *Vali* heard this loud singing, he turned to his assistants, saying, "Are you aware how much the Jews love their leaders?" In the meantime the *rav* returned home with those accompanying him.

In spite of this bizarre scene, *sinyor* Y. F. lived just about a month![29] This was the second "blow" that deeply scared everybody.

28. Because wine cannot be consumed unless it is kosher, the rabbi is reluctant to drink anything red for fear it could turn out to be wine. This episode is curious because the *Vali*, who as a Muslim would be forbidden from drinking wine, would not have been likely to offer it to a guest.

29. This is contradicted by Nehama's claim that he moved to Constantinople with his brother at a later date. See Nehama, *Histoire des Israélites de Salonique*, 7:720.

Chapter 5

Third Blow

[6b] Until the year 1845 many newly married young women died of pneumonia and tuberculosis. Prominent *sinyores hahamim* such as *h"r* Avraam Gatenyo, *h"r* David Yosef [d. 1867], and *h"r* Shelomo Pipano[30] started to investigate the cause and origin of this situation. They would gather around 3 p.m. at the home of the wealthy and scholarly *h"r* Yeoshua Modiano [d. 1853], who had retired and handed over his business to his older son, who was *sinyor* Alatini's[31] partner at that time. Usually, he stayed at his home, while visitors stopped by to spend time with him. However, the above-named *sinyores* would come every day in the afternoon to spend some time with him and discuss various community matters. In the course of these conversations the subject of the recurring deaths of these young women was broached in order to find a way to fight these diseases and to eliminate the deaths of the newlyweds. One of the visitors expressed his opinion that this might be traced back to the cold water of the ritual bath[32] that affected their health due to their lack of experience with this new habit.

The second one expressed another opinion. At that time it was customary for parents to give their daughters two furry *yurdis* as part of their trousseau, in addition to all the clothing and household objects. One of them, called *yurdi nafé*, was of multicolored fabric, and the other, called *yurdi chilibi*, of red fabric, was lined with weasel fur, with edges and a collar of the same material. But because not everyone could afford their own new fur, they would buy used trimmings and ornaments from Turkish ladies who had no use for them, having switched to the new style of a *feredje*. Some of these were brought from out of town, but no one knew who had worn them previously. It

30. Pipano was a communal *dayyan* (judge) at this time.

31. The son of a prominent Franko physician, Dr. Moshe (Moïse) ben Eliezer Allatini (Alatini) (1809–82) studied medicine in Livorno before returning to Salonica, where he became one of the leading Jewish figures in the city, instrumental in the fields of industry, education, and philanthropy.

32. In this context the reference is to the religious practice of immersion in water for purification.

could be that they had tuberculosis, which then contaminated the local young women.

[7a] The third to speak among them was *h"r* Avraam Gatenyo; his was the most plausible opinion of them all. He thought somewhat deeper about these young ladies, who, as young girls, were accustomed to dress lightly. But as married women, they wore these furred *yurdis* and covered their hair with a white scarf for their visits. Clearly, in the height of the summer heat, they would be drenched in sweat. At their destination, with *yurdis* and scarves removed, their bodies continued to sweat. To cool themselves, they looked for a breezy spot, while also fanning themselves with a fan that dried their sweat over their skin and caused a sudden cooling leading to a disease like pneumonia. And if not well treated, this led soon to tuberculosis.

Now, *sinyor h"r* Yeoshua, who was such a fine person, studied the three opinions and found *Rav* Gatenyo's opinion the most compelling. They then thought how to solve this matter. The *Rav* Gatenyo suggested to get rid of the furs in these *yurdis* and to introduce a reform of wearing plain *yurdis*, similar to the robes worn by men. Soon, they had a meeting among themselves, and the *sinyor Rav h"r* Asher Kovo joined them and immediately acquiesced to this solution.

Yet, they thought that the people would not follow them, simply because they had said so. It might be necessary to have a meeting at *sinyor h"r* Shaul's house, because [they thought] if he does not concur with us, our entire plan collapses. They all agreed to go to *Rav h"r* Shaul's house to inform him what they had discussed among themselves and the solution they found. He immediately called the "Seven Honorable Citizens," except for the *Rav h"r* Asher, who was left out. He became angry because he was not invited and managed to convince three among the "Seven Honorable Citizens" to boycott the assembly's meeting. Nevertheless, those who attended the meeting decided to go along with the plan. As a first demonstration they brought the *yurdi* belonging to the *robissa*, and they ripped the edge of the fur lining. **[7b]** To complicate things, the lower edge of her fur was embroidered. But the *gevirim* could not wait; they had three and a half yards of red material brought to them from the market. They then called a seamstress to complete the sewing without delay between that evening and nighttime, so that members of the assembly could go the next morning on a visit to see if all the furs had been removed from the *yurdis*. After that, women, even the *robissa*, would visit each other for two to three days in a row, dressed in these fashionable *yurdis* to serve as exemplars for the entire community.

The *sinyor rav* ordered all beadles, including the *Kolel*'s beadles, to proclaim that henceforth no woman may wear *yurdis* with fur. At the entrance of every public bath, he placed two beadles to prohibit any woman wearing a furry *yurdi* from entering. They had no choice but to return home, rip their furs, and only then proceed to the bathhouse. Similarly, when a woman wished to visit someone, she had first to rip her fur and then continue her visit.

Let us now recount a tragedy that resulted from this event. Two among the "Seven Honorable Citizens" could not be found when they came to invite them. The third, who disliked attending the assembly all by himself, answered by saying that he was busy but that he would come later. *Sinyor Rav* Shaul sent word saying, "If you come immediately, it will be fine. But if you don't, you might as well never come to my house!" But the latter was unwilling to revoke the promise he had given to *Rav h"r* Asher; he never showed up at the assembly. Habitually, this gentleman passed by *Rav h"r* Shaul's house mornings and evenings, on his way to his business and when returning to his house. Now, after closing his store, he used a different route, unfamiliar to him. This was a narrow and dark alley called Kandiantis. He was an old man, missed a step, fell down, and broke his right hip. He was carried home with the help of a few people. News about him spread throughout the city that it was for the sin of disobeying *Rav h"r* Shaul's summons, who had said, "If he doesn't come immediately, he might as well never come to this house!"

[8a] All the women were scared by this incident and immediately removed all the furs from their *yurdis*; they also stopped including fur lined *yurdis* in their daughters' trousseaus. Yet, there was a ray of hope in two areas: first, the savings involved in the purchase of these furs; and the other, protecting young women from the disease of tuberculosis. Needless to say, the fear and shock created by these unusual developments occurred during the rabbinate of *h"r* Shaul.

There were other similar cases, but we shall not evoke them here, in order not to bother our readers. Thus, the entire population of our city and its suburbs came to view the *Rav h"r* Shaul as if he were the prophet Jeremiah, who, after uttering a curse, saw it fulfilled, so he, too, became notorious by spreading fear among the superstitious population.

By nature, he took seriously, with no further investigation or inquiry, the words of anyone reporting to him something unusual, even for reports patently baseless, simply because he was a fair man and thought likewise about others. Once, someone reported to him about a certain observant individual who had shaved during *Lag la-'Omer*.[33] Immediately, the *rav* dispatched the beadle to his house and excommunicated him. Now, this was an honest man, loved by all, and when he returned home that evening, he found his wife crying. He asked her why she was crying. She replied, "What happened between you and *Rav h"r* Shaul?" His answer was that he hadn't even passed by his street. His wife answered that *Rav h"r* Shaul's beadle came to excommunicate him. When he heard this from his wife, he became furious and went immediately to ask for a satisfactory explanation. The *sinyor rav* answered, "Because you have transgressed a rabbinic injunction by shaving during the *'Omer*." While this gentleman defended himself that this was a lie and a slander, those who were present there said that it can be proven otherwise.

[8b] Immediately, he bared his head and showed them his bald head. The *rav* quipped, saying, "Witnesses came to me testifying that they saw you at the barber." He answered, saying, "It is true that I go daily to my barber, but it is also true that I have *alopecia* in the middle of my scalp, and he carefully removes any dead hair with a pair of tweezers, then applies an ointment; without this treatment, I run the danger of losing even the whiskers of my beard." To this, the *rav* answered that he must have had another sin that was forgiven with the *onus* of this slander "and your sin shall be forgiven" (Isaiah 6:7).

33. Shaving during the period of the *'Omer* (that is, between Passover and *Shavu'oth*) is avoided by observant Jewish men. However, different Jewish communities have various interpretations as to whether and when shaving is allowed during this period. Unlike Ashkenazim, Sephardic Jews would not shave on the day of *Lag la-'Omer*, a holiday that occurs during this period, but were permitted to shave on the day after the holiday.

Chapter 6

The Sinyor Behor Varsano Incident

Another similar incident happened when someone reported to the *sinyor rav* that during a celebration, after everyone was drunk on wine, a man named Varsano placed his hat on the table and collected one *metalik* from all those who hit it with their fist. The *rav* was furious and sent a memorandum to a beloved and influential *gevir* asking him to send an official note to the *Porte* to arrest this man called Varsano and to punish him with two hundred lashes for disobeying the *rav* in accordance with current custom. Without delay the *sinyor gevir* sent the memorandum and the chief *kavas* sent him two *kavases*. In the meantime he sent for a young *haham*, also named Varsano, who was a scribe that wrote official documents. This was a recently married young man. He tucked his silver writing set in his sash and a ply of parchment paper in his bosom, thinking that this gentleman was planning to draft a document. As he entered the store of said gentleman, he greeted him and asked him how he could help him. His answer was, "You wicked, you dishonored the Tora!" Immediately, he ordered the two *kavases* to arrest him. When this poor young man saw himself under arrest by two *gendarmes*, he started to scream and cry. But the *gevir* paid no attention to his outcry.

[9a] When this young man saw himself held by two *gendarmes*, he resisted by latching himself to the corners of some of the five hundred coffee sacks in the store. As the *gendarmes* were dragging him and he was holding on to the corners of the sacks of coffee, a pile of sacks tumbled down, almost crushing him and the *sinyor gevir*. Now, this bazaar had its own group of porters. When they heard the noise of the tumbling sacks, they rushed inside, freed the young man, and helped him escape. He immediately ran home, collapsed, and fainted. When the women saw the fainted young man, they started to scream. Immediately, the young man's *sinyor* father came and, when he saw that he had fainted, called a doctor, who revived him. To his father he appeared annoyed and quite angry, and he asked him what this business was all about. He told him the full story. Now, his father as a trousseau appraiser was known by all the influential people in town, as well as a frequent visitor at *Rav h"r* Asher's house, and so he told him the entire incident. But *Rav h"r* Asher felt often intimidated by *Rav h"r* Shaul, even though he was well-known for his knowledge and wealth. He sent a message to the *gevir* to find out the reason behind this incident. He answered by saying that he had received a memorandum from the *Rav h"r* Shaul asking him to send it to the governor's mansion to punish the young man with two hundred lashes on his feet for dishonoring the Tora. Immediately, the *Rav h"r* Asher donned his judicial robes and, accompanied by the father and his son, went to ask a satisfactory explanation from *Rav h"r* Shaul. Upon entering the room, where the *Rav h"r* Shaul was, they greeted each other formally as the latter had *Rav* Asher take a seat next to him. Following some small talk, *Rav h"r* Asher inquired about the cause of this incident. The *rav* replied that during a celebration last night, this wicked person was determined to get money from those who were drunk. And so, he placed his hat on a table to collect a *metalik* from anyone who could hit his hat with their fists. When he heard this, *h"r* Asher let the father and his son enter the room, asking, "What was the celebration that your son attended last night, creating this scandal?" The father answered **[9b]** that his son had just left the *huppa* and that last night they had celebrated the groom. Obviously, he could not have participated in any other celebration. Then, the *Rav h"r* Asher called in the witness who claimed that he had seen him with his own eyes. *Rav* Asher pointed at the young man to see if he was the one who was doing what he just described. The witness declared, "I don't know this young man!" "And whom did you see?" "Oh dear, who doesn't know this Varsano who goes to play music at weddings?" The witness figured out that he must have been *h"r* Yaakov Varsano, who is still alive as we are writing this story. Today he is eighty-eight years old, but at the time, he was an inexperienced organizer and music player at festivities. Needless to say, both the *rav* and *h"r* Asher were amazed by this news.

The *Rav h"r* Asher asked the *sinyor Rav h"r* Shaul, "Had the porters not rescued this young man, would he have had the two hundred lashes?"

The *Rav h"r* Shaul, unperturbed by this question, added, "If he had more serious sins, he would have been subjected to the two hundred lashes, but his sins must have been light, and as of now, even they have been forgiven "and your sin shall be forgiven" (Isaiah 6:7).

Another Incident

It happened to a *talmid haham* from a good family.

Once, the head of a family went to Gumuldjina[34] on business, while his family stayed in Salonica. Every other month, he sent money for the needs of the family. Once, he found someone who was leaving for Salonica, so he gave him some money to deliver to his family. But this person tried to keep the money by withholding both the letter and the money from the family. Soon, his wife was worried that for quite a while she had received no funds from her husband, so she wrote him asking why for some time he hadn't sent her any money. The head of this family wrote back **[10a]** that he had sent money with somebody. Again, his wife wrote that she had received nothing. Her husband rushed back to Salonica to inquire about the man and was told that he was fine and running his business nicely. He then found that individual and asked him why he hadn't given the money to his family. His answer was that on the way, he had been robbed by thieves. But when he asked around, he discovered that his wife wore a necklace valued at about one thousand *grushes*. He informed his four sons who were brave young men. Three of them went to this man's house knowing full well that he wasn't home. They asked his wife where her husband was. In all seriousness she answered that he had left home half an hour earlier. The strongest of them slipped behind the woman, turned her around and held her by her arms. The other two put their hand on her neck, removed her necklace and they left. When this woman's husband learned about it, he went clamoring to the *Rav h"r* Shaul to report this incident to him. With no delay the *rav* circulated a proclamation throughout the city excommunicating them, but this head of family and his sons just ignored curses and excommunications. Also, the oldest was an outstanding *talmid haham* beloved to all those who dealt with him. One of his colleagues asked why the *rav* had excommunicated them. They answered that he had transgressed the prohibition of "thou shalt not enter his house" [Deuteronomy 24:10]. The son who was a *talmid haham* answered that this was not a case of "thou shalt

34. Gumuldjina is current-day Komotini, in northeastern Greece.

not enter his house," because this man is a thief who stole my money, as it is written in the books of the *Posekim* in such and such a place, under such and such paragraph, where they ruled that it is permissible to enter a thief's house to retrieve stolen objects. But because the *sinyor rav* felt offended by a younger *talmid haham*, he answered that as one who "points at his borrower in front of his companion," he deserves judgment. He immediately wrote a memorandum to one of the *gevirim* asking him to write to the authorities to have him punished with two hundred lashes. And so it was. Even before he had a chance of gathering his thoughts, this *talmid haham* was seized by two *kavases* **[10b]** who took him to the *Vali*'s mansion. In the courtyard they threw him on the ground, and after raising his calves, they placed his feet in the *falaka* and administered two hundred lashes before imprisoning him. But because the father of this *talmid haham* had numerous acquaintances among the European business people, a consul intervened with the *Vali*, who released him from prison. In the meantime this *talmid haham* threw in the towel and gave up studying altogether, resulting in some rumblings among the *hahamim*. But the *Rav h"r* Shaul feared no one; totally oblivious of the rest, he did only what pleased him.

During the fourteen years of his rabbinate, *Rav* Shaul made many enemies among the *hahamim* and the *dayyanim*. One of these was a certain *haham* who lived through worrisome days because of the *rav*. Unfortunately, this *haham* fell ill and found himself in dire circumstances. Even though he felt that he was on his deathbed, he gathered his strength, and in a moment of extreme courage, he let him know that he did not believe in baseless curses, so that *Rav* Shaul should not conclude that his death was due to one of his curses, rather that his time finally had come.

Another incident occurred when a rich, powerful, and also very scholarly *sinyor haham*, who was a member of the rabbinic tribunal, threw a party in honor of his grandson's wedding. Following a number of receptions, he had a final reception on the "day of *El Pishkado*" when he invited all the *hahamim* and *dayyanim*, including *h"r* Shaul. After they ate and drank, he allowed a singer to sing any song requested by the guests. The very first demand was for a Turkish song picked from his repertoire. The *Rav h"r* Shaul hated Turkish music and, like a hypochondriac, he could not stand the Turkish language: **[11a]** back home that evening, he excommunicated that singer. The singer totally ignored this. But when the groom's father, who was the son of the above-mentioned *rav*, heard this, he was so upset—and on a full stomach—that he had a complication and died eight days later. Because this tragedy and the sorrow at the death of his son had left the *sinyor haham* heartbroken, he closed his business and emigrated to Jerusalem. These series of incidents were not brought about by Providence; they were the outcome of imagined sins. Furthermore, the people were so superstitious that they believed that surely the *sinyor rav* was one of the messengers of God, and whatever he asked from Him, He granted him, to the point that even he came to trust this delusion.

Chapter 7

The Aversion to Turkish Music

The *sinyor Rav h"r* Shaul had a strong aversion to the Turkish language to the extent that he would excommunicate anyone singing Turkish songs. Not only Turkish songs, but even a Jewish liturgical poem chanted in a Turkish mode or copying a known Turkish song.

Let me tell you a story, my dear readers! I did tell you earlier that I, the author of this account, lost my father at the age of five or six and my mother at the age of sixteen or seventeen and that I was left with a ten- or twelve-year-old brother who had kidney disease. Under these circumstances I dedicated myself body and soul to my printing business, but my income was pitiful. I had a great love of the art of singing, given my promising voice. **[11b]** Among Jews we had a certain *maestro* who knew many Hebrew songs. He knew some twenty *fasils* in varying *makams*, with three *peshrevs*, *bestes*, *kiyares*, *samayis*, etc. etc.[35] He also knew the chants of the Days of Awe. His name was *h"r* Aaron Barzilay. In a previous celebration he had heard me sing a couple of Turkish songs I was taught by the Turkish master singer Murteza Izeddinoglu, who had an extraordinary voice. This *maestro* liked me almost as if I was

35. The Hebrew songs in question are set to these Ottoman modes. See glossary.

his own son and used to ask me to sing with him in various festivities. *Maestro, h"r* Aaron Barzilay also took me under his wing, teaching me all that he knew.

At that time a certain rich and scholarly *sinyor haham* had to marry his son. This *haham* was *h"r* Yeuda Alkalay [d. 1849],[36] who ran the Great *Yeshiva* of *rabbanim* in his house, called the Alkalay Yeshiva. Twice a year, he held a reception for the *hahamim*, with me and my young brother as singers.

A day before the wedding, he invited me to sing in his house for the eight days, on condition that I arrange a new song for the *kiddush* chanted during wedding ceremony. I composed a melody based on the *kaddish*, while I also asked four to five handsome young men to join me for rehearsals to prepare them to sing it. The synagogue was filled with *rabbanim*, *hahamim*, and the entire aristocracy of Salonica before the arrival of the groom. When the time for the singing of the *kaddish* came, my colleagues and I ascended the *bima* to sing the *kaddish* in the *hüzzam* mode. The multitude of people in the synagogue attending this wedding were overwhelmed with this *kaddish* they were hearing for the first time in this brand new melody. All of them congratulated me for my skillful rendition of this *kaddish*, except for the *sinyor Rav h"r* Shaul, who paid no attention to my singing the *kaddish*, **[12a]** having never in his lifetime enjoyed any singing. When he went home accompanied by eight to ten of his friends, he removed his cape and sat on his elevated cushion for some rest; he was asked if he had enjoyed the *kaddish* that Sa'adi had arranged based on a Turkish melody. The *sinyor rav* hit the roof when he heard this question, saying, "What a wicked person to sing a Turkish melody inside the synagogue! Immediately, go and tell *h"r* Yeuda that he cannot employ such a wicked one for his celebration."

When *h"r* Yeuda heard the words of the beadle, he became incensed and turned red like a beet. He said, "Is he also trying now to order us around to do this and not that?" All those important people who had been invited to this wedding were equally infuriated to hear such talk. But *sinyor Rav h"r* Shelomo Pipano begged *h"r* Yeuda not to get too

36. Alkalay was a publisher of rabbinic works, including a commentary on the *Zohar*, and was reputed to have a very large private library.

upset, because he would be able to convince the *Rav h"r* Shaul to retract the message he sent. He went at once to see the *rav* and to demand a satisfactory explanation, telling him, "By what right did you send a message asking him not to hire this singer for his celebration?" His response to *h"r* Yeuda was that "this singer is a wicked person because he sings in the Turkish style and sang the *kaddish* in synagogue according to the Turkish style." To these words *h"r* Shelomo retorted, "Aren't all of our liturgical poems written in our sacred tongue chanted in the Turkish style? Please, refer yourself to the book composed by the Rav Nadjara [1555–1625],[37] and you will notice that every one of them bears the mention of a Turkish mode.[38] Rabbi Yeuda a-Levi [c. 1075–1141][39] composed his liturgical poems for the Days of Awe, specifically those of the Day of Atonement, based on Arabic modes." Having never known anything about music his entire life, *Rav* Shaul was utterly surprised to hear *h"r* Shelomo's words. He was finally convinced! He sent word to *h"r* Yeuda that this was an involuntary mistake, that what he heard had misled him, and that now he was free to do as he pleased, on condition that there be no Turkish-style songs.

Chapter 8

[12b] As I mentioned earlier, earnings from the business of printing were not enough. Therefore, I devoted myself to my singing career, first because at that time there was no one else to compete with me and, second, because I was well-acquainted with an impressive repertoire of Jewish liturgical poems, as well as Turkish songs and melodies passed on to me by both *maestros*. There was scarcely a celebration or a banquet

37. Israel ben Moshe Nadjara (c. 1555-1625) was a famous poet, kabbalist, and musician. Born in Damascus, he died in Gaza.
38. Because there existed a controversy about using Ottoman musical modes in liturgical texts as part of a Jewish prayer service, the *maftirim* are considered paraliturgical (see introduction). While various pieces in the traditional liturgy were composed according to Arabic prosody, full awareness of their origin disappeared over time.
39. Yeuda a-Levi (aka Yehuda Halevi) was a renowned philosopher and poet of medieval Muslim Spain.

where I was not invited to sing; especially at a time when it was not customary to have Turkish musical entertainment during celebrations, I, my younger brother, and a colleague had a virtual monopoly. Up to that time, music players and singers for celebrations or banquets were drawn from the group of the religious *minyan* who could sing a few popular songs for dancing. But as soon as the people learned to enjoy listening to Jewish liturgical music *a la turka*, those old music players rushed to the *Rav h"r* Shaul, reporting to him that "last night so-and-so attended such-and-such celebration and was singing some dirty Turkish songs!" Never missing a beat, the *Rav h"r* Shaul would send excommunication instructions directed at me. As for me, I was compelled to go and seek his forgiveness, not because I was afraid of his excommunication, but I did dread the lashes, if I did not seek his forgiveness.

This happened three times a week. By the fourth time I was uncertain that I could ever win, until the day came when he excommunicated me for what happened the previous night. Two hours later, an organizer, who was my namesake, came to invite me for that night. He was also an honorary beadle at the home of the *Rav h"r* Shaul who had three beadles, one of whom was *ham* Chelebon Mordoh, the excommunicator. My answer to this man, who invited me for that night's celebration was, "It is scarcely two hours ago that the *sinyor rav* has sent me a hostile message." He answered me, saying, "Please, do come tonight, **[13a]** and tomorrow you can work on two releases for the effort of one!" [quoting a Turkish phrase], "pay me for one, I'll count it as two". I accepted his challenge and joined him immediately. While the guests were arriving, I started a conversation with this organizer, also called *ham* Sa'adi a-Levi, hoping to find ways of escaping from the wrath of the *sinyor rav*. He answered, saying, "If you are not afraid of his excommunication, why do you keep going each time to seek his forgiveness?" My answer was, "The excommunication is not the reason why I ask his forgiveness; it is rather the fear that if I do not ask his forgiveness, he goes on with a foot beating [*falaka*], in keeping with the custom that the *sinyor rav* sent a memorandum to one of the *gevirim* who in turn dispatched two *kavases* to pick up the culprit, enough to scare one to death." Then he told me that when the *sinyor rav* proceeds with an excommunication, he never records who was excommunicated today and who was excommunicated yesterday, simply because he rarely limits himself to one or two a day. Instead, he issues excommunications for the slightest thing, up to twenty-five to thirty a day without his remembering those involved! Taking to heart this explanation, I henceforth quit going to the *rav* to beg for his forgiveness.

Once the *rav* was having a conversation with two or three *talmide hahamim*. He was told about a new book [being published in my printing press] by a *haham* from Izmir which refuted the *Shulhan Gavoa*,[40] whose author was his *sinyor* grandfather. He immediately asked to be shown some galley proofs to find out about the refutation. By coincidence, this also reminded him of my failure to go to him for his forgiveness after a number of excommunications. So now, he sent a memorandum to a *gevir* to issue an official note to the chief *kavas* to send him two *kavases* to pick up the culprit and administer two hundred lashes on his feet. He then hid the *kavases* in his kitchen, while at the same time called me, under the pretext of the refutations in this book concerning him. As I showed him the printed books, he yelled at me, saying, **[13b]** "You wicked man! Why didn't you show up earlier for forgiveness after so many excommunications?" Wasting no time, he called *ham* Chelebon, saying, "Hand him over to the *kavases*." Suddenly, I felt two iron arms, each one grabbing one of my limbs, as they dragged me on the way to the *Vali*'s mansion. I screamed, but no one heard me. He, too, was screaming, "You, the accursed, this will teach you to sing songs of the gentiles!" They rolled me down the stairs, then up the stairs to the Fishermen's Synagogue. As they climbed the last step, I was plotting my escape. When we reached the street, I could see that we were across from *Chilibi* Moshon Mizrahi's[41] front door. As a way to free myself from them, I said to them [in Turkish], "Allah, why are you holding me as if I were a murderer? I haven't killed anyone, I haven't robbed anyone, I haven't dishonored anyone, have mercy on me, and I will go wherever you want."[42] My plea worked; they let me

40. The *Shulhan Gavoa* was a rabbinical commentary by Yosef Molho (1692–1765) that was published in four volumes in Salonica between 1750 and 1784.

41. Presumably the influential merchant Moshe Yaakov Mizrahi, who died in 1885.

42. This Turkish sentence, which is transcribed in the Ladino text that follows, provides proof of Sa'adi's familiarity with the language, at least in its spoken form.

walk freely with them until we reached *Chilibi* Moshon's open door, when I raced like an eagle almost flying to the last floor, and I hid under a bed. Some *kokonas* were sunning themselves on the veranda. At the sight of the *kavases*, they got up with their canes and their umbrellas and their chairs, running after the *kavases*, warning, "How dare you enter the home of a Franko?"[43] A mob of passersby and businessmen had already filled the courtyard. Word had been sent to *Chilibi* Moshon's office; within five minutes the Fernandes brothers[44] and their *kavases* were already on their way, but when they saw the unruly crowd, they didn't know what to expect. In turn the *kavases* of the Fernandes brothers succeeded in throwing out these persecutors by force, vacating the premises and locking the doors. Then they wanted to know why this had happened. The *kokonas* told the *chilibis* that a certain Sa'adi who participates in our **[14a]** celebrations with Murteza is hiding upstairs. I was called at once and asked about the reason for my escape. I answered, "Frankly, even I don't know why they arrested me to take me to the *pasha*'s mansion." Insisting, they said, "Did you commit any crime?" In my defense I said, "No, I didn't commit any crime, other than I was dragged from *Rav h"r* Shaul's house to the governor's mansion to be flogged, for singing in Turkish, which the *sinyor rav* has categorically banned. Singing is my livelihood, but he keeps excommunicating me: My only choice is to disobey him." The *chilibis* understood that I was right and decided to go to the *pasha*'s mansion for a satisfactory explanation. The *pasha* was flabbergasted to hear that the chief rabbi and the *gevirim* could dispatch someone to be flogged for singing in Turkish. He called the chief *kavas* and admonished him, "Don't you ever dare accept an official note from the Jewish community without first showing it to me"; immediately, the *pasha* sent a note to the *gevirin* with the warning that henceforth all such matters should be channeled through him only. This freed me from beatings and excommunications.

This is how they managed fifty years ago. What are the thoughts of our contemporaries concerning the slavery we Jews endured under the heavy-handed tactics of our religious leaders?

43. See the discussion of the Frankos in the introduction.

44. Leading members of a significant Franko family.

Chapter 9

About the Incident of the Janissaries

A "Moorish"[45] Jew called Liachi the miller (flour dealer) was a troublemaker and a friend of the Janissaries. Whenever the Janissaries needed money, he would give him the names of wealthy Jews. The chief of these bandits made it a practice to send to some wealthy Jew two or three bullets wrapped up in a handkerchief, **[14b]** implying that each bullet was for a hundred *grushes*. At this point, and depending on the information given by this troublemaker as to the victim's worth, the Janissary would send that wealthy person anywhere between two to three up to ten bullets, asking for the immediate dispatch of the amount corresponding to the number of bullets. Without any hesitation the involved party would agree to send the requested sum. But if he refused, he was dealt with the same number of bullets. In this way the troublemaker blackmailed the affluent and the mighty.

The *sinyores hahamim* summoned this evil man, asking him to desist from his evil conduct, but he refused to comply, persisting in his wicked ways. As for the Janissaries, it took the government to get rid of them, and the *hahamim* used this occasion to wreak their retribution on him.

In that period of history, when the government dismissed a *pasha*, it was incumbent on Ahmed Bey, the assistant administrator, to fill the vacant post until a new *pasha* was nominated. About the same time, a certain *gevir*, who was Ahmed Bey's treasurer, was asked to incarcerate this man. And so it was. Yet, while in prison, his visitors told him to appeal to the *hahamim* to forgive the evil deeds he had committed. Instead, he started insulting the *hahamim* and the *gevirim*, saying that once released from prison, he would mete out on them worse than what he had done before. On their part the *hahamim* passed a sentence that he deserved the death penalty, pleading with this *sinyor* treasurer to have him hanged. This *gevir* who was Ahmed Bey's treasurer was reluctant to have blood on his hands. The *hahamim* reacted by drafting a duly

45. The descendants of Sicilian Jews who lived in Salonica, who were mostly fishermen, were called "Moros."

signed note, assuming full responsibility for this crime.[46] On a Friday, said treasurer [15a] went to Ahmed Bey, greeted him on behalf of the *hahamim*, saying that this prisoner should be hanged. With no hesitation Ahmed Bey had this prisoner hanged around 5 p.m. on that Friday. By 6:30, they took him down and buried him at a separate cemetery without any religious ceremony. I witnessed this incident with my own eyes as an eight- to ten-year-old.

I remember another type of incident from this same period. When someone was caught committing the sin of sexual intercourse with a married woman, he was judged and severely sentenced to be flogged, then imprisoned and heavily fined. But if the accused had time, they could flee to another city, as was the case with two individuals who had the same first name, but different last names, one called A. R. and the other A. N. They both had advance notice that they would be arrested and fled to Jerusalem, spent a number of years there, and then came back.

Then, it was noticed that a certain unmarried young girl was pregnant and that her boyfriend had fled. The *hahamim* ordered her caught. She was brought before the rabbinic court and sentenced to get one hundred lashes in the *Talmud Tora*. Then, they confined her in one of the storerooms of the *Talmud Tora*, putting her through a torture press. In that very place she gave birth to a baby who lived only a short while. This incident was publicized throughout town; both Turks and Greeks heard about it. A correspondent of a London paper wrote an article about it and sent it to the entire press. When this despicable act reached the British government, they sent a protest to the Turkish government asking for a satisfactory explanation of this wanton act. The government [15b] contacted the *Vali*, inquiring if such an incident ever occurred in the city, in order to punish those who committed it. Then the *Vali* convened the city's dignitaries for them to explain who took part in this senseless act. When the *hahamim* felt the pressure under which they were, they called this young girl and promised her anything she wanted. On condition of denying everything when summoned by

46. That Sa'adi labels this a crime speaks volumes about his views of rabbinical authority. The sentence of capital punishment by the rabbis was used rarely and always executed by non-Jewish authorities.

the *Vali*, she was helped by the *hahamim*, who married her using funds from the *kolel*. Thus, when she appeared before the *Vali*, she denied everything that was said about her.

Whenever the communal leadership wanted to spend money frivolously, they used the *kolel* fund; as a result this public fund became depleted. This plague has lasted to our own day.

Chapter 10

The Earthquakes of 1828

Our city experienced almost a whole month of earthquakes with at least one or two aftershocks every day and every night. The *hahames* convened and decided to organize *selihoth*, in the *Talmud Tora*. They sent criers all over the city inviting the people to come to the *Talmud Tora*. Thus, by the end of the day the *Talmud Tora* was swamped with all the Jews. The *hahamim* who attended this colossal gathering read the entire book of Psalms. After that, the *Rav h"r* Shaul, who was a skilled performer in pulling heaven down to earth, rose as the prayer leader for the occasion. In the middle of the *selihoth*, or penitentiary prayers, there was so much wailing and crying, that *Rav* Shaul caused a new earthquake, as the *Talmud Tora* and those within it started to shake. The ensuing clamor was so potent that some started singing the liturgical hymn "God, listen to Your destitute" (Psalm 69:34), while others intoned the hymn, "God, awesome in deeds" (Psalm 66:5). Finally, for fear that the *Talmud Tora* **[16a]** might collapse and crush them, some started to run away from the *Talmud Tora*. All this wailing lasted for another few days.

Chapter 11

Fourth Blow

At that time there was no Turkish musical entertainment during festivities. All they had was tambourines for women and men to dance. However, during the festivities of the wealthy, there was Turkish musical entertainment and a renowned singer called Murteza.

One of *Chilibi* Menahem Faradji's sons got married at that time. This *sinyor* was our city's prominent banker and the government's chief banker, because in those days there was no separate treasury.[47] All proceeds from the income of the province were sent in a case to the *pasha*'s office, who then sent them to Istanbul in protected containers. The wedding celebration was carried out with great pomp at *Chilibi* Menahem's mansion, which is today the house of *sinyor* Merkado Yeoshua and *sinyor* David Nehama, and finally belongs now to the community. It stretched from the entrance to the *Talmud Tora* to the street corner. *Rav h"r* Shaul's house, which today belongs to *sinyor* Shaul Shaltiel, was behind this mansion. There was a wall separating the house of *Rav h"r* Shaul from this mansion. One night during this celebration, they were playing music using their violins, tambourines [illegible in the Ladino text, suggesting other unidentified musical instruments].

After dinner that night, *Rav h"r* Shaul went to bed but had a hard time falling asleep because of the sumptuous and noisy celebration, topped by the sound of the violin, which seemed to him like a crying old lady. He had never in his life heard the sound of a violin. He asked his wife to silence this hammer. **[16b]** Laughing, his wife told him that there was neither an old lady, nor a hammer, but the sound of the violin that they were playing at the celebration. He retorted that he had never heard such a sound except for cheap whistles blown by kids in the streets. They replied, "What you are describing is not a violin, but a simple whistle." They showed him half a dry gourd and a fiddle-stick that when moved produced this sound. He concluded that this is forbidden by [Jewish] law as an "imitation of the gentiles." He immediately sent his beadle to tell them that they cannot use this musical instrument. They told *Chilibi* Menahem about the messenger sent by the *Rav*. He retorted that he had no right of interfering in private celebrations, unless there were two adjudicators deciding the law, when such behavior is possible. Without even taking a bite from the food, the messenger returned and conveyed

47. Faradji was a tax farmer. These moneylenders would lend money to the treasury in return for the exclusive right to collect taxes from a region, taking a cut in the process. Some Jewish figures became involved with this system of financing the central administration as early as the sixteenth century.

his full conversation to the *rav*. Without wasting any time, the *sinyor rav* sent his beadle to excommunicate everybody attending this celebration: the host and his guests. They in return threw the beadle out.

The next day, the *chilibi* brought a handyman to wall a small door that opened to the mansion at the end of the corner. This caused an upheaval with maledictions and strong curses, but the *chilibi* ignored all this. But it served to further strengthen fanaticism. We already mentioned that *Chilibi* Menahem was the chief banker managing the income and the expenditures of the province.[48] After paying all government employees their monthly salaries, the balance of the revenue was sent in protected containers to Constantinople for deposit at the Haten Bank. A short while after this incident mentioned above, *Chilibi* Avraam Haten arrived in Salonica. He was received at the home of **[17a]** *Chilibi* Menahem with great honors. They organized a few extraordinary banquets where he was impressed by the delicious food, the succulent fruit, and also by the jewelry of the women, the furniture of the house, and the silk fabrics. He figured out that a similar lifestyle in Istanbul would cause the collapse of big banks. In *Chilibi* Menahem's office there were three partners whose business was run by five of their married sons. All these expenses came out of the same pocket. As he analyzed this setup, he reached the inescapable conclusion that this business would soon be wiped out.

In his wisdom *Chilibi* Avraam Haten decided to sever his ties with this partnership. He turned over all his files relating to *Chilibi* Menahem to the government, and by doing so, *Chilibi* Avraam was in fact terminating this partnership. In a short time this business disintegrated to its very roots, unable to pay a very large sum to the government.

The government dispatched two high officials to Salonica who immediately seized their houses and the business, sending all three partners to jail in Constantinople. The government confiscated their furniture, and *Chilibi* Menahem's mansion was turned into housing for government officials. *Sinyor* Avramachi's house became the City Hall, and the house of *Sinyor* Izakucho Nahmias, the third partner, was turned into offices for the secretaries. After some time, *Sinyor* Avramachi Nahmias

48. See the explanation of tax farming in the previous note.

was freed because he claimed that, as the chief banker[49] of Monastir [current-day Bitola in Macedonia], he used to send sealed money bags to *Chilibi* Menahem's bank. After checking his records, they returned his mansion to him. However, both *Chilibi* Menahem and *ham* Yishakucho died in misery, "restless wanderers in the land" (Genesis 4:14) to this day. Now, let our readers decide: How could fanaticism not gain strength among our population, so long as they thought that the curses of the *Rav h"r* Shaul had caused all this?

Chapter 12

Our Cruel Teachers

[17b] In my time there was a rule that small children ages four to five years old attend the *Talmud Tora* when their parents "sent them to the *rubi*." After one or two years, sitting on the floor of the synagogue, they taught them the Hebrew alphabet and its vowel-points, until they learned to combine consonants and vowels to make words. Class by class, the *Talmud Tora* leaders tested them, and those they considered ready were promoted to another teacher, who taught them the chanted poems of the morning service. After a similar test the following year, they promoted them to another teacher, who taught them the second section of the *parasha*. The following year, another teacher taught them to read the fourth section of the *parasha* with the musical notes. After that, they advanced to *parasha* in Ladino with a teacher who taught them how to sing the *parasha* in Ladino without understanding what they were saying. He also taught them the musical signs by singing the name of each sign [in Hebrew] along with its Ladino meaning, such as: an upside down *shofar* precedes a small arrow. Students loved this type of song, not realizing that it was the Ladino of "an upside down *shofar*!"[50] Then, the students went through eight grades, until they reached the classroom of the

49. Nahmias was also a tax farmer.

50. The *shofar*, or ram's horn, that would be used during the religious service curves upward; any depiction of it turning downwards would be perceived as strange and humorous.

haham who taught them the entire *parasha* and *haftara* in Ladino, along with prophetic readings from Jeremiah and Isaiah, etc. and a section of the *parasha* with the Rashi.[51] This teacher, whose name was H. M. S., was one of the most cruel tutors of the *Talmud Tora*; he was of medium size, heavy, and hairy like Esau. On summer mornings he would come to his office, baring his chest, undressing himself, then removing his outer shirt and his hat, with his naked feet stinking to high heaven. He would roll up his pants to his knees and his sleeves up to his elbows that were covered with hair and looked like a scorpion fish. **[18a]** His chest was full of hair, and his eyes protruded like bowls. To those students who took a look at him, he seemed like the Angel of Death. He grabbed a dry beef tendon to use as a whip and a twig of cornelian cherry before sitting on a sheepskin rug.

When the students started to recite the *parasha*, he looked for any excuse to beat up the students. Moreover, when a parent complained about his son,[52] he would grab his *falaka* from his cabinet, hurl it from one end of the veranda to the other, producing a thunderous noise.

Such outrage on the part of the teacher utterly scared the students, as they wondered whose bad luck was next. Then, the *haham* would signal one of the monitors to grab the child, throw him on the floor, and put his feet in the *falaka*. He, then, would descend on him like a lion and gnashing his teeth like a tiger, he would start to beat him on his feet brutally up to fifty, eighty, or a hundred lashes, the number left to his discretion. Finally, when they lifted up the child, he could not stand on his feet because of the blisters that now plagued him.

For extra cruelty this brutish teacher had the child run around the entire veranda with two monitors holding him on each side. The child's suffering then was more excruciating than the original beating.

Finally, this fate fell often on a number of young boys who could not tolerate it anymore: three of them left and converted to Islam. At the same time, he even started to treat me like them. I, as an orphan, complained to my *sinyora* mother, telling her that I couldn't take this life anymore.

51. Here Sa'adi refers to reading the *parasha* with the pertinent Rashi commentary.
52. It is not clear if this parent's complaint concerns the child's misbehavior at home or the teacher's mistreatment of the pupil at school.

My *sinyora* mother called this *haham* **[18b]** to our house and complained to him that he shouldn't beat me again. Gnashing his teeth, his response was simply to quote the [Ladino] proverb, "It takes blood to learn every letter." He then grabbed me by the arms and took me to the *Talmud Tora*. As I sat on the bench, he grabbed the *falaka* as usual and locking his eyes on me and threatening me with his bullish head, he hurled the *falaka* in his customary fashion. I immediately understood that he would pour out his wrath on me. With one jump I took off and flew like an eagle. He sent eight to ten youngsters after me to catch me, but their efforts were useless. I went to the house of my *sinyora* grandmother, who was the mother of my *sinyor* father who was still alive and lived with her oldest daughter called Bula Miryam, wife of *ham* Yusef Ezrati.

When my *sinyora* grandmother saw me so frightened, pale, and half-fainted, she gave me a hug and a kiss, as I was her only grandson from her son's progeny. She inquired about the reason of my escape. I told her in detail all about my suffering. Leaving me in the custody of my *sinyora* aunt, she immediately put on her *kyurdi* and her head-scarf and went to my *sinyora* mother's house, screaming and yelling. She said, "This is the only bough that I have left. Do you wish to lose that, too? Please, take him away from this cruel teacher." That is how they placed me in the Talmud *Berahoth* class, where I found some peace of mind. But unfortunately, I was left far behind from mastering the Bible. This is the individual responsible for my remaining an ignoramus. I was then quite eager to deepen my knowledge of the Holy Scriptures, but the only materials I found for reading were **[19a]** a few pamphlets in Ladino. My reading list consisted in *{Da'd} [Eldad] a-Dani*,[53] the *Ben Sira* pamphlet,[54] and a short tract by Yosef dela Reyna,[55] all of which was next to nothing for me.

53. This refers to the popular account of his travels by the ninth-century merchant and traveler Eldad a-Dani. The first Ladino translation was published in Istanbul in 1806.

54. The Ladino translation of *The Wisdom of Ben Sira*, a noncanonical Hebrew text from the second century BCE, was published in Vienna in 1818 and in Istanbul in 1823.

55. De la Reyna was a fifteenth-century kabbalist. The Ladino translation of his work was published in Vienna as *Rekuerdo de Yosef de la Reyna* in 1852.

About that time the first Protestant missionaries came to Salonica bringing thousands of Jewish Bibles, printed in two columns of facing Hebrew and Ladino texts on each page.[56] On my own I started to read these texts for the Hebrew and the Ladino and was able to understand whatever was easy for me to grasp. Yet certain prophetic passages were hard for me to penetrate. Through my conversations with the Protestant missionaries that had arrived, I made some progress in the study of the Bible; nevertheless, I know that I am an ignoramus when compared to scholars who have studied the holy tongue in depth. In short, these cruel school teachers are directly responsible for the harsh reality of those of my generation who have nothing to show but our ignorance. I consider myself the more knowledgeable among them! Clearly, it was the unconscionable behavior of these teachers that sank everyone in deep and dark ignorance.

Chapter 13

The Plague

Earlier, I mentioned that I lost my father at the age of five or six and my mother at the age of fifteen or sixteen, and that I was left with a handicapped brother. Severed as I was from my parents, I said to myself, "If I am not for myself, who is for me?" (Avoth 1:14), so I tried to secure my own livelihood. I decided to embrace my father's printing business, where **[19b]** a veteran employee hired by my father was still working, together with two typesetters and an employee to dispense ink. By this time, as our fonts were quite worn-out, I decided to cast new ones with molds and matrices we already owned, and I proceeded with this job. But as our foreman was unwilling to teach me the proper timing needed for each mold, it took me almost two months to complete casting all the letters. Also, because my bellows were deficient, my fonts were not up to par. Soon, I was convinced that my foreman's reticence

56. The London Society for Promoting Christianity Amongst the Jews, a Protestant missionary organization founded in 1809, was particularly active in the Ottoman Empire in this period. It had minimal success in converting Jews.

to teach me the proper timing to get decent fonts caused my failure, and I fired this foreman from our printing press.

At that time the *sinyor haham*, our teacher, *h"r* Gatenyo entrusted me with the printing of his book, entitled *Mehoshkim Kesef* [1837], just as the incipient pestilence of 1837–38 suddenly intensified to a higher number of deaths per day.

But the rabbi, fearing that he might die from this implacable disease and leave his book unfinished, maintained a steady flow of his manuscript to conclude this project as soon as possible. Despite this pestilence, I managed to make ends meet. Unfortunately, the only drawback was that the book was printed with poorly configured fonts.

However, all those who saw me working so hard at the time of the pestilence were amazed and said, "What a fine seventeen-year-old youngster this is who is working so hard without any fear for his life." Everybody had halted their businesses, all the markets were closed, half of the population had fled **[20a]** to foreign towns, and those afflicted by this disease were dying by the hundreds every day. Yet I lived in the same room with my younger brother, impervious to the fears of the people about satans, damaging spirits, and ghosts. Of all these I never had any fear, nor did I ever take them seriously.

In those days, according to a commonly held false belief, a person's sins were carved on their forehead, so when Satan saw them in the street, he would cast on them the curse of pestilence, smiting them and causing their death. Many of these fanatics covered their foreheads with a scarf, so that the devil would not see the writing on their foreheads. As early as 6 p.m., the men cloistered themselves in their homes, covered their windows with black fabric, ate dinner, and went to bed in the dark around 7 p.m., for fear that the devil might peek through a window and discover the presence of people inside.

My second sister came to live in my house to escape from a contaminated neighbor. Her husband, who was a peddler going from locality to locality, owned guns that he hung on the walls of his room. I planned to kill the cats because they roamed around, from homes with afflicted people to homes of healthy people, contaminating the healthy. I took one of my brother-in-law's guns and filled it with gunpowder and buckshot, and after climbing on the terrace, I saw a cat on the roof of my neighbor['s house], who was a *talmid haham*; I fired my gun and killed the cat. Under this roof there was a woman in labor. As soon as she heard the sound of the gun, she gave birth to her child. The *haham* peeked through a curtain in my house and excommunicated me. I responded **[20b]** using dirty language. Furious and without thinking, he, too, retaliated in kind.

In a hurry he went to see the *haham*, *sinyor Rav h"r* Shaul to tell him all about this incident. At once, he summoned me to ask me why all day long I was firing bullets and scaring everybody. In my answer I said that I was not firing for fun but as a favor to my neighborhood to save them from potential contamination. He objected, saying, "Look, here was this woman in labor who gave birth as a result of your gunshot." I answered that this, too, had a favorable outcome as it speeded up her delivery! The *haham* requested that I remove the dead cat from his roof because it would get maggots in the sun. I took a metal bar, climbed on his roof, and threw the cat on the awning.

Let us now talk about what this disease called pestilence was. Doctors in those days claimed that this disease came from a small fly found in the refuse of frogs living in the swamps of Ethiopia (Indies)[57] and that the inhabitants of those places usually suffer from this disease comparable to malaria in Europe. When travelers from these places entered Egypt, they contaminated Egypt. And from Egypt, Turkey became contaminated, because at that time the practice of quarantine was not known in Turkey. But at European borders they had lazarettos for passengers coming from Turkey for isolation before they were allowed to enter.

When Mehmed Ali *Pasha*[58] was appointed *Khedive*, Europe signed a treaty with Mehmed Ali *Pasha* to set up a quarantine three days before entering Egypt, so that travelers from Ethiopia could not enter Egypt without a quarantine (forty days). **[21a]** This quarantine is still enforced to this day. That is how this terrible disease was eradicated

57. Sa'adi erroneously equates Ethiopia with India, which is known as *las Indyas* in Ladino.

58. Known also as Muhammad Ali, he seized control of Egypt while serving as the Ottoman governor there in the early nineteenth century and, while remaining nominally under Ottoman rule, established his own ruling dynasty in the region.

from the world. Now, at this writing, it has been three years since this disease has disappeared; earlier, it recurred every fifteen, twenty, twenty-five years. Whenever it reappeared in Turkey, it spread panic everywhere because of the immense losses it caused that year; in every city thousands of people contracted the disease during the three months of the summer. At that time, in 1838, I was eighteen years old, but I felt none of the fears that people lived through.

That is when my older sister caught the disease, without my being aware of it. It was customary then to call a physician specializing in the nature of this disease. He was called *ham* Yaakov Haten. By his side stood an employee of the *kolel*, whose name was *h"r* Moshe Ezrati and who was an uncle of my brother-in-law. When I went to call the doctor along with Moshe Ezrati, I brought them in through a small, secret door. He examined her by feeling the three areas where pestilence was visible: her neck, under her chin and the lower part of her side, including her groins, for a swelling the size of a cucumber [typical symptoms of the plague].

This physician was so skilled that he could predict whether a patient was facing life or death. Apparently my sister's case was light and not life-threatening. But because my brother-in-law's uncle didn't wish to upset him or cause him undue expenses, he suggested to keep the matter to himself and unpublicized. The physician prescribed ointments to be applied **[21b]** on her affected areas. In this way she was healed from her disease in less than ten days.

The floor of my house was level with the street. Every night, dogs roamed around barking. The next day, my sister would tell us that evil spirits had come and were tearing up the sidewalk of our street. I, for one, who attached no credence to this nonsense, would go outside every morning to see that not a single stone had budged from its place. My sister, who was sharing her room with our brother, urged me to spend a night with them, even though I had my own room. I refused. But my younger brother, who empathized with my sister's fears, insisted I move my bed to a secluded corner in their room. In the middle of the night I heard a terrible noise that, indeed, sounded like they were tearing up the sidewalk. It was a moonlit night; I raised my head to look through a crack in the secret door, and I could clearly see a pack of dogs, a mother and her pups, playing with a bone and everyone pulling in their direction: This is what the noise on the sidewalk was all about. I grabbed a heavy club I had ready by my side and opening the door without making any noise, I went outside and hit them fiercely, making them run in all directions. Then, I retrieved the bone, brought it inside and closed the door.

When my sister and my brother-in-law heard all that commotion in the street, they started pulling their hair. My sister's fear was so intense that she soon came down with a large boil on her back, presumably in atonement for her sins. For my part, I showed them the bone, adding, "Here is the digging fork to tear up the stones of the sidewalk; **[22a]** I have taught the demons a good lesson; they will never come back here."

During the time of this epidemic, they had from thirty to forty male caretakers and from fifteen to twenty elderly female caretakers staying in some houses in the courtyard of the *kolel*, ready and on call to take care of the sick. They also had a chief caretaker who sent one woman along with men, that is one woman with two men, to the home of the victim. He was tall, heavyset, red-haired, and in normal times was a house painter. When the physician alerted them that there was a patient in a given house, he was in charge of emptying the house of all relatives. They would gather outside, and he would send them to a separate location where, after removing their clothes, they would wear clean clothes and stay in this very place for ten days of quarantine. The house of the patient, with all its contents, remained in the custody of these caretakers, as if they were its owners, with all maintenance expenses paid by the home owners. In the morning he sent them breakfast, lunch around noon, and the same for dinner. There was a daily charge of an *altilik* [Ottoman unit of currency] per person collected by the chief caretaker. *Raki* was supplied to them in *binlik* bottles and wine by the barrel. If the patient died, they carried the deceased to the cemetery, while the house remained closed for forty days. The caretakers in the homes of the 5 percent who survived kept eating, drinking, and getting drunk. On the forty-first day they all took the patient to a Turkish bathhouse. They also soaked all the linen for one or two days, then thoroughly washed it. That is when all the relatives returned home. **[22b]** As for those patients who died from this disease or were killed by the caretakers, this was caused by such high fever that they went into delirium that pushed them into violent behavior. To continue with their drinking, the caretakers would seize the patient, throw him on his bed, and smother him with his comforter. Then each one sat on either side of the comforter until the patient ran out of breath and died.

A tragic event occurred at that time when a young girl who had been plagued by this disease was assigned two female caretakers and one male caretaker. This young girl was very beautiful, especially when she was running a high fever; her cheeks turned red like a rose. Her caretaker, who was then drunk, got excited and tried to assault this young girl. But because she was an honest person, this young girl did not let herself be dishonored, in spite of her disease and her unbearable high fever. When her caretaker realized that his nefarious plan would not succeed, he suffocated her with her comforter, and this is what caused her death! This caretaker sent the two female caretakers to wash her linen and committed his despicable act, even after the death of the young girl. The female caretakers secured the evidence against the despicable act perpetrated by this accursed man and handed it over to the chief caretaker, who immediately went to inform the *sinyor Rav h"r* Shaul about this evil deed. The *sinyor rav* convened in the *Talmud Tora* a number of *hahamim* and *gevirim*. They dispatched two robust caretakers to capture this assassin and bring him to the *Talmud Tora*. Following his interrogation, he confessed to his despicable act, blaming it on his drunkenness. They threw him on the floor of the courtyard in the *Talmud Tora*, tied him to the *falaka* and flogged him with five hundred lashes, until **[23a]** he passed out. The two caretakers picked him up and carried him to the caretakers' jail, which is a horrible place, and confined him to a dungeon. I never found out whatever happened to him.

This incident was not something reported to me but one that I saw with my own eyes. This caretaker called *ham* S. M. T. was blind in one eye and went around wearing a loose robe. When the people heard about this scandalous act, no family entrusted anymore their afflicted patients at the hands of these caretakers. When a family was afflicted, either parent stayed with their child to safeguard their loved ones. That is how they were able to save many a relative from death.

Chapter 14

Nizam Soldiers

After the massacre of the Janissaries at the Hippodrome [in Constantinople], Sultan Mahmud the Second proved to be a wise and courageous man.[59] He was lion-hearted, as is often mentioned in royal chronicles. He succeeded in gaining to his side the *Agha pasha*, who was head of the Janissaries, thanks to the promises the sultan made to him. He convened and addressed at the Hippodrome the entire Janissary corps, who numbered forty thousand souls from the Istanbul barracks, to convince them to give a satisfactory response to the sultan. The *Agha pasha* returned to the sultan. In the meantime he had twenty thousand souls dressed in vests and pants, arming them with rifles, while he also prepared two artillery batteries, one on one end at the entrance of the street leading to the Hippodrome, and the other one at the other end, with ten thousand souls behind each battery. **[23b]** On the other side, by the sea, he armed all the battleships to open fire from their guns at the first sign. Upon his return from the sultan, he went up to an elevated spot and said to them, "The Sultan doesn't need to give an accounting to anyone. As head of the nation, he knows best how to rule over his empire."

When the Janissaries heard this answer, all in unison shouted a call to vengeance, unaware that the entrances to the Hippodrome were blocked with special soldiers. The Janissaries were headed toward their barracks to pick up their weapons but encountered artillery fire and bullets from the guns. When they turned toward the sea for their escape, they met with artillery coming from the navy. In the space of a couple of hours, forty thousand souls perished, and the Hippodrome became a carpet of bodies. At the conclusion of this incident the sultan ordered the demolition of all the Janissary barracks where the Janissaries held their meetings.

After an interval of cease-fire the sultan sent out criers carrying the holy flag and companies of armed soldiers prompting the people to

59. The following is a description of the 1826 abolition of the Janissary Corps, a major division of the Ottoman army that had become an obstacle for reform. In Ottoman accounts this is known as "The Auspicious Event."

open their stores and their shops and run their businesses with peace of mind. He also dispatched to all the major cities soldiers dressed European style to get rid of any remaining Janissaries in many localities.

He sent to Salonica eight to ten battalions of soldiers who rounded up anyone who belonged to the Janissaries, incarcerating them in the White Tower. Every night, they killed from ten to fifteen of them, according to how many they arrested that day. For each one killed, they fired a bullet; this informed the population about how many had been killed that night.

[24a] This is why this tower was formerly called "Bloody Tower" until our sovereign, Sultan Hamit II [Abdul Hamid II, 1876–1909], ascended the throne and ordered that henceforth it should be called the "White Tower." Immediately, they brought a number of whitewashers, and they whitewashed it, transforming it into a "white dove" as seen today.[60]

When these soldiers came to Salonica with their military brass, consisting of a lieutenant colonel, a colonel, a regiment paymaster, an army major, and a captain, they were all wearing gold filigreed uniforms. Each one of these high officials occupied a mansion for his private use. This also was the beginning of calm for all the religious communities.

These high officials were not accustomed to wearing European-style shirts. When they decided to dress in the European style,[61] they asked a certain *ham* Daniel Andjel, whose shop at the Women's Market was their meeting place, to help them get such shirts. He inquired about who sold such shirts, but he didn't find any simply because sewing machines were not available. And those worn by Frankos had been handsewn by my *sinyora* mother, who inherited this craft from her mother and her grandmother. Then, *ham* Daniel needed to call on my *sinyora* mother to sew a dozen shirts for each one of them, and he tried to take my *sinyora* mother to see these gentlemen. My *sinyora* mother replied that she was unwilling to go to a Turkish home, but anyone

60. This tower, known in Ladino as the *Torre Blanka*, became iconic in the imagination of the Salonican Jewish diaspora as of the early twentieth century.

61. After the abolition of the Janissary Corps, the new Ottoman army adopted European-style uniforms.

who wished was welcome to her house to be measured for her to sew the shirts. The *sinyor* Daniel asked how much she charged for sewing a shirt. She answered that she charges all consuls and businessmen one *altilik* [Ottoman unit of currency] to sew a shirt. *Ham* Daniel replied that he would charge a 100 percent commission on the total amount of her sale to these gentlemen.

[24b] My *sinyora* mother replied, "Fine, if they pay me two *altiliks*, you will get the second one." This *sinyor* said to her, "I'll bring here three people for you to sew a dozen for each one." My *sinyora* mother thought that only three people would be coming; yet by the time she heard the sound of the twenty armed horsemen who accompanied each one of them, the streets were filled to capacity with all these people. To be precise, streets around our home were alleys rather than streets, varying between three and two *pikos* in width. As soon as mother looked through the window and caught a glimpse of the gold-embroidered uniforms and the hanging swords, she immediately hid my three maiden sisters in one of the rooms. In came the three top military officers, accompanied by four to five majors. She didn't even have enough chairs for sitting! She had to borrow extra chairs to seat them all—tall, hefty, and covered in gold embroidery. *Sinyor* Daniel was no less impressive: He was quite fat and tall, wore a silk turban around his head, and his body was wrapped in a loose robe of red damascene fabric, an alpaca robe with a sash from Tripoli. He sent his employees to the market to bring bolts of embroidered fabric. They brought in about forty to fifty bolts of this fabric to make about a dozen shirts each. When my *sinyora* mother took a look at this fabric, she reacted by saying that her original price was inadequate because this is a thicker fabric, hard to sew. *Ham* Daniel agreed on three *altiliks* to get half of it for himself. As for the customers, they had no interest in these price changes, beyond what he told them, especially because *Chilibi* Menahem's coffers paid any bill that came. My *sinyora* mother took the measurements of every one of them for the fabrics they chose, making sure to set aside one-tenth of the fabric from each dozen shirts, sum total two robes, **[25a]** five half-shirts, and five jackets for my wedding. As soon as they left, my *sinyora* mother with her three daughters and three helpers started the work, and within a month they finished eight dozen shirts. The day the job was finished, these three gentlemen came, and each one tried his shirt, and the remainder was packed and sent to their homes. They brought along a pouch full of altiliks to pay my *sinyora* mother. After that, *Sinyor* Daniel came to get his own half, but my *sinyora* mother started to give him a hard time. He defended himself, saying, "You are not the only one that I charge 50 percent; I charge the same percentage from those who supply sand to the barracks." This is how this man became a millionaire. But what a shame that there is no lasting recollection of him, neither of his wealth nor of his three sons who died with no male progeny. Only his youngest has survived; he lives in Jerusalem, is seventy years old, but has no sons.

Chapter 15

The Fire of 1839

On the first night of *Rosh a-Shana* at 9 p.m., when everyone was at home, we heard two artillery shots signaling a fire, which started at the Shoemakers Building and engulfed it on four sides. The fire spread all the way to the Women's Market, surrounded all markets in a fire ring, continued to Hamza Bey and burned the entire European quarter to the Gate of the Vardar, then turned around to the Marine Tower, consumed everything all the way to the Market and the *Es Hayyim*[62] quarter, burning also the slaughterhouses and turning everything into a wasteland before reaching the Aragon Synagogue. When the members of this synagogue realized that it, too, would burn, they tore down all the houses surrounding the synagogue. That is how they succeeded in saving the synagogue. At the end it can be said **[25b]** that this fire destroyed almost half of Salonica, even beyond the fire of 1890.[63] The following day, when I went out to view this fire's devasta-

62. *Es Hayyim* was the oldest Jewish synagogue in Salonica. This was in the first Jewish district near the port.

63. Known as *el fuego grande* in Ladino, this devastating fire began in the shop of a *raki* manufacturer behind the Saint Theodora Church on September 3 or 4, 1890 (according to the Gregorian calendar). The fire destroyed approximately thirty-five

tion, I was able to see from the corner of the old Business Court all the way to the Gate of the Vardar with no obstruction whatsoever. As I turned toward the sea, one could actually catch a glimpse of the sea and the ships. Truly, this was a huge fire, but it did not involve residential areas, rather mostly businesses and markets and the European quarter where every house had a large garden and a long courtyard. In those days there were no insurance companies in our city, and even some rich people were left without their goods and their valuables.

To continue (2) [continuation missing in manuscript]

The Removal of Rav Matalon

In that year the *hahamim* were opposed to some things that the *Rav* Matalon [d. 1847] was arbitrarily doing and were up in arms about them. The ultimate showdown came when *h"r* Yeoshua Modiano's [d. 1853] wife passed away. As a scholar and a wealthy person at the peak of his vigor, he tried to find a pleasant wife of his choosing. Among the many prospective women, he chose a beautiful wife from a good family, and not too old. They got engaged.

When the news reached the *Rav* Matalon, he informed him [Modiano] that he could not marry this woman, because she was an Ottoman subject, while he was Italian. When this woman would have children, they would become Italian citizens. Therefore, he could never marry this woman.[64]

With his wealth and knowledge, *h"r* Yeoshua [Modiano], who was a prominent figure in the city, insisted on marrying this woman. The *rav* advised him that he would not allow anyone to perform their wedding. **[26a]** In case of disobedience he would inform the authorities.

Feeling threatened, *h"r* Yeoshua sent intermediaries to the *rav*, asking him to stop being stubborn; they were instructed to offer him some

---

hundred homes and left approximately six thousand families (twenty thousand people) homeless. Among the homeless were some five thousand Jewish families.

64. Relations between Frankos who had foreign protection or were foreign citizens and the vast majority of other Jews were frequently fraught with tensions and conflict.

money. He asked for such and such an amount. Eager as he was to satisfy his wish and obtain that woman, *h"r* Yeoshua sent the full amount and married this lady.

Soon, the *Rav h"r* Avraam Gatenyo and the *Rav h"r* David Yosef [d. 1867], who spent lots of time with *h"r* Yeoshua, brought up during their conversations the subject of his encounter with *Rav* Matalon. But as they were already incensed by his previous behavior unbecoming to a *rav*, they called a general meeting of *hahamim* and *gevirim* and decided to remove him from office. In the name of all the *gevirim*, they sent him two important *talmide hahamim* to tell him that henceforth he was not recognized as a *rav*. Upon seeing himself accused, he threw the imperial decree appointing him chief rabbi to their faces.

Chapter 16

Weddings

In my time weddings were arranged in such a covert fashion that the engagement of a boy and a girl was decided at the pleasure of their parents. The bride and the groom never met each other, nor even saw each other, before their wedding day, as the groom was forbidden from passing by the street of the bride's residence. When my engagement was decided, my sister and brother-in-law announced, "You are engaged," without my even meeting the father of the bride.

As the date of my wedding approached, I still didn't have the foggiest notion about marriage, thinking that a wife was about **[26b]** laundry, cooking, and taking care of the house. By my wedding day, the women had completed all the necessary arrangements. At 4 p.m. I saw relatives and my sisters coming in all their finery. After a while they went to bring the bride. As they were returning, I saw a group of women I never met before; among them were my sisters and a creature, half-woman and half-man, like a mermaid. I asked my friends, "Where is the bride?" With their fingers they pointed at this woman who was surrounded by my sisters. I said to myself, "Is this my bride?" Her outfit was neither that of a maiden nor that of a woman, wearing on her head a tiny bonnet decorated with silver threads and a veil with gold settings. Well, well! Usually, a woman's dress consisted of a cape, a robe, thin-soled boots, and yellow shoes. Is this a bride? Seeing this, I became utterly confused. In appearance she was not so ugly, yet with her bizarre accoutrements she looked to me like a mermaid. "Patience," I said to myself. They told me to shower her with Jordan almonds. I was so dazed that I scattered them pell-mell.

As the bride was climbing the few steps leading to the house, there stood this old lady with a piece of red hard candy. As soon as the bride was near her, she stuck it into the bride's mouth who moved it to the side, where it protruded, looking as if she had an egg in her mouth. To me she looked as if her face was swollen and red as a result of the depilation done the previous day. In short, she looked like someone who had just got over a serious disease.

Meanwhile, my relatives came; they dressed me in a linen robe **[27a]** from Bursa,[65] another loose robe of white fabric, and a well-adjusted turban. You can imagine what I looked like without beard or mustache, yet wearing this *memma* [turban]. They made me look into a mirror; I took one look, but what I saw was so bizarre that I spat on the mirror. They took me to the synagogue and as they were singing the *kaddish* and the *kedusha*, it seemed to me that they were chanting the *sidduk a-din* [burial prayer] for me.

When we returned home, the cantors started to wail again. They asked me to place a ring on her finger. They showed me a finger sticking out from under her veil, and I nailed that "hoop" on that "stump." Then, the cantors chanted the *Shiv'a berahoth*,[66] which to me sounded like the dirges sung on the Ninth of *Av*, and we went indoors. Once inside, I kissed my sister's hand sitting for the mother of the groom, my brother-in-law for father of the groom, the bride's brother-in-law for her father, who was out-of-town, and her stepmother, who gave me five gold coins for the "kissing-of-the-hands." After that, two old ladies, holding tambourines in their hands the size of huge pans and three tin rattles, started to sing.

Then dancing started, first with two old ladies, followed by women dancing in pairs. In the meantime they were preparing the tables, while

65. City in northwestern Anatolia and the first Ottoman capital.

66. Colloquial for *shév'a berahoth*, the Seven Blessings chanted at weddings.

the groom and his party were first to sit down and eat. But before that, my bride and I were put in a room to talk to each other and to exchange a few words as I was previously instructed, such as, "good evening," and to offer her some *raki*, which she refused! I drank the whole thing, also tossed some Jordan almonds and one gold ducat at her lap. We then came out of the room.

[27b] As soon as I opened the door, my relatives kissed me and hugged me as if I was returning safe and sound from war.

They made me sit at the table. After eating and drinking, they took me to the bedroom. But earlier, the women had taken the bride to the bedroom, some playing music, others dancing. Some elderly women, who had even blackened their faces with soot, looked like witches and posed before the bride with their tongues out. They undressed her and put her to bed, which was covered with some drapes, but gave her nothing to eat as was the custom.

As for me, they picked me up from the table, and two men carried me on their shoulders, while singing "he shall offer a perfect male" (Lev. 1:3), with lit tapers all the way to the bridal chamber. Those who were carrying me on their shoulders tried to enter the room through a small door without lowering me, banging my head on the lintel. At that time they had hooks to hang phylacteries. A hook smacked my forehead causing a swelling the size of an egg. My friends placed a coin on the swelling and wrapped it with a kerchief.

After that, they undressed me and put a white turban on my head that made me look like a *mulla*. Then, they all left the room locking the door from the outside, like those condemned to imprisonment with hard labor.

As I went to bed, my glance caught a woman with funny-looking cheeks caused by the depilation done the previous day, lying in bed, looking like a patient suffering from chickenpox. In turn, when she saw me with that white turban and a tightly bound headband, both she and I were immobilized **[28a]** as if spellbound. To me she looked like a midwife; to her I must have looked like some *imam* who arrived from Mecca.

Dear readers! You can well imagine the horrible situation in which both she and I found ourselves. I, for one, couldn't utter a single word because of the sharp pain I was still feeling from hitting the lintel, deepened by my bizarre-looking bride, with her funny-looking cheeks as seen on a sunburned traveler. As far as she was concerned, she was not allowed to talk prior to being addressed by the groom, especially because she must be assuming that a *hafiz* is lying next to her, and that I cannot speak Spanish, and she doesn't know Turkish, yet she was instructed to ask for a sip of water. For this is how they advised future brides: the first word uttered by a bride is to ask for a sip of water from her groom. However, at this stage she dare not look me straight in the face. Tell me, my dear readers, how can one enter into marriage in such a dire situation?

Finally, both of us spent that night in great discomfort, as if we were at the peak of a typhoid fever.

The next morning, they woke us up and found out that it didn't go so well. An hour later, I noticed that they were bringing a well-built woman, wearing *a fez* over an elaborate hairdo, attached on either side. While female music players were roaring, they seated my bride next to me.

I seriously contemplated the idea of killing myself, but I had not as yet decided how to go about it, to show to my sister and my brother-in-law in what a terrible position they had put me. Even though I spent the rest of the festivities in deep anxiety, I renewed my patience by repeating *Allah kerim* [God is beneficent]!

Once out of the "bridal canopy," I went straight to my job **[28b]** to earn a living for me and my wife (and my younger brother left behind after my father died. He was then in my mother's womb and died of kidney disease at the age of seventeen).

In the meantime, with hard work and determination I was able to provide for all the needs of my family. Almost without noticing it, within a year we had our first daughter. After three years of marriage, we had two daughters; after five years we had a son, three children in all; and after seven years, another son, four children in all.

It is during this period that the great cholera epidemic emerged. We had to flee from the city. A friend of mine and I, with our families, had to rent a room in *Orundjik*. This cholera epidemic was quite strong at the beginning, to the point that hundreds were dying every day.

During the peak of this epidemic my friend with whom we fled caught this disease and passed away within five hours. When I saw myself surrounded by four children in an isolated place, I said to myself that there was nothing better than to return to the city. Thus, my wife and I packed everything and moved back home. The next day, I went out to the market to buy some food; all I could see was less than 5 percent of the population that were in town. For every three passersby, there was one dead body they were carrying like meat of the butcher shop. All I managed to do was fill a bottle with *raki*, buy a chicken, slaughter it, and bring it home. After some small talk, I drank like water a couple of shots of *raki* and went to accompany the dead.

The next day, I came down with a strong cold and went to bed with a very high fever. In the meantime **[29a]** one of my sons caught cholera, died, and was buried without my being aware of it. The following day, my physician saw that I had sweated[67] and prescribed some quinine. I asked my wife where my little boy was. She answered that she had moved him to another room to avoid my relapse. While we were talking, my other boy also got sick, and within two hours he, too, was gone.

Now, we were left only with our two daughters; and with circumstances going from bad to worse, we managed to conclude this terrible year. As the cholera abated, everyone returned to the city, and everyone started to assess the situation.

The following year, my wife gave birth to a daughter. Poor woman! Having lost two sons who were not being replaced by other ones, she took this greatly to heart and could not bear her life without sons. She did not take care of herself and could not arise from the bed where she gave birth. This disappointment caused her death. Subsequently, I married a maiden to avoid marrying a widow or a *divorcée*.

(1) to continue. [Continuation missing in manuscript]

67. For a carrier of infectious disease, sweating was considered to portend recovery.

Chapter 17

The Death of the Rav h"r Shaul [1849]

As we have already said, the *Rav h"r* Shaul had distinguished himself for quite some time as a holy man who performed miracles and had spread fear among the people. At the advanced age of eighty-eight years, his time to depart from this world had come. When he fell sick, the people believed that this man could not die. But as his condition worsened, a segment of the population never failed holding a vigil day and night. Toward evening the day he expired, the entire population came to lament and recite dirges; the streets were full all the way to Lube square.[68] They spent that entire night **[29b]** sitting on the pavement, with their Ninth of *Av* books, some reading the *Book of Lamentations* and some chanting dirges. The next day, many among them fasted. The entire Jewish population came to escort him, with various groups of teachers singing dirges and thirty-two cantors with their Psalm singers chanting funeral melodies. The funeral cortege lasted until the evening. All day long, there wasn't a single store, office, shop, or market open: they were all closed. All other religious communities were amazed by the funeral ceremony of this man, who was known to all the religious communities. And whenever a gentile had litigation with a Jew, rather than going either to the archbishop or to the local authorities, he used to go to the *Rav h"r* Shaul, who satisfied both sides. And so, until he died, there was universal fear of his religious authority among the people.

Afterward, the leaders of the community named the *Rav h"r* Asher [Kovo] as chief rabbi and *h"r* Hanania Saporta [d. 1857] as head of the rabbinic court.

The first blow that *h"r* Asher wished to administer was in the matter of prostitution. He appointed a number of inspectors to monitor the streets of the prostitutes and find out who was going in and out of houses of ill repute by bringing him reports about each one. He then summoned them to his office to judge and sentence them according to whatever offense he discovered. Some were beaten at the *Talmud Tora*;

68. Unidentified location.

others received lashes. Among these, someone who in his youth was a *talmid haham* and from a good family was seen leaving the house of a Greek. Because of adverse circumstances he had not been able to continue studying; instead, he went into business as a broker for a Greek businessman. As is well known, Greeks are named after the saint in whose festival day they were born, such as **[30a]** those called Basil celebrate their birthday on Saint Basil's day, when friends and relatives come to visit him. The name of the above mentioned person, who had become the broker of this businessman, was M. G. He went to visit his boss, but the inspectors saw him going in and out of this house and reported him to the *Rav h"r* Asher. He asked him what business he had entering the house of a Greek. In his answer he said that he was not accountable to anyone about his comings and goings. Hearing such an unexpected answer, the *rav* became angry, mistreating him for his audacity for using such language in his answer. This man was quite daring because of his extensive religious background and insisted on defending his behavior. Without wasting any time, the *rav* had him sent to jail. While in prison, he used insulting language against the *rav*. Immediately, his words were reported to the *rav*. He was so furious that he sent a note to the *Porte*, the seat of authority, saying, "He has cursed my religion and my faith, dishonoring me, the Chief Rabbi. Let him join the shackled prisoners to sweep the streets with chains on his feet and a placard around his neck." They paraded him in all the streets. When the people witnessed this scandal, it created a major uproar and extremism loosened up somewhat.

He wished to inflict another blow in a case involving a certain *haham* from Sheres [Serres], called *h"r* Sh. H., who adjudicated the case of two individuals. Earlier, the *Rav h"r* Asher had issued a ruling about these two individuals who, upon returning to Sheres, resubmitted their litigation to this *sinyor haham*. The aforementioned *sinyor* reversed *Rav h"r* Asher's ruling, who then found out about this ruling issued in Sheres.

But to demonstrate his influence and thereby **[30b]** disgrace this *haham*, the *Rav h"r* Asher attempted to bring him to Salonica with the help of the authorities. However, this *sinyor haham* wasn't less erudite than him in religion, even though he wasn't as wealthy.

At that time, Sheres depended on Salonica in religious matters. Yet the people of Sheres loved their rabbi, and they sent two of their influential members to intervene in Constantinople. Putting forward their best efforts, they spent an enormous amount of money and managed to make Sheres independent of Salonica, freeing their *sinyor haham* from having to go to Salonica.

A similar case happened in Salonica after the rabbinic court of the *Talmud Tora* issued a sentence. The convicted person went and informed the *Rav h"r* Asher about it, and he reversed the verdict upon studying the case. They, in turn, ordered and pressured him to obey their sentence. His answer was, "I do not recognize your law, other than the law of the *sinyor Rav h"r* Asher." The head of the rabbinic court was called *h"r* Sh. P. and was one of Salonica's greatest and most respected scholars. Just for the audacity displayed by the beadle of the *Rav h"r* Asher to speak against this *haham*, *h"r* Sh. P. sent his own beadle to excommunicate the beadle of the *Rav h"r* Asher. Then, *h"r* Sh. P. went to the Alkalay *yeshiva*, where all the sages congregated, and reported to them the full story. They grew extremely angry against the *Rav h"r* Asher.

His scholarship and especially his wealth made him so arrogant that he wanted to outshine all other scholars in town. The gravity of this situation caused such a serious upheaval in town among the old and the young that it called for the establishment of a group of appointed controllers.

Chapter 18

The Memunnim [Appointed Controllers]

[31a] A group of young people held a meeting to challenge and also learn about the rules of the community. They discovered irregularities in the practices of the community, first among them the thievery that constituted the outrageous gabelle[69] on meat, which angered all the young people. By custom, every year one of the *gevirim* bought the right to collect the gabelle, a different *gevir* bought the right to collect another gabelle. This process was repeated every year, with the amount

69. The gabelle was a tax levied on various kosher foods. It supplied the principal portion of the communal budget that supported various welfare funds.

fluctuating from thirty-two thousand to thirty-four thousand [*kurush*] according to their estimation. Whoever bought the gabelle for a given year was sitting on profits enough to purchase bread and delicacies. The young people called on two major butchers and asked them how many heads of cattle they slaughtered annually. They replied, from seventy-five hundred to eight thousand [*kurush*], amounting to a gabelle of thirty *gass* [Ottoman unit of currency] per head of cattle. When these young people noticed the enormous income generated by the gabelle, they got even angrier. They then began to investigate the gabelle on wine and cheese and concluded that it amounted to an enormous income for the community, while the poor were crying and languishing in the streets, with no one listening to them. Then the entire population started protesting in the streets and demanding the creation of a special committee in our city. A young man called D. B. emerged as the voice that proclaims and challenges. They started by dealing with simple matters; they designated two *hahamim* with authority for this task. One of them was called *h"r* Sh. M. and the other *h"r* R. Sh., who started with the cheese makers. The cheese gabelle was for the *Bikur Holim*, which received forty thousand to fifty thousand *gr.* [*gurushes* or *kurushes*] per year. The rest of the money generated was squandered or stolen. **[31b]**. The year the controllers took office, proceeds jumped to 110,000 *gr.* Finally, they dealt with the ritual slaughterers and found out about two illegal slaughterers without a license who had an income of 160,000 *gr.* a year. At that point the controllers said, "How come the ritual slaughterers get 160,000 *gr.* while the gabelle in the meat generates 35,000?" It also happened that there was plenty of lamb that year, so that the gentiles were paying one hundred *gr.* to the *okka*, while the Jews 6.20, so that the Jews protested saying, "Why do the gentiles pay 100 *gr.*, while the Jews 6.20? By adding 50 *gr.* to the 100 *gr.* per lamb, the price of the *okka* would increase by 10 *gr.*, or 3 *gassim*, where is the excess 3 1/2?"[70]

70. Without knowing the value of the *gas* coin, the meaning of Sa'adi's calculation is unclear. What this section does highlight is the corruption that accompanied communal taxation on kosher food, the bulk of the revenue of which was diverted to various parties.

Besides the community gabelle, there were also small, secret gabelles. Then they drafted a written proclamation in due form: "This is a call to the people to inform them about shortcomings and irregularities that exist in our city." They managed to rescind the licenses of the ritual slaughterers and abolish the small, secret gabelles, and to establish a committee to organize in the future all the income that was being lost now. In this way the controllers were able to attract competent people. In view of all this, backers of the *sinyor Rav h"r* Asher tried to find a way to strengthen their position to compensate for their weakened influence. To that end they advised the *sinyor rav* to submit his resignation, thinking that the entire population would rise up against the controllers, especially in Istanbul, where they and the *sinyor rav* had their own supporters who would object **[32a]** to his resignation.

For this he had to insist as a condition that they should get a *firman* from the *Porte* allowing him to punish at his discretion, without any interference from the authorities.

In spite of all these speculations, the acting chief rabbi of Istanbul [Rabbi Yakir Gueron, 1813–74] accepted immediately and his resignation was published in the *Djurnal Yisraelith*. As soon as this news was known, everybody was filled with sadness. The backers of the *sinyor rav* filed an appeal to Constantinople, stating, "We won't let him leave his position, disregard his resignation." The acting chief rabbi answered them, saying that the *rav* himself had to convey his change of mind in writing. That is how, he sent a message, saying, "The people are disconcerted with my decision; I am, therefore, retracting my resignation." In this way he stayed in his position, which however had become weaker. Then, a council was assembled [1870] to implement a number of reforms during the lifetime of *sinyor* Shaul Modiano [1816–83],[71] who was then the president. But after his death the council became perfunctory, and to this day it continues to languish.

Income is big, but expenditures are even bigger, and meetings are very rare. Since the council's inception until now there has been no financial report to inform the people how all that money is being spent.

71. Modiano, a Franko banker and philanthropist, was one of the wealthiest men in nineteenth-century Salonica.

For this reason, when elections for a new council are held, they don't even mention the number of invitations sent in view of the deterioration of those who are joining the council. Let us see how long it will take before they decide to run the business of the community as it should be. "One generation goes, another comes, but the earth remains the same forever" (Eccl. 1:4). Many times *La Epoka* has lamented this situation, but it has always been, "a voice calls in the desert" (Isa. 40:3).

Chapter 19

The Schools and the Hesed 'Olam Fund

[32b] Forty years ago ignorance reigned supreme in our city among our fellow Jews. In an attempt to bring civilization to the people of Salonica, the tireless and enthusiastic *sinyor* Moizé Alatini, of blessed memory, in cooperation with *sinyor* Shelomo Fernandes[72] and the *Rav h"r* Avraam Gatenyo, *z"l*, held a few meetings and thought of creating a special fund, called *Hesed 'Olam* [everlasting kindness], open to the participation of all the Jewish bankers and businessmen.

Then they called a general assembly of the entire aristocracy of the city in the house of the *sinyor Rav h"r* Asher Kovo and agreed to have twenty-four deputies, with *sinyor* Alatini and *sinyor* Shelomo Fernandes as presidents, the *Rav h"r* Asher as honorary president, and the *Rav h"r* Avraam Gatenyo as secretary. And they put a tax on all purchases and sales to which all of Salonica's merchants agreed with their signature. Also, to protect the privacy of each merchant's income and expenses, they used a closed and sealed box, with a slit, for them to drop their taxes [in]. Every two months, they audited their books, while also inviting all merchants to attend. As they arrived, each one dropped the amount of his tax into the box, without divulging to anyone the ex-

72. A wealthy Franko and the brother-in-law of Moïse Allatini, Fernandes served as consul to the Duchy of Tuscany in Salonica. After moving to Constantinople, as of 1874, he headed the Regional Committee of the Alliance Israélite Universelle, playing a major role in the development of the organization's network of schools in the Ottoman Empire.

penses or incomes. When the collection ended, they opened the box, gathered all the money, placed it in a sack, and deposited it in *sinyor* Fernandes's safe. This fund was established a few years before the creation of the *Alliance Israélite* in Paris [1860].

[33a] First on their agenda was the education of children in the *Talmud Tora*, which until then was based on deplorable teaching methods. For the teachers to earn an adequate living, they paid them weekly. They had twenty-six teachers organized now in pairs, one to gather the students every morning, while the other welcomed and settled them down. They fixed the morning teaching period until noon and the other from noon until the early evening, they also trained the teachers in educational methodology.

Next, they reviewed the income of the *Bikkur Holim* fund. In addition to the gabelle on cheese, oil, and salt provisions, they created new income to keep up with the expenses of the *Bikkur Holim* fund. To mitigate the suffering of the poor, the two salaried physicians they had were increased to eight.

After that, they tackled the job of establishing schools for boys and girls. Yet the *talmide hahamim* started to grumble, saying, "Foreign languages should not be taught in the school, since we do not know any of them." For that, *sinyor* Alatini had to obtain a *firman* from the imperial government stipulating that every Jew who can support the work of the schools has the obligation to give his maximum support to it. The *talmide hahamim*, headed by the chief rabbi, had to help the proponents of said work on behalf of schools to teach foreign languages as well as the language of this country. This *firman* was read in the presence of the General Assembly and the entitled *hahamim*. In 1856 the first school for boys opened **[33b]** with sixty paying and forty tuition-free students. They also brought a teacher from Paris whose name was *Musyu* Lipman[n],[73] who was extremely smart and knowledgeable in both our religion and the French language. He also had a sturdy and most healthy body.

73. Sa'adi is referring to Rabbi Joseph Lippmann, who in fact hailed from Strasbourg. The school he was brought to teach in opened in a section of the *Talmud Tora*. Moïse Allatini obtained an imperial decree authorizing its establishment and, in so doing, more or less forced the institution onto the rabbinical establishment.

But because they were accustomed to wild behavior, our kids brought him real suffering by giving him much trouble. On a three-year contract he spent two and a half years in our city, the last six months suffering from dysentery.[74] *Sinyor* Dr. Alatini and his colleagues tried very hard to save him. In the end it became impossible to heal him locally from his disease, so they paid up his three year contract and sent him back to his hometown.

Sinyor Alatini had invested much effort and took pressure from his entourage to create the *Bikkur Holim*, the *Talmud Tora*, and the school. Yet our gentlemen from Salonica, instead of rewarding him for his good services and the benevolence he showed to the Jewish population, tried to foment a plot that forced him to resign. He had a proclamation printed and distributed to everybody letting them know the effort he had invested and the pressure he took and the duty we all have to do good to our fellow Jews. And whoever has the means of doing that, yet refrains from it, has sin on his hand.

When he quit, submitting his resignation, many from our community begged him to withdraw it, but he insisted he would not, for he was a man whose "yes" was "yes!" and whose "no," was always "no!" In our city we always had the bad luck that goodness never lasts. If this good man was spared all the pressures he was subjected to, he would have continued to introduce many new reforms to our community. By now we could have had our own European-style hospital, an idea dear to his heart. Yet it was the bad luck of the poor who acted like the devil at the instigation of bad individuals to make him quit for good.

[34a] We made reference to the efforts deployed and pressures sustained by this good man. Let us now describe some of these pressures and the details of the plot.

Personally, I got to know some of them. The fact was that those who sent their children to the *Talmud Tora* or to a private class were accustomed to pay the teachers a small fee of four to five *gr.* a week per child. Yet, when their children entered the schools of the wealthy, each one of them was evaluated according to his means. Then the deputies assessed them, establishing three categories of tuition, as follows: first class, one

74. Most other accounts mention that he stayed five years.

Turkish *lira* a month per child; second class, half a *lira*; and third class, one fourth of a *lira* a month. When they had two or three children, the first class tuition for the second child was that of the second class and for the third child, that of the third class, namely wealthy parents with three children in school would be paying one lira and three quarters monthly tuition for the three children. As for the second class, the tuition for the first child was half a *lira* and for the other two, a quarter *lira* each per month.

In the third category tuition was one quarter *lira* a month for each child.

For fathers who were accustomed to pay an *altilik* a month for their children, this new assessment was hard to swallow.

At the beginning, monthly payments were disbursed regularly. But by the end of the first year, there were some arrears. By the second year, the arrears were **[34b]** more substantial. Also, subscribers to the *Hesed 'Olam* Fund started to put less than their dues in the box, to the point that an important businessman even dropped a counterfeit coin in it. This occurred in the presence of four deputies, the echo of the metal coin was clearly heard as this contributor was the last person to come.

As it was late, they had me open the box, and the piece of metal was on top of all the money in the box. I showed it to them, saying, "Here is the coin you heard fall through the slit." They saw that it was indeed counterfeit!

The *sinyor haham h"r* Avraam Gatenyo took me aside and asked me if I could find out to whom this coin belonged. I told him that I could. *Sinyor* Alatini, too, asked how I could identify him. I told him that I would find a way so that the businessman would not know about it. The businessman had sent this coin with his employee from his office to be put in the box. So, I went to this employee and I said to him, "You should know that the coin you put in the box is counterfeit; try to find out who gave it to you." He took it and exchanged it for a real coin.

Now, the *si[nyor] haham* and *Si[nyor]* Alatini knew me as a capable man who knew everybody, who was honest and who was not, for having proven myself on many occasions; they had also noticed the people's slackness from the decreasing revenues of the fund; they convened an assembly to rejuvenate it. However, this time they were unable to set the people of Salonica back on the right track; indeed, **[35a]** proceeds dwindled soon to a pittance.

On the other hand, payments by parents of school children were falling behind. When *Si.* Alatini saw that they were unable to pay for the school's vital expenditures, because coffers were almost empty, he told me one day to urge, on his behalf, those with arrears to pay their debts. Twice a week, I approached each one of them with my standard speech. In spite of my efforts, they kept procrastinating. Among these was a father who had three sons in school and owed three bimonthly payments for all three sons. I contacted him in his office to pay at least half now and the other half after a while. It so happened that a partner of *Si.* Alatini, who was also one of the twenty-four deputies, was there and encouraged me. I gently broached the subject on behalf of *Si.* Alatini, thinking that the presence of this official would embarrass him and he may pay me.

You can imagine my disappointment when I witnessed that, even before I spoke to the businessman, this deputy opened his mouth and, scolding me, said, "You rely on *Si.* Alatini to keep bothering everybody! While everyone is worried about his business, you choose those days when ships arrive, which is a time when everyone has to take care of his correspondence on Fridays, in addition to having to pay bills. But *Si.* Alatini doesn't have any of these worries! Therefore, good day to you!"

It can be readily understood that in spite of my daring, when I heard the harsh language used by this *sinyor*, I turned for a moment into a marble statue. I went back to my business.

[35b] When the *si.* partner returned to the office, he complained about me to *Si.* Alatini, saying, "This collector is abusing your name, embarrassing merchants by going after them in their busy time." He also suggested to him to get a new collector and also warn me not to bother the merchants so much. *Si.* Alatini was a very patient man. He knew that his partner thrived on gossip but that I was very faithful in his service, for he had tested me many times. Therefore, he immediately sent three to four employees from his office to find me. When they found me, they sent me to *Si.* Alatini's house rather than his office. I promptly went there and found him in his private office. This time, he wanted to test me to get to the truth. He started by asking me nonchalantly why I wasn't collecting owed debts, because the treasurer, *h"r* Moshe ben Veniste, informed me that there was no cash in the coffer, monthly salaries had to be paid to the teachers and employees, and I had not brought any funds. My answer was that I was doing my duty but that the merchants keep procrastinating from one week to the other. And in the end they are not paying me! What can I do? He said to me, "Maybe, you are not using my name." "It is true, *Si.*, that sometimes I do, sometimes I don't, not to abuse your name."

He asked me, "When did he give you the stubs of those who owe money?" I had them in good order and alphabetically arranged. By coincidence, the first debtor was the gentleman where the incident occurred and who owed three bimonthly payments, namely eighteen monthly payments for his sons. *Si.* Alatini did not wish to check anybody else having understood the tale-telling they were doing about me.

[36a] He simply said, "I understand; Godspeed to you and try to collect as much as possible." As I left him, I was utterly confused, and I didn't want to cause him more anxiety. That is why I didn't tell him what had happened to me earlier. I had gone directly to the *Si. haham, h"r* Avraam and reported to him the entire incident, begging him to accept my resignation, for I was losing three times the monthly pay I was getting. The *si. haham* comforted me, saying that *Si.* Alatini had great esteem for me, I shouldn't worry as he never doubted my loyalty.

That Friday, I went to see *Si.* Alatini to ask if he had a job for me. He told me to go to the *si. haham* [Avraam Gatenyo] and tell him when he planned to come to his house; that is what I did.

In their conversations the *si. haham* told him that *ham* Sa'adi was very annoyed with all the things happening to him, but he cannot report them to you. He also related to him the fact that I wanted to resign. But *Si.* Alatini answered, "I am satisfied for having tested him many times, not once have I discovered any false behavior in him, and I do know my partner intimately. He has always liked to bad-mouth people, even me; this is his nature."

On another occasion I learned that they were trying to foment a plot to curtail the influence that *Si.* Alatini had in our city, and curiously, his partner was among them.

As for this secret plot, I was the one to inform the *si. haham* about it, rather than *Si.* Alatini, for I had observed this gentleman's fervor and passionate love for his fellow Jews.

[36b] One day, the *si. haham* divulged the story to *Si.* Alatini, who could no longer tolerate the discord prevalent among his colleagues and their jealousy of him. He then thought of quitting and formally resigning. He drafted a detailed list of all the accounts of all the schools and the *Bikkur Holim* with their incomes and expenditures, and he distributed it to everybody to show them the work he did during these past five years.

He called me to his house, let me sit in one of his rooms, and gave me a penholder, ink, and paper. He had me copy that list as he dictated it from the Italian, and I wrote it in Spanish letters [in Ladino cursive, *soletreo*].[75]

In this memorandum was a paragraph showing the effort and hard work it took him to create income for the *Talmud Tora*, the *Bikkur Holim*, and the schools. Also [it showed] the extent of the people's lack of cooperation, as they tried to destroy the seeds he had planted. Later on, more about this. Let us now turn to the plot they were planning.

Then, I stopped writing. He asked me, "Why don't you continue to write?" I answered that "some day, they will hang me by my ears when they learn that I was the one to disclose this plot. Rest assured that one day, they will come up with a pretext to harm me."

Si. Alatini gave me his gentleman's word that he would never allow harm even to one of my nails. So, I fulfilled his order and printed it secretly; no one knew about it. I kept them in my safe until he asked me to distribute them. On the first day of the intermediary days of Passover, he called me and gave me permission to distribute all of the one thousand notices, along with **[37a]** a financial report. An hour later, the *Bikkur Holim* committee came to plead with him not to withdraw from leading them, as everything was running well because of his patronage. He answered them, saying, "No, I am not dissatisfied with the *Bikkur Holim* committee." But in case his presence will be needed, he would do his utmost not to let the *Bikkur Holim* services to the poor deteriorate!

After a while, he had to take a trip to Europe. The night before his

75. This anecdote provides proof that Sa'adi understood at least some Italian.

departure, he had dinner with his brothers and his sons, and he was kind enough to recommend me to them, so that in case of need, they should protect me. And so it was. After a short while into the trip of the *sinyor cavaliere* [*Doctor* Alatini], an Imperial Decree came from Constantinople ordering all types of printers to obtain a license from the government before printing anything.

As for me, I was totally unaware of this recommendation. I turned to *Si.* Emanuel ben Rubi, a benefactor and dear friend of mine, who was also very well acquainted with *Si.* Alatini and Fernandes, and told him that now I couldn't print anything without a printer's license. Before I even finished my sentence, he took me to the Alatini brothers and related the facts to them. Immediately, they gave me a letter addressed to *Chilibi* Avraam ben Zonana asking him to do everything in his power to obtain a license of printing equipment. That is when *Si.* Emanuel ben Rubi told me that before his departure, *Si.* Alatini had recommended me, for that night he was there for dinner.

I was also carrying another letter from *Si. Rav h"r* Asher for the *Si. Rav* Avigdor [1794–1874][76] of Constantinople, and left immediately for the capital and presented my letters to the concerned. They promised me not to worry, for in a few days they would obtain my license for printing equipment. And so it was.

Chapter 20

The Fire of Skilich

[37b] It was almost in the year [5]617 [1856/1857 according to the Gregorian calendar] when the news spread that there was a fire in the European quarter, in the house of a merchant, and until help came, the fire had widely spread. Two to three houses away was the house of the [Greek] merchant *Si.* Skilich, who, besides his regular business,

76. Acting chief rabbi in Constantinople, Avigdor, who had been chief rabbi since 1860, was removed from his position in 1863 after his opponents complained of his attempts to create a European-style Jewish school with the support of the wealthy Franko banker Abraham Camondo [1781–1873].

was also involved in the illegal trade of gunpowder that he secretly sold to foreigners from his basement, where he managed to store five hundred barrels of gunpowder.

At that time of the year he wasn't living there but was staying in his summer home. When his agent, named *Si.* Y. B. Sh., saw that the house was on the fire line, he ran there as fast as possible, opened the office, took all the money that was there, and carried it to his own home, without anyone seeing him. Within fifteen to twenty minutes fire reached said house, in spite of all the efforts made by the firemen and those working with grapples, who were unaware that underneath, there was gunpowder stored in the basement. As the burning house collapsed on top of the basement, all the barrels of gunpowder caught fire and exploded, lifting up the burning house to the sky and scattering debris all around the adjacent houses, as far as the ships and boats in the harbor. The intensity of the explosion was such that it was heard from a distance of two hours away, and the ground split, creating a huge cavity like a small lagoon. The helpers were propelled into the fire, which killed a considerable amount of people who were buried under the ruins. The survivors started to run away like crazy people. Others, whom the intense explosion had thrown on the ground, were now trampled by the more than two thousand bystanders who were watching the fire, so that their number exceeded those killed by the fire!

[38a] That night reverberated as a major catastrophe, with everyone mourning loudly the death of sons, husbands, and [other] family members.

The next day, they kept bringing all the dead to the *Talmud Tora*; it was extremely sad to see people coming to lament their loved ones, dead and trampled during this catastrophe; there was deeply felt sorrow all around. *Si.* Skilich was caught and imprisoned, but *Si.* Alatini used all his influence; and with money, he escaped from the grip of those who had already condemned him to be hanged. But nobody figured out how he was allowed to escape from the grip of the authorities. After a while it became known that he was living in some European city from which he could not be extradited. Yet the *si.* agent Y. B. Sh. kept all the money; no one challenged him. What he managed to lay his hands on must have been quite a substantial sum, for after a short while, this man's wealth was apparent, and he kept using it unashamedly until today. By nature, I am very cautious, and never in my entire life have I gone out to watch a fire. But that night was an exception because this fire was approaching the house of *Si.* Shelomo Fernandes. I rushed to help him move his belongings from his mansion to his office, as he was the president of the *Hesed 'Olam* Fund. That is the main reason why I found myself in his mansion during this fire. I was inside his mansion rather than outside, and when the big explosion occurred, it shook the mansion and shattered the glass in all the windows. When I heard the screams and the clamors of the wounded and the trampled, I tried to escape through a secret door, exiting at the Malta corner. Running fast, I went through the Brokers' Market and reached home. My wife was waiting for me; both of us hugged and cried, **[38b]** unaware of the total death toll.

The following morning, we learned the extent of this disaster as we heard also the bad news about friends who had perished from the fire embers or as a result of being trampled to death.

Chapter 21[77]

The Visit of His Majesty Sultan Abdul Medjid [1839–61]

This is about the visit of His Majesty, Sultan Abdul Medjid, to Salonica on Wednesday, July 25, 1859. When the sultan decided to travel, he sent an imperial decree to the local *pasha* twenty days before his departure, stating that preparations should be made in every stop on his itinerary, as well as here, in Salonica.

The first thing they did was to cut all the bay windows from the marina to the *pasha*'s palace, until they finished cleaning all the streets and decorated some places with fancy material, that is:

1. The *pasha*'s palace,
2. The mansion and the villa in the garden of Yusuf *Pasha*,

77. Even though Sa'adi's memoir already contained a Chapter 21, its author must have felt that the visit of Sultan Abdul Medjid deserved its own chapter number and title. In shaky handwriting, he squeezed this text immediately after Chapter 20, creating duplication.

3. The mansion of the Tannery Tower. They also built a new pier facing the same tower toward the sea.
4. They built a special place for the sultan in the upper level of the Santa Sophia Mosque, when he is there for the Friday Noon prayers.
5. The house of *Si.* Dario Alatini,[78] may God protect him, amen, was set aside for Captain Mehmet Ali[79] *Pasha*, the sultan's brother-in-law. **[39a]**
6. The house of *Si.* Shelomo Fernandes, may God protect him, amen, was set aside for the minister of war. They also notified all the artisans to set aside two days to clean the road going from the New Gate to the Lodge of the *Mevlevi Dervishes*, as well as the road to *Orundjik* and *Besh Chinar*.[80] They took notice of it.

The great pier of the marina was also repaired, and at its end they built a sturdy staircase, wide like that of a house of eight yards in width. They prepared a long piece of broadcloth to cover the area from the pier to the Egyptian Market[81] for the day of the sultan's arrival. After that the local *pasha* sent a note to all the heads of the religious communities to prepare the schoolchildren to be dressed all in white. He issued an order to teach them a few nice songs to welcome the sultan on the day of his arrival with all the heads of the religious communities in their clerical attire.

Instructions were also issued to keep all stores in the market open and well lit every evening of the sultan's stay in our city. Similarly, the entrances of the houses were to be lit until 11 p.m. to 12 a.m. Everybody was pleased to follow these orders.

Then, *Si.* Alatini and *Si.* Fernandes and the twenty-four deputies

78. Dario Allatini was the brother and business partner of Moïse Allatini.

79. Mehmed Ali served in various capacities in the Ottoman administration, among other things as head of the navy and Grand Vezir.

80. Salonica's oldest public (municipal) park, then situated at the western outskirts of the city.

81. Situated next to the gate of the harbor and east of Besh Chinar, the Egyptian Market specialized in sugar, spices, coffee, linen, and other items associated with Egypt in the public imagination.

held a meeting at the house of the *si. rav*, putting me in charge of teaching the children the appropriate music for this occasion. I composed a song in the *adjem makam* and another one in the *huzzam makam*, with my name as an acrostic and another one in the *rast makam* specially written with an accompaniment to the Judeo-Spanish composition mentioned above.

And three days before the arrival of the sultan in our city, ten frigates anchored in our harbor, while the sultan arrived on July 27, 1859, with six **[39b]** cruisers; he was accompanied by his brother, Aziz *efendi*,[82] his three sons, and his brother-in-law, Admiral Mehmet Ali *Pasha*, and the minister of war, Riza *Pasha*.

As soon as they anchored, Riza *Pasha* emerged in a hurry to inspect the places for readiness before they landed. Immediately, he returned to the sultan's cruiser and informed him that the villa of Yusuf *Pasha* was the appropriate place for him to stay. For himself he designated the villa in the garden of Yusuf *Pasha*, for his brother and his sons the *haremlik* and *disharilik* of the same villa, for his brother-in-law *Kaptanpasha* the home of *Si.* Dario Alatini, for Riza *Pasha* the home of *Si.* Shelomo Fernandes, and other places for the rest of his retinue.

And among these were all the heads of the religious communities with their entourage, as well as the schoolchildren, who moved from where they were stationed and started to parade from the corner of the pier to the entrance of the Egyptian Market. All the bands and the imperial guard were positioned on both sides of the street, arranged militarily from the start of the Egyptian Market to the last soldier at the edge of the city. The children of the Turkish schools and their *hodjas* were ready in the field along the seashore from the end of the Egyptian Market to the Gate of the Marina. On one side were the Greek bishops and their entourage; on the other side, there were fifty Greek children and fifty young men, all dressed in white, the young boys holding a green branch and the young girls a bouquet of roses, ready to be thrown in front of the sultan as he approached them.

Then in the city from the Gate of the Marina to the Fountain of the Customs were seventy Jewish young men, uniformly dressed in white,

82. Aziz *efendi* was the future Sultan Abdulaziz (1861–76).

well-kempt, wearing their black *fezes* decorated with *medjidies*. Each one of them had a red button appended on his lapel. Each one of them was wearing white **[40a]** gloves and holding sheets of music in various colors to sing as the sultan approached them.

On the other side there were some two hundred children, well-dressed in the Turkish style, to answer *amen* to what those on the opposite side would say. And our teacher, the *Rav* Asher Kovo, and his entourage were standing in front of the Fountain of the Customs. All the streets, from the corner of the pier all the way to where the sultan had to go, had been filled with sand.

By 11 a.m., the sultan emerged from his ship and boarded a well-furnished boat, with the *Kaptan Pasha* holding the rudder, while all the frigates and ships were showing their colors. And from the moment he left his ship until he stepped on the pier, there was a continuous gun salute from the frigates, the ships, and the forts. However, the sultan refrained from stepping on the broadcloth; instead, he walked over the uncovered side all the way to the horse-block. He then climbed on the horse prepared for him, while the bands played their music and the children started singing, a really magnificent spectacle for the eyes and the ears.

The following protocol was observed: First, the important personalities of Salonica, then Yusuf *Pasha*, accompanied by the then commanding *pasha*, Mehmet Ali *Pasha* and Riza *Pasha* and their retinue and five royal horses covered with invaluable jewelry of all kinds. Following them were close to one hundred people dressed in red with epaulets and crowns on their heads with multicolored feathers. Behind them was the sultan, wearing his diamond crown topped with an aigrette. After him came his brother with his three sons, wearing diamond crowns on their heads. As mentioned earlier, the sultan went to the villa in the garden of Yusuf *Pasha*, while his brother and his three sons went to the mansion of said individual, Mehmet Ali *Pasha* **[40b]** went to the house of *Si.* Dario Alatini, and Riza *Pasha* to the house of *Si.* Shelomo Fernandes, with their emblems on display on each street door. After he rested for an hour, the sultan left by horse for the New Gate, as he entered the Tower of the Tannery through one gate and exited from the other. From there he went to *Besh Chinar*, where tents were ready and waiting for him, his brother, and his sons. He spent two hours at *Besh Chinar* and returned for dinner to the mansion of Yusuf *Pasha*. Half an hour later, he went back to *Besh Chinar* again on horseback. His brother and his sons stayed at *Besh Chinar*, where they spent the night. The road from the New Gate to *Besh Chinar* looked like a street lit with colored torches; all the frigates, the ships, and the Tower of the Tannery started displaying fireworks of all colors. The entire city was aglow with fireworks, a spectacular view to watch. All the while he rested at *Besh Chinar*, there were court chamberlains going back and forth with great speed to the city on horseback to carry out the sultan's orders. He stayed at that place until 11 p.m. and then returned by carriage to sleep at his mansion. He left for the country home of *Si.* Abot [Abbott][83] in *Orundjik* on the second day, Thursday, July 28, after lunch, at 1 p.m. by a two-horse carriage; he drove himself, without a coachman. When he reached said place, he went for a walk on the hills of *Orundjik*; then he proceeded to *Si.* Abot's country home, which was well prepared and ready, with a broadcloth on the ground, yet he did not step on it but walked on the sides, and he stayed there almost fifteen minutes.[84] He then returned by carriage that he himself drove to the Yusuf *Pasha* mansion. After resting almost half an hour in his mansion, he left again by carriage for *Besh Chinar*, where he dined and stayed **[41a]** until 11 p.m., with lit torches and fireworks like the previous night, leaving for the Yusuf *Pasha* mansion to spend the night there. On Thursday evening, July 28, he sent a written notice to the governor [*Vali*] Sait *Pasha*, inviting all the councils, the heads of the religious communities, and the consuls to be ready for Friday, July 29, at 3 p.m., to introduce themselves to the sultan at *Besh Chinar*. On Friday, at 11 a.m., he left his mansion with his entourage as he had done the day of his arrival, in full uniform for the Noon Prayer at the Saint Sophia Mosque, where they had specially furnished a place for him.

83. John Abbott was a member of a wealthy English mercantile family that had long since settled in Salonica and had become Greek Orthodox through conversion and intermarriage. His wealth resulted from the monopoly he exercised over the export of leeches to Europe, where they were in demand for medical use.
84. This action of the sultan's was widely perceived as a snub of John Abbott.

After he finished his prayer, he came out of the mosque, changed his clothes for regular ones, and then left in his two-horse carriage, which he himself drove. He drove passing by the New Gate in the direction of *Besh Chinar*, to his red tent, open on all sides. Behind his tent there were other tents prepared for the guests who started to arrive there. The sultan was standing in front of his tent, facing the city, with all the soldiers and the imperial bands ready to play. Also present there were the *Kaptan* Mehmet Ali *Pasha*, Riza *Pasha*, their chamberlains, and four other *vizirs*: Ismail, military commander in chief in Monastir;[85] Abdi Vali *Pasha*, [governor] of Monastir; Sait *Pasha*, the governor of Salonica; and Yusuf *Pasha*. He immediately ordered his chamberlains to start introducing the guests:

1. The four *pashas*, who are Ismail *Pasha* of Monastir, Abdi Vali *Pasha* of Monastir, Sait Vali *Pasha* of Salonica, and Yusuf *Pasha*.
2. The great council of Salonica.
3. The Criminal Justice. **[41b]**
4. The bishop of Salonica with three Greek businessmen and the bishops of Salonica's districts who presented the sultan with a pillow well embroidered by the local schoolgirls, valued at four to five thousand *grushes*, and the sultan accepted it.
5. A commission of the local inhabitants.
6. Chamber of Commerce.
7. The French, British, Austrian, Russian, Tuscan, and Dutch consuls, who presented him a well-written speech, welcoming him to Salonica, read by the Russian consul.
8. Our teacher, the *Rav h"r* Asher Kovo, *h"r* Moshe ben Veniste,[86] and five businessmen: *Si.* Shalom Hekim,[87] *Si.* Yishak Moshe Tiano,[88]

85. Monastir, currently known as Bitola, is in Macedonia.
86. Ben Veniste was a close colleague of Chief Rabbi Asher Kovo.
87. Hekim was a financier from the city of Larissa in Thessaly.
88. Tiano was a member of the "Seven Honorable Citizens" of Salonica; see glossary under *Shiv'a* for more information.

Si. Yishak Yeoshua Modiano,[89] *Si.* Shaul Modiano,[90] and *Si.* Yaakov Moshe Mizrahi.[91]

9. The ranked *beys*, minor class, all of whom were introduced by one of the sultan's chamberlains. He spoke to everyone a few words about their concerns. After each of the sultan's words, no response was required, except an oriental salute.

When our teacher the *Rav* [Asher Kovo] and his entourage were introduced by Riza *Pasha*, minister of war, they gave the sultan the oriental salute, while Riza *Pasha* said, "This is the Chief Rabbi." The sultan answered that he was very pleased. He then asked about the others and was told that they were prominent figures of the religious community [*millet*]. In his answer the sultan said that he was very pleased and reminded them to take care of the poor. Immediately, Riza *Pasha* intervened, saying, "Because these gentlemen do not know your language,[92] they have appointed your servant as their representative to tell you that day and night, they never fail to pray for you and your kingdom's welfare." Delighted, the sultan repeated that he was very pleased; then they returned to their places.

[42a] Following all this, the bands started playing, and everyone returned to their places. The sultan and his entourage stayed at *Besh Chinar* until 10 p.m., where he dined, in similar fashion to the merrymaking of the previous nights.

The same day, in the evening, Sait Vali *Pasha*, governor of Salonica, sent a written notice to all the religious communities [*millets*] and councils to get ready for the next day, July 30, with all the children to accompany the sultan on his departure similar to what took place on the day of his arrival. And this was done.

On Saturday morning everyone was ready, occupying the same

89. Yishak Yeoshua Modiano was also a member of the "Seven Honorable Citizens" of the city.

90. For more on Shaul Modiano, see note 68 above.

91. Mizrahi was a leading notable of the community who was related to other notables through descent and marriage.

92. This intriguing comment suggests that none of the leaders of the community had working fluency in Ottoman Turkish.

places they held on the day of arrival, and the sultan was ready to leave, as all the *pashas* were waiting outside Yusuf *Pasha*'s mansion.

At that last moment Riza *Pasha*, minister of war, happened to come with *Si.* Shelomo Fernandes and *Si.* Moshe Alatini, and immediately introduced them to the sultan, who was standing in his room; after a brief silence, *Si.* Alatini and *Si.* Fernandes thanked the sultan for his kind visit to Salonica, who answered that he was very pleased to meet them.

Then Riza *Pasha* answered, "Sir, these are the two gentlemen I mentioned to you yesterday who are constantly looking after the welfare of the city regardless of self-interest." Again the sultan answered that he was very pleased.

Then, *Si.* Fernandes started to speak, saying, "Sir, we gave your servant Riza *Pasha* a letter to show you at your convenience." The sultan answered in French,[93] "This city will thrive greatly." Because of this event, the sultan was delayed by ten to twelve minutes, while, as we said, everybody was waiting outside in the heat of the sun. As soon as *Si.* Fernandes and *Si.* Alatini left, the sultan headed **[42b]** on horseback to the pier of the marina, accompanied by his entourage as on the day of his arrival.

At 7 a.m. he boarded his ship with great pomp and was greeted with a continuous gun salute from the forts, the frigates, and the ships until he entered his ship. They lingered at port until noon, and then they left in peace. Again, there were more gun salutes from the forts, the frigates, and the ships; apparently, he was so pleased with our city and *Besh Chinar* that he only spent six hours in Chios[94] after he left here on his way to Constantinople.

As monetary gifts for the three communities—i.e., the Turkish, Greek, and Jewish—he left twenty thousand *grushes* [*kurush*] for each school; in addition, he left another sixty-five thousand *grushes* of charity for the *hodjas* and all the poor, of which the Jews received twenty-six thousand, while the Greeks received five thousand *grushes* in *beshliks* to acknowledge the pillow given to him in *Besh Chinar* by the schoolgirls.

93. It is striking that the common language of communication between the sultan and these leading Frankos is French rather than Turkish.

94. Chios is an island in the Aegean Sea off the coast of Anatolia.

In addition, he also distributed the following gifts: a beautiful cigarette case to the local governor, Sait *Pasha*, and another one to Mehmet *Pasha* of the arsenal and some ten pocket watches to the hosts who accommodated his entourage in their own homes.

Following the departure of the sultan, they took possession of the money left by the sultan, which ultimately was entrusted to the *rav* and the community. The distribution was carried out at their pleasure. As for me, they allocated me five hundred *gr.* for my work of composing the songs and of training and rehearsing the children to sing them after I had spent twenty days selecting one hundred youngsters. They also gave 150 *gr.* to each one of the two assistants that worked with me. An itemized list of the five hundred *gr.* that they set aside for me was shown to *Si.* Alatini, **[43a]** but he got upset, saying, "This is not enough for someone who spent twenty days training the children and also composed three wonderful songs." Even though they offered to increase my stipend by three hundred *gurushes*, he insisted that they should give me fifteen hundred *gr.*

It was to no avail! I had to spend another thousand *gr.* out of pocket to recover from all the hard work and exhaustion I went through. I was bedridden for a whole month. But my hard work and my efforts to excite the children to perform to everybody's satisfaction was appreciated by old and young alike.

Chapter 21

[43b] *The Two Weddings*

A year after the arrival of Sultan Abdul Medjid in Salonica, there were two big celebrations. The first one was the wedding celebration of the daughter of *Si.* Shelomo Fernandes with *Si.* David, his brother's son. The bride was the *sinyorita* Ortensya, marrying *Si.* Djon Fernandes. Her father was consul of Tuscany, which added a unique charm to this ceremony, the likes of which had never been seen before. By coincidence, French warships happened to be visiting our port at that time. Among those invited were the admiral and all the commanding officers of the frigates, as well as the diplomatic corps, the governor general with all the high officials, the *Si. Rav H*[*am*] Asher and the *Si. haham h"r* Avraam Gatenyo, signatories of the *ketubba*, or marriage contract, the archbishop and the Greek community, and the entire Jewish aristocracy. Finally, it was a pleasure to see all the high officials, such as the consular corps and those from the French frigates, in their uniforms, with soldiers lining both sides of the street. And, from the door of *Si.* Shelomo's house to the groom's house, the street was covered with a red carpet for the bride to walk on. Thirty young men, dressed in white, with boutonnieres on their lapels, were singing, while ahead of the bride the band of the French frigate was playing. Except for good luck, this was a ceremony that no amount of money could ever buy.

That was also the first time that I ever printed gilded invitations.

Like a *sukka*, the tables were covered with a light fabric and ready in the courtyard. All the table settings were made of fine silver, arranged for the banquet of that evening. [44 a] A few weeks later, the second celebration took place when the son of *Si. Rav h"r* Asher, called Hayyimachi, married the daughter of *Si. Haham h"r* Yakovachi Kovo, who was the son-in-law of the *Si. rav*. Although this celebration was rather low-key, it was similar to what took place in the weddings of rabbis, where ten cantors and thirty young men chanted the *peshrev* of *sos tasis* [you shall surely rejoice], from the house of the bride to the house of the groom. Here, too, all these singers were chanting most gracefully while they were leading the bride.[95]

The same was done on the way to the synagogue. On returning home from the synagogue, the groom was brought home as they sang Hebrew songs.

In this celebration, too, there were many high officials who came to accompany the *si. rav*. The *kiddushin* and the *shiv'a berahoth* were sung with a new melody carefully composed beforehand and rehearsed by the young men.

That evening, there was a special banquet for 120 women who, under the rich lights shining on the jewels they wore on their heads, of-

95. As was true of Sa'adi's own wedding (see Chapter 16), it appears that only the groom goes to the synagogue, while the bride moves from her father's house to that of her future husband.

fered a magnificent view; and the weight of the sum total of these pearls could easily have reached ten to twelve *okkas*.

The second night was for the men; the tables were set as on the first night for the 120 guests, all of whom belonged to Salonica's high society. The evening extended until the next morning, with songs, and also peppered with jokes making fun of the *si. rav*.

Chapter 22

The Alliance Israélite of Paris

[44b] After the resignation submitted by *Si.* Alatini, Jews in Salonica still had to send their children to the schools, even though the primary school had fallen apart and its director had left. Its leaders became aware of the mistake they committed by not supporting *Si.* Alatini in the good deeds he performed and the excellent results the boys' school had yielded within a mere three years.

Musyu Shalem,[96] the first one to graduate from this school, opened his own small school and started to work with twenty to twenty-five students. Another graduate of the same school, called [Be]n Ardut, also opened a small school with a handful of students. He, too, included elementary French in his curriculum.

Just about this time, a French teacher (whose name I don't recall) arrived in Salonica; and the reverend *h"r* Yeuda Nehama [1824–99][97] formed a committee and opened a school in a big house with the help of this teacher consisting of about one hundred tuition-paying students. There were also about thirty high-paying boarding students. By hiring some teachers' aids, they established a school with classes taught in French, under the direction of *Musyu* Shalem, the Hebrew teacher. This school had a good start, but after a while it began to stumble. In the course of those years the *Alliance Israélite* was established in Paris.

96. The school opened by Haim Shalem(1840–1904) lasted until the founder's death.

97. Nehama was a well-known Salonican Jewish intellectual and reformer who was in regular contact with the leading eastern European *maskilim* of the time.

Its goal was to enlighten the Jews of the Orient, and its curriculum was geared to spreading the French language, the national language of the country, as well as Hebrew. **[45a]** They printed flyers, which they sent to every city in the Orient, especially to the city of Salonica, with a card addressed to the reverend *h"r* Yeuda Nehama, asking him to recruit members interested in participating in this *Alliance*. The reverend *h"r* Yeuda Nehama did his utmost to recruit the highest possible number of new members to join the *Alliance* in Paris, whose annual membership was six [French] francs.

Yet he could not reach a sufficient amount of subscribers. He then wrote a letter to the *Alliance* in Paris, explaining to them that in order to reach their goal, they had to turn to *Si.* Alatini and beg him to get involved in this project, which earlier had been his brain child and now coincided with what the *Alliance* was promoting anew.

Then the *Alliance* in Paris and its president, the famous attorney *Musyu* Kremyo [Adolphe Crémieux, 1796–1880],[98] wrote a most engaging letter to *Si.* Alatini, which he couldn't turn down, especially as this was actually what he wanted to hear.

He then called a general assembly, and they decided to mail flyers calling on all the Jewish inhabitants of the city to become members of this association, everyone at his own level. The lowest subscription was twelve franks, of which six franks were for Paris and six franks were placed in a separate box for the work of the *Alliance* school.

Thus, he was able to recruit close to 250 members, and this list continued to grow unfailingly.

The *Alliance* in Paris promised to send a qualified director, whose salary would be partially paid by them and the remainder to be covered by our community. **[45b]** Then after figuring out the total income from tuition-paying students and some help from the community, as well as creating new incomes for the said school, work was started with the help of the twenty-four deputies. They rented two large houses, one for the boys' school and another for the girls' school.

Before sending a director, the *Alliance* sent a delegate named *Si.*

98. Adolphe Crémieux, a leading public figure of French Jewry, was at this time also president of the Alliance Israélite Universelle.

Kazes,[99] who tested both paying and nonpaying students, drafting a complete list of all the students by their names and assigning them to their appropriate classes. Soon thereafter they sent a director called *Musyu* Maks [Marx],[100] who upon arrival placed every student where he belonged.

This director may have not been such a tall man, but with his ability he was truly one of the rarest directors ever found in any of the schools of the Orient. Unfortunately, four to five years later, when the director of the school in Paris[101] passed away, he was recalled to fill his position there. In his place they sent *Si.* Israel Danon as director, who headed the school for fifteen years. However, in spite of all the efforts, incomes by then were insufficient to cover the mounting expenses.

In the meantime the philanthropist and king of charity, the Baron [Maurice de Hirsch] Hirsh [1831–96],[102] of blessed memory, came to Salonica to survey the railroads and was a guest at *Si.* Alatini's house. After breakfast he and *Si.* Karlo[103] went, in the company of two other people, to the railroad station, then proceeded by special train to Gevgelya [in Macedonia], and returned by noon to have lunch at *Si.* Alatini's.

At the lunch table their conversation revolved around the schools **[46a]** and their annual deficit. He asked with how much can this deficit be covered. *Si.* Alatini answered, saying, "If they owned the school buildings, this deficit could be covered by not having to pay two hundred to three hundred *liras* annually."

He asked how much was needed for these two buildings. *Si.* Alatini answered that with one hundred thousand [French] franks one could purchase two buildings suitable for schools. He answered, "Let the

99. David Cazès was born in Tetuan, Morocco, in 1851 and was among the first Sephardi Jews who attended an Alliance school, subsequently joining the organization as a teacher and director. He was the founder of the Alliance schools in Izmir and Tunis.

100. Maurice Marx was one of the first teachers in the Alliance network.

101. Sa'adi is referring to the *Ecole Normale Israélite Orientale*, the teacher-training school of the Alliance.

102. Hirsch, a German/Belgian banker and philanthropist, was a leading supporter of the Alliance Israélite Universelle, and a financier of railroad concessions in the Ottoman Empire.

103. Carlo was the son of Moïse Allatini.

city's affluent people launch a fund-raising campaign and I shall provide the balance in matching funds."

Upon the departure of the philanthropist, Baron Hirsch from Salonica, *Si.* Alatini wasted no time in calling a general assembly of all affluent people in Salonica. With four hundred *liras*, he emerged as the top contributor. *Si.* Shaul Modiano, who was accustomed to contributing half of *Si.* Alatini's donations, followed with two hundred *liras*. Then came contributions from the Sayases,[104] the Tianos,[105] and the al-Hasids,[106] etc. etc. Thus the sum of forty-five thousand franks was reached; a note was sent to Baron Hirsh, who provided the difference of fifty-five thousand franks, for a sum total of one hundred thousand. When these funds arrived in a strongbox, they bought a spacious and large house for twenty-two hundred *liras* to be used as a school for boys and the house of *Si.* Dr. Palombo and the attached spacious yard. A kindergarten for girls was built in a section of the yard. In another corner of the yard they built living quarters of three to four rooms for the principal, and as of this writing, these schools have been running well.

Yet in spite of what we said, and the annual donations generated by deaths and celebrations, there is still a deficit.

We also heard that a letter was sent by *Si.* Alatini to the Baroness [Clara de Hirsch, 1833–99].[107] **[46b]** To be better informed, the baroness sent a letter asking about needed things in Salonica.

Si. Alatini answered with a letter in which he listed all the needs of Salonica, such as the suffering of the poor people and the lack of a hospital in our city.

When the baroness saw the details of this report, she immediately

104. The Sayases were a prominent Jewish family who founded a cotton factory in Salonica in 1873. Shalom Sayas also established a *yeshiva* in the city.

105. The Tianos were an important Jewish Salonican family who imported European industrial products such as steam engines, motors, and pumps.

106. The al-Hasids built a textile mill, created a *yeshiva*, and were involved in communal administration.

107. Clara de Hirsch, wife of Baron Hirsch and a philanthropist like her husband, provided funds in 1890 for the construction of a new Jewish quarter and Jewish hospital in Salonica.

sent ten thousand franks to be distributed among the poor people. These funds arrived at the opportune time of Passover eve by helping a number of honorable families of limited means; may their blessings reach the heavens and may divine Providence lengthen the life of this queen of charity. She also promised *Si.* Karlo Alatini to send later on one of her trusted representatives to investigate what else needed to be done in this city. To this day we are impatiently looking forward to his arrival. We hope that when this representative arrives, he will relate to the baroness the extent of deficiencies in need of correction that he will have observed with his own eyes; we also hope that a sorely needed hospital will finally be built.

Perhaps she will succeed in covering the schools' deficit that is close to thirty thousand franks; it is our hope that in the future, too, the baroness will continue to be active.

Unfortunately, it has been six months that this heavenly angel has left this world,[108] plunging us into despair. She had already sent us twenty thousand franks to build three (dispensaries) out-patient clinics, two hundred thousand franks to build a hospital, with the promise to send annually thirty thousand franks to cover necessary expenses and sixty thousand franks for the construction of the Great *Talmud Tora*. But her heirs cancelled all of her pledges.[109]

Chapter 23

Si. Danielucho's Printing Press

[47a] We have already mentioned *Chilibi* Menahem Faradji's bankruptcy, which in turn caused the failure of another limited partnership managed by *Si.* Behorachi Shaki, who maintained many business ties with the businessmen from Vienna, one of whom owed him a large

108. As Clara de Hirsch died in 1899, this reference confirms that Sa'adi's text was being updated over the years until his death in 1903.
109. Nevertheless, the Jewish hospital established in Salonica in 1908 was named after her, suggesting that some of the funds she had earmarked were ultimately used for the purposes she intended.

sum of money. This businessman owned a printing press. As he was unable to collect his debt from him [Menahem Faradji], *Si.* Shaki got ownership of this printing press *in lieu* of payment and transferred it to Salonica. It was adequate in every respect, such as twenty molds with their matrices, two hand presses, and five hundred sheets of basic materials to cast new letters, etc., etc.

When *Chilibi* Menahem's bankruptcy occurred, his younger son, *Si.* Danielucho, found himself powerless; he gathered all these tools and moved them elsewhere, to a plot he had rented, where he built a large warehouse and with the help of two of my *si.* father's employees, he installed these machines there. They started to cast all kinds of letters, such as *Rashi* type, size eight, ten, twelve, as well as square Hebrew letters of all sizes. He also managed to convince three businessmen and one *talmid haham* with some means, as well as another *haham* who was a book seller, to join him. He showed them a list of out-of-print books that were selling then at high prices, books that, if reprinted, would have a lower cost. In books such as the *Zohar*,[110] the *Tikkunim*,[111] *Hok le-Yisrael*,[112] *Sefer a-Berith*[113] in Ladino, they could earn up to 80 percent. This was their partnership: he contributed the printing press as his capital, and the other partners invested the necessary funds.

Their plan failed because they **[47b]** overpriced their books at a time when their readership was limited.

Based on their projection of profit, they printed by the thousands, when buyers numbered barely 5 percent. Thus the remaining 95 percent went into storage in a warehouse they rented for safekeeping. In the meantime, while they kept printing and saving the money from

110. The *Zohar* was composed in the form of a commentary to the Tora by Moses de Leon in Spain in the thirteenth century and became the most important book of Jewish mysticism.

111. Recitations conducted on specific dates and times in the religious calendar.

112. This is a book ascribed to the sixteenth century kabbalist Hayyim Vital (1543–1620) that presents some of the commandments in the Hebrew Bible with Talmudic and kabbalistic commentaries.

113. Pinhas Elijah Hurwitz published this book in 1797. Its mixture of scientific observation and mystical commentary made it popular reading material among Ashkenazi and Judeo-Spanish communities.

sales, *Si.* Danielucho was putting it to good use, spending it on fat turkeys and old wine. This lifestyle lasted four to five years, until the workmen of this printing press started to produce shoddy work. Finally, he got angry with them and tried to appoint me as director to correct the shortcomings of his business. But my older brother-in-law, whom I respected as my father, was against my leaving my own job to go and fix somebody else's problems. Meanwhile, I cast about thirty to forty thousand *Rashi* letters and accepted to print for them in my printing press parts of the *Zohar* at a price convenient to me. When his partners saw the impeccable work I was doing, a big quarrel started between him and his associates who were providing the money; they then decided to draw up a balance sheet of the last few years' turnover and noticed that *Si.* Danielucho had already consumed twice his original investment in the printing press. In spite of all that income, there wasn't even one penny left in the coffers, except for unsold books: one thousand of some, fifteen hundred of others, and from eight to ten items of certain books. They tried to sell them wholesale but failed to find a single buyer even at 20 percent of the cost. Finally, they took away the printing press and all its equipment from him and sold it practically for nothing to the reverend *h"r* Yeuda Nehama,[114] who hired a mason and built for himself **[48a]** a shed in a corner of his backyard. But he was unable to set up the presses, nor was there anyone to use them. *Si.* Nehama took me as his partner, and my work there lasted almost a year, while I collected all the cash. However, the rather low purchase price of this printing press created an obstacle—"in front of my wine, don't you sell vinegar"—he also saw that the earnings were meager, and he was compelled to sell me the other half, until I rid myself of this competitor.

The Masá

After *Si.* Danielucho got rid of his printing press, he convinced someone else, who owned a factory, to produce *masá* and to sell it ready-made by the *okka*. This was truly an excellent idea, as in those days the homemade *masá* was such hard work that everybody cursed their life until they brought the *masá* home; that is, they had twenty public ovens

114. See note 97.

for people to bring their semolina sacks they had purchased from the mills, which they unloaded in one of the rooms of these ovens. Thus, sacks belonging to family heads kept arriving and were stored in this place. Even though bakers charged a fixed price per *okka* of *masá*, still everyone wished to have the *masá* delivered urgently to their homes. And even though they were working day and night, they were unable to satisfy everyone; they had to tip the workers, the young girls, and the baker for faster service. They also had to bring their wood, **[48b]** oil for the lamps, and *raki* for the workers. In the middle of the night, come rain or snow, the owner of the semolina was summoned to come and supervise the actual baking, failing which barely half the amount of the *masá* would be delivered.

Another group of people insisted on consuming only carefully sorted food [*mundado*][115] on Passover, which called for extra labor as required by their fanaticism. It consisted in purchasing the same wheat, bringing it home, gathering ten to twelve women from the neighborhood, and going through the wheat grain by grain in search of some barley grain. Then, they carried this wheat to a mill, taking along some clean sheets, and after grinding it, they would fill their sacks and bring them back home. They also had professional "sifters" who went from house to house, three of whom sat on the porch: one set aside the flour, the other the semolina, and the third one the bran, so that one hundred *okkas* of wheat barely yielded fifty *okkas* of semolina.

This was sent to the bakery, which charged twice the price to cover the requirement of boiling once more all the equipment needed to manufacture this special *masá*.

Our readers will readily understand the labor and drudgery entailed in producing a piece of this *masá*. Yet the first year when ready-made excellent *masá* sold by the *okka* was available, it was an eye-opener for the entire population. The following year, another four bakeries selling by the *okka* opened.

After *Si.* Alatini began this machine-operated mill [1854], all the horse-operated mills closed. As for the bakers, they now purchased

115. The careful sorting of food was meant to ensure that all leavened products were removed before Pesach, as dictated by Jewish law.

ready-made semolina from *Si.* Alatini's storehouse, baked their own *masá* with it, and then sold it by the *okka.*

[49a] And even though the cost per *okka* is one more *grush*, it is worth the ease with which we can go and buy *masá* at any time. In summary, this is the legacy left behind by *Si.* Danielucho Faradji.

Chapter 24

The Lag la-'Omer Ceremony and Gemiluth Hasadim Printing Press

Forty years ago on *Lag la-'Omer* night, some heads of household in our city organized a night of festivities, called *illula* of Rabbi Shimon,[116] to which they invited some relatives, as well as eight to ten disciples of the sages. They read selections from the *Zohar*, followed by a banquet until dawn, eating, drinking, and singing. Some of them repeated this during the following day.

Out of the blue a stove-maker had an idea. For the sake of money he started to preach a sermon about the story of Rabbi Shimon at the Aragon Synagogue on the eve of the festivities. He embellished some marvelous episodes, which the audience took for the ultimate truth expounded by this preacher. Also, the previous evening, they prepared tapers labeled with the name of Rabbi Shimon and Rabbi Elazar and their associates, which he sold for kindling by purchasers. As he soon noticed, results were lucrative. He extended this practice to *yarsayat* evenings similar to the evenings of Rabbi Meir, Moses our teacher [the prophet Moses], etc. His profit turned into real money.

Later, he came up with a smarter innovation. He made small tin boxes, sealed, with a hole on top, and a stamped label on the box, stating, "For the *zehuth* or merit of Rabbi Shimon." Following the lighting of these tapers, they would continue singing in one voice the liturgical poems of *Bar Yohay* and *Yah Ribbon 'alam ve-'alemayya*.[117] **[49b]**

116. Shimon Bar Yohay was a second-century CE Jewish religious figure erroneously believed to be the author of the *Zohar*.

117. This Sabbath hymn by Israel Nadjara is sung on Friday nights in Ladino in Sephardic and in Aramaic in Ashkenazic synagogues.

Other labels read, "the *zehuth* or merit of Rabbi Meir," for "the *zehuth* or merit of Moses our teacher." He hung these boxes on every column of the synagogue, so that in the morning, congregants placed their donations in these boxes. Every month, he opened these boxes to find God's blessing.

Every Saturday he delivered a sermon to a multitude of ignorant people who came to listen to his short stories on various topics; on the Saturday of *Purim* he recounted the story of Haman in exaggerated imagery that made everyone laugh. With every story he told, he knew how to choose its appropriate intonation, just as a *karagoz* [Turkish shadow show]. He also had made a sugar-paste puppet in the effigy of Haman at a candy store, which he hung in the middle of the synagogue, provided with an extended string, so that as they mentioned his being hung there, they began to pull that string, while everybody joined him in shouting, *isa*, *isa*, *isa* [also the name of Jesus in Turkish], or pull, pull, pull. They raised it, then lowered it until it hit the floor and was shattered. This scandalous game took place in front of the Holy Ark, a sacred place where prayers are offered to God. Yet our religious leaders failed to notice this farce until [my] newspaper, *La Epoka*, criticized this, pointing out that someone from the other religious communities seeing this couldn't help but identify it with Christ. Then the acting chief rabbi forbade the repetition of this scandal.

In the meantime the *hahamim* started to mind that this person was addressed with the title *h"r* and complained. What did this sneaky schemer do? On *Lag la-'Omer* eve, he invited forty to fifty *talmide hahamim* and asked them to read about two psalms each to the end of the book of Psalms,[118] **[50a]** followed by a reading from the *Zohar* appropriately selected for this circumstance. Then, carrying showy paper ornaments, he walked in a procession the entire circle of the synagogue.

Following the afternoon and evening prayers, they would sing as usual, while he distributed money: two *altiliks* per *dayyan* [judge], one *altilik* per assistant judge, and a *beshlik* to the subordinates. Thus, he succeeded in silencing their complaints.

For the purpose of starting a new source of income, but also to en-

118. The full book contains 150 psalms.

dear himself, he even nominated a commission where he proposed to make one thousand tin boxes similar to those found in the synagogue. He distributed these among the heads of household for them to contribute one coin per person every week, and as much as they pleased if they were sick or in the event of some birth.

Finally, every month he went from house to house to open the boxes with his small key, emptying them in a larger sack. Having skimmed his share, he carried this sack to the treasurer of the commission, where they counted the funds collected monthly, making sure that he also charged 20 percent for his labor.

In this fashion he carved a nice position for himself; and every year he came to my printing house to order fifteen hundred labels for the tin boxes.

Within four to five years other preachers with similar skills emerged. They established an identical ceremony in every synagogue, then came to my printing house and ordered similar labels. When the above-mentioned gentleman learned about this development, he complained to the commission, saying, "Now, we have competitors to imitate what we are doing, surely our income will shrink."

They called me on the carpet, asking me, "Why are you offering our business model to others?"

[50b] I answered them, saying, "My printing house is not the monopoly of an individual. I must print any job that any customer brings me." This was my vigorous defense in this case.

The top schemer in this affair also told them that there was much money to be made in the printing business. Daily profit can be two hundred *grushes*: after an order is placed, it is delivered the next day, with a charge of two hundred *grushes*; and needless to say that other similar jobs are available the same day. Since we have cash in our coffers, we should start a printing press and earn double the money. This plan was well received by the commission.

The Printing Press of Gemiluth Hasadim [Giving of Loving Kindness]

The *sinyor* treasurer of the commission, who never liked me, advised them to open a printing press with the easy money they had effortlessly accumulated in their coffers. They wrote to Vienna and imported some

Rashi [print mold] characters, various square Hebrew types; they also rented a room in Papuchilar Han, purchased a used printing press from a Greek who had closed his business, and then even managed to steal the head typesetter of my printing press.

The Inauguration of This Printing Press

At that time a businessman was about to marry his son. The commission, led by the *sinyor* treasurer, contacted this businessman to offer their services to print his invitations as part of the inauguration of their printing press.

Now, this was an honest businessman whose answer was, "I don't want to be the first to promote competition against the head of a family. Moreover in my mind, these invitations are in the same category as the person who will run the actual banquet. *Ham* Sa'adi, who runs these banquets, will not come to mine if I were to print these invitations in your printing press." He courageously defended his position that he could not possibly **[51a]** abide by their request.

In the end they came back empty-handed and disappointed; they never again advertised to print invitations for feasts, yet they started to compete with me in other areas.

After two to three years, as they were checking their balance sheet, they discovered that in addition to waste incurred during printing, not only were they not earning a return on their investment, but that they had a deficit. This compelled them to close their printing business. For a year or two they even had to pay rent for their closed storage room. Finally, they tried to sell it but failed to find any buyers!

In their conversation with a friend of mine, they asked, "What to do with this printing press?" My friend answered them, "if Mordecai is of Jewish stock, you will not overcome him, you will fall before him to ruin" (Esther 6:13), trying to convince them to sell it to *ham* Sa'adi, if he wants it. They agreed to have my friend offer it to me. One day, as my friend was paying me a sick call, he brought up the idea for me to purchase this printing press. I authorized him to buy it for a certain price, if he could.

He returned to the commission, and after trying hard, he managed to buy it for 46 *liras* instead of the original price of 160 *liras*.

But what happened to all the income from the tin boxes and the

46 *liras* from the sale of the printing press? Into which pocket did this money go? Asking such a question is forbidden!

Chapter 25

My Personal Story Starts Here

[51b] I have mentioned earlier that to secure my future I lightened up my work at the printing press, as I started supervising the work morning, noon, and evening as director, by appointing one of my employees to replace me, so that I could resume my singing career. Obviously, singing was my love, and my voice helped me in this vocation. At that time our city was graced by the masterful cantor, *h"r* Aaron Barzilay, who, upon hearing me sing, called me and said, "You have a lovely voice; it would be nice if you attended my rehearsals to learn a number of *pizmonim* that your own *sinyor* grandfather, who was the top cantor, taught me."

Then I gathered five to six handsome friends and introduced them to this rehearsal, where I started to learn *pizmonim*, in all kinds of *makams*, becoming soon famous throughout Salonica. Due to the lack of qualified and knowledgeable singers of Hebrew and Turkish songs like me, there was no banquet or celebration to which I was not invited to sing.

However, my *si.* master was qualified to sing only Hebrew songs. Otherwise, he earned his living as a tailor, in which profession he reached the top in fashion and tailoring in Salonica. He enjoyed immensely teaching me and passing on to me all his knowledge, training me in mastering all the melodies of the prayers recited during the Days of Awe; he even invited me to assist him at the Neve Shalom Synagogue where he was a *mezammer*, which he himself had learned from a certain *h"r* Yaakov Kamhi from Istanbul.

[52a] During that time my *si.* teacher, assisted by me and my colleagues, rejuvenated the choir of the *Talmud Tora* that sings every Saturday morning, which had a long-standing tradition but had also deteriorated as a result of its aging members.

After I established a choral group of twenty young singers worth listening to, people from all over town would flock every Saturday morning to listen to us.

By the time we came to the synagogue, there were already some two thousand people assembled in the *Talmud Tora*. Meanwhile, my teacher was getting old, so he allowed me to proceed with the *taksim* that precedes the *fasil*, all composed in the same *makam*. I had also acquired a book by the *Rav* Nadjara in which every final verse in each *bakkasha* is followed by biblical verses appropriate to that *bakkasha*.

I used to sing these biblical verses as a final *taksim*. This book contained specific verses for the Torah portion of every Sabbath, verses that were appropriate for such a *taksim*. I would consistently set up the *taksim* based on these biblical verses according to the *makam*, of the *fasil*, we were about to sing. In the long run I produced a *fasil*, of ten to twelve pieces of *peshrevs*, *bestes*, and *semais*, which lasted more than an hour to sing. Finally, I assumed the role of master director, esteemed by everybody who supported me. Yet my master teacher had two sons who started to be jealous of me; luckily, their voices could not measure up to mine. I also loved the discipline of prosody, not only in Hebrew verse but even more so in Ladino verse. For family celebrations I composed "special toasts" of welcome tailored to each individual. In every case I wrote a series of compositions suitable to that circumstance, such as an appropriate poem for the dedication of the renovated *Talmud Tora*. In my repertoire I even had some *romanzas*.

[52b] After that, I started to write a book of poems for *Purim*, similar to those well-known among the inhabitants of Salonica; it was well received and is cherished to this day. On the occasion of His Majesty, Sultan Abdul Medjid's visit, I also composed three songs whose words and music were mine, two in Hebrew for his arrival and one in Ladino for his departure. By then, I had become deeply involved in this career, but "jealousy, lust [and vainglory] remove a man from this world" (Avoth 4:21).

Soon, not only my singing career prospered, but thanks to my leadership, I was invited to run every "fund" and "association" that was established in our city.

First among these was the *Hesed 'Olam*, and the second was the tuition collection for the newly established schools. After that they charged me with the task of rehearsing the children to sing on the occasion of the arrival of the sultan, as well as preparing for the parade at the entrance of the city. I was so successful that young and old thanked me. Even in this setting the jealousy of some was never absent; they tried to persecute me. But as a *protégé* of *Si.* Alatini and the *Rav h"r* Asher and the *Rav h"r* Avraam Gatenyo, they couldn't hurt me. This lasted until the interests of certain people, who never liked the truth or justice, were affected.

When the "Society of Good Deeds" was established,[119] its younger membership was quite influential, and as I mentioned earlier, they tried to improve the management of our city by supporting the gabelle on wine, meat, etc.

They observed that the profits of ritual slaughterers were five times higher than the proceeds from the meat gabelle. Therefore, they issued **[53a]** a proclamation appealing to the people. They gave me this notice asking me to have it signed by all the dignitaries. Those who were opposed to me suspected me for advising the officials of said society and started to further consolidate their animosity against me.

We have already mentioned that this notice created a strong reaction among the people, with the group of controllers emerging later on.

Also, the *Si. Rav h"r* Asher had submitted his resignation during one of my trips to Constantinople. At that time an influential Salonican relative of these people, who also opposed them, happened to be in Constantinople.

He drafted a letter for the acting chief rabbi in Istanbul to accept the resignation of the *Rav h"r* Asher, even though I knew nothing about this resignation. This *sinyor* called me and asked me to deliver this letter to the acting chief rabbi, and yet I was completely in the dark as to its contents. The following Friday, as the *Djurnal* [*Yisraelita*] appeared, my friend *Chilibi* Yehezkel Gabbay[120] informed me about this resignation, an event that totally surprised me.

Soon, I became suspicious that the letter this *sinyor* gave me might be

119. Reconstituted from the remnants of the *Hesed 'Olam* society under the new name *Sedaka va-Hesed*, the "Society of Good Deeds" was supported by Moïse Allatini.

120. Gabbay (1825–98) was editor of the Ladino newspaper *El Djurnal Yisraelit*, founded in 1860, and, like Sa'adi, he was a supporter of reforms.

the root cause for the acceptance of this resignation. However, a week later, I read in the newspaper [*Djurnal Yisraelita*], that this resignation had been rejected.

When this *sinyor* saw that the resignation had been rejected, he feared that on my return to Salonica I might report what took place between him and the dignitaries in Istanbul, in view of my frequent visits to the house of *Si. Rav h"r* Asher. To avoid being suspected, he sent a letter to the *si. rav*, informing him that *ham* Sa'adi was responsible for the acceptance of the resignation; **[53b]** therefore, having been a double-dealer, I should not be welcome to his house.

When I returned to Salonica, I went to pay a courtesy call to the *si. rav* soon after I came home. I noticed his lukewarm welcome, and I asked him why this was so. He simply referred to the contents of the letter sent by the *sinyor*.

I defended myself categorically, saying, "As an intimate of this house, how could I commit such a deception? Moreover, what power do I have in Constantinople to push for the acceptance of a *rav*'s resignation? I am a plain person with no connections in Istanbul. However, were you to reveal to me the identity of the sender, I might disclose something of interest to you." His answer was that the writer of the letter said that we shouldn't divulge his name to you.

Then I said to him, "This must have been an ill-mannered person, inferior to me, to fear my knowing his name." He answered me that "he is another dignitary." Then, I said to him, "if he is indeed a dignitary, why should he care if I knew his name?" While this conversation was taking place, the *Si.* Yaakov Kapuano, a conscientious man, was there. After they looked at each other, he said to the *si. rav*, "I am convinced that this is a trickery by the *sinyor* whom both of us know well; as for me, I know *Si.* Sa'adi as a person incapable of planning such an absurdity." The *si. rav* answered me saying, "I am ready to be convinced with your words, yet it is your job to approach Hayyimucho[121] and convince him." When I met with Hayyimucho, I asked him for a clarification about this letter. He wouldn't let me finish but jumped like a lion, saying, "All that is stated in the letter is true; you are the culprit."

121. Sa'adi refers here to Hayyimucho Kovo, the son of Rabbi Asher Kovo.

I tried in vain to defend myself, but he never took **[54a]** my words into consideration. From that day on, he developed a hatred toward me, always acting vindictively against me. After this came the matter of the notice. Conspiring with a group that was intent on hurting me, he reached an agreement with all the ritual slaughterers to establish a society with monthly dues of one *grush*, with the aim of helping members in case of need. In no time they recruited from among themselves a horde of four hundred to five hundred members: the rabbinic segment and a large group of lower-class individuals.

Their very first initiative was to create a Jewish city council[122] provided with a balance gauge to check the *dirhem* weight units of the swindlers. Anyone whose weights were deficient had to pay a fine of one *beshlik* per *dirhem* weight unit.

Then, they established five to ten groups of these lower-class individuals, with a young *haham* heading each one of them. Every Saturday, each one of these took up a position either at each of the city gates or at the coffeehouses, stopping every passing young man, checking his pockets for money or tobacco, which they confiscated, and also beating them up; those in the coffeehouses were subjected to the same treatment. This new policy spread an incredible terror among the young men.

This way they started to gain new advantages, leading them to make their rounds with greater audacity. Their success grew stronger as the Jewish people in those days were very fainthearted, especially when they saw the "holy flag" flying in front of them. The more they succeeded, the more they tried to reach their real purpose of weakening the Society of Good Deeds, their ultimate goal.

As we have already said, they tried to ensnare me **[54b]** yet failed to discover the proper tool for it. What to do? As a tool, they picked my son with some wrongdoing, to get to me. Now, they could accuse me, too.

But this was not so easy to carry out. So, they bribed a poor man with some money to testify that he saw my son smoking on the Sabbath. Thus, the following Sunday, April 26, 1874, they called a meeting of all the rabbis, also inviting the most rogue young men among their members. They gathered at the house of his eminence, and they looked

122. The Jewish City Council was created in 1870.

like a gang of rebels. But neither the *si. rav* nor the communal council was aware that I was their ultimate goal; they started first by vilifying some other people, whether they had found tobacco or money on their person, or for transgressing the prohibition of going to a coffeehouse, and others for having been seen entering public entertainment places.

Included among these was my son, who was attacked for a similar wrongdoing, as testified by a witness who had seen him smoke the previous day.

In order for my readers to judge whether my words are true, or if this situation was connived by them to reach their coveted goal, I will make an observation that anyone can readily understand. Indeed, summoning my son first seems a normal course; but why summon me first? If it is true that my son broke the law, why did they look for me? But the truth was that they wanted me rather than my son, for indeed, by summoning my son, they were in reality chasing after me!!!

Thus, they summoned me before my son, and I was caught unaware, nor did I think that they were determined to concoct such a plot. Further evidence that this was a false testimony: First of all, this witness was a vile individual, a porter of the lowest class, so much so that he walks barefoot even on the coldest day, consuming food in the streets like an animal; even though he has plenty of money, he is ostracized by fellow porters. **[55a]** All this is irrelevant, except to show that they were unable to find an honest man to give false testimony.

Another unassailable proof is that my son was out of town on that Saturday, April 25, 1874. It happened that a prominent family wished to entertain in one of the resorts of *Orundjik*. The previous Thursday, they hired a well-known restaurant owner and ordered all the food needed for a banquet of twenty people. When all necessary preparations were finished, this restaurant owner, who was a friend and even a relative, asked my son to join him there as a helper and server to attend the table of this high-class family.

My son didn't turn him down; instead, he, the restaurant owner and his servants, along with the food, left on Friday, April 24, arriving at the resort at 4 p.m. Then by 6 p.m. they completed all preparations for breakfast and lunch for the following day and returned to Salonica Saturday night at 11:30.

Yet when they summoned us to uncover their plot, those who were eager to attack my son, as well as my honor, had no inkling about my son's whereabouts on that day. We, too, were completely unaware of the scheme these people had in mind; we just went and presented ourselves before the assembly of all *si. hahamim*.

The *si. rav* started to speak, saying, "Do you know that your son is accused of committing a sin about which the Law of Moses warned us not to light a fire on the Sabbath?" My answer to him was, "Yes, when was this sin committed?" He answered me, "Yesterday." Then I asked him, "Where was this sin committed, in town or out of town?" He answered me that the witness saw him smoking in a coffeehouse in Salonica.

When I assured myself that it was supposed to be within Salonica, I asked about this testimony: "In case I can reliably prove **[55b]** to the satisfaction of those present that this testimony is false, what will be the verdict against this liar?" He answered me that the penalty applied to your son in case he is convicted would apply to him, too. My answer was, "This is fine."

I answered him, saying, shouldn't the witness identify himself publicly? "And out came this calf" (Exodus 32:24), "and God opened the ass's mouth" (Numbers 22:28). He parroted what he was told to say, saying that he had seen the cigarette butt as it was thrown out of the window of a certain coffeehouse. At that point I called in the restaurant owner with his three servants and presented them to the judge.

They answered that Hayyim Sa'adi a-Levi was with us on Friday from 3 p.m. until Saturday night, 11 p.m. to 12 a.m., in the tower of *Orundjik* serving the Alatini, Fernandes, and Matalon families. The *Rav Si.* [Asher] Kovo, the *Si. Rav* Gatenyo, the *Rav* Arditi,[123] the *Rav* Nahmias,[124] and all the judges didn't have the slightest idea that this bunch of young rabbis, ready on the other side, were all of them waiting for the slightest hint to unleash their violence against me and my son in order to remove us from among the living; we, too, couldn't possibly have known that this was the design of the entire plot, and even that their society had been established with this goal in mind.

123. See page 10.
124. Ibid.

As the *si. rav* heard the four witnesses that I brought forward, he showed his satisfaction. However, when these people realized that the plan they came up with had failed, one of them, a sleazy hothead, got up, opened his mouth, and addressed our witnesses, saying, "Do you know that we shall bring witnesses to testify that indeed Hayyim Sa'adi a-Levi was yesterday in Salonica? When these witnesses, too, show up, you will be declared liars, and you will be subjected to the same sentence as the accused." **[56a]** Truly, I could never understand how this young rabbi got up in front of such distinguished company and felt free and audacious enough to use such language.

I immediately realized that this devil wanted to confuse my witnesses. I tried to figure out a suitable way to demolish the position of this unfortunate opponent. My only alternative was to get up and nonchalantly ridicule this "blessed" young rabbi, saying: "I have good news for you, *si.* judge!" Then turning to the *sinyores rabbanim*, I said, "Gentlemen!!! Allow me to suggest that this new judge should occupy a place next to you." And to him, I said, "Please, *sinyor* new judge, take your seat, as the words that you just uttered should come from persons entitled to judge and not from a simple rabbi."

My *sinyores* readers!

I can swear by the utmost sanctity that in all that I told you now there is not a single word said in that assembly that I did not mention here. Indeed, the great majority of those present in this encounter are still alive, and they can testify before God and people.

My heart aches and my body is crushed, my legs and my arms are paralyzed by this nonsense. As I write this biography that took nine years to finish, I still remember that dark and cursed day; would that the sun had not risen on that day, or at least, I had been sick rather than live through this anguish. I sure pray to God that none of my loved ones live through a similar experience; "perish the day on which I was born" (Job 3:3).

Suddenly, a strong uproar was heard among the members of said committee of the "Execution Society." Amidst that uproar, made incomprehensible by the shouting, a single voice was heard urging: "Hit them, kill them, both the father and the son, O God!"

[56b] Indiscriminately and even without understanding why, all their associates started beating us and our supporters with such cruelty that we had a hard time figuring out how to escape from their grip. Anyone trying to protect us was also beaten up.

Until we managed to flee through the gate of the garden in order to reach the door of my house half dead, there were five hundred more people gathered there who as they arrived and heard the yelling, "Hit them for the sake of God," also turned into monsters. They pursued me and my son, as well as ten of our friends, who were subjected to the same cruel treatment, mercilessly beating us. Ultimately, a point was reached when if one were to ask, "Why all that vindictiveness," he would be answered, "Who knows? We are doing this for the sake of God!" It was a miracle that we survived. But this was not enough for them. They entered my house, broke all the windows, mirrors, and they stole everything from clothing to copperware. A few Turks and even some gendarmes ran to help us, but unfortunately it was in vain as they were outnumbered a hundredfold.

Finally, in order to save my life, without even thinking of my family, I climbed through a kitchen window, to my neighbor's porch, barefooted and bareheaded, but surrounded by members of the "Society of Good Deeds," until I reached safety in *Si.* Alatini's office. That is when members of the "Society of Good Deeds" learned about this sad situation. First, they wanted to organize a counteroffensive, but when *Si.* Alatini heard about it, he calmed them down, saying that he would seek a satisfactory explanation of this catastrophe.

Always a cool-headed individual, *Si.* Alatini understood that at such times disastrous developments can occur on **[57a]** each side.

Immediately, *Si.* Alatini had the idea of dispatching a messenger to the *si. rav*, saying, "What is this uprising of the people all about? Have we Jews now inherited those damaging actions for which we criticized the Turks in the days of the janissaries? This is a time when our sovereign, the Sultan has promulgated *kanunnames* [legal codes], forbidding anyone to act as a judge except for duly constituted government tribunals." The committee of the "Society of Good Deeds" was comforted for a while to hear the message that *Si.* Alatini had sent to the *si. rav*. As we said earlier, *Si.* Alatini had a good heart; he always tried to smooth matters, never letting any animosity between two parties get out of control. On the other hand, as a true humanitarian, he couldn't conceive that the messenger he would send could behave as a scandalmonger. But unfortunately, someone who happened to be there volunteered to carry this message; he immediately went and carried out his mission.

But how did he go about it? He spilled sulfur at one end and tar at the other, as he was always wont to do. He brought back a positive answer, saying that the *si. rav* took no part in this affair, but that in view of his message, the *rav* had already sent his messenger to disperse the people. But immediately after this mission he went to the opposition, where again he rekindled the sulfur and the tar more intensely than before. They welcomed it and sat down to devise a new plan designed to distort the truth.

Yet in order to restore credibility with the people in justifying their plan, they started publishing all kind of lies and possible deceptions to convince the people. First, they spread rumors that my son and I had insulted the rabbinic corps to their face. Second, that we offended the honor of the Tora. **[57b]** Third, that this man is opening their eyes to ideas about the joys of this world. That very night, all these sleazy people reached an agreement for everyone to assume his assignment for the next day. The next morning, they all gathered together. They started by dividing the markets among themselves, going from office to office and from store to store, proclaiming, "Whoever is for the Lord, come here" (Exodus 32:26); let every Jew, proceed to the Great *Talmud Tora*! They also invited the rabbis to the Ashkenazi Synagogue. And this is what they did.

All merchants, small and big, were walking or running in groups, unaware why they were being summoned under the "holy flag." When they saw that the *Talmud Tora* and the Ashkenazi Synagogue were full of people, they sent a messenger to the Ashkenazi Synagogue, asking the rabbis to join them at the Great *Talmud Tora*.

They moved all the children to the center of the courtyard of the *Talmud Tora*, while bringing in thirteen ram's horns like machine guns, corresponding to the thirteen attributes of mercy. With the Holy Ark open as usual, they started to shoot continuously, while signaling the children to say "Amen." As people were hearing the sound of the ram's horn, echoing near and far, they were shaken to their bones. Now, they started to read Psalm 109 with eyes uplifted in an ecstatic mood and shedding crocodile tears to prove their hypocrisy to the people.

Following this sad religious ceremony, they proceeded to a prearranged place where they produced a statement in Hebrew stipulating horrible conditions to be signed by everyone present, both laypeople and rabbis, who had never read it beforehand or examined its contents. Blindly, they came forward to sign, so much so that an uncle, who was a brother of my wife's mother, and also a nephew, put their signature against us on this medieval decree of execution. However, four to five high-level rabbis **[58a]** refused to sign it, claiming that they could not endorse a sentence to kill innocent souls.

This statement had some loose paragraphs clearly objectionable to any conscientious reader. Here is a summary of what a friend of mine read in it, such as no Jew can greet me, no Jew can do business with me, no matter how small. Needless to say that no Jew can read anything published in my printing press; same prohibition for religious books. No one is allowed to print invitations at my press, neither can they retain me as an organizer, etc. Anyone who will do any favors to my family will be considered a sinner. Finally, we are all duty bound to "destroy, massacre and exterminate all the Jews . . . children young and old" (Esther 3:13). Yet all this was done without the acquiescence of the *si. rav* and the other rabbis. Also, no Jew could count me as part of a *minyan*. Since then, I stopped going to the synagogue.

Despite this upheaval that took place in the morning, they were still dissatisfied. By coincidence, their anxiety had increased because of the lack of rain at that time. They organized penitentiary prayers called *selihoth* for 4 p.m., with town criers calling on every Jew to come to the Great *Talmud Tora* to petition God for rain. At the appointed time, everybody closed their businesses, came to the *Talmud Tora* to pray for rain. An emissary[125] from Lemberg got up and, turning to the rebels, said, "Gentlemen! As an emissary coming from Tiberias, I am authorized to excommunicate on behalf of the rabbis of that city. And now by

125. Emissaries from Ottoman Palestine were sent to Jewish communities in the diaspora to collect funds for Jews of the Holy Land.

the authority of the heavenly tribunal and of this court below I came to excommunicate the sinner Sa'adi a-Levi, and his entire family."

No sooner had he uttered these words than "the floodgates of the sky broke open" (Genesis 7:11), **[58b]** except that this year, the rain coming down from heaven was like "fire and sulfur and a scorching wind" (Psalm 11:6), not enough even for seeding. With all that, they were still dissatisfied the next day.

Now, they drafted an official note to the *Vali* to imprison me for insulting the chief rabbi. They also immediately sent an unaccredited lawyer to the chief rabbi.

[This lawyer had been jailed for escaping during a cross-examination, but had picked up some legal vocabulary allowing him to act as a lawyer. This was enough to entrust him with his defense.][126]

At that moment he sent to my house ten gendarmes to incarcerate me and my son. All day long they searched attics and basements! In addition, 250 very observant Jews, all of them select dregs of society, came to help them. In the end, when they found absolutely nothing, they came back like . . .

[With all this hoopla and frenzy they created, they imagined that I would die the next day either from fear or worry. But I appealed my sentence. On review, it seemed appropriate to the court to grant a concession to the fanatics, passing a sentence of thirty-one years. I went to the court of appeals and retained as my lawyer who was an angel to me, Refael, and he submitted documentation that came back with specific clauses. Then, they gave me a thirty-one-year sentence. By now twenty-eight years have already passed, with three more to go. After that, Allah will be gracious.][127]

This entire hoopla reached the ears of *Si.* Alatini. Also, the deputies of the "Society of Good Deeds" approached him, aware of all that had happened. He was deeply shaken and fearful of the loss of any life, in fulfillment of the saying, "either way, woe to the daughter of Jephthah"

126. This barely legible paragraph, obviously added later, appears at the end of the page with an asterisk, indicating it should be inserted into the main text here.
127. This paragraph, also barely legible, appears on the right side of the page with a circle indicating its location here, making it clear it was added in 1902.

(Judges 11:31–35); so he decided to call Shemuel Ben Rubi, his treasurer, and commit me temporarily to his custody for my safekeeping in his marvelous mansion in Chavush Manastir[128] for a couple of days.

So I was taken to the home of this gentleman and treated like a prince by his noble family. They knew where I was hidden, but frustrated by their inability to get me out of there, they caught my son, yet they wanted only me.

But the *si. cavaliere* was fully aware of the seething fanaticism that prevailed, **[59a]** and wished simply to extinguish that fire. For my protection he ordered his treasurer to take me to the "army major" on Wednesday night, saying: "The Jewish merchant Alatini sends his greetings. He entrusts this man into your power until he asks for his release. This is the man you wanted by order of the Chief Rabbi."

When *Si.* Shemuel Ben Rubi broke this news to me, I immediately accepted to go at 9 p.m. He called his valet, kindled a lantern with two tapers, and the three of us set out as if to a celebration. He turned me over to the custody of the "major," who placed me in his room and treated me well.

Then, *Si.* Ben Rubi came back and informed the *si. rav* [Asher Kovo] that *Si.* Alatini had fulfilled his wish. But the *si. rav* was not so impressed by this action, because it was he and the body of deputies who were playing this game. In fact, the *si. rav* took no interest in this, neither was he kept abreast of these developments.[129]

But *Si.* Ben Rubi, too, had his game to play, as our readers are well aware. He is reported to have said that *Si.* Alatini had fulfilled his wish and that he hopes to gain his release by 3 p.m. tomorrow. This statement by *Si.* Ben Rubi hit them like a gunshot, because they didn't appreciate the way he took me to prison by order of *Si.* Alatini, which they construed as an honor for me; what they wanted was to send me to prison accompanied by ten gendarmes and five hundred people

128. Chavush Manastir was a district in the upper city near the only active monastery in Salonica. This area was inhabited mostly by Greek Orthodox Christians and also by Muslims.

129. At this time Chief Rabbi Asher Kovo was old and ill: he was to die soon after this incident.

walking behind, like someone condemned to death. Also aggravating to them was *Si.* Ben Rubi's statement, "Let them release him by 3 p.m. tomorrow."

The next morning, they had a big meeting; after much discussion and nonsensical arguments, they decided to inform *Si.* Alatini **[59b]** that "they" would find the means to release me from prison the following day. But because his wish had not been met, he gave a cold reception to the delegation. When they realized that they were not well received, they decided to let me go the next day. A courier was instructed to come and tell me that I shouldn't leave without *Si.* Alatini's consent. At 4 p.m. I was contacted by the communal executive council telling me that "the Chief Rabbi has forgiven your sin and we allow you to leave."

In my answer to them I said that I had never sinned against the chief rabbi, nor that he had ever imprisoned me, but it was *Si.* Alatini who ordered me sent here with one of his employees. But if you so wish, *Si.* Alatini can send here one of his men, similar to when he sent me here, so that I can leave immediately. When the council heard my logical answer, they sent me back.

The person they sent to release me communicated my answer to them [his opponents] after spicing it with salt, pepper, and lemon juice. When they heard it, they became furious and piled additional charges on me, saying that I wasn't worthy of leaving prison by their command. They did this to convince the people that from the very beginning, I had not been sent to prison by them.

On Friday *Si.* Alatini went to the *Vali Pasha*, saying, "At 6 p.m., I shall be sending you the same employee who had brought here an individual. Please place him in the custody of this employee, with a gendarme to accompany them to his house." In his answer the *Vali* said that yesterday the chief rabbi had sent someone to free him. But he refused, saying that he hadn't been imprisoned by order of his eminence.

The *cavaliere* answered, "It is true that I sent him to prison to satisfy the *si. rav*. But he feared a new harassment, and he was unwilling to leave without my **[60a]** employee at his side." Then the *Pasha* told him, "I have already been informed by the British and Italian consuls and I'll be glad to send my report on this matter to the Chief Rabbi."

Finally, at 6 p.m., *Si.* Ben Rubi rushed to the office of the [Ottoman] major and obtained my release in the company of a gendarme. We went to the home of *Si.* Ben Rubi, where we stayed until Monday morning. In the meantime we have not stopped, nor should we ever fail to pray to God on behalf of this kind man and his noble wife, who had never been less generous than her honorable husband for her charity and love of humanity. Both were to me guardian angels then and at all times.

Before concluding my narrative, let me talk about the patience of this generous and philanthropic *cavaliere*. While this benefactor was active, he was waging war on two sides. To one of them his advice was not to dismiss the people in this matter, saying, "Don't you know that the ignorant people are under the influence of the rabbinic side? It is necessary to enlighten them with lots of patience and some finesse to gain their approval." To the other side his appeal was that people should be handled according to circumstances rather than from a position of strength. Finally, for all the times when he had held meetings in his house with interested parties to mediate such problems, this time he was told that now he had to call on his eminence, where the entire matter should be concluded. This most fortunate being, with a dove's heart, said to them that if this is all, I can go personally to expedite matters.

However, he sent two honorable people, *Si.* Avramucho Mizrahi[130] and *Si.* Moshe Shaltiel,[131] ahead of him, and they brought back the reply that with his coming the matter **[60b]** would be closed, following so much pain.

And this is what happened. The admirable and praiseworthy Alatini went to see his eminence, and after a few words he was successful; yet my opponents were unwilling to close this matter simply because the plan they had devised would be thwarted. Then, to satisfy *Si.* Alatini, they came up with an idea; they sat down beside his eminence and issued a made-up release [from the *herem*]. However, *Si.* Alatini, who was unaware of such tricks, was happy to see them studying and moving back and forth and concluded that he had won a war.

130. Avramucho Mizrahi was the brother-in-law of Moïse Allatini and the future director of Salonica's *Talmud Tora*.

131. Shaltiel was a merchant and communal leader.

He got up pleased and thankful for the honor they bestowed upon him and left immediately for his office.

Right away, he called *Si.* Ben Rubi, saying, "On your return tomorrow, you may bring *Si.* Sa'adi with you, as I was able to obtain his forgiveness without him being present before them." Out of much respect *Si.* Ben Rubi did not elaborate but thanked him for his efforts.

That night, *Si.* Ben Rubi brought me the news. I immediately understood that they had deceived him, but how can one say to God's angel that they deceived him? This might cause him some anxiety on my account, as I did not deserve this gentleman's solicitude for my misfortune. Finally, I could not sleep all that night, trying to decide whether I should tell him that he had been deceived or if I should keep quiet; I was hesitating because tomorrow someone else might tell him about it. The next day, I came back to the city with *Si.* Ben Rubi who took me to see *Si.* Alatini. He was happy and elated as if God's light were shining on his face.

He started advising me better than a father would do, saying that it is necessary to move ahead very carefully: "I can assure you that this matter is now closed; go on with your business as usual, and don't dwell on the past anymore." **[61a]** Unable to give him an answer, I simply said, "I am very thankful to you for being so good to me." But I couldn't express my true feelings to him in stronger terms. I left him with tears in my eyes and went directly to see *Si.* Avramucho to tell him all that had happened. He assured me that he would inquire how this ridiculous development came about. That evening, he went to the house of *Si.* . . . , with *Si.* Moshe Shaltiel. They asked what kind of joke was it to deceive *Si.* Alatini and issue a release in the absence of the accused?

His curt answer was, "We have given a satisfactory answer to *Si.* Moisé! Why are you still meddling in this affair?" They said, "That is fine, since *Si.* Alatini needs no further satisfaction; final closure is his only wish in this matter rather than leaving things half cooked." But their claim was that he was satisfied with what he saw. After further deliberation, these two gentlemen decided that this entire thing was a farce, because as long as this vindictive document [of the *herem*] was not destroyed, all the efforts of the tireless *Si.* Alatini would go to waste. "He" [the unnamed person] answered that "this was just to forgive him, but the sentence itself can never be abolished." They answered that this man did not need a release, as he never recognized the original excommunication. "Therefore, it was your desire for vindictiveness that started all this." [The *Si. Rav* Hayyim Gatenyo also had advised him that he was not in need of a release, adding, "If you really need one, I have plenty of unused releases for you to wear."][132] When these two gentlemen saw that their mission had failed, they immediately went back to inform *Si.* Alatini. . . . Let us go back in time; the news had spread among the other religious communities, and anyone hearing this incident gnashed their teeth. The British and Italian consuls filed their complaints with the governor. They claimed that allowing a religious leader[133] to commit such scandalous acts, with potential bloody consequences, could tarnish his honor and his position; **[61b]** in the end the authorities would be responsible.

Reacting to the reports of the two consuls and other important figures, the *Vali Pasha* sent an official note immediately to his eminence written in sharp words. He also warned him that in case of recurrence, he would have to accept full responsibility for it. Also, with reference to the Jewish fanatics who have constituted a city council of their own, if they ever come before me, they shall be punished, because the government has its own city council chartered with its laws and privileges to administer its legal functions.[134] Finally, "according to the information I have received, this man whom you have jailed as a sinner is just an independent thinker who happens to act contrary to your wishes. Right now, send someone to get him out lest this cause you some shame."

132. In the original manuscript this bracketed text appears at the bottom of the page.

133. By all accounts Chief Rabbi Asher Kovo, old and enfeebled at the time of this episode, was not, in fact, the principal actor in the issuing of the *herem*. One source claims that his son Hayyimucho Kovo and his son-in-law Yaakov Kovo were the principal parties behind the plot.

134. The *Vali*'s note provides clear indication that new Ottoman institutions were at this point claiming legitimacy in matters that would have been left to the *millets* in the years prior to the Tanzimat Reforms.

It was in response to this official note that he had ordered my release, except that I was unwilling to comply, as I mentioned earlier. This will illustrate the extent of their animosity, as their scheme to start a business, based on checking the weights and charging a *beshlik* per defective unit, had collapsed.

Let us return to my business. After leaving *Si.* Alatini, I went home, but I was unable to go on with my work. They had ruined my business; my printing press was closed because they were not allowing anyone to bring their printing jobs to me.

A week, a month, two months passed, and I kept providing for my family of twelve from my meager past savings. Yet the fanatics felt assured that I would soon die, either because of their deep conviction in the power of the extraordinary excommunication that they had organized with such pomp or because of the anxiety I had after the loss of my business and the closing of my printing press. **[62a]** Worse than that, they printed invitations for life-cycle events at an unfamiliar printer. Their purpose was to eradicate me and my family's very existence with mortal vindictiveness. But the opposite happened, as the proverb says, "they may build, but I will tear down" (Malachi 1:4). They thought that "for one reason or another, he will die; we will then scare the people and thus reestablish our religious domination."

In spite of all their nefarious thoughts, Providence kept them from fulfilling their wishes. First, the notion of excommunication didn't bother me. As for my livelihood, I was not in such despair, because my innocence and particularly my enlightened friends kept me strong. This is exactly what happened. The first to help me was *Si.* Hayyim Faradji, a recently arrived lawyer from Shirin. The second was *Si.* Ezra Nigrin, who brought me work from Ioannina consisting of some *Pirké Avoth*[135] pamphlets in Judeo-Greek printed with Hebrew letters. To me this person was an angel. To both of them I owe an eternal debt.

The *si.* lawyer brought me a brochure of the newly established society in Shirin. They also asked me to print a new story entitled *The Secret Killer*, and another one, *The Obsession of Gambling, the Youth of the Cercle*

135. This classic text of the Mishna is a compilation of Jewish ethical teaching dating to 200 CE.

des Intimes;[136] to this day, I will never waver in my gratitude to these brave young men.

But neither two nor twenty-two can measure up to the thirty-two [teeth], as I kept wondering what my future can bring me by scraping the bottom of my limited finances.

Those young men asked me if I wanted to import printing equipment to establish a newspaper. As I reviewed the procedures to obtain a *firman*, I realized that my petition to the *Vali Pasha* would have to be approved by the chief rabbi, an impossible task. **[62b]** You will readily understand, dear readers, that this was a time when anyone who brought them a negative report about me was handsomely rewarded. Needless to say that a petition by me to start a newspaper would never fly, at a time when they were so eager to close the *Gazeta de Viena* or the *Nasyonal de Konstantinopla*[137] for having published so many articles against them concerning my episode.

You can rest assured that instead of helping me, this would cause more harm to me.

Therefore, my only hope was to go back to my eager benefactor. One day encouraged by my friend, *Si.* Ben Rubi, I went to visit him and told him all that had happened to me. He listened to me most attentively. Moreover, he had been quite disappointed by the trick they had played on him because of me. And also, he was unwilling to intervene so as not to compromise his standing among these people.

He readily understood that my downfall was at hand, but in his genuine compassion, he encouraged me to restart my printing business by importing Turkish, Roman, and Greek [printing] types.

As for money, I shouldn't worry about it. I told him that I had a few resources utterly insufficient for the necessary expenditures. He wouldn't let me sell them but suggested that I place them in his treasurer's safekeeping. I was at a loss finding words to thank him. Furthermore, he gave me a handwritten letter of recommendation for one of

136. The *Cercle des Intimes* came into being in 1874 to fight for the reform of the Jewish community and for "modern" ideas.
137. Sa'adi is referring here to *El Koreo de Viena*, which was a Ladino newspaper published in Vienna; *El Nasyonal* was a Ladino newspaper in Istanbul.

his friends in Constantinople to help obtain an imperial decree to publish a newspaper and another letter for a friend in Vienna for the supply of all the necessary items for the printing press.

When I arrived in Constantinople, I went to see *Si.* Tiano, to whom I transmitted *Si.* Alatini's letter. He immediately called **[63a]** *Si.* Gabbay[138] and told him, "I would like you to take care of this matter in complete secrecy." As this *sinyor* Gabbay was also a close friend of mine, he answered that he would do his utmost.

That same day, he introduced me to the acting chief rabbi [in Constantinople],[139] who treated me with great respect. He asked me to sit down and offered me coffee. Truly, this was the first time that I saw such an intelligent yet so humble a religious leader.

Briefly, *Si.* Gabbay related my entire story to him, adding that *Si. Rav* Gatenyo had always supported me against those who sought my downfall. He asked me if I was carrying any letter of recommendation from him; I immediately presented it to him. After he read it, he urged *Si.* Gabbay to do everything possible to help me.

The next day, he took me along to *Bab-i Ali* and introduced me to an acquaintance of his who usually handled such matters. He inquired about the health of a friend in Salonica and suggested that I should get a letter of recommendation from this Jewish friend. I happily accepted his idea, as long as he was a friend of mine; but I feared that he might be one of my opponents. He promised me that with a letter of recommendation from said person, he would use all his influence to obtain an imperial decree without bothering anybody.

It was a total surprise for me to see [the plan of my accusers] was unraveling [and working in my favor]. On learning that that person was my son, my joy knew no bounds, especially when I asked for his address and he answered, "Hayyim, the bookseller." Then, I told him, "This is my son!" As soon as he heard that this friend of his was my son, he hit the roof and told me that he would immediately start implementing this matter. **[63b]** Doing the impossible, he managed

138. See note 120.

139. The acting chief rabbi was then Moshe a-Levi, who occupied this position until 1908.

within three weeks to have the imperial decree sent to me all the way to Salonica.

As you read this narrative, you will have an idea of God's miraculous ways to help an innocent person.

Now, our readers must have an important question to ask, "How come, so many people are opposed to one man? Surely, there must be among them a few fair-minded people; why then have such animosity and subject a large family to such mortal vindictiveness by ruining their livelihood and persecuting them to obliterate their name?"

Dear Readers!

You are fully justified in raising this question, but retribution is according to human nature. When one deeply feels that his friend has offended or harmed him—absent a clear explanation—he can be sure that a deep root of animosity survives in this friend's heart, as was the case with *Si.* Hayyimucho [Kovo]. All those who pursued me to death had their own reasons; on the other hand, I was right and not they.

And this is what I mean: First, some imagined that I was instrumental in prompting the people [in Constantinople] to accept the resignation of the *si. rav*. Second, when the "Society of Good Deeds" was active, I was the one who informed the committee and recruited new members considered hostile to my opponents; yet it didn't suit them to remember that I was just an employee, doing his work honestly, and that I was not guilty.

As for the others, they cannot express their true reason, even to themselves, as it would be shameful. Whenever they were invited to some celebration, **[64a]** they acted as if it was all for them, so that they could linger around day and night eating and drinking nonstop.

However, the host of a celebration could not ask them to leave, letting me find ways to ease them out. As an organizer I was in charge of concluding the banquet, so that they could start preparing the tables for the next crowd. This frustrated their enjoyment. They would start grumbling among themselves, uttering insults, and saying that I was the culprit in spoiling their party.

Another excuse was their game of interpreting Hebrew words based on their numerical value to make quite inappropriate jokes. When I faced such a revolting situation, I would demolish their enthusiasm by quoting a contradictory verse. They had difficulty deciding how to kill me but were unable to do so.

All these pretexts, and many more, kept accumulating in their hearts; their animosity gained strength until the appropriate time arrived for them. They persisted in reaching a climax, but Almighty God thought otherwise.

As the proverb says, "Many designs are in a man's mind, but it is the Lord's plan that is accomplished" (Proverbs 19:21).

It seems that the Almighty ran out of patience as He prompted them to continue their incredible scandal the likes of which even old-timers had never seen in its cruelty.

Up to now the people avoided hearing the sound of this old weapon of excommunication until they saw the gatherings and the machine guns, with thousands of adults and children answering "Amen," at the sound of the blowing horn, **[64b]** as well as thirteen *shofaroth* (one of these thirteen was mine, leaving only twelve), reading Psalm 109, replete with curses. Yet this had no effect on my person or my family. They fired a cannonball at me; I fired back in kind. This convinced even the fanatics to conclude that this weapon of excommunication was now obsolete and that it had lost its power. And since then, they themselves have not used it at all. Said differently, having spent their entire arsenal on me, they had now exhausted the effectiveness of this weapon when they realized that they were holding in their hands and showing to the public a pistol without a spring. However, now that the people knew how ineffective this weapon of excommunication was, they stopped showing it, as the Turkish proverb goes: "His skullcap fell, his baldness appeared."

For the time being I am grateful for every day of my life! Even though I am not feeling well as I write this story, I give thanks to God that thanks to me, the population of Salonica was saved from this leprosy still prevalent at that time. As for me, I have forgiven them and have never asked in my prayers to God for vengeance against my opponents, even though their intention was to bring so much evil upon me and my family. On the contrary, I always pray to God for His forgiveness, so that He may change their hearts for good, Amen. May He also not forget me and my children, Amen.

Chapter 26

The Es Hayyim Printing Press

As funds in their treasury were increasing, they established a printing press called *Es Hayyim* [Tree of Life], simply because they couldn't come up with any other suitable scheme to compete with me. The initial printing equipment they had imported fell into the sea as it was being unloaded from the ship to the warehouse. What a shame, it was insured. With the money paid by the insurance they reordered the same materials. This printing press has been in business for the past twenty-eight years. Its directors are not professionals in this trade; it is run by its employees and has lost five hundred to six hundred *liras*. Initially, they printed rabbinic books that have a meager profit margin. Later, they took on other smaller jobs. The only reason why it is still functioning is because it does not belong to any one person but is funded by the members of the Society [*Es Hayyim*].

To compete with me even more they established a newspaper with the name *El Avenir*; but I hope to God that this will not survive for long.

Chapter 27

[65a] *Clothing of Men, Women, and Maidens*

Men's clothing falls into four categories. Some wore a fur cap, a man's robe, and loose robe. Others, who were the majority in Salonica, wore a round cap. Middle-class men wore a turban in the style of a round cap with a *fez* underneath. Lower-class individuals wore a twisted turban.

On Saturdays this category of people wore a red or a blue robe edged with a striped ribbon. Red robes had blue edges and blue robes had red edges.

The youth of these people wore wool breeches on weekdays and baggy trousers on Saturdays. In the winter they wore dark baggy trousers and in the summer white baggy trousers with white outer shirts that required a full piece of white cotton fabric. These were called clothes of "rice starchers." Later on, prominent people stopped wearing their fur caps and wore instead turbans edged with blue silk. The next class of people wore a fitted turban during the week and a bonnet in honor of the Sabbath.

Much later, the fashion changed again: young people started dressing in the European style and this continues to this day. Lower-class individuals changed their fashion, too; some dressed in the European style, others wore a loose robe and a men's robe, and some carried their men's robe on their shoulders, others beside them, while eating pumpkin seeds in the streets. Now, after twenty-five years, the bonnets have survived among the rabbis. The rest of the people wear only a *fez*; some young people changed their fashion again by wearing modern hats, even though they are not European.

[65b] *Traditional Clothing of Women*

Some women wore on their heads an Aleppo style scarf. It was shaped as a hood made from embroidered silk fabric. This hood was edged with a gold embroidered filigreed lace and had a number of feathers on it. During festivals they wore diamond flowers on their heads, but this fashion was short-lived.

Women from Yenishehir [Larissa] or Istanbul wore skullcaps on their heads. This skullcap was in the shape of a small towel of cotton fabric. The entire edge was made of blue velvet; these women also wore diamond flowers on their heads during the festivals, but they were rare in Salonica; after a while even this fashion changed.

Our own women in Salonica dressed the same way as they dress today, namely a *fez*, a *kofya*, a *sayo*, and an *entari*. What has changed is that they used to wear *mestas* and yellow shoes, but now they wear ankle boots or shoes. During festivals they wore gold bracelets and gold necklaces. Recently, the fashion of their necklaces has changed; now they wear pearl necklaces and a *tokado*. Earlier, they used to wear earrings of precious stones, hanging at the corners of this hairdo. But after a while they stopped wearing these earrings.

Traditionally, when women went out, they would wear a *kurdi*, made of red material and lined with fur, which was a weasel fur. On the outside there was a thin edge of fur; they would cover their heads with a white scarf that made them look like angels. After a while this fashion also changed; instead of *kurdis*, they started to wear *kirims*, lined with sable. As for the *kofya*, it stayed the same, except that now they are shorter than before, when they had reached almost one meter. Also, the *fez* they wore with their hairdo was larger, whereas now it is much smaller. **[66a]** Recently, there has been a faster change in fashion, as one-fourth of the women are now wearing European-style clothes. Needless to say, the majority of maidens also dress the same way for their wedding.

A long time ago maidens dressed in the Vlach style.[140] They wore on their heads a *fez*, similar to a skullcap, covered with a small, blue silk tassel, held with a strap placed under the chin. Their hair was done in braids looking like ribbons, with each braid ending in a tassel of short hair. Their clothing consisted of printed fabric, a dress two to three strips wide, and a narrow *fermele* [braid used as trimming as an edging]; and when they went out, they wore a *djubbe*, in the Vlach style. The waist was very narrow and the sleeves were so tight that there was barely room for their bracelets. The hems had white, silk shamrocks, while their slits were less than one yard long. They covered their heads with a shawl, while each end dangled from the opposite side of their shoulders, an unusual style. The shoes they wore barely covered their toes.

Chapter 28

Wedding Customs of the Past

They brought the bride dressed in married woman's attire with cape, loose robe, thin-soled boots, and yellow shoes. On her head she wore a small gilded fur cap, called *findjan*, like a metal mug, and a veil with gold embroidery. To display the bride's trousseau, a family celebration called *alvorada* was held eight days before the wedding. The day before she went to the Turkish [ritual] bath, a Jewish servant came with a small pot containing a piece of *pelador*, or hair-removing wax. Facing the bride, she applied this wax **[66b]** to her forehead, her cheeks, even

140. The "Vlach style" refers to the clothing of an ethnic group in the region who spoke a dialect of Romanian; from Wallachian, current-day Rumania.

under her eyebrows. When it attached itself to her face, they pulled it off forcefully, tearing it off, while the bride would be screaming with pain. Woe to the bride whose skin was delicate and who would inevitably bleed. Some of them would have swollen cheeks that made them look as if they had chicken pox. When the bride was brought to the house of the groom, who had never met her before, at first sight she must have looked to him as if she had chicken pox. As she was climbing the steps into the house, an elderly lady from her family was ready with a piece of rock candy about fifteen to twenty *dramas*, which she placed in her mouth, while she kissed her on both cheeks. Under the wedding canopy was set the bride who had a large swelling on one side of her face caused by the candy she was not supposed to eat but let slowly melt in her mouth. As for the groom, they dressed him up and seated him in a porch facing the gate of the courtyard through which the bride would enter. They put on his shaven head a white scarf embroidered with silver threads and hanging tassels, making him look like an *imam* recently arrived from Afghanistan.

Later on, they removed his white scarf and dressed him with a bonnet and a robe, to go to the synagogue accompanied by his parents. When he returned home, they sang the *Shiv'a berahoth* in the presence of the bride and the groom. Then they seated the in-laws on each side; the groom would get up and kiss the hands of his father, his father-in-law, his mother and his mother-in-law, who would give him a golden ducat as a gift. Then the groom was taken to another room to sign the *ketubba*, or marriage contract, while the bride started dancing, accompanied by two old lady musicians. In the meantime, as it got dark, the groom joined his parents and friends for a meal, while the bride was led to her bedroom with music and love songs. They seated her at a small table with a dish of Jordan almonds and a small bottle of *raki* and two cups. The groom would join her in that room **[67a]** for what was called the *avlar*. As the groom sat next to the bride, they would lock the door from the outside. He would fill a small cup with *raki* and offer it to the bride. The bride would raise her head and signal her unwillingness to drink. As the groom took a look at the bride covered with tinsel, he would first drink his *raki* and then, taking a handful of Jordan almonds, would place them in her lap with his gift; he would then leave the room. Then the women as a group entered that room, took the bride outside, with song and music. They seated her in the porch, where she continued to fast, while the groom and his friends sat at a separate table, eating and drinking. They took the bride, who had still not broken her fast, to her bedroom, singing love songs full of advice for the bride, who would say, "Dear mother, in this new beginning, I need your guidance to deal with my first love. He loves me and I do want him." "Dear daughter, keep repeating those words all through this night." As for the groom, they carried him singing religious poems, lifting him up in the air and taking him to the bridal chamber, undressed him and put him to bed; they then left the room. The groom bolted the door and the rest is obvious.

Chapter 29

[67b] *Eating Habits During Festivities*

This is how banquets during festivities started. On the day of the *kiddushin* upon the return of the groom from the Turkish bath, with his friends, they set a table for about twenty to thirty people, depending on how many friends he had. The menu consisted of fish, meat, rice, and fruit. The same menu was used for the night before conjugal privacy, with separate tables for men and women. The following night, called the night of the in-laws, was attended by all the invited guests from the groom's as well as from the bride's side.

The same thing was served [for lunch] the following Saturday and Saturday night, with all kinds of additional banquets given during the wedding week.

On the "day of the fish" there was a special banquet for the *talmide hahamim* who received monetary gifts.

Fifty years ago, the average room was from eight to ten meters long and the living room measured four meters and was furnished with elevated cushions and pillows. There were round, copper trays on each table. The tablecloth was surrounded with a seven- to eight-meter-long towel in lieu of napkins. In the living room just mentioned there were three tables. Some would sit on the elevated cushions, while the pillows served as chairs to sit on. On the table were two to three glasses, a few wood spoons to eat rice, and a black bottle containing from one thousand to two thousand [*dramas*] of wine. There was always one person who held the bottle between his legs and poured wine for whomever he pleased. They would place a platter of fish in the middle of the table from which people helped themselves with their hands. This was followed by a large, round, and shallow platter of meat and vegetables. The first to stretch his hand grabbed the best of the meat, followed by the second and third persons who snatched the next best, and the rest of the people licked the bones. Then came the poultry platter. The person with the longest arm grabbed the best piece, and those who couldn't reach were left with just a bone in their hands.

[68a] After that, barely cooked rice was served; its grains looked like bullets. It came in large tureens, covered in so much sugar and cinnamon that one could barely see the rice. When the top layer was consumed, they had two plates full of sugar and cinnamon on the ready to top it off again. The clever ones would save in their laps spoons from the previous dish; those who couldn't reach a spoon used a leftover bone from the chicken they just ate, and those who had neither used their bare hands as a spoon.

At that time it was customary for men to have long beards; obviously, part of this half-raw, half-cooked rice, landed on their beards, and those black beards turned white with all the rice that fell on them.

After the meal the groom started to dance with his friends and was followed by his guests dancing two by two.

The musicians consisted of the organizer and an additional musician who sang according to the tunes they improvised, in three categories: dancing music, jumping music, and *cicek havasi*. While some danced, wine lovers sat at the tables drinking wine until the black bottle was emptied. They then played the *morra* game; the loser paid for a pitcher of wine, and the drinking continued unabated. When the dancing ended, the joking started; some would wear a fur coat inside out; others would place a pot of water on their head, covering it with a bedsheet, and then came to play with the organizer, who was wearing a big bonnet. Contestants in this game started to scream, arguing, "You owe me, I don't owe you; you told me, I didn't tell you." Finally, the person who was carrying the pot of water covered with a bedsheet would bow down in front of the *si. haham* pretending to tell him something and would then spill the water, soaking him from head to toe. **[68b]** All the guests were paying attention to learn the final verdict, even though they were dead drunk.

Now, the women and the bride, who had also finished eating, would join the men in the hall to watch this funny scene and would laugh heartily. The groom and the bride joined the crowd in laughter, fulfilling the phrase, "rejoicing the groom and the bride" [from the *shiv'a berahoth* in the marriage ceremony].

Then, they would pick two people who sat on the floor facing each other. They would tie together their feet and their hands, and fill the space in between with pillows until they couldn't breathe. They called this "loading the ship." After rowing with the two tied men, a self-appointed captain would warn that this ship would sink, unless it is repaired again. They would fetch two mortars and pestles and would start hammering on them, singing like sailors, as the repairman said, *ya isa!* In turn, the guests responded to this appeal.

Such were the celebrations and jokes in bygone days. At a time when there were no luxuries in the homes, our ancestors were preoccupied almost exclusively with eating and drinking. A typical house had a tiny curtain on the windows, five to six rudimentary chairs, and a small, framed mirror, barely sufficient to reflect one's face. Their clothing consisted in a cotton wrap for weekdays and Saturdays, which they left behind as an inheritance for their children.

Therefore, the little they earned was sufficient for eating and drinking.

Chapter 30

[69a] *The Leeches*

Since time immemorial, the first medicine for a sick person, whether for a cold or for some pain in the pit of the stomach or any other part of the body, was to apply fifteen to twenty leeches on the pit of their stomach. There was hardly a house without a bottle of twenty-five to thirty leeches for such emergencies. As we just said, leeches were immediately applied on anyone who had any pain in any part of the body.

At the end of Passover, also called "spring," the majority of the people applied to themselves at least ten to fifteen leeches to cleanse their blood. It is also true that the affliction of hemorrhoids was not as prevalent as nowadays.

At that time there were eight to ten people who earned their livelihood from this trade. When *Si.* Abot [John Abbott][141] was in London in his youth, he found out that leeches were worth one shilling apiece and that they were sent from Salonica. He was also aware that the going price in Salonica was two for one *metelik*, or ten *paras*; and so, he was the first to start this business.

As he came back *via* Constantinople, he managed to obtain there an imperial decree granting him the right to trade in leeches. This authorization was granted to him for a number of years.

Upon his return to Salonica he prohibited all those who dealt in leeches to sell them but hired them as employees who had to bring all the leeches to him for sale.

Thus he started to reap extraordinary profits by shipping barrels full of leeches to Europe. Over the swamps where the leeches lived, he placed the scum of the city as guards who even once dumped a man into a swamp where he died.

These guards were assassins from the mountains, now hired as bodyguards after they had submitted to his authority. He also purchased a large plot with many trees in *Orundjik*, **[69b]** where he built himself a country home.

On his second trip to London, when he was extremely rich, he fell in love with a young girl taken captive during a war waged by the British and wanted to buy her for himself. Her owner said to Abot that "if he ever were to sell her, it would be on condition that he marry her rather than take her as a mistress."

This girl was from Jewish extraction. So, her owner sold her to *Si.* Djon [John] Abot on condition that he marry her. He was happy to comply, and he married her according to the law prevalent then.

141. See note 83.

When he brought her to Salonica, she was a very beautiful and unblemished young girl who bore him a son and a daughter. Later on, he built in Malta [Street], where today the Lombardo Building stands, a very beautiful mansion with four to five offices for himself in its courtyard.

A few years later, his love for her turned into hatred, and as the womanizer that he was, he started keeping mistresses. To help him in his adventures, he even had someone who procured women for him; money was not a problem in satisfying his desires.

He bought a house for each one of these women, complete with servants. At his whim he would take along one of them to his country house in *Orundjik* to satisfy his passion, as this was his only preoccupation.

He kept enlarging his business activities and became the top banker in Salonica. His influence was such that he could do anything he wanted. Then, his first wife complained to the British consul, who called Abot and warned him that according to British law he couldn't divorce his wife. Yet he insisted that he no longer wished to recognize her as his wife. But the British consul couldn't twist his arm, because as we said earlier, he was a very influential individual.

The consul wrote to England, explaining this entire story. A ruling from the British government came back stipulating **[70a]** that full compliance with the consul's orders was required.

Therefore, the British consul compelled him to buy a separate house for his wife, complete with maids and a servant to bring her anything she asked for. He also fixed for her an adequate monthly stipend. But because this gentleman couldn't accept the consul's orders, he wrote slanderous letters about him to London, causing him so much grief that he ultimately died.

However, this consul was a good and fair person, to whom God had given a very capable son to avenge his father from all the hardships that this gentleman had brought on his father.

He caused him much pain at the time when he was bedridden about to die. As mentioned earlier, his house, his offices, and his business records had burned during the Skilich fire. [The consul] sued his brother, *Si.* Bob Abot, claiming that he could not prove his partnership with his brother for lack of appropriate documentation as a result of the fire that had destroyed everything. His brother brought two first-class lawyers from London, paying each of them ten *liras* daily, plus traveling expenses.

When they came to Salonica, they examined this matter and decided that the brother was right, that he was a partner.

Now, as this brother was rather tight with money, never spending it like *Si.* Djon, he grabbed the cash. *Si.* Djon was the exact opposite in spending, as when he built a stone mansion—today's Ottoman Bank—where he spent close to ten million franks during the fifteen years of building it and tearing it down until it was finished. By now, his business was in the red, and his debts in London reached a large sum of money.

At this point they designated as executor the consul, *Si.* [John] Blunt, who was the son of the old consul avenging his father, to take over the remaining property and to sell it in an auction.

The consul had town criers announcing that all those who wished to buy valuable goods **[70b]** should come to the mansion, next to the bank. Every day, merchants would show up as the town criers auctioned them off, and the *sinyor* from his bed was placing his signature for the sale of so many goods that cost him a fortune. The consul managed to sell everything that was in the house, turning it into cash. Then, *Si.* [Abbott's] son came to Salonica to get something from his inheritance. All he found was empty shells because even the houses of his father's mistresses had been sold. The thousands of magnificent plants and all the statues he had in the garden of his country home in *Orundjik* were sold almost for nothing in the presence of this sick man, who died in anguish and torment. This was his vindication for the distress he caused the consul's father. It has been more than twenty-five years that this consul has been in our city; he was always a good and an upright man, getting along with everyone. He is a humble benefactor that even the youngest child adores. Now he has left for America as an ambassador.

Chapter 31

Tenants in the Month of Nisan

Forty years ago, tenants used to move out in the month of *Nisan*, or April. The *si. hahamim*, in agreement with the *Rav h"r* Asher, took into consideration the hardship caused by the winter, combined with extra expenses needed for Passover, and tried to alleviate this problem.

They issued a *haskama*, that tenants should move in September rather than in April.

There were many discussions about this, but finally they prevailed. When the move occurred during the month of *Nisan*, it meant fifteen days of lost rent until Passover, so many tenants were left without a house until *kal hamira*, or the day before Passover.[142]

Landlords were reluctant to go along because when Passover came, they liked to collect their rents, but now they compelled them to collect the proper rent from April to September.

[71a] Therefore, a notice was issued that no landlord can compel his tenant to pay him rent for the full year but only from April to September.

They also asked me to read this notice in the *Talmud Tora* on Saturday during the month of *Adar*.

This is the rule used to this day.

Chapter 32

The Massacre of the Consuls on May 6, 1876

On the fifth of the current month, the train coming from Skopje brought a Bulgarian young woman, dressed in the Turkish style, who wanted to appear before the authorities to convert to Islam. As soon as she got off the train, she begged the attending gendarmes to take her immediately to the authorities to inform them about her decision. They had barely walked a few steps when a bunch of Greek youth, who had been advised of her arrival, seized the young woman from their hands, publicly removed her veil and her Ottoman-style coat, and put her in a carriage.

142. If a home was rented to a Jewish tenant prior to Passover, that is, in the month of *Nisan*, the space would have to be koshered twice: once immediately, according to standard dietary laws, and once again in preparation for Passover. In compelling landlords to allow tenants to rent for a partial year (from April to September), the rabbis sidestepped the strict observance of the laws of kashrut.

The few gendarmes who were present were unable to prevent this. So, too, the Turks who were in the coffeehouses celebrating the *hidrellez*, or spring festival, were shocked and displeased, witnessing this scene.

At noon the next morning, which was Saturday, the Turkish people, the Albanians, and foreigners who were in town went to the authorities to insist that this young woman wished to convert to Islam, that she should be brought to the authorities to inquire which religion she preferred, Islam or Christianity.

The authorities replied that they were looking into this matter. When they heard this, they all gathered at the *Saatli Djami*. The governor took notice of this upheaval, and he was trying to get hold of her **[71b]** but didn't know where the young woman was hidden.

Then, the *pasha* sent five to six honorable persons to calm down those assembled in the mosque so that everyone would go back to work.

Their response was that since he and his council were looking into this matter, they would not leave the premises until they got back the young woman. However, *Si.* Sarito [unidentified first name] Abot, the German consul, and *Si.* Jul Mulen [Jules Moulin], the French consul, wanted to see the *pasha* for mediation, but unfortunately, they went instead directly to the mosque where the entire population was impatiently waiting. In so doing, they hoped to calm down the highly agitated people, even though, while on the way there, they had been warned that this was not the appropriate time for them to be seen there. However, they misjudged the severity of the situation, continuing on their journey; when they entered the mosque, they found themselves in the middle of the people.

In turn, when the *Vali Pasha* learned that the consuls had entered the mosque, he and his entire council went immediately to the mosque to prevent a potential instigation [to violence]. As the *Vali Pasha* entered the mosque, the entire population stood up, unanimously proclaiming that no matter what, they were determined to get the young woman back by force, if necessary. When the *Vali* saw the seriousness of the situation, he and his council begged the consuls to see to it that the young woman be brought back because of the extreme complexity of this matter. Their answer was that because the young woman was in hiding, it was very hard to locate her but that they were trying to find her. But the

Turks lost their patience, insisting again that unless they brought the young woman, they would not let the consuls go.

It reached a point when the consuls realized that the situation was quite grim. They wrote pressing messages, asking to have custody of the young woman in view of the great danger in which they found themselves. But unfortunately, the answers were late in coming. Because of their delay, the Turks attacked the consuls, broke the iron bars from the windows, and entered the room where the *Vali*, **[72a]** his council, and the consuls were meeting. But as there were not enough soldiers to defend the people, they started beating them angrily with the iron bars they had removed from the windows. Unfortunately, the two consuls perished as victims of the mob's anger, in spite of the presence of the *Vali*, who was desperately trying to protect them to no avail. The members of the council were also beaten and even the *Vali* himself was mistreated. The commander of the gendarmes received many blows; a captain was beaten so severely that he was bedridden; and they also wounded many gendarmes.

While these things were taking place, they did bring the young woman, but, unfortunately, it was too late.

Many revolver and pistol shots were fired in the air. Following this, everyone returned to their homes. The two bodies were moved Saturday night, the German consul to his house and the French consul to the custody of the Catholic nuns.

The *Vali Pasha* cabled neighboring Monastir to send immediate military help to prevent a potential revolt.

Around 10 or 11 a.m. on Sunday, soldiers from nearby localities started to come, and one thousand soldiers arrived by train from Skopje. Our city was then totally closed; numerous patrols circulated in the streets, but after these measures it was hoped that everything would return to normal.

The entire city was hurt by those cruel events that took place, and all the religious communities participated in this common grief. Within three days warships of certain powers started to arrive. Tuesday morning, the ship *Gaulois* arrived, bringing the French vice admiral.

Around 8 p.m. the same day, a large number of guards began patrolling our city to make it safer. On the pier a large number of infantry and cavalry were stationed, forming an impressive barrier. The people were perplexed, **[72b]** seeing such intense preparations on the heels of the secrecy of the meetings and the trial. An hour later, six of the most guilty prisoners were seen being brought from the Turkish jail. Simultaneously, admirals and foreign officials, accompanied by our *Vali Pasha*, left the corvette and stepped into various little boats coming from the shores of the pier. Within less than half an hour, the sentence of the six guilty assassins who perpetrated this evil deed was administered.

Following this execution, the French, German, and Turkish frigates exchanged official, military salutes, and everyone returned to their normal life and their work.

About 6 to 7 p.m., they moved the bodies to the hospital, and they were buried the following morning.

On Wednesday all the members of the various councils, as well as the *muhtars*, or village elders, were invited to the governor's mansion. All the officials lined up, and His Excellency the *Vali Pasha* stood in their midst. Eshref *Pasha* delivered a magnificent speech, mentioning all the trials, which had been conducted with extreme care and evidence based on valid testimonies.

On Saturday, the twenty-sixth of the current month, he announced that the remaining culprits, too, would be penalized according to their guilt, assuring the people not to have any fear for the future.

We never doubted that His Excellency Eshref *Pasha* [the *Vali*] would not continue to keep the peace as before or that everything would be forgotten so fast.

But we were very sorry to have lost these two victims who were brave and worthy individuals; they perished in the prime of life. And besides, the population of our city has always demonstrated our mutual fraternity, no matter what our religious background. Hence our hope was that those unfortunate events would certainly not change or lessen the new feelings of brotherhood among us.

[73a] *The Funerals of the German and French Consuls*

On Thursday night, the eighteenth of the current month, notices were posted on the walls announcing the funerals of the French and German consuls for the next morning.

The first took place at 6 o'clock and the second at 8 o'clock European time. At dawn Friday we saw large military units patrolling all the streets. Each street corner that intersected the main street was cordoned off, with soldiers blocking traffic, making it difficult for the people to reach those roads through which the caskets of the deceased would pass.

At 10:30 in the morning Turkish time[143] [5:30 a.m.], we saw His Excellency the *Vali Pasha*, accompanied by Vahan[144] *efendi*, counselor to the *hakim* [judge], as well as all the consuls and the French and Prussian delegates with their interpreters. All of them, wearing their uniforms, went to the pier, where they waited for the French vice admiral to disembark. At eleven Turkish time [6 a.m.] Turkish soldiers preceded and also followed companies of soldiers belonging to the various nations disembarking from their ships, along with their vice admirals, their commandants, and officers of each warship anchored in our port. Together, they all marched toward the Catholic church.

The church was covered with flags and other mourning signs.

All the notables of Salonica belonging to the various religious communities were waiting for the arrival of the *Si.* Chief Rabbi *Rav h"r* Avraam Gatenyo, accompanied by representatives of our community, ten *hahamim* and a group of young men as mourners. Also entering the church was the Metropolit *efendi*, accompanied by representatives of the Greek community. The two heads of community met and greeted each other and then proceeded inside together. The funeral ceremony inside the church lasted about half an hour, and then the cortege moved on toward the cemetery.

It is impossible to describe this funeral scene, which saddened **[73b]** everyone, with such expressions of emotion.

Three rows of Turkish soldiers walked in front and behind the *Vali*, joined by Vahan *efendi* and the Turkish admiral. Then came all the soldiers belonging to the various powers, with their guns upside down, walking very calmly and in perfect formation. Then came the Metropolit

143. According to the Muslim calendar, a new day starts at sunset, which is then considered to be 12 a.m. The liturgical date in the Jewish calendar also starts at sunset.

144. Vahan was an Armenian civil servant.

efendi and the Catholic priests, followed by the casket held by French sailors. After them came all the consuls, vice admirals, commandants, and officers belonging to all the warships anchored in our port, together with the French and Prussian delegates, the *si. rav* with his representatives, and then, all the notables of the city. All of these were dressed in mourning attire; rows of Turks ended this cortege. The funeral cortege left the church, followed the road to the Ottoman Bank, and made a turn at the street of the theater and another turn toward the main street. After that it veered again, headed toward the avenue of the market that took them directly to the pier. They were met there by various French officers in a boat decked in mourning, where the casket was deposited and attended by two Catholic priests affiliated with the French navy. As soon as the boat carrying the casket started to move, a multitude of gunshots was heard coming from all the frigates until the casket was placed on board the frigate *Gaulois*. After that the entire cortege was headed toward the new Greek church called Saint Nicholas to offer the German consul the honors he deserved. The religious ceremony was conducted with everyone's participation. They left the church in less than an hour to form a procession. As before, the soldiers came first, then the *Vali* with Vahan *efendi* and the Turkish admiral, the *si. rav* with his retinue, and then came the Greek priests, German sailors carrying the casket, and then all the representatives as was done before. The cortege moved through the best and widest streets until it reached the Metropolit cemetery, where the deceased was buried.

[74a] At that moment, too, the sound of the artillery was heard as half-mast flags of mourning were raised back to full mast.

Everything unfolded with the utmost calm and respect, thanks to the excellent and wise measures taken from the beginning by His Excellency Eshref *Pasha*.

Chapter 33

The War Between Turkey and Russia (1877–1878)

Following the catastrophe of the murder of the consuls, Europe found the right time to raise some questions asking Turkey to adopt reforms guaranteeing the lives of all its Christian citizens. Especially worried was Russia, whose schemes between *Si.* Ignatief[145] and Sultan [Abdul] Aziz were in jeopardy. By his extensive spending, amounting every year to a sum of more than a million gold *liras*, the sultan was ruining his government. The press reported that he was importing up to forty extra expensive carriages annually from Europe, one of them even costing one hundred thousand *liras*. In addition, he had many palaces full of women; up to one thousand women were maintained and governed themselves with funds from the treasury. The *Valide* [Sultan's Mother] eagerly fulfilled every one of his wishes, until the ministers were sick and tired and couldn't stand him anymore. Every day he would change his ministers because they refused to agree with him to change an old law requiring the older son to rule at the death of the reigning sultan. He wanted to gather backers to sign a legal proposal for his son, Yusuf Izzeddin, to rule after him. But the *Sheh [Sheyh] ul Islam* wouldn't allow him to pursue this whim, and the ministers backed the *Sheh [Sheyh] ul Islam*.

[74b] He would become angry with his ministers and would fire them, replacing them with others to see who would go along with his capricious ideas. But none of them would agree with him. This worry drove him to insanity by doing things unworthy of a sultan, ruler of the whole nation.

He was even determined to sell Constantinople to Russia and move his capital to Baghdad when he got in touch with the Russian ambassador called *Si.* Ignatief.

His ministers, the *Sheh [Sheyh] ul Islam*, and the *ulema* agreed to institutionalize him and declare prince Murat[146] as sultan in his place. And this is what happened. They made all the necessary preparations, placing all the warships in front of the palace; on land, too, they stationed two armed battalions headed by a *pasha*. At midnight, a *pasha* came to the palace, holding a *firman*, signed by all the ministers and by Sultan Murat, along with a *fetva* from the *Sheh [Sheyh] ul Islam*.

145. Count Nicholas Ignatieff was the Russian ambassador who served in Constantinople from 1864 to 1877.

146. Murat V reigned as sultan for a few months in 1876.

When they knocked at the door of his bedroom, he woke up and got very angry.

He wanted to know who had dared disturb him at such an hour. They answered that it was Ambassador Ignatief who had come on a pressing matter. Then, he pulled the latch and opened the door. When the door was opened, the *pasha* read him the *firman* and *fetva*, issued by the *Sheh [Sheyh] ul Islam*.

When he heard these words, he grew extremely angry and tried to give orders to his imperial guard, but they had already agreed to back the ministers. The *pasha* who brought him the *firman* and the *fetva* said to him, "Sir, it is useless for you to look for a way out; from your window, you can observe that by land and by sea, everything has been taken care of."

As he looked through a window, he was convinced that everything was indeed blocked both **[75a]** by sea and by land. That is when he was extremely scared, got up from his bed and got dressed.

They fetched the *Valide* [Sultan's Mother] and the *sultana*. He was placed in a *caique*, while the Queen Mother and the *sultana* were placed in another one, both headed to the palace in *Sarayburnu*. Everyone was placed in separate apartments, including his son Yusuf Izzeddin, who had his own apartment. Watchful guards were patrolling the area, so that they would not communicate with each other.

The same night, they brought Sultan Murat to the palace and they enthroned him as sultan. The next morning, the first day of *Shavu'oth* of that year, 101 gunshots were fired from the fortresses to announce the enthronement of Sultan Murat. When this news was heard, happiness and joy could be read on the faces of the entire population of Istanbul, because they had come to know Sultan Murat as a conscientious and patient man who was familiar with European politics. They knew that with him the empire would be better organized.

Two days later, the news spread that Sultan Aziz had punctured a vein in his arm with a pair of scissors and had bled to death. Then they brought nine of the most [famous] doctors to examine him, and they concluded unanimously that Sultan Aziz had committed suicide. But later on, the real truth of this death was known, as the physicians seemed to have been in agreement with the ministers.

When the Russian government learned all about this development, they started to realize that their entire plan had collapsed and that the Turks were not that naive. The Russians instigated their vassal states such as Serbia, Bulgaria, and Rumania to revolt by raising new questions in Bosnia-Herzegovina. In no time Turkey moved to action. Then Serbia was pushed to the forefront; but again they were shown their true strength under pressure from Turkey, who had started to march toward Belgrade.

[75b] Then, Serbia asked for an armistice that was granted by the Turkish government. Peace with Europe was established, and, to compensate for Serbia's size, which was deemed too small, Turkey was asked to give back all the territories it had occupied during this war. It was General Abdul Kyerim [Kerim] *Pasha*[147] who had won this war. To reward him for his bravery, the Hungarians who were friends with Turkey sent him a sword studded with diamonds.

Russia sent a note to the six great powers stating that, with no direct benefit for themselves, they were eager to save all their Christian brethren and declare war against Turkey. Then they sent an ultimatum to Turkey, saying that they were about to declare war.

Because Russia could not attack Turkey on land, the Turkish government sent Abdul Kyerim *Pasha*, the commander of the whole army, to block the entire coastline of the Danube. Thus, Abdul Kyerim *Pasha*, as head of the army, moved to Ruschuk[148] to block the crossing of the Danube by Russian soldiers.

However, Ignatief, who knew the personality of Abdul Kyerim *Pasha*, informed his government that it was easy to convince this person with a handful of gold rubles. And that is how Russia set up with much ingenuity some bridges over the Danube made of water buffalo hides to transfer its army across the river.

On a night when the Russians were busy building, the *Karahanlis*[149] came to tell Abdul Kyerim *Pasha* what was going on. But because he

147. Abdulkerim Nadir *Pasha* (d. 1884) was commander in chief of the Ottoman army in the Balkans.

148. Ruschuk refers to present-day Ruse, a Bulgarian city by the Danube just south of Rumania.

149. In all likelihood the *Karahanlis* were a local Turkic tribe.

was "drunk" with the gold rubles, he told them that the Russians would never dare step on Turkish soil. Yet that night, Russia crossed the river with one hundred thousand soldiers; this war had indeed started with much strength. They marched all the way to the city of Plevne, where general Osman *Pasha*[150] was headquartered. **[76a]** When he suddenly saw himself facing so many thousands of Russians, he performed an act of real bravery. On a dark night he started firing all his cannon guns and killed ten thousand Russian soldiers.

But the Russians had ten times more soldiers than Osman *Pasha*, who was also short both on ammunitions and food. He sought help from [headquarters] but got no answer because they were "drunk" with Russian gold. Thus Russian soldiers held Osman *Pasha* and his soldiers under a tight siege, so that he could not escape.

He and his army were compelled to surrender because they were unable to resist before so many millions of Russians. For him and his soldiers it was a complete surrender as prisoners of war. The Russian commander treated Osman *Pasha* as a hero, warmly greeting him and his army, and sent them to a nearby locality. The Russian army began advancing fearlessly until it reached San Stefano [Yeshilkoy, near today's Istanbul airport].

When England saw that Russia was advancing with no opposition toward Constantinople, they placed six warships on either side, threatening that if they took one more step beyond where they were, their entire army would be annihilated by their frigates. Russia immediately understood that they could not fight against England; they stopped their army in San Stefano. When Turkey perceived the great danger that threatened it, it sent representatives to San Stefano, where peace with Russia was concluded under most unfavorable conditions, with the stipulation that Europe be the arbiter to judge if these conditions were fair and appropriate.

Russia complied with this last condition because the other six powers had not participated in these talks that had been conducted bilaterally; they, too, had to evaluate them.

150. Osman Nuri *Pasha* (d. 1900) became an Ottoman hero for his defense of Plevne.

[76b] Then, they met at the Berlin Congress [1878] with six delegates from the Powers and one delegate from Turkey, to decide the terms for fair and appropriate conditions. They also fixed Bulgaria's borders as a principality, ruled by a prince to be approved by Turkey and Russia. Many candidates applied for this office, but Russia couldn't accept any of them because, in her opinion, she wished to appoint a prince who would side with her. But when the Bulgarians sensed that they would be called Russians rather than Bulgarians, they chose Aleksandro [Alexander] of Batemberg [Battenberg] as their prince, even though he did not have Russia's recognition as a prince. During his tenure as prince of Bulgaria, he was pressured by both the Russian and Bulgarian sides, feeling obligated to leave his position and to return to his homeland. Later, they chose Prince Ferdinand, but Russia was unwilling to recognize him, too. However, in order to be accepted by Russia, the latter baptized his son in the orthodox church, which met Russia's requirement that the prince belong to that church. In this fashion he was acceptable to both Russia and Turkey. After a while, as Turkey noticed that this prince was humble and obedient, she appointed him governor general of eastern Rumelia.

Chapter 39

The War of April 17, 1897 [Greek-Turkish War]

During the Congress of Berlin, Turkey was forced to cede Thessaly to Greece in return for one hundred million franks, to be paid in installments; Turkey was also given a map with new borders that specified the cities in Thessaly to be ceded, and this is what happened. After a while Greece requested to be given two more cities in order to better adjust its borders. This turned into a pretext for Greece not to pay its debt. As if this wasn't enough, every so often Greece kept instigating the Christians of Crete, and each time there was an insurrection, it cost the **[77a]** Turkish government a bundle of money. As of this writing, they now wished to annex all of Crete to Greece. The Turkish government turned to the six powers who proclaimed that these places should remain under Ottoman rule on condition that adequate reforms be adopted, and that is how an agreement was reached.

Thinking that this question was now resolved, Turkey withdrew its forces from Crete.

When Greece saw that the Turkish army had withdrawn from Crete, she sent about four to five battalions, causing a new revolt. Each one of the big powers had to send two to three warships to quell the revolt.

But this didn't help a bit, as bloody incidents occurred every day.

As for Greece, apparently she had been preparing for this war against Turkey for the past eight to ten years. Thus, she kept bothering Turkey almost daily by pouring companies of insurgents across the border.

When Turkey became aware of this tactic, she lost patience and sent Edhem *Pasha* with a strong army to the Turkish-Hellenic border, backed by many commanders and their troops.

In addition to all that, the rebels were trying to capture Preveze and Ioannina, but the commanders with their troops taught them a good lesson, causing them to flee after they had abandoned the border. When the regular troops from Greece tried to help these outlaws, Edhem *Pasha* was ordered to stop and even to pursue them. Thus, open war was declared between Turkey and Greece.

Now, Edhem *Pasha*[151] was well educated in the art of war and was familiar with the map of the entire world, which he had thoroughly studied. He issued orders to his commanders about suitable strategies to reach victory. The soldiers, full of enthusiasm, acted like lions and, thanks to the strength **[77b]** of their batteries and bayonets, soon occupied the enemy's fortifications, as well as the cities where they had been besieged, killing many of them and taking lots of prisoners, seizing thousands of boxes of bullets, guns, and cannons. A survey of the places captured by the superior Turkish army, such as Chataldja, Vlestino, Dimo[ti]ko, and Djemre[152] reflects the bravery of the Turkish soldiers and the extraordinary zeal with which they fight for the love of their religion and motherland.

Also, it was evident that Providence had helped them, as it was an unjust war waged by Greece. When all of Thessaly was lost and left in the hands of the Turks, they got their just deserts. The Turks fought this

151. Edhem *Pasha* was the commander of the Ottoman armies.
152. These are towns located in Thrace. Djemre is unidentified.

war bravely with plenty of soldiers and money, while the Greek government and its king were in dire poverty, unable to feed their army. The Greek citizens were in a state of open revolt against the deputies of both chambers and their king when they found themselves threatened by Germany for not paying their old debts and the fine imposed on them by the powers. The press in those days was reporting that King George, his family, and the heir to the throne would leave their positions to rejoin his father, the king, in Denmark.

Therefore, the war lasted barely a month. It has been three months since the cease-fire, but the terms of a final peace are still pending. Let us see when a lasting peace will be concluded.

Chapter 40

[78a] *The Beginning of the Rav HaRibbi Avraam Gatenyo's Rabbinate and His Dismissal*

The *Rav h"r* Asher died in the month of *Tevet*, or January, 1874. A few days later, the Council[153] named as rabbis the *Rav h"r* Avraam Gatenyo as first, the *Rav h"r* Mair [ben Yaakov] Nahmias [1804–87] as second, and *h"r* Shemuelachi Arditi, who were three of the most prominent rabbis.

At that time the notables of the city tried to introduce some reforms, among them not raising new taxes and limiting expenditures to the income from the gabelles. But the *Rav h"r* Avraam, who was familiar with the income and the expenditures of our *Kolel*, objected to this reform because the income was insufficient to cover the expenditures and many poor people would find themselves without any help. But because the notables wished to defend their own well-being rather than that of the poor, they were determined to remove him from office. They sent a message to the Chief Rabbinate of Constantinople, complaining that the *Rav h"r* Avraam was acting against the interests of the *Kolel* and that they should get an *irade*, naming *h"r* Shemuelachi Arditi to the position of chief rabbi.

153. The Council here refers to the self-constituted Jewish council created in 1870. See page 58.

So the community spent much money to get an imperial decree obtained through the Chief Rabbinate of Constantinople and brought here by its steward, Jak Gabbay *efendi*. He brought it here with great pomp, but the *Rav h"r* Avraam Gatenyo took it as a personal insult. Prior to that, the influential people of the city had sent couriers to the *Rav h"r* Avraam, asking him to acquiesce to their wishes. They then met in the house of the *Rav h"r* Mair to have some rabbis join them and sign a document that the *Rav h"r* Avraam not be recognized as chief rabbi. His answer was always, it was the people who had chosen him as chief rabbi, so that the burden of the poor was mainly on his shoulders. "Hence, I cannot sell the Jews to them as they have not sold them to me."

I remember witnessing an extraordinary event. The last evening before they signed this document, they sent a courier to the **[78b]** *Rav h"r* Avraam to tell him that this was the deadline for this document and that if he agreed, all would be fine, and if not, he was finished. "As for me, I shall never call on you again," said the courier. The *si. rav* answered, "With God's help, may you never come back here again!" This courier was a member of the assembly and a relative of the *Rav h"r* Avraam. He returned to the assembly and reported his last word. This sealed their decision.

This *sinyor* courier and relative went to his home as soon as the final decision was taken. He fell ill and died within eight days, in fulfillment of the words of the *si. rav*, who had said, "With God's help, may you never come back here again."

After a short while two to three of his colleagues started to depart from this world. When the rest witnessed this sad miracle, they started to get alarmed, sending feelers to the *si. rav* to learn if he could see them and grant them his forgiveness. The *Rav h"r* Avraam, the humble man that he was, didn't turn anyone down. One by one, the *talmide hahamim* as well as the influential people, everyone started to parade before him and ask for his forgiveness. He forgave them all, adding, "I forgive you; may heaven, too, grant you forgiveness."

However, this incident did leave a bad taste in every mouth.

After the death of the *Rav h"r* Avraam, his son *h"r* Shemuel examined all the papers written in his handwriting that his father had left behind. He found a document written before his death that was a very precisely drafted balance sheet, going back to the time he was manager and treasurer of the Fund for Orphans and Widows. He had five hundred copies of this document printed and distributed among the people.

When they saw this balance sheet, everyone was amazed and surprised. The most surprising one was the case of a widow who had given him one hundred *grushes* **[79a]** to manage. This widow gave him her name and her husband's name. Thirty years later, these one hundred *grushes* became six hundred, but as this widow had no children, there was no one to claim the money. One day, two litigants came to him and mentioned the family name of her husband, who had a "legal case" against him. When the *haham* heard the family name of the husband of the widow who had given him the one hundred *grushes*, he said to this person, "Send me this person you have mentioned because I have some money to give him." He immediately went and informed that person, from whom he asked, "If you give me 25 percent, I can show you a source where you can get some money." The two made an [oral] deal among themselves.[154] He immediately took him to the *Rav h"r* Avraam, who cross-examined him and ascertained that he was indeed the son of that man who [presumably] had died without sons. He ordered his scribe to draft a receipt so that he could have his money. And this is what happened. He also explained to him what the one hundred *grushes* had become and gave him the money in a pouch.

When they went out in the street, the informer requested his 25 percent. They started an argument because he now reneged on his promise.

Just as he was stepping out, the beadle of the *si. haham* saw them arguing; he went back and informed the *si. haham* about what was going on in the street. He immediately called them in and said to the heir that [you] should not give him anything *kon behoth*.[155]

A similar incident happened when, forty years ago, a woman had deposited a sum of money with the *si. haham*, but until that balance sheet was published, nobody knew to whom these funds belonged.

154. The word *oral* has been added here for clarity by the editors in anticipation of the ending to this story. When the heir in question reneges on his promise, both litigants appear before the rabbi, who declares: "No undocumented claim should be paid simply based on *kon behoth* [weeping]."

155. See *behoth* in glossary. According to rabbinical law, undocumented claims based on oral agreements and backed by shouting could not be honored.

Even though town criers made an announcement in all the synagogues and the *Talmud Tora*, no heir was found. In the absence of any heir the influential people of the community decided to use this money to print the second volume of the book entitled *'al a-kesef*.

That is when the influential people of the community started to recite confessionary prayers to atone for the scandal they had caused the *si. haham*: they visited his tombstone and asked for **[79b]** his forgiveness.

When *h"r* Shemuelachi [Arditi, 1811–87] found himself as the sole *rav* of the community, he started ordering the notables of the city to apprise him of all occurrences. As the notables resented this move, a conflict started among them. At that time the notables wanted to requisition a few stores located in the Women's Market, which formerly belonged to a woman who had donated them as an endowment to the *yeshiva* at the Gate of the *Talmud Tora* of her time. On weekdays, morning prayers took place in this *Talmud Tora*. At the conclusion of this service they would go up to this *yeshiva* to listen to an exposition dealing with the *asara batlanim*.[156] But lately, morning services in this *Talmud Tora* had been discontinued; the rabbi who presented the expositions had died, and the academy remained idle. Therefore, this endowment belonged to the community, and the stores should have reverted to the community. Yet because the *Rav h"r* Shemuelachi was the manager of one of the descendants of the rabbi of said academy, called Nissim, he was opposed to this request. Instead, he sent his steward with the wife of this descendant to make a formal deposition to the government stating that this woman is the granddaughter of the woman who formerly owned these stores. She was the one who gave it as a gift to her husband with a formal deposition, now his property under the name of "the Nissim Foundation."

As this transaction was deemed as a secret trick by the *rav*, they tried to remove him from his position. They sent a message to the Chief Rabbinate in Constantinople. The *rav*, too, sent a message to the Chief Rabbinate explaining the situation from his angle. In response the *rav* from Constantinople sent a letter to the council urging them not to pursue this matter.

156. See glossary, *batlan*.

In fact, the Notables, too, gave up their request but continued to worry about him until the day he died.

Following the death of the *Rav h"r* Mair Nahmias, they managed to give this position to *h"r* Yakovachi [ben Hanania] Kovo [1827–1907],[157] an intelligent man who was also familiar with business life, thanks to which he succeeded in gaining the goodwill of all the members of the council. His title was that of *kaymakam* and honorary president of the council. To this day he has been managing all Jewish matters in our city.

Chapter 41

[80a] *The Fire of 1890*

On August 29, 1890, while they were distilling *raki* in a *raki* store, the roof of the store caught fire, which soon engulfed the adjacent buildings, and because of the strong winds, it spread to the entire neighborhood. The huge flames were almost flying from neighborhood to neighborhood. The firemen were unable to control it because the flames were coming from all sides. Its area extended from the *Placeta* [Small Bazar] to the *Ahche Medjid* and from *Ahche Medjid* to the seashore, consuming numerous mansions and recently built brick buildings. Whatever belongings poor people managed to salvage to a safer place, the flames would soon arrive and consume everything there, too. Almost two thousand poor families were left destitute on the heels of this fire, the likes of which never happened before in our city. There were also two people who fell victim to this fire, an old man and a young man. As for the houses of the poor, none of them was insured.

But recently built houses whose owners were well-to-do had insurance both on the building and the furniture. The entire insurance bill amounted to 125,000 *liras*. Therefore, the insurance companies sent their agents and compensated everyone to the last penny.

However, some insurance agents made a fortune from customers

157. Yakovachi Kovo was the son of R. Hanania Kovo, Asher Kovo's brother, and was also Asher Kovo's son-in-law. Founder of *Hevrat Es Hayyim* [1874], he was the last Salonican-born chief rabbi of the city.

eager to be immediately compensated in return for a percentage. Some preferred to be paid in napoleons[158] instead of English pounds sterling. After a short while, when the insurance companies learned about these schemes, they replaced these agents with more trustworthy ones. Also, after this fire no one built a house without first buying an insurance policy. As of this writing today, it has been three years since this fire, and only 20 percent reconstruction has taken place, mostly full-brick or half-brick buildings.

[80b] The municipality drew very beautiful maps of the new buildings, shown in blocks with wide streets. The widest street is approximately twenty *pikos* wide stretching from the pier to the Albanian Oven, with a very sturdy sewer in the middle going to the sea. On both sides they also built a footpath two meters wide with large stones, which is about to be finished. These same stones are being used to pave the streets. On both sides they planted saplings on the edges that within five to six years will transform this street into a splendid boulevard that people will use for their walks. There are also streets that are sixteen *pikos* wide, while the narrower ones are twelve *pikos* wide. In twenty to twenty-five years, when this place is totally rebuilt, the entire burnt area will turn into a showcase for the city.

But for the time being, the price of plots has fallen down to half of their former value, as the middle class is now short on capital, and needless to say that it is worse for the poor people. Rents, too, have come down by 20 to 25 percent of their former levels.

Chapter 42

[81a] *The Revolt of Kasandra [Cassandra]*

I forgot to tell the story of the event at the fort of Kasandra,[159] a revolt that occurred when I was very young, barely eight years old when the

158. Gold coins.

159. The Revolt of Cassandra refers to an episode in the Greek War of Independence that took place in Cassandra, one of the peninsulas near Salonica. During the revolt, 430 Greek Orthodox Christians resisted 3,000 Ottoman soldiers under the

Greeks of Kasandra rebelled. At that time, they had no *nizam* soldiers [reformed army]. Only when war was imminent, they sent notices throughout the land, calling on men to come and defend the motherland. Immediately, the top janissary posted scribes in every main building with a drum accompanied by clarinets and a flag. Right away, the Turks of every village rushed to the buildings, armed to the teeth with pistols, *yatagans* (curved knives), spades, and carbines to register. They also appointed corporals, captains, and majors over them. As soon as a battalion was formed, they were immediately issued ammunition and would leave with great joy in anticipation of their return, loaded with objects and money from the looting. In the aftermath of their departure for Kasandra, they engaged in all sorts of vandalism: those who brought back young men and women as slaves had the young men circumcised and taught them to play various musical instruments, while they took the young women as wives.

Many times, I have had some of these slaves by my side playing music in Abdur Rahman *Bey*'s mansions and farms, who inherited them from his father, Ahmet Bey, former army chief in Kasandra.

It was during this war that the fort had been built in front of the Jewish cemetery, as it came rather easy to the builders to remove all the tombstones from the graves that belonged to the very first Jews who arrived from Spain. These tombstones were located near the fort they were building, which explains why the date of the first sages **[81b]** who arrived and settled in Salonica is still unknown. As if it wasn't enough for them to steal the tombstones from the graves, every day some Jews had to do hard labor by carrying earth in sacks. For eight days all the markets were closed because the fort had to be built in a hurry. With no exception, old or young, grown-ups or children, even rabbis, everyone had to come and carry earth.

Then they drafted the *toran* [unidentified word] *h"r* Shelomo Mordoh [c. 1760–c. 1850], may he rest in peace. I was told that this gentleman was very well versed in astronomy. One night, he woke up Ahmet *Bey* and told him that this was the most propitious time to

---

command of Mehmed Emin *Pasha* of Salonica. The resistance was broken, and numerous Greek Orthodox Christians were killed, taken prisoner, or enslaved.

defeat the enemy. That is how they sounded the trumpets; they all got up like lions and carried out a very bloody killing. Of those who remained, some resisted and perished; others were taken as slaves. This was the battle that concluded the war. However, the leaders never forgot *Si. h"r* Shelomo; they gave him many gifts because they respected him as a holy man. Every year, they would buy a calendar in Turkish from him. Those who had a correspondence with them were prominent people, three of them Greeks who were killed by the sword: the archdeacon, *Si.* Menekshe[160] and *Si.* Polardos. Since then, the Greeks have lived in fear.

[Epilogue][161]

[82a] Following my misfortune of April 26, 1874, those who were jealous of me, seeing how successful I was in my business, tried to seek revenge. But Providence consistently foiled their plans. As of my writing today in 1902, twenty-eight years later, I am proud of all my accomplishments. I dedicated myself to my printing business, working very hard; and thanks to the continuous help I got from the philanthropist, *cavaliere* Moizé Alatini, may he rest in paradise, and the sound advice of the *Rav h"r* Avraam Gatenyo, I always advanced in my business.

During these twenty-eight years I managed to marry off nine daughters and three sons. I expanded my printing press, and I also built my house without asking anyone's help, but with just the rewards of my labor. To those who sought my downfall, I say, "They collapse and lie fallen, but we rally and gather strength" (Psalms 20:9).

During these twenty-eight years, my body endured various diseases from which I emerged in good health, as I always obeyed God's will.

By now, some of my persecutors have passed away. I have already forgiven them, but they remain few in number. As for the others, whenever they see me, they do greet me albeit begrudgingly, as they are still

160. Christos Menexes was a Salonican notable and a member of the Greek revolutionary organization, the Society of Friends.

161. This title does not exist in the *soletreo* text but is found in an imprecise transliteration/translation of the original made by Sa'adi's grandson, Leon David Levy.

waiting for my demise. And when one of them dies, those who survive are crippled with fear, as the number of these hate-mongers keeps diminishing.[162]

By now, some of my persecutors have passed away. I have already forgiven them, but they remain few in number. As for the others, whenever they see me, they do greet me albeit begrudgingly, as they are still waiting for my demise. And when one of them dies, those who survive are crippled with fear, as the number of these hate-mongers keeps diminishing.

[93b] The song I wrote in the *Adjem Makam*
welcoming Sultan Abdul Medjid
to Salonica on Wednesday July 27, 1859
acrostic [in the Hebrew]: Sultan Abdul Medjid[163]

The eternal King, who is a merciful father, A.[164] is king
Who brought us to the proper time and occasion, A. is king
To glimpse the face of the invited king, long live the king
Our Sovereign, our Master our lord, the king
The victorious Sultan, Abdul Medjid *Hân*. long live the king,
amen

O blessed King, creator of man, A. is king
Who chose for himself a ruler over man, long live the king
He granted honor to mortal man, long live the king
Our Sovereign, our Master our lord, the king
The victorious Sultan, Abdul Medjid *Hân*. long live the king,
amen

162. The following paragraph in a different handwriting is a repetition.
163. This and the following poem, written in Hebrew, were appended to Sa'adi's memoir. They do not appear in the romanized transcription of his memoir, which refers only to Sa'adi's Ladino-language text.
164. "A." is traditionally used for *Adonay*, "my Lord," or "God" for fear of uttering the ineffable name in vain.

He is a unique king, girded with a sword on his right, — long live the king
Which his creator granted him, — long live the king
In whom his entire population put their trust, — long live the king
Our Sovereign, our Master — our lord, the king
The victorious Sultan, Abdul Medjid *Hân*. — long live the king,
amen

He is an accomplished king, the delight of our heart, — long live the king
Good and beneficent, the light of our eyes, — long live the king
The crown and joy of our glory, — long live the king
Our Sovereign, our Master — our lord, the king
The victorious Sultan, Abdul Medjid *Hân*. — long live the king,
amen

He is a king with a reliable and fearless heart, — long live the king
Endowed with a mighty arm, — long live the king
His immense glory radiates like the sun, — long live the king
Our Sovereign, our Master — our lord, the king
The victorious Sultan, Abdul Medjid *Hân*. — long live the king,
amen

[94a]

He is a king who rules over a vast kingdom, — long live the king
Highly praised, omnipotent indeed, — long live the king
Whose exalted kingdom grows steadily, — long live the king
Our Sovereign, our Master — our lord, the king
The victorious Sultan, Abdul Medjid *Hân*. — long live the king,
amen

He is a an upright king like no other, — long live the king
He has a pure heart, merciful and compassionate, — long live the king
Dearly honored, for he is exceptional, — long live the king
Our Sovereign, our Master — our lord, the king
The victorious Sultan, Abdul Medjid *Hân*. — long live the king,
amen

You are a great king, welcome in God's Name, — long live the king
To a community called the people of God, — long live the king
As we walk in God's path, — long live the king

Our Sovereign, our Master | our lord, the king
The victorious Sultan, Abdul Medjid *Hân.* | long live the king,
amen

O king, this day is a day of jubilation, | long live the king
It celebrates the power of your reign, | long live the king
To render to you honor and greatness, | long live the king
Our Sovereign, our Master | our lord, the king
The victorious Sultan, Abdul Medjid *Hân.* | long live the king,
amen

He is a king, who seeks welfare for all his people, | long live the king
With no hesitation let us trust him, | long live the king
With one voice let us welcome him, | long live the king
Our Sovereign, our Master | our lord, the king
The victorious Sultan, Abdul Medjid *Hân.* | long live the king,
amen

He is a great king, master of his throne, | long live the king
With his stature praised among royalty, | long live the king
His throne will endure for his people, | long live the king
Our Sovereign, our Master | our lord, the king
The victorious Sultan, Abdul Medjid *Hân.* | long live the king,
amen

Our king, shall be mighty forever, | long live the king
Always prospering in his ways, | long live the king
Blessed by the eternally Present, | long live the king
Our Sovereign, our Master | our lord, the king
The victorious Sultan, Abdul Medjid *Hân.* | long live the king,
amen

[94b/95b]

Our king is blessed by his bounties, | long live the king
May the star of his fortune shine over him, | long live the king
May his days of rule be lengthened, | long live the king
Our Sovereign, our Master | our lord, the king
The victorious Sultan, Abdul Medjid *Hân.* | long live the king,
amen

acrostic [in the Hebrew]: Sa'adi

Our king relies on God's will, long live the king
May the angel Michael walk with him, long live the king
All Israel wishes him well. long live the king
Our Sovereign, our Master our lord, the king
The victorious Sultan, Abdul Medjid *Hân*. long live the king,
amen

[Makam] *Hüzzam* acrostic [in Hebrew]: Sa'adi a-Levi *Hazak*

My Rock and my fortress, ruler of land and sea,
You appointed a sovereign king over mankind,
The star of his fortune shines like the light of the sun,
His hand is outstretched like a bronze bow.
Long live our Sovereign, our Master.

Show us, O King, a miracle for good,
God has freely bestowed on us a great kindness.
We found favor in his eyes, a tremendous love,
May we enjoy these to the end as in the beginning.
Long live our Sovereign, our Master.

He immediately sought to distribute charity,
From his treasury, he gave directly a large sum.
Willingly, the king started to distribute funds,
To youngsters singing a new song.
Long live our Sovereign, our Master.

On Wednesday, the king and his ministers arrived,
On Tammuz 25, 5619 [July 27, 1859].
Young and old, we all rejoiced,
Day and night, there were three days of festivities.
Long live our Sovereign, our Master.

He who grants kings lasting victory,
Bestow upon him a crown of grace and charm,
To hear our prayer and abide with us.
May his kingdom be an inheritance for him and his sons.
Long live our Sovereign, our Master.

[95a/95a]

May he be strong and blessed, may his success endure,
With long days and goodness over his kingdom,
To content well with us, a people dear to him,
That we may bless him morning and evening.
Long live our Sovereign, our Master.

[96a] This poem was composed by *Sinyor* Sa'adi a-Levi
For the day when his majesty Abdul Medjid Han
Left Salonica for Constantinople
On Saturday 28 Tammuz 5619 (July 30, 1859)
In the *Rast Makam*

1. Praise God, O chosen people,
the good and perfect king has come.
He is such a wise and most accomplished man,
He left his home by God's command.
Live, long live the king, he is welcome.

2. *Be-siman tov*, may his coming be for good,
May this be a lasting joy for us.
During his happy days we have satisfaction,
For the sake of the king's *zehuth* who is worthy of it. *Live, long live*

3. *Grand Sinyor* he is called and that is his name,
Among royalty great is his fame.
He greatly loves his citizens,
With a good heart and with deep feelings. *Live, long live*

4. On Wednesday, at two o'clock [9 a.m.],
Turks, Christians, and all the Jews,
We all felt joy and happiness.
We sang with our voices and loudly. *Live, long live*

5. *Allah* is great, He made this king magnificent,
Never his equal existed, he is unparalleled.
Let us in advance pray to God,
May our king live, he was chosen by God. *Live, long live*

6. May he have a long life, favored by God,
With acts of goodness to render us happy.
May his power overwhelm his enemies,
May he be strong with his sword. *Live, long live*

7. Great was our luck, we, his people,
To live on the land of this kingdom.
Surely, holy God made him beloved,
We see how well he rules over us. *Live, long live*

8. July was the month when our king arrived,
All Turkish citizens declared it a festive day.
May our blessing rise continually,
Almighty God on high is beloved to us. *Live, long live*

9. May we have prosperity during his good days,
And may his coffers always be filled.
May he live one hundred years, no less,
This is our universal wish. *Live, long live*

10. Let us invoke our great and mighty God,
That this kingdom always know peace.
Long live our king, always courageous,
With success throughout the world. *Live, long live*

11. Together, let us all pay homage to our king,
With deep pleasure and much enjoyment.
Our king is fair in every respect,
His acts of loving-kindness are numerous. *Live, long live*

12. The Ottoman kings have always been fair,
They have excelled by ruling with mercy.
Surely, this was a special favor from heaven,
This merit brought them steady victory. *Live, long live*

[96b]

13. Brethren, let us offer our prayers,
All the Religious Communities, bless him.
For the sake of our king's welfare,
Receive, God almighty, our good intentions. *Live, long live*

14. Our fame grew as our king arrived,
He is handsome to behold, tall as a cedar.
Yesterday the entire population was unanimous,
Everyone who saw him recited a blessing. *Live, long live*

15. Sultan *Abdul Medjid* is a handsome king,
He is worthy to rule, for he is most merciful.
May he always be content, cheerful and joyous,
With good luck accompanying him everywhere.
Long live the king, may he always be welcome,
May he return safely with his retinue. *Live, long live*

16. This glorious king left behind sweet memories,
Abdul is his name, *Medjid*, the most fortunate.
Let us invoke God, the most powerful,
To guide this monarch speedily to his beloved home. *Live, long live*

Sa'adi

[My Last Request][165]

My last request from my children is to print this story as soon as possible and by all means, either in our printing press or in Vienna, or in Belgrade, so that not to transgress my request. After you have improved on some sentences and taken care of some difficult words in Turkish and Hebrew, be certain to keep a copy in book form. After incorporating the oath of *Purim*, to this story, be sure to print everything in the *Rashi* script. Following these, add also all the poems without exception that you will find in the small sack. Thus you will be blessed and enjoy prosperity and bliss in everything, Amen. Sa'adi a-Levi.

165. This title does not exist in the *soletreo* text but is found in the transliterated text produced by Sa'adi's grandson, Leon David Levy. The paragraph itself constitutes a loose fragment found between pp. 27b and 28a in the original manuscript.

Prefasyon

El eskopo de dita estorya es por dar a saver a los *doroth* vinideros komodo trokan los tyempos, de dyentro de medyo sekolo ke non asemeja de el todo a los uzos de agora, tanto en los ombres komo en las mujeres, tanto en las vistimyentas komo en los mobles de kaza, *afillú* las moradas mizmo. Non kere dicho en el komer i el bever, masimame[nte] los mansevos ilas mosas ke son unas kozas muy kuryozas. El kese akodra de akel tyempo, a ver lo de el tyempo preze[n]te, ande mas el komportamyento delos ombres i mujeres, ijos i ijas, parese vinir de un mundo vyejo a un mundo otro. I los mansevos ke meldaran dita estorya, unos se van a burlar, i otros se van a riir, i otros se les va a dezazer el korason en dizyendo, este modo sufrian muestros padres en los tyempos antiguos, a kavza dela inyoransa i el fanatizmo komo lo veran adelantre de dyentro dela estorya.

En tanto, rogo alos ke meldaran dita estorya ke non me akulpen ke si veran algunas kozas ke devian eskrivirsen despues i se eskrivyeron de antes, ilo de antes ke se keria eskrito despues, syendo ke non me akodro las datas prechizas. En mezmo tyempo, syendo ke les kyije dar a saver los fatos, i non me okupi delas datas. I por la verdad es ke en los tyempos antiguos non eskrivian muestros padres, de mezmo ke ni yo eskrivi los nasimyentos demis ijos. Non es por mi solo ke lo digo, si non ke el 99 por syen delos Djidyos eran ansi. I yo vo a avlar loke vide kon mi ojo solamente, i loke oyi kon mi oyido, i algunas kozas ke sinti de djente verdadera. Dita estorya es empesada a eskrivir del 24 Iyyar 5641 [23 May 1881] i endelantre, i es la pura verdad.

Sa'adi a-Levi

Kapitolo 1

Estatistika

[1a] Yo, el soto eskrito, so vinido de un syerto Sinyor Besalel a-Levi Ashkenazi en el anyo de 5580 [1820] *b'a"'a,* [bendicho para syempre]. Era un mansevo vistido al uzo Eshkenazi. El era savyo ke en vinyendo en Salonik lo risivyeron komo un *shaliah,* ma el non era menesterozo, ni vino por *shelihuth.* Estonses uzavan a risivir a los forestos *ahnasath orhim.* I le dyeron por *ba'al a-bayith* en kaza del si. *Rav* Modiano, *n"'E,* [su repozo en Gan 'Eden]. En los dias ke estuvo en dita kaza, konversando kon el si. *rav,* le demando a ke okazyon vino a Salonik. El le respondyo ke non vino por *shelihuth* natural, syendo ke iva bushkando lugar a estabilirse, syendo konosia a el ofisyo de estamparia, i era artizano. El si. *rav,* vyendo el ermozo mansevo, vino en su ayuda para avrir una estamparia i estampo munchos livros delos savyos de aki; entre los kualos se topa en mi poder el livro estampado de su propya mano en anyo 5512 [1752] ke se yama *Meoré Or.* El si. *rav* lo izo kazar en muestra sivdad, i tuvo dos ijos, el uno se yamava Avraam, el otro Yeuda a-Levi Ashkenazi. El ijo Avraam muryo sin deshar ijos. Mi sinyor papu Yeuda bivyo *chirka* 90 anyos, kelo alkansi a konoser yo, syendo muryo despues dela muerte de mi padre ke no alkanso ala mitad de su vida. Mi sinyor papu tuvo dos ijos, el grande se yamava Sa'adi, el kual muryo ala mitad de sus dias i sin deshar ijos, i eredo la estamparia mi padre. Mi padre muryo tambyen a la edad de 36 a 37 anyos, deshando su mujer kon 4 ijas, i a mi a la edad de 5 a 6 anyos. Mi padre alkanso a kazar una ija, i en este anyo muryo en deshando ami sinyora madre prenyada de 5 mezes. I a su tyempo paryo un ijo ke lo yamo *Chelebon* el kual tuvo una hazinura de mal de pyedra. Kijendo azerle la operasyon, el muryo a los tres dias ala edad de 18 anyos. Syendo la sensya de la medikeria estonses non estava avansada, i non avia munchos medikos estudyados en muest[r]a sivdad, solamente un syerto sinyor Parsakaki. El le izo la operasyon a su pareser, le kavzo la muerte.

Yo yevo el nombre de el ermano de mi padre, syendo avia murido mi sinyor tio ala landre de [5]574 [1814], i me desho de eredad un aniyo de su nombre Sa'adi a-Levi ke es i mi nombre mezmo. Mi sinyora madre me lo metyo en el dedo ala edad de kinze anyos, i ke lo yevi syempre sin kitarlo de el dedo chiko asta el dia el este ke eskrivo dita esta estorya. Tambyen yo lo vo a deshar de eredad despues de mi **[1b]** a uno delos ijos ke alevantaran el nombre mio, syendo en muestra *mishpaha* non uzamos a alevantar el nombre en vida de el otro.

Kapitolo 2

La Kavza dela Muerte demi Padre

Mi padre era un ombre relidjyozo, i syendo ke en akel tyempo todos los Djidios uzavan a mantener las reglas dela relidjyon, por egzemplo nochadas de meldados de noche de *Shavu'oth*, i nochadas de *Selihoth, Osha'na Rabba, Shevi'i shel Pesah.*

Una noche de *Shavu'oth,* despues de komer, se fue al meldado komo uzo de todos los Djidyos de akel tyempo, kenon kedava ningun ombre en kaza, i todos se ivan alas *keilloth.* I syendo la nochada chika, ke amanesia alas sesh i medya, algunos tornavan en kaza a komer la enkyusa i el arros kon leche, i se echavan a durmir, ise alevantavan a las 6 o 7, [1 or 2 PM], de el dia. Otros se ivan a pasear por las guertas, i el puevlo de tersya klasa inchian un kanistro de komanya, komo enkyusa, *sutlach, raki* i guevos enhaminados ise ivan kon sus famiyas en alguna guerta despues dela sivdad, ise emborrachavan i kedavan durmidos en las yervas, i lo mas de eyos se azian hazinos.

Mi sinyor padre, despues de la orasyon, se fue para la oria de la mar kon uno de sus empyegados dela estamparia por tomar [aver] fresko. Syendo estonses non avia ni vapores, ni postas, las kartas ke mandavan de el ajeno las traian los kapitanes i las davan a kyen era el dirito.

[2a] Mi sinyor padre, vyendo vinir un *kaik* de Esmirni, syendo el echo de la estamparia era lo mas delivros delos savyos de Esmirni, se ayego para la oria de la mar i vido en la kapa de el *kaik* espandido kartas delos negosyantes. Entre eyas, una karta al adreso de el sinyor *Rav* Gatenyo de estonses ke el era *maggi'a* i korespondyente delos savyos de Esmirni. Mi sinyor padre, pensando ke non le ivan a yevar la {la} karta asu mano, la tomo para mandarsela kon su empyegado, ke podia ser eskrivia en la karta alguna koza por su entereso por algun livro. Le paresyo mas, porke non penára el *haham* kyen le avriera la karta, el se la dyo a un Grego kese la despegara; se avrio la karta, se la mando kon su empyegado. Este empyegado, pasando por su kaza, se entro adyentro i izo la *se'uda.* Komo de uzo, le tomo el esfuenyo, se echo a durmir asta la tadre. En alevantandose, non se akodro dela karta ke yevava en su aldikera. Ala noche sigunda, dito empyegado se fue a otro meldado. Ala manyana, izo komo el primer dia, komyo ise echo a durmir fina la tadre. Al dia despues de *Shavu'oth,* se vino a la estamparia por meterse ala ovra. Mi padre le pregunto sila karta fue yevada asu patron. El empyegado se dyo la mano en la kara dizyendole ke se olvido de todo punto. Mi padre le disho al empyegado ke se la yevara apunto i ke lo eskuzara en dizyendole, esto ke la topa avyerta es por la razon ke fue de *Shavu'oth* kela risivyo, i la izo despegar por ke non tuvyera pena para ke sela avrieran.

Myentres ke el empyegado fue a yevar la karta al *haham,* mi padre se asento a dezayunar kon un pedaso de enkyusa sovrado de *Shavu'oth,* i unos kuantos biskochos estupandos, i un pedaso de kezo fresko, i una partida de serezas. En eskapando de dezayunar, torno el empyegado de ande el si. *haham,* el kual non le disho todo lo ke le enkomendo mi padre por non toparse akulpado. El sinyor *haham* le demando, "de ande tomates esta karta"? El le respondyo ke, "me la dyo el si. maestro *H[am]* Besalel tal akual komo la ve". **[2b]** En su repuesta del sinyor *haham* le mando adizir kon el empyegado ke el paso la *lavá* de *ribbi* Yeuda Hasid. Mi sinyor padre, syendo muncho relidjyozo, sintyendo el nombre de *ribbi* Yeuda Hasid, le paresyo ke este *ribbi* Yeuda Hasid era el *malah a-maveth,* i ke vinia kon la espada desvaynada en su mano para matarlo. De el espanto, estando akavado de komer, se le izo un afíto, i se echo ala kama kon un friyo fuerte, i ke en tyempo de 9 dias, a la noche de 18 Sivan el eskapo de bivir, el muryo en 18 ~~Sivan~~ de 5586 [23 June 1826].

Ah, povre padre! Pedrites la flor dela vida por un espanto de una dicha de un ombre ke izo un livro de todo "non se puede": non se puede kazar Yisrael kon Kohen; non se puede deshar una gaina ke kanta komo el gayo biva, ke la degoye; non se puede de kazar un mansevo ke tyene el nombre desu esfuegro; i dos {i} kosfue[g]ros de un nombre non se puede konsograr; non se puede degoyar pato en *teveth* i *shevat, echetra, echetra, echetra.*

Ma esta enkomendansa les fue buena para los *shohatim,* syendo ke el ke degoya pato es menester ke koma karne de el pato mezmo ke degoyo a esta okazyon. Syendo los patos son godros en este tyempo, eyos se toman la kavesa kon la papada i el kueyo; ke este uzo non se baldo asta este tyempo ke eskrivo, ke por ke alos *shohatim* les es agradavle la sena.

Dunke—ke por unos espantos ke metyeron los vyejos en algunas kozas tan vanas— murian la djente de el espanto de el fanatizmo, komo vos kontare mas adelantre munchas kavzas de semejantes fatos.

Kapitolo 3

La Estatistika i la Muerte de mi Sinyora Madre

[3a] La *mishpaha* de mi sinyora madre, me kontava eya, ke vinia de un sinyor Morpurgo vinido de Italya, i se estabilio en Saloniko. El tuvo una ija, i la kazo kon un syerto si. Avraam Kovo, el kual tuvo ijas, i se le muryeron, i kedo mi madre sola de este ombre. Le metyo por nombre Djantil, ma a kavza de las ijas ke se le muryeron, i kedo regalada, le trokaron el nombre ila yamaron Merkada. Eya konosia el ofisyo de shastreria de kamizas ala franka, eredado de su madre, i la madre de su sinyora vava, syendo este ofisyo lo trusho de Italya. Si komo estonses non avia el artifisyo de makinas de kuzir, era todo el travajo ala mano. Todos los konsolatos de Salonik, i los altos personajes, i todos los negosyantes vistian sus kamizas de el travajo de mano de mi sinyora madre. Si komo ami me desho chiko de 5 a 6 anyos, la estamparia kedo en mano delos mosos, non abastesia para mantener a sinko ijos de la ganansya de la estamparia. Fue kon lazerya de sus manos a mantenermos sesh almas. Eya reusho a kazar tres ijas, ma por desgrasya, yo non tuve la ventura de kazarme en tyempo de mi madre.

Estonses era ke los grandes negosyantes i konsolos la mandavan a tomar kon sus *kavazes*. I syendo el kuartyer franko era vazio de todos estos magazenes ke se topan oy, era asolapado, i tenian en sus *konakes* unos *kelavim* muy fuertes por espanto de mal azedores. Tanto eran fuertes los *kelavim* komo unos leones ke el dia eran enserrados i atados kon kadena estas fuertes bestyas. Un dia ke la mando ayamar la Madama de Musyu Rika—este ombre era el venerable delos Masones—un perro fuerte de esta kaza ainda no estava enserrado, estava en el kortijo dezatado. En entrando de la puerta kon el *kavaz*, sintyendo—ala vista de este perro, mi sinyora madre—i el grito, **[3b]** tuvo un espanto fuerte i kovro unos frios dekuartanas ke los *kulaneo* munchos mezes. Estonses, los medikos le ambezaron ke bevyera vino azarado. Este vino azarado era de un vino vyejo, i echado adyentro una kuantita de limadura de fyero, i lo metian al sol un{a}[os] kuant{a}[os] dias, i de este vino iva bevyendo 3 kopos el dia, kuarenta dias en *sira*. En eskapando esta melizina, sele konkrio la hazinura de tropika. Ala fin, i eya muryo de esta hazinura en el 15 Ellul de 5597 [15 September 1837]. Estonses kedi yo i mi ermaniko ala soledad.

Kapitolo 4

El Espanto de el Fanatizmo

De mi chikes, me akodro de los *rabbanim* ke muryeron—de estonses fina este tyempo—la muerte de el *Rav* Romano, ז"ל, 5588 [1827][1]. Estonses, metyeron por *rabbanim* los *Shiv'a Tove a-'Ir* al *Rav, h"r* Nehama, al *Rav, h"r*Yaakov Menashe, i al grande delos *shohatim, h"r* Moshe Beraha. Ala muerte de estos 3, metyeron otros tres *rabbanim, h"r* Avraam Soriano, *h"r* Shaul Molho 5595 [1835], *h"r* Behor Matalon. Ala muerte de estos tres, metyeron a *h"r* Hanania Saporta 5614 [1854], al *Rav, h"r* Asher Kovo. Ala muerte de estos 2, metyeron al *Rav, h"r* Avraam Gatenyo 5636 [1876], *h"r* Mair Nahmias, *h"r* Shemuel Arditi. Ala muerte de estos tres, metyeron por *kaymakam* al *Rav, h"r* Yakovachi Kovo, però el mas poderozo i respektado de estos *rabbanim* ke kontimos fue el *Rav, h"r* Shaul Molho, el kual dyo un espanto entre el puevlo ke al ke maldizia el, le kavzava la muerte. Ande es ke tuvo una shans, antes de entrar por *rav* tuvo unas kombinasyones i kavzos de muerte ke fueron por la maldisyon suya. **[4a]** En syendo dainda un *shohet*, el puevlo de sigunda i tersya klase lo adoravan komo si fuera uno de los *neviim*.

Primer kavzo ke dyo el espanto en djeneral fue el pleyto de los *hahamim* kontra los *gevirim* i el *Rav* Nehama, syendo el era *rav a-Kolel*. En este tyempo, se metyeron de akodro el *rav* kon los *gevirin* de pujar una *para* en la kuarta de vino de el presyo ke era taksado de antes.

H"r Shaul enflamo a todos los *hahamim* i una partida del puevlo. Eyos mandaron un mesajero, un barragan, *h"r* Yaakov Djenyo, ake se retiraran de la idea de pujar la *para* de la gabela en una kuarta de vino. La komunita i el *Rav* Nehama sostuvyeron sus kaprichos, i non ovedesyeron. Tórna, mandaron a amanazarlos kon palavras fuertes ala komunita i sus repuesta. Los *gevirin* i el *rav* mandaron a aprezar a *h"r* Yaakov Djenyo, i le izyeron meter kadenas ensima de el.

Estonses, se ensanyaron *h"r* Shaul i sus kolegas, kitaron pregon por *charshis* i plasas kon la palavra de uzo, *mi le-a-Shem, elay,!!!* [ken por a-Shem, a mi, (Exodus 32:26)]. El puevlo serraron sus butikas i vinyeron al *talmud tora a-gadol*, los *hahamim* avrieron el *ehal a-kodesh*, ensendyeron una kuantita de kandelas, i trusheron tanyedores de *shofar*, i *enheremaron* kon el *herem* de *kol bo*.

Los *gevirim* se ensenyaron i fueron ande el Governador i le dyeron denota ake izyera *surgun* a 3 o 4 *hahamim*, a *h"r* Shaul primero, i 3 de sus kolegas. En akel tyempo, se topavan en Salonik el rikisimo bankyer de Kostan, *Chilibi* Yeoshua Adjiman, el kual tenia sempatia kon *h"r* Shaul a kavza ke tuvo en su kaza al ijo, *h"r* Behor Molho, en Estambol. El akonsejo al Pasha i alos *gevirin*, dizyendoles ke, "si en kavzo vash a ensistir en guestras ideas de el *surgunluk*, yo levo a dizir al Pasha ke kale ke mande a 3 de los *gevirin* kon los *hahamim* a Kostan **[4b]** para ke ai se djuzgen i miren kyen tyene la razon". Los *gevirin*, sindyendo esto de *Chilibi* Yeoshua, se repintyeron dela mala echa.

Estonses, fueron a demandar al Pasha el retiro dela petisyon. El les respondyo ke non podia ser, syendo ya avia dado avizo a Kostan de este echo, i ke izo a este efeto munchos gastes. Los *gevirin*, mirando ke la tenian apretada, fueron konstretos de dar una *djeza* de dozyentos mil *groshes,* i vazyaron la kasha de el *Kolel,* i tomaron a kam[b]yo de bivdas *togarmas* a 20 por syen de enteres para tomar atras la petisyon. I malgrado todo esto, vino la desgrasya dela muerte de el *Rav, h"r* Nehama ke non alkanso a gozar de el *rabbanuth* ke sálvo 31 dia.

Este fue el primer golpo de el espanto ke dyo la maldisyon deel *Haham, h"r* Shaul Molho a todo el puevlo.

Estonses, desharon la komunita la gabela de el vino para la mantenisyon delos *rabbanim* i *dayyanim, echetres.*

Estos meldadores non krean ke el *Haham, h"r* Shaul era de una talya alta i grosa. Al kontraryo, el era un puerpo muy flako i muy basho ke apenas mezurava un metro i 25 puntos, ma el grito i la severidad i el animo era de un leon de vente anyos ke entrara en *rabbanuth* ~~sin ser metido~~. El ya enfluensava sovre todo el puevlo basho, ilos djuzgava a su buen pareser, a un ke non era savyo a fondo, ma el era un ombre djusto i derecho. El tuvo 4 ijos, todos eyos *talmide hahamim,* ma el grande [de] eyos ke su nombre, *h"r* Behor Molho, tenia una otoridad superior ala del si. padre. El era alto komo un pino, de buena konstruksyon, i una vista de andjel ke le dava un ayre de respekto a todo el ke lo aserkava, i nunka de su boka kito palavra de *herem, afillú* al ke era akulpado. De este modo se gano la sempatia de todo el puevlo.

[5a] Malgrado todas estas buenas kualidades, el muryo mallogrado ala edad de 44 anyos. La kavza de su muerte fue de el espanto dela muerte de *Chilibi* Behor Karmona. El se topava esta mizma noche en la kaza de *Chilibi* Karmona a *musafir,* i kuando vinyeron los *yaveres* de Sultan Mahmud kon una eskrita en sus mano, i una *chevere* de oro kon la kuala lo aogaron en echandosela en el kueyo. Se entyende ke ala pavor de esta triste vista le entro una hazinura en el korason, i sufriyo muncho tyempo. Ala fin, esto le kavzo la muerte ke fue yorado amargamente de toda la populasyon Selanikyota.

Sigundo Akto de el Espanto de Fanatizmo

Kuando entró por *rav* en anyo 5595 [1835], estonses los ijos delos rikos salian de el *Talmud Tora* inyorantes, syendo non avia eskolas. Los padres rikos non les davan ofisyo a sus ijos. Eyos ivan de kafe en kafe, i de paseo en paseo, pasando sus tyempos, kon kelos padres les taksavan una mezada a kada ijo porke tuvyeran de *harshlik* en sus *djepes,* i non savian mas otro ke komeres i beveres, i djugos de kartas, invyerno en sus kazas, en el enverano en los paseos. Se azian *bolukes, bolukes,* i se ivan por mezadas enteras a azer *djumbushes* en las kampanyas, kualos a *Orundjik,* kualos en *Sedes.* I eyos se metian de akodro ke kada dia mandavan kon *sira* el komer i el bever, kada uno de sus kazas, i pasavan la ora. La manyana kon sus dezayuno, ila medyo dia armorzos, ila noche lo mezmo. Eyos durmia[n] el dia; alas ocho, mueve [3-4 PM] se alevantavan ise ivan a kasar. Uno de estos *pazara yiden,* vyendo kasar pasharikos ike los asavan, i se los komian, non pudo somportar de el pekado ke via el ojo. **[5b]** Se alevanto i fue se lo komuniko al *Rav, h"r* Shaul de todo loke vido. El si. *rav* supyendo todo esto, non tadro a azer la ezekusyon.

Devista, mando al *shammash* ala plasa a pregonar ke, todo *ba'al Yisrael* vinyeran al *Kal* de Sichilya *yashan* (Peshkadores), i izo ensender kandeleria en la *keilla,* i avrio *ehal a-kodesh,* i *enheremo* a todos los de esta parea kon *shofar.* Entre esta manseveria, se topava un mansevo yamado Y. F.[2] Tomando avizo de este *herem,* se fue ande el konsolo, reklamando su onor. I se fueron el konsolo i los paryentes de el mansevo ande el *Pasha* a demandar satisfaksyon. El *Vali* mando dos *kavazes* a tomarlo al *Rav, h"r* Shaul. El mando avizo alos *Shiv'a Tove a-'Ir,* i a los *gevirin* los kualos non se desharon muncho a esperar. Uno de los *gevirin* trusho un kavayo de su *ahir* byen adovado, i lo suvyeron al sinyor *rav* i todos eyos delas dos partes de el kavayo, detenyendolo al sinyor *rav,* por primera vez ke suvia a kavayo. I el puevlo, tomando avizo de esto, koryeron de vista a tomar parte en esta shena, i se akojeron *chirka* dos mil personas, i lo akompanyaron asta el *konak* de el *Vali.* El *Vali,* echando una ojada por el *shanish,* i vyendo vinir una armada de Djudyos, el *Vali* se metyo en penseryo, demando ke koza era este *yurultu,* syendo en el *konak* entero de el *Vali* non avia ni vente *kavazes.* Estonses non avia ni djandarmeria, ni polisia. El se aparo ala varanda i vido en el kortijo una suma grande de ombres, i abashando de el kavayo, un ombre dezmizeryado i enkolgandole la kapa, mas elguenga de su puerpo. I tomandolo por los lados, los grandes de la komunita, ilo suvyeron ariva. El *Pasha* salyo asu enkontro arisivirlo, lo tomo por la mano, i lo entro adyentro el salon, i lo izo asentar en una poltrona. El konsolo i todos los ke se toparon ai se alevantaron en pyes, i le izyeron una reverensya al sinyor *rav,* ke non savia una palavra en lingua turka. Izo por mano de uno dela komunita ake izyera *terdjumanlik.* Le demandaron al *Vali* ake eskopo era la yamada del sinyor *rav.* El *Vali* respondyo ke tyene *davadji* al konsolo porke *enheremo* a uno desus suditos. **[6a]** El sinyor *rav* respondyo ke el non tuvo *enheremado* a ninguno, otro ke el izo el komando de loke eskrivyo un *rav* de antes de el: kito desu pecho un livriko dizyendo ke el sinyor papu del sudéto sinyor ke dize ke yo lo *enheremi,* eskrivyo en este livriko ke, "todo elke kome ave sin degoyar kon el kuchio de el *shohet,* merese ser *enheremado".* Dunke, yo non lo ize de mi veluntad, si non ke kumpli la eskritura de el sinyor papu suyo ke se yamava *R'* Sh. P. Etonses, kedaron maraviyados todos los sintyentes. El *Vali* topo de djusto de dizirle a el sinyor Y. F. ke se alevantara, ke le bezara la mano, i ke lo perdonara. I el konsolo lo topo esto de djusto, i todos los paryentes de el sinyor Y. F. le bezaron la mano. El *Vali* tambyen le demando ke lo bindishera ael, i el sinyor *rav* le kumplyo su demanda i lo bendisho. Despues de esta shena, trusheron refreskamyentos, i le ofrieron un vazo de *vishnada.* El sinyor *rav* pensando ke era vino, disho ke el non bevia koza korolada. I le dyeron un vazo de limonada blanka. En retirandosen, los Djidyos ke esperavan abasho kon despasensya, supyendo la novidad ke el sinyor *rav* salyo libre, echaron un grito de alegria todos en una dizyendo,

"Patishaimis chok yasha, Pasha efendimis chok yasha". En suvyendolo al kavayo para tornar a kaza, se metyeron a kantar, *"yom geulla, yom geulla,"* todos en una boz. El *Vali,* sintyendo todos estos gritos de kantes, disho a sus *yaveres,* "estash mirando ke *karar* de amor tyenen por sus kapo los Djidyos"? I el *rav* e[n]tro a su kaza kon los akompanyadores.

Malgrado toda esta shena, ke el sinyor Y. P. non bivyo mas de otro un mes, esto fue el sigundo kolpo ke dyo el espanto a todo el mundo en djeneral.

Kapitolo 5

Kolpo Tersyo

[6b] Asta el anyo 5605 [1845], la muerte de las rezin kazadas Djudias era konsideravle ke murian de hazinura de puntada i de tikia. Los sinyores *hahamim* grandes, *h"r* Avraam Gatenyo, i *h"r* David Yosef, *h"r* Shelomo Pipano tomaron a ezaminar esta kavza de ande provenia. Eyos se adjuntavan de las 8 de el dia ande el riko i savyo, *h"r* Yeoshua Modiano, el kual abandono sus echos i enkargo a su ijo el mayor de estar mirando los echos de su negosyo, ke era estonses *haver* delos sinyores Alatini. El estava arepozado en su kaza, i ke ya le vinian djente por pasar el tyempo. Ma kada dia, despues de el medyo dia, vinian los sinyores nombrados ariva a pasar el tyempo kon el, i konversavan en diversos rijos de la Komunita. Entre sus konversasyones, se avriyo la kuestyon dela muerte de estas djovenas muchachas, i bushkar el remedyo a konbatir estas hazinuras, i la muerte de las rezin kazadas. El uno de eyos disho su *sevara* ke es ke podia ser a kavza dela *tevila* ke era la agua yelada, i non se savian konportar en el rijo de su salud, syendo era un ofisyo muevo para eyos.

El sigundo de eyos disho otra *sevara*. I es ke en akel tyempo davan los padres en la ashugar alas ijas, enresparte de todos los vistidos i obdjetos, tambyen 2 *yurdis samarrados*. Uno se yamava *yurdi nafé* de panyo de kolores, el otro *yurdi chilibi* de panyo kolorado, *samarrado* de *po[n]dekyi* por adyentro, i por afuera los *prevazes* ila *yaka* desu matyer. I syendo ke kualunke non podia alkansar el, su *samur* muevo, merkavan unas ka[r]nitures de algunas *hanumes* ke avian abandonado de vistirlo, i ke izyeron moda de vistir *feredje*. Estas ka[r]nitures tambyen vinian de afuera la sivdad, ke non se savia de ke puerpo eran vistidas estas *samarras*. Podia ser de algunos puerpos entikiados i se atakavan ditas djovenas mujeres!

[7a] El tersyo de eyos, ke era el *Rav* , *h"r* Avraam Gatenyo, la *sevara* mas puntual a estas dos, dizyendo ke el pensava mas afondo, syendo las muchachas en syendo mosas, embezadas a vistir un fostan solo, i kuando eyas kazavan, se ivan en las vijitas, vistyendo este *kyurdi* de panyo *ensamarrado,* i un maraman blanko kuvryendo la kavesa. Se entyende ke en tyempo de enverano, kon las kalores fuertes, eyas se banyavan en la sudor. I kuando arivavan en kaza de la vijita, se deznudavan el *yurdi* i el maraman, kedavan sus puerpos estopados en el agua de la sudor, i bushkavan de asentarsen ande avia un poko de vyento para arefreskar. Aventandosen kon el aventador, se les enshugava la sudor en las karnes, i les kavzava una desfriasyon fuerte de alguna hazinura de puntada. I non byen mirada, se les azia hazinura de tikia.

El sinyor, *h"r* Yeoshua, ke era un ombre tan fino, estudyo las tres *sevaroth* i topo ke la *sevara* de el *Rav* Gatenyo era la mas emportante. Eyos pensaron estonses el remedyo de este echo. El *Rav* Gatenyo disho de abandonar las *samarras* de los *yurdis,* i azer una reforma de vistir *yurdis sades,* komo las *djubbes* delos ombres. A esta *sevara,* un dia se adjuntaron a eyos i el si. *Rav, h"r* Asher Kovo, ke devista i el acheto a este remedyo.

Ma eyos pensaron ke, kon ke sus dichas, el puevlo non van a achetar. Es menester de azer un ko[n]bido en kaza de el si. *Rav, h"r* Shaul, porke si el non acheta a muestra opinion, es derrokado todo muestro plano. Eyos se alevantaron todos en una, i se fueron en kaza de el *Rav, h"r* Shaul, i le dyeron a saver todo loke paso entre eyos, i el remedyo ke toparon. Mando de vista el *rav* a yamar alos *Shiv'a Tove a-'Ir,* ma en esta reunion el *Rav, h"r* Asher non lo konbidaron. Esto le vino afuerte de no toparse i el en la asamblea. El tomo de su parte a tres de los de *Shiv'a Tove a-'Ir,* ake non fueran en la asamblea. En tanto, los ke se toparon en la asamblea dechidyeron de azer la egzekusyon. La prima vista, fue traido el *yurdi* de la sinyora *rabbanith* i deskuzido el *prevás* en la *samarra* de adyentro. **[7b]** Por mas mal, en el *kyenar* debasho el *samur,* por abasho, avia oria. Non se desharon mas esperar los *gevirin,* mandaron al *charshi* i trusheron tres pikos i medyo de panyo kolorado, yamaron a un djastre a kelo akavara de kuzir entre la tadre i la noche sin falta. I ke ala manyana, devian de salir a vijitar los de la asamblea, todas kitadas las *samarras* de los *yurdis,* i irsen a vijitar de unas alas otras, dos, tres dias en afila, i mizmo la *rabbanith,* kon estos *yurdis* ala moda, por dar enshemplo a todo el mundo.

El sinyor *rav* dyo orden a todos los *shammashim,* i a los *shammashim* de el *kolel* apregonando ke ningun modo de mujer puede yevar *yurdi* kon *samarra.* I metyo en kada puerta de banyo 2 *shammashim* a non deshar entrar mujer kon *yurdi ensamarrado.* Eyas tornavan en kaza, la deskuzian la *samarra,* ise ivan al banyo. Lo mizmo kua[n]do se iva ir alguna mujer a vijitar, enprimero se deskuzia la *samarra,* i despues se iva a vijitar.

Diremos a gora el akontesimyento tradjiko ke sudesyo de este fato. I es ke entre estos sinyores de *Shiv'a Tove a-'Ir,* los 2 non se toparon para kombidarlos. El otro non kijendo toparse en la asamblea, mando a dizir ke el estava embarasado, i non podia ir, otro ke mas tadre. El si. *Rav, h"r* Shaul mando adizirle, "si vyene en este momento, va byen. En tanto ke non, ke non venga mas por su kaza"! Este ultimo, non kijendo renosyar ala palavra ke tuvo dado al *Rav, h"r* Asher, non fue deel todo punto a la asamblea. Este sinyor, era su kamino de la tadre i la manyana de delantre la kaza de el *Rav, h"r* Shaul al ir al *charshi* i al tornar la tadre en kaza. Kuando serro su gruta, se fue por otro kamino ke el non lo konosia, ke era la kaledjika yamada Kandiantis muncho estrecha i eskura. I el syendo un ombre aedado, izo un paso falso, i se kayo i se le rompyo el gueso de la pyerna derecha, i fue yevado a kaza entre munchas personas. Este fato fue puvlikado por la sivdad entera, en dizyendo ke por el pekado ke el non ovedesyo a la palavra de el *Rav, h"r* Shaul, i ke le mando a dizir ke, "si non vyene *pishin,* ke non venga mas por su kaza".

[8a] Devista, todas las mujeres, espantadas de este akontesimyento, se kitaron todas las *samarras* de *kyurdis,* i en todo modo de ashugar non asementaron mas *kyurdi asamarrado.* Ma esto fue dos provechos: uno, el avánso de moneda ke kostava esta *samarra* de *samur;* i la otra, ke se avanso tantas desgrasyas de las muchachas dela hazinura de tikia. Ya se entyende de suyo la pavor i tembla ke dyo en estas kombinasyones akontesidas en el tyempo de el *rabbanuth* de, *h"r* Shaul.

Uvo otros kavzos semejantes. Por non enfasyar a munchos meldadores non los asenyalamos aki. En tanto, el puevlo entero dela sivdad i de los entornos lo tomaron al *Rav, h"r* Shaul komo si fuera el profeta Yermiya, ke todas las maldisyones ke, echando el profeta ivan akontesyendo, en este modo fue la fama ke tomo, i el espanto ke dyo a todo el puevlo fanatiko.

El tenia una natura ke todo el ke le vinia a kontar algunas kozas demudadas, el las tomava devista en konsiderasyon sin azer ninguna *hakira u-derisha*—si komo era un ombre djusto, le paresia ke todos eran komo el—ande es ke uvo akontesimyento ke non tenian dingun fondamyento. I una vez, le vino uno kontando ke tal fulano, un ombre relijyozo, se arapo en tyempo de *Lag la--'Omer.* El *rav* devista mando a su kaza al *shammash* i lo *enheremo.* El ombre, syendo de fama i estimado de todos, kuando el vino en kaza ala tadre, topo a su mujer yorando. El le demando por kuala razon eya yorava. Eya le respondyo, "ke koza le paso kon el *Rav, h"r* Shaul"? El le respondyo ke non paso ni por akeya kaye. La mujer le respondyo ke el *shammash* de el *Rav, h"r* Shaul vino a *enheremarlo.* Sintyendo esto de su mujer, le suvyo la sangre ala kavesa, i de vista se fue a demandar satisfaksyon. El si. *rav* le respondyo, "por kavza ke pasates *divre hahamim*, i vos arapatesh en el *'Omer"*. El se defendyo en dizyendo ke es mintira, ke fue una kalumnia. Los ke se toparon prezentes disheron ke se podia azer la preva.

[8b] Devista se deskavenyo i mostro su kavesa pelada. El *rav* le disho ke, "ami, me vinyeron *edim* ke vos vyeron al *berber"*. El le respondyo ke "es verdad ke kada dia me vo al *berber*. I es ke tengo en medyo dela kavesa un *sach kiran*, ke me los kita los kaveikos malos kon la penseta, i me unta inguente, ke si non me miro a tyempo por melizinarme, me pueden kayer *afillú* los kaveyos dela barva". A esta repuesta, el *rav* le respondyo ke algun pekado otro tenia, i se le vino a perdonar kon esta ensulta ke es *ve-hattatehá tehuppar*, [I tu pekado sera perdonado, (Isaiah 6:7)].

Kapitolo 6

El echo de si. Behor Varsano

Otro un fato semejante paso ke un ombre le vino kontando al si. *rav* ke en una fyesta ke, despues ke ya estavan estofados en el vino, uno ke su nombre Varsano metyo en la meza su bonete, i todos los asistyentes, ke[n] dava un punyo ensima el bonete, le dava un *metalik*. El *rav* se ensanyo i mando un *teskyere* a un *gevir* enfluente, el kual el *rav* lo adorava, dizyendole ke mande un *takrir* ala Puerta, i ke lo aferren a este de Varsano, i ke le agan dar 200 palos, ke esto era el uzo de estonses, ke kuando alguno non ovedesia al *rav*, era esta la penalità. El si. *gevir* sin retardar mando el *takrir*, i le mando el *kavas bashı* dos *kavazes*. Myentres mando a yamar a un *hahamiko*, de Varsano su *alkunya*, el kual era un *sofer* ke eskrivia *shetaroth*. El ombre, apena salyendo dela *huppa*, metyo su eskriveria de plata asu *kushak*, i un pligo de papel a su pecho, i pensando ke este si. *gevir* keria alguna koza de eskritura. En entrando en el magazen de dito si., lo saludo i le demando ke ay por sirvirlo. En su repuesta, fue, *"rasha,* izites *bizzayon* ala Ley". I devista lo dyo en mano de los 2 *kavazes,* i ke se lo yevaran. El povereto, vyendose en mano de dos djandarmes, empeso a esklamar i a yorar. Ma non metyo oyido el *gevir* asus esklamasyones.

[9a] Este mansevo, vyendose aferrado de 2 djandarmes, el se aferro de las orejas de los sakos de kafe, ke avia una suma de 500 sakos de kafe. Los djandarmes travando a el, i el travando las orejas delos sakos de kafe, ke kayeron una montanya de sakos, ke por poko non lo tomo debasho a el i al si. *gevir.* En este *charshi* avia una partida de *hammales.* Al sonete dela kayidura delos sakos i las esklamasyones de el mansevo, entraron adyentro i lo kitaron delas manos a el mansevo, ilo izyeron fuir. El se fue devista asu kaza i kayo en un desmayo. Las mujeres, de verlo al mansevo desmayado, alsaron guayas. Devista vino el si. padre de el muchacho, ivyendolo desmayado, yamo mediko i lo retornaron. I vyendolo desbrochado i aravyado, le demando el padre ke fue la kavza de este echo. El {ke} [le] konto todo el páso. El si. padre, syendo konosido de todos los grandes dela sivdad—el era el presyador delas ashugares en akel tyempo—el era muncho entrado en la kaza de el *Rav, h"r* Asher, i le konto todo el fato. El *Rav, h"r* Asher, aun ke era ombre afamado por su sensya i su rikeza, kon todo se espantava de el *Rav, h"r* Shaul. El mando asaventarse de el *gevir* ke fue la kavza de esto. En su repuesta fue ke el risivyo un *teskyere* de parte de el *Rav, h"r* Shaul kelo mandara al *konak* i ke le izyera dar 200 palos en los pyes por lo ke izo *bizzayon a-Tora.* El *Rav, h"r* Asher devista se vistyo el *benish* i se fueron en djunto kon el padre i el ijo onde el *Rav, h"r* Shaul a demandar satisfaksyon. En entrando en la kamareta ande estava el *Rav, h"r* Shaul se saludaron de uzo i lo izo asentar asu lado. Despues de algunas palavras de seremoniya, le demando el *Rav, h"r* Asher ke fue la kavza de esta echa. El *rav* le respondyo ke este *rasha* anoche en una fyesta, por tomar paras de los ke estavan borrachos, metyo el bonete ensima la meza, i ke estuvyeran dando un punyo kada uno, i ke le dyeran a un *metalik. H"r* Asher sintyendo esto izo entrar al padre i a el ijo adyentro, i demandandole, "en ke fyesta estuvo anoche guestro ijo i izo este eskándalo"? E[l] padre respondyo **[9b]** ke el ijo ay dos dias ke salyo de la *huppa,* i anoche tuvo *misvat tefilla,* se entyende ke non estuvo en ninguna fyesta. Estonses el *Rav, h"r* Asher izo yamar el *'eduth.* El si. respondyo ke el kon su propyo ojo lo vido este echo. I lo amostro al mansevo si era este ke izo loke esta dizyendo. El *'eduth* respondyo ke "a este mansevo non lo konosko". "I kyen es este ke vites"? *"A djanim!* Kyen no lo konose a este de Varsano ke va alas bodas a tanyer", azyendo kuento ke era *h"r* Yaakov Varsano, el kual dainda bive en el tyempo ke eskrivimos dita estorya. Oy es patron de (88) ochenta i ocho anyos ke en akel tyempo era *yeni chikma* konbidador i tanyedor en las fyestas. A esta shena, kedaron enkantados todos 2, el *rav* i *h"r* Asher.

El *Rav, h"r* Asher le demando al si. *Rav, h"r* Shaul ke si a este mansevo non lo eskapavan los *[h]ammales* ke entraron adyentro, iva a komer los 200 dozyentos palos?

El *Rav, h"r* Shaul, sin azer ningun kavzo de esta demanda, le respondyo ke si tenia mas pekados pezgados, iva a komer los 200 palos, es ke non fueron otro ke livyanos los ke tenia. I agora, i estos sele perdonaron, *ve-hattatehá tehuppar,* [i tu pekado sera perdonado, (Isaiah 6:7)].

Otro un Fato

Ke akontesyo en un mansevo *talmid haham* i de buena famiya.

I es ke un padre de famiya tenia su echo en Yumuldjina, i la famiya estava aki, en Salonik. En kada un mes a dos, les mandava moneda por el menester dela famiya. Una ves topo a una persona ke iva partir por Salonik, i le dyo una partida de moneda, ake se las konsinyara a su famiya. El ombre bushko de komersela esta moneda, non les dyo ni la karta, ni la moneda ala famiya. La mujer, vyendo tadrar tyempo kyenon le mandava paras, le eskrivyo porké non le manda moneda, syendo ay muncho tyempo ke non le manda. Este padre de famiya eskrivyo keya le **[10a]** tuvo mandado por mano de fulano. La mujer tórna le eskrivyo ke non tuvo risivido nada. El ombre se metyo en kamino i se vino a Salonik, i demando por el fulano, i le disheron ke esta en buen estado, i esta azyendo buen echo. El lo topo al dito ombre, demandandole porke non le konsinyo la moneda a su famiya. El respondyo ke lo *soydearon* por el kamino los ladrones. El si. se asavento i supo ke la mujer yevava un buen *yardan* en el kueyo ke valia *chirka* (1000) mil groshes. El se los izo saver a sus (4) kuatro ijos, i eran byen korajozos. Los (3) tres se fueron a su kaza, supyendo ke el marido non se topava ai. Eyos le demandaron ala mujer ande se topava el marido. Eya seryamente respondyo ke avia medya ora ke salyo de en kaza. I uno, el mas forsudo, se paso por dedetras dela mujer ila arrodeo detenyendole byen los brasos. Los otros dos le metyeron la mano en el kueyo, le kitaron el *yardan,* i se fueron. El marido, tomando avizo de esto, se fue esklamando ande el *Rav, h"r* Shaul i le konto la echa. El *rav* sin tadrar mando i los apregono por toda sivdad. Ma este padre de famiya i los ijos non azian tanto kavzo de maldisyones i de *heremoth.* Tambyen el mayor de los ijos era un *talmid haham* de primer rango i amado de todos los ke lo aserkavan. Uno de sus kolegas demando por ke kavza los *enheremo* el *rav.* Le respondyeron porke pasaron el *lav, lo tavo el betho,* [no entraras en su morada (Deut. 24:10)]. El ijo *talmid haham* respondyo ke esto non es por pasar *lo tavo el betho,* [no entraras en su morada], syendo ke este ombre se yama "un ladron ke me rovo la moneda", komo ya esta eskrito en los livros de los *posekim,* en talugar i en tal lugar, en tal *simman* i en tal *simman,* ya kortaron la ley ke un ladron, le puede ir en kaza i tomarle los objetos ke tyene. El si. *rav,* vyendose ofendido de un *talmid haham* mansevo, respondyo ke este ombre es *mare a-love bi-fene re'o* [el ke apunta al devdor delantre de su kompanyero] merese el *mishpat.* Devista eskrivyo un *teskyere* a uno de los *gevirin* a ke lo mandara ariva i ke le dyeran (200) dozyentos palos. I ansi fue. Este *talmid haham,* sin pensarlo, lo aferraron 2 *kavazes,*

[10b] i lo yevaron al *konak* del *Vali*. En medyo el kortijo, lo echaron en basho, le alevantaron los *baldirin*, le metyeron la *falaka* i le dyeron los 200 palos ilo metyeron en prezo. El padre de este *talmid haham*, tuvyendo muncha relasyon kon los merkaderes frankos, fue el konsolo ande el *Vali*, i lo izo kitar de prezo. Este *talmid haham* devista dyo el bonete en basho inon kijo ir mas a meldar, i uvo un murmuramyento entre los *hahamim*. Ma el *Rav*, *h"r* Shaul non se espantava de ninguno i no lo metyo ni en tino, el izo lo ke le plazyo.

En el entervalo delos katorze anyos de *rabbanuth* ke tuvo izo munchos inimigos kon los *hahamim*, i los *dayyanim*. Entre estos, uvo un *haham* ke le paso una *merikia* kon el si. *rav*. Por desgrasya, este si. *haham* se echo *hazino*, i vyendose en oras apretadas, ma aun kon todo ke vyendose para murir, el akojo sus fuersas. I kon un fuerte koraje, el le mando a el ke non entyenda ke es por la maldisyon suya ke el aya se va murir, otro ke vino su tyempo; i syendo el aya non kree en maldisyones sin fondo.

Otro un fato paso ke un si. *haham* muy savyo—i era [de] *beth din* de *rabbanuth*—riko, potente, izo una fyesta en el kazamyento de su nyeto. Despues de azer tantos kombites, "el dia de el pishkado" izo un kombite a todos los *hahamim* i *dayyanim*, *bi-helal* a *h"r* Shaul tambyen kombido. Despues de komer i bever, le dyo lesensya a un kantador ake kantara todo lo ke les plazia alos kombidados. De eyos, le demandaron ke kantara alguna *sharki* turka de las ke savia. El *Rav*, *h"r* Shaul, ke aborresia tanto el kante turko, i kaji el tenia una ipogo[n]dria ke non podia sintir kantar en lingua turka, **[11a]** indose a su kaza, le mando a *enheremar* al kantador. El kantador non izo kavzo de esto. Ma el padre de el novyo, ke era el ijo de el si. *haham* ke dishimos, sintyendo esto, akavado de komer, tanto *sehora* se tomo, ke sele izo un afito fuerte, i se echo en kama, i de dyentro de ocho dias el muryo. I [el] si. *haham*, de *merikia* de esta desgrasya ke le akontesyo, i la ansya ke le kavzo la muerte de su ijo, el aresento sus echos, i se alevanto se fue a Yerushalayim. Estos fatos ke ivan akontesyendo, a un ke no eran dela Providensya, otro de kombinasyones imajinadas. Ma syendo el puevlo fanatiko, lo tenian por siguro ke el si. *rav* era uno delos *shelihim* de el Dyo, i todo lo ke Le demandava de El, El le respondia, a tanto ke él mezmo yevava este enganyo.

Kapitolo 7

La Antipatia por el Kante

El si. *Rav, h"r* Shaul tenia una antipatia kon la lingua turka, a tanto ke el ke kantava kantigas en lingua turka, el lo metia en *herem* devista, non solamente kantiga turka, *afillú* un *pizmon* ke kantavan en el son i alguna kantiga turka.

Vos kontare, si. meldadores! Ya vos dishe mas antes ke yo, el eskrivedor de dita broshura, syendo kedi guerfano de padre a la edad de sinko a sesh anyos, i guerfano de madre a la edad de 16 a 17 anyos, kon un ermaniko de edad de 10 a 12 anyos, ma ke tenia una *hazinura* de mal de pyedra. Estonses pensando por mi avenir, me di puerpo i alma al lavoro de la estamparia, ma era un ganar mizeryozo. Yo fui *sevdali* de el arte de kante, i syendo la boz me lo permetia. **[11b]** Avia entre los Djidyos un syerto maestro ke konosia munchos kantes en ebraiko. Tenia unos vente *fasiles* de diversos *mekames* i en kada *fasil* dos, tres *peshrefes, bestes, kiyares, samayis, eche, eche.* Tambyen konosia los kantes de *yamim noraim.* El se yamava *h"r* Aaron Barzilay, el kual, sintyendome un dia kantar en una fyesta unas kuantas *şarkis* ala turka, ke me eran embezadas de un maestro kantador yamado *Murteza{n} (Iz-Eddin Olu)*, ke tenia {una} i una bos ekstraordinarya. Yo me ize byen kerer de este maestro, a tanto ke me amava komo su ijo, i me yamava kon si alas fyestas ande iva a kantar. El maestro , *h"r* Aaron Barzilay me metyo i el asu lado i me embezo todo loke el savia.

En este tyempo, un si. *haham,* riko i savyo, tuvo de kazar un ijo. El se yamava *h"r* Yeuda Alkalay ke el poseia la grande *yeshiva* de los *rabbanim* en su kaza ke era la *yeshiva* grande, nombrada *Yeshiva[t]* Alkalay ke dos vezes al anyo les azia kombite a los sinyores *hahamim.* El kantador de estas fyestas era yo i mi ermaniko.

Un dia antes de la fyesta, me disho ke keria ke estuvyera los ocho dias dela fyesta para kantar en su kaza, a kondisyon ke le izyera un kante muevo en el *kiddush* de los *kiddushim.* Yo enventi un kante de una *sharki* ensima del *kaddish,* i adjunti ami lado kuatro, sinko mansevikos ermozos, i se los ize *meshkiye* i me pronti para kantarlo. Antes ke abashara el novyo a la *keilla,* estava yena de todos los *rabbanim* i *hahamim* i de toda la aristokrasia de Saloniko. Kuando vino la ora de kantar el *kaddish,* me apari ala *teva* kon mis kolegas, i kanti un *kaddish* de el *mekam* de *huzzam.* El puevlo ke asistia en la *keilla* a muchidumbre kedaron todos imobil, syendo ke por la primera ves ke sintyeron kantar *kaddish* kon el son muevo. Todos me felisitaron por la buena manera de el kante de el *kaddish.* Ma el si. *Rav* , *h"r* Shaul, ke en sus dias non tenia sintido koza de kantar, **[12a]** non atino el son de el *kaddish.* En indose akompanyado asu kaza de 8 a 10 personas, despues de kitarse la kapa ise arepozo a el *mindel,* le demandaron si tomo *has* de el *kaddish,* syendo era un kante muevo ke lo asento Sa'adi de una *sharki* turka. Sintyendo esto, el si. *rav* salto en alto dizyendo, "este *rasha* de dyentro dela *keilla* kantar kantiga en trukuesko"! Presto, andad dizilde a *h"r* Yeuda ke non lo puede tener a este *rasha* en la fyesta.

H"r Yeuda, sintyendo las palavras de el *shammash,* le suvyo la sangre ala kavesa, i se izo entero komo una *pandja[r]* kolorada, dizyendo, "i sovre mozotros kyere emplear la enfluensa a komandar a ke esto ke agas i esto non". Ma los asistyentes ke se topavan en el salon de los *kiddushim* se indinyaron de sintir tal koza, syendo eran todos djente grande los ke se topavan ai. El si. *Rav, h"r* Shelomo Pipano tomo la palavra i disho a *h"r*

Yeuda ke non se ensanyara muncho ke el iva a ser kapache de azerlo tornar atras esto ke mando a dizir el *Rav, h"r* Shaul. Se alevanto devista i se fue ande el *rav*, demandole satisfaksyon, "kon ke derecho le mando a dizir ke non tome a este kantador en la fyesta"? A *h"r* Yeuda, el respondyo ke este kantador es un *rasha* ke kanta en trukuesko, ke el *kaddish* lo kanto en el son trukuesko en la *keilla*. Le respondyo a estas palavras *h"r* Shelomo ke, "todos los *pizmonim* ke tenemos en *leshon a-kodesh* son destos turkos. Tóme el livro de el *rav* Nadjara, i vera ke ensima de kada *pizmon* ke el kompozo son de *sharkis* turkas. I el *Rav, ribbi* Yeuda a-Levi, ke izo tantos kantes en *Yamim Noraim,* masimamente en *Yom a-Kippurim,* son tomados de kandes arabos". Ma si komo el non supo de koza de kantes e[n] sus dias, estas palavras de *h"r* Shelomo le vinyeron todas muevas. Estonses el se konvensyo, i le mando a dizir a *h"r* Yeuda ke fue un yerro envolontaryo, ke le disheron otro modo a el, i ke aga lo ke le plaze en su fyesta kon kondisyon ke non kante en turko.

Kapitolo 8

[12b] Ya tuve dicho ke la ganansya de la estamparia non era sufichente. Yo me di en la karyera de el kantar, i syendo en akel tyempo non avia otro ke me izyera konkorensya, syendo yo me asaventi kon el un maestro i el otro una partida grande de *pizmonim* i una partida grande de *sharkis* i *bestes* en turko. Non avia fyesta ni *ziafet* ke non me yamavan ami para kantar, syendo en akel tyempo non uzavan *chalgi* en las fyestas, era yo kon mi ermaniko, i algun kolega mio. Estonses los ke tanyian ikantavan en las fyestas i *ziafetes,* tanyedores i kantadores de alguna djente de el ~~a-minin~~ *minyan* ke savian kantar algunos handrajos para baylar. Kuando ya tomaron el gusto la djente de sintir kantar ala turka *mizmorim,* etch. estos tanyedores vyejos ivan ande el *Rav, h"r* Shaul i le dizian ke fulano anoche estuvo en tala fyesta i estuvo kantando kuanta kantiga en turko suzya ayi. El *Rav, h"r* Shaul non se deshava esperar, devista mandava i me *enheremava* sin demandarme satisfaksyon. Yo era konstreto de ir a demandarle *mehila,* non porke me espantava de el *herem,* solamente ke me mandava a dar palos si non le demandava *mehila.*

Esto era 3 vezes en la semana. Al 4, yo non me podia dechidir de ganar; ma asta ke vino un dia ke me mando *enheremar* por la noche de antes. Pasando 2 oras, me vino a kombidar para una fyesta para la noche un kombidador ke se yamava de mi nombre i mi *alkunya,* i ke el era el *shammash* onoraryo dela kaza del *Rav, h"r* Shaul, ke el kual tenia tres *shammashim.* El uno era el *enheremador* ke se yamava *Ham Chelebon Mordoh.* Yo le respondi al ke me vino a kombidar para fyesta de la noche ke no ay 2 oras ke me mando a sepelear el si. *rav.* El me respondyo, ven esta noche **[13a]** ala vista, amanyana iras a tomar una *attara* por dos (*bir verirsan, ikyi sayarum),* [si me das uno, yo lo konto por dos]. Yo ovedesi, i me fui kon el a [la] fyesta. Myentres ke estavan vinyendo los kombidados, tomi a konversar kon este kombidador ke se yamava *Ham* Sa'adi a-Levi, demandandole ke me bushkára un remedyo para eskapar delas manos del si. *rav.* El me respondyo, "syendo tu non te espantas de el *herem,* para ké vas kada ves a demandarle *mehila"?* Le respondi ke non es por el *herem* ke vo a demandarle *mehila,* si non ke es por el espanto ke, si non le vo a demandar *mehila,* me manda a dar palos, ke ansi era la uzansa, ke el si. *rav* le mandava un *deskyere* a uno de los *gevirim,* i lo mandava a tomar kon dos *kavazes,* i le arreventava la fyel. El me disho estonses ke el si. *rav,* kuando manda a *enheremar,* non lo eskrive en *defter* akyen *enheremo* oy, akyen *enheremo* aer, syendo non es uno o dos *heremoth* ke echa el dia, si non por la mas chika koza lo asolta el *herem;* andemas ke vente i sinko, trenta *heremoth* el dia echa, i non se akodra a kyen echo, i a kyen no! Estas palavras las tomi en konsiderasyon, i non fui mas por ande el *rav* a demandar *mehila.*

Un dia estavan konversando kon 2, 3 *talmide hahamim.* Le disheron ke un livro se esta estampando de un *haham* de Esmirna, i ke vyene kontra de el *Shulhan Gavoa,* ke era su si. papu. El demando presto ke trusheran estos pligos para ver ke es lo ke kontradize. Estando en esto, se akodro ke ya me tenia *enheremado* munchas vezes, i yo non fui por ayi. Mando un *teskyere* a un *gevir,* "a ke mandara un *takrir* ande el *kavaz ba shi* a ke le mandára 2 *kavazes,* i ke a el ke van a traer le enklavas 200 palos en los pyes". De vista, i alos *kavazes* los eskondyo ala kozina, myentres me mando ayamar kon el achake ke los pligos ke kontra dizia asu eguardo. Yo le prezenti los livros estampados; el, echo un grito de leon, **[13b]** "*rasha!!* Ya son tantas vezes ke te mando a *enheremar,* i tu {non} non vyenes a demandar *mehila".* El, yamo devista *Ham Chelebon,* "daldo en mano delos *kavazes".* Devista, me vinyeron 2 brasos de fyerro, i me aferraron uno de kada braso, i me empesaron a travar para me yevar al *konak.* Yo esklami i non uvo kyen me oyera. I el iva gritando,"*mehoram,* kantaras mas *shire a-goyyim"!* I me abasharon dela eskalera, i empesimos a suvir otra eskalera ke era la *Keilla* de Peshkadores. En suvyendo asta el trazer eskalon, yo iva pensando kon ke artifisyo yo me iva fuyir de sus manos. Kuando vinimos ala kaye, yo atini ke era *vizavi* la puerta de *Chilibi* Moshon Mizrahi. Para desbarasarme de eyos, les dishe: "*Allah, ne tutarsinis beni katil yibi, ben kyimsei oldurmedim, kyimseden chalmadim, kyimsenin irzina dokulmadim, kyonul verin, nerde isterseniz yidelim",* ["O Dyo, ke me estash tratando komo un matador? Yo no mati a dinguno, no me rovi de dinguno, ni a la onor de dinguno toki. Azéme una piadad i iremos ande vos gusta"]. Eyos se *kandirearon* i me soltaron, i empesi yo a kaminar adelantres *serbes, serbes.* Kuando vinimos allado la puerta de *Chilibi* Moshon ke estava avyerta, me arodji komo una agila, i kon un bolo, suvi la eskalera de pyedra, i me suvi al andar de ariva, i me eskondi debasho de una kama. Las kokonas ke estavan en el varandado, en vyendo alos *kavazes,* se alevantaron todas las kokonas, kyen kon un baston, kyen kon un *chadir,* kyen kon una siya a sigirlos alos *kavazes,* en dizyendoles, "kon ke ozadia entratesh en kaza de franko". Myentres ya se incho el kortijo de djente de los pasantes, i dela plasa, i ya mandaron ala gruta de *Chilibi* Moshon avizo, ke dyentro de sinko puntos ya koryeron los si. Fernandes kon sus *kavazes*; i vyendo el *bazbilik,* non supyeron ke pensar. I los *kavazes* de los Fernandes izyeron kitar kon la fuersa a los presigidores afuera, i a toda la djente, los kitaron afuera, i izyeron serrar las puertas. Eyos demandaron ke fue la kavza de esto. Las madamas les respondyeron alos *Chilibis* ke un syerto Sa'adi ke vyene kon *Murteza{n}* en muestras **[14a]** fyestas, fuyo de manos de estos djandarmes, i esta eskondido ariva. Me yamaron devista i me demandaron la kavza de esta fuida. Yo les respondi ke non lo se ni yo, porke me aferraron para me yevar al *konak* de el *Pasha.* I me demandaron, "algun *kabaet* izites"? Yo les respondi ke, "non tengo ningun *kabaet,* otro ke me tomaron de la kaza de el *Rav, h"r* Shaul para yevarme al *konak* i darme palos por la razon ke kanto en trukesko, i el si. *rav* me defyende de kantar. I syendo es mi mantenisyon, el me manda a *enheremar,* yo non lo ovedesko". Los *Chilibis,* sintyendo mi razon, devista se fueron al *konak* de el *Pasha* a demandar sadisfaksyon. El *Pasha,* sintyendo ke por una persona ke kanta en turko mandan adarle palos de parte del *haham bashi* i los *gevirim,* el *Vali* mando a yamar al *kavaz bashi* ile disho, "otra ves non tengas la ozadia de risivir *takrir* de la komunita delos Djudyos sin me lo mostrar ami". Devista mando una eskrita el *Pasha* alos *gevirin* ke, "de endelantre non sea ke se adresen a otro afuera ke ami". Estonses eskapi delos palos i delos *heremoth.*

Este modo era los rijos de akel tyempo ke ay *chirka* sinkuenta anyos. Ke pensan agora los de esta epoka sovre la esklavedad ke teniamos los Djidyos debasho el pezgo de muestros pastores?

Kapitolo 9

En el Kazo de el Yeni Cheri

Un Djidyo yamado Liatchi, el farinero, ke era amigo de los

djanisares, el era un entrigante (Moro). Kuando algun *yenicheri* se topava manko de moneda, el les dava avizo de los djidyos ke eran rikos. El kapo de estos bandidos mandava a algun riko djidyo en una punta de riza atado 2 a 3 *krushumes.* **[14b]** Esto keria dizir ke un *krushun* era syen groshes. Estonses, sigun el avizo de este entrigante ke le dava al *yenicheri* ke *karar* de riko era. Estonses, mandava el djanisaro a akel riko de 2-3 asta 10 *krushumes* ke le mandaran devista la moneda dela kandida de los *krushumes* ke le era demandado al ke le ivan estos *krushumes.* Sin refusar, el achetava a mandarsela, ke si refuzava a non mandar el *sikkum* demandado, ala noche el ya era aprimado kon los mezmos *krushumes* ke le mandara atras. En este modo fue azyendo este ombre estrasos en todos los poderozos.

Estonses, lo yamaron los sinyores *hahamim* a este malo ombre en rogandole ake se ripintyera de esta mala echa. El ombre non ovedesiya i kontinuava en su negrigura. Kuando al *yenicheri,* el governo se desbaraso de el; los *hahamim* toparon el tyempo de vengarse de el.

En akel tyempo, era ke kuando a un *pasha* lo azia *aaz[l]* el governo, en el tyempo vakante, asta ke mandavan a el otro *pasha,* era Ahmed Bey, el *musellim* ke komandava komo *pasha.* Estonses rogaron a un gevir ke era su *hasnadar* de este *bey* ake lo aprezara a este ombre. I ansi fue. Ma estando en prezo, le ivan la djente ala prezyon a dizirle ake mandara a rogar alos *hahamim* ake le dyeran el perdon de todos sus malas echas ke izo. En su repuesta, fue ke enpeso a dezonrar i alos *hahamim,* i alos *gevirim,* i en dizyendo ke kuando sarla de en prezyo[n], el ara mas negro de lo ke izo asta agora. Los *hahamim* izyeron un *pesak,* (setensya), ke era meresedor de muerte, i rogaron a este sinyor *hasnadar* ake lo izyera enforkar. Este *gevir,* ke era su *sarraf* de Ahmed Bey, se espanto de verter sangre por su mano. Los *hahamim* le dyeron un papel firmado por sus manos ke eyos tomaran la responsabilidad de este krimen. Dito *sarraf* en dia de vyernes **[15a]** se fue ande Ahmed Bey i lo saludo departe delos *hahamim,* dizyendole ke este aprezado sea enforkado. Ahmed Bey non se desho muncho arogar, ke devista dia de vyernes, dyes la ora, mando i lo izo enforkar. Onze i medya la ora, lo abasharon ilo mandaron a enterrar en un *beth a-hayyim* aparte, sin azer ninguna seremonia relidjoza. Este fato, lo vide kon mis odjos en syendo de edad de 8 a 10 anyos.

Otro un fato me akodro en estos tyempos, ke alguno ke se aferrava kon el pekado de *zenuth (esheth ish),* era djuzgado i apenado fuertemente kon darle palos, i aprezado, i *djeza* fuerte. Ma si el akulpado tenia el tyempo de fuirse a otra sivdad, komo ya uvo en dos personas semejantes, ke eran todos dos de un nombre, ma las alkunyas trokavan, el uno se yamava A. R., el otro A. N. Estos, tuvyendo avizo ke ivan aser aferrados, se fueron a Yerushalayim, i estuvyeron ai unos kuantos anyos, i despues tornaron.

Estonses, una muchacha se aferro ke estava prenyada, en syendo mosa sin kazar, el muchacho fuyo. Los *hahamim* izyeron apanyar ala muchacha ke se yamava fulana. La trusheron delantre *beth din,* ila djuzgaron ke le dyeran syen palos en medyo de el *Talmud Tora.* Despues, la enserraron en una gruta de el kortijo de el *Talmud Tora,* i la metyeron al *trimbuk.* En este lugar mezmo paryo una kiryatura ke non bivyo muncho tyempo. Este fato se puvliko por toda la sivdad, i lo supyeron turkos i gregos. Un konrespondyente de la gazeta de Londra lo izo un artikolo i lo mando a publikar en las gazetas. Vinyendo ala konosensya de el governo inglez esta mala echa, mandaron a kesharsen al governo turko, i demandando satisfaksyon de esta mala echa. El governo **[15b]** mando a asaventarse de el *Vali,* si uvo tal fato en la sivdad, i ke apenara alos ke izyeron la ezekusyon. Estonses, mando el *Vali* alos grandes dela sivdad ayamar ake le espyegaran kyen fue el ke tuvo parte en esta mala echa. Los *hahamim,* vyendosen en el apreto ke se topavan, yamaron ala muchacha i le aprometyeron todo loke demandava. I eyos la kazaron dela moneda dela kasha de el *kolel,* i ke enyegara en yamandola el *Vali* de toda esta echa. I ansi fue ke kuando vino en prezensya de el *Vali,* eya se desnyego de todo loke le estavan dizyendo.

En tanto la kasha de el *kolel* la yoro ke kuando kerian azer algun kapricho los de la komunita, era kon la fuersa dela kasha publika. Esta *makka* es un uzo ke turo i asta muestro tyenpo prezente.

Kapitolo 10

Los terretemblos del anyo 5588 [1828].

Uvo en muestra sivdad kaji un mez de te[m]blamyentos de tyerra ke non deshava dia i noche atras sin aver uno o 2 terretemblos. Los *hahames* se adjuntaron i dechidyeron de azer *selihoth* en *t"t,* kitaron pregoneros por la sivdad azyendo una yamada a el puevlo a ke vinyeran todos a *t"t.* I ansi fue ke a la fin del dia, el *t"t* se topava embutido de toda la djuderia. Los *hahamim* ke se topavan en el *mabbul,* meldaron los *teillim* enteros. Despues salyo por *hazzan* el *Rav, h"r* Shaul, el kual savia azer munchos djestos i travar los syelos abasho. En medyo de el *selihoth,* tanto fue los djemidos i yoros, ke izo te[m]blar de muevo la tyerra i *t"t* kon los ke kontenia adyentro se empesaron a menear. Estonses, la esklamasyon fue tan fuerte ke unos esklamavan יה׳, שמע אביוניך [*Yah, Shema Evyoneha, Yah,* eskucha a Tus proves (Psalm 69:34)]; otros אל נורא עלילה, [*El Nora 'Alila, El,* temerozo en echas, (Psalm 66:5)]. Enfin, empesaron a fuirsen **[16a]** del ת"ת *Talmud Tora* del espanto non sea ke kayera ת"ת i los tomara de debasho. En tanto, estos djemulamyentos turaron otros unos kuantos dias.

Kapitolo 11

Kolpe Kuatro

En este tyempo, non avia koza de *chalgi* en las fyestas. Era solamente un pandero ke valia para azer bayles a las mujeres i a los ombres. Ma, en las fyestas delos rikos, ya avia *chalgi* i un kantador muy alavado el kual se yamava *Murteza{n}*.

En este tyempo, kazo un ijo de *chilibi* Menahem Faradji. Este sinyor era p{i}rimer bankiyer de la sivdad, era el *sarraf bashi* del governo, syendo un tyempo non avia *hazine* partikolar. Ande el *Pasha* era ke vinia toda la moneda dela entrada del *Vilayet,* vinia en su kasha, i el despues mandava *haznes* a Estambol. La fyesta se izo kon gran pompa enel *konak* de *Chilibi* Menahem ke es agora la kaza de el si. Merkado Yeoshua i si. David Nehama. Agora apartyene ala komunidad. Era dela entrada del *t"t* fina la *kyoshe.* Detras de este *konak,* era la kaza del *Rav, h"r* Shaul, ke agora {el} es el patron el si. Shaul Shaltiel. Espartia una pared entre el *konak* de *Chilibi* Menahem a la kaza del *Rav, h"r* Shaul. Una noche de la fyesta, estavan tanyendo *kyeman,* i [illegible], i [illegible], i pandero.

Ala noche, despues de komer, el *Rav, h"r* Shaul se echo en su kama. El non pudo tomar esfuenyo dela *saltanat* ke se azia enla fyesta i el sonete del *kyeman* le paresia komo una vyeja ke estava yorando, syendo en su vida non tuvo sintido sonete de *kyeman.* Demando a su famiya ke izyeran a azer a kayar a este martiyo. **[16b]** La famiya, en riendo, le respondyo ke non era ni vyeja, ni martiyo, si non la boz del *kyeman* ke estavan azyendo a la fyesta. El disho ke esta boz non tyene sintido nunka otro ke los chufletes ke vyenen de *bazarya* ke tanyen los ninyos por la kaye. Le disheron ke akeyo non es *kyeman* otro ke chuflete. Le mostraron una medya kalavasa kon una flecha, i en meneando dicha flecha es ke aze este sonete. Estonses, disho el si. *rav* ke es אסור *[asur]* de la Ley, i se yama שתי וערב *[shethi va-'erev,* (Leviticus 13:48 and Hullin 109b)*]*. De vista, mando a el שמש *[shammash]*, dizyendoles ke non pue[d]an sirvirsen de este enstrumento de tanyer. Estonses, le dyeron avizo a *Chilibi* Menahem del שליח *[shaliah]* ke mando el *rav*. I le mando a dizir ke non tyene dirito de se emmeskar en fyestas dela djente otro ke kuando le eran 2 personas a דין תורה *[din Tora]*, ke aga lo ke kere. El שליח *[shaliah]*, torno sin gostar de dinguna koza dela fyesta ile komuniko ael toda la dicha a el si. *rav*. El si. *rav* sin tadrar mando a *enheremar* a todos los de la fyesta entera, a el patron i alos kombidados. I al שמש *[shammash]*, lo echaron dela puerta afuera.

Al dia, el *chilibi* mando i trusho un *yapidji* i le serro una puertizika ke dava para el *konak* ke era kavo de *kyoshe*.

Estonses uvo una barana i unas maldisyones קללות נמרצות *[kelaloth nimrasoth]*. El *chilibi* non izo kavzo de todo esto. Na otra kombinasyon para enforteser mas el fanatizmo. Ya dishimos ke *Chilibi* Menahem era *sarraf bashi* delas salidas i entradas del *Vilayet*. Despues ke pagavan los *aylikes* a todos los funksyonaryos, el resto mandava en *haznes* a Kostantinopoli, al adreso de banka Haten. Un poko tyempo despues dela shéna ke kontimos ariva, *chilibi* Avraam Haten vino en Saloniko, i fue risivido kon munchas onores en kaza de **[17a]** *chilibi* Menahem, i le izyeron unos *ziafetes* ekstraordinaryos ke el kual kedo enkantado de todas las komidas delikadas, i de todos los frutos ermozos, las djoyas delas mujeres, los mobles de kaza, de estofas. Izo un kalkolo ke si en Estambol se aze este modo de fyestas se derrokan bankas grandes. En esta gruta de *Chilibi* Menahem eran 3 *haverim* ke kontinuan a 5 ijos kazados kada uno. I todos estos gastes salian de un djarro. I egzaminando la koza, vido ke en poko tyempo se iva a rovinar este echo.

Chilibi Avraam Haten, kon su fineza, kijo eskabuyarse de esta *hevra* i paso todas las korespondensyas de *Chilibi* Menahem al governo, i *Chilibi* Avraam se aparto de esta *hevra*. Non paso poko tyempo, esta gruta se rovino asta las simyentes, i non pudo pagar una suma grandisima al governo.

El governo mando 2 altos funksyonaryos en Selanik, i devista le siyaron la kaza i la gruta, i los mandaron prizyoneros a {do} todos 3 en Kostantinopla, i todos los mobles pasaron al governo i lo izyeron al *konak* de *Chilibi* Menahem morada para los fonksyonaryos. La kaza de el si. Avramachi Nahmias la izyeron *hukyumat*, la kaza del si. Izakucho Nahmias, el 3 *haver*, se izo *dayres* para los *kyatipes*. Despues de tyempo, si. Avramachi Nahmias salyo libre kon dizyendo ke el era *sarraf bashi* de Manastir, i mandava los grupos a la banka de *Chilibi* Menahem. Miraron los kuentos i le tornaron el *konak* atras. Ma *Chilibi* Menahem i *Ham* Yishakucho muryeron desfortunados i kedaron נע ונ{ע}[ד] עד היום *na' va-na{'}[d] 'ad a-yom*, [i sere meneado i esmovido, (Genesis 4:14) fina oy]. Ke miren muestros melda{ron}[dores]. Komo ke non se enrezyára el fanatizmo entre el puevlo? I pensavan ke las maldisyones de el *Rav, h"r* Shaul kavzo todo esto.

Kapitolo 12

Los *melammedim* krueles

[17b] En mi tyempo, el *Talmud Tora* tenia una regla ke los chikitikos, de 4 a 5 anyos, los mandavan los padres ande el *rubi*. I despues de un anyo o dos de estar en el tavlado dela *hevra*, le embezava la אלפה[3] ביתה *[alpha beta]* kon los puntos asta ke les embezava adjuntar los biervos. Los *parnasim* de *t"t* egzaminavan klasa por klasa, i los ke vian kapaches de los *talmidim* delos *rubisim*, los pasavan a otro מלמד *[melammed]* ke les embezava las זמירות *[zemiroth]*. Al egzamen del otro anyo, los pasavan en otro מלמד *[melammed]* por meldar שני *[sheni]* de פרשה *[parasha]*. Al anyo, en otro מלמד *[melammed]* de רביעי *[revi'i]* de פרשה *[parasha]*, kon los טעמים *[te'amim]*. Despues, lo pasavan a פרשה *[parasha]* kon ladino. En este מלמד *[melammed]*, embezavan los elevos la פרשה *[parasha]* en ladino, komo kantar sin entender lo ke estan dizyendo. I les echava el ladino delos טעמים *[te'amim]* en kantando. Por egzempyo, שופר מהופך קדמא זקף קטון *[shofar meuppah kadma zakeph katon], shofar* aboltado akonantado asta la chika. Esto, a el elevo le plazia, ke era una kantiga non savyendo ke es el ladino de שופר מהופך *[shofar meuppah].* Despues, los pasavan asta 8 klasas, asta ke vinian en la meza del *haham* ke meldava פרשה *[parasha]* i הפטרה *[aftara]* entera en ladino i נביאים *[nevi'im]* komo ירמיה *[Yermiya]* i ישעיה *[Yeshaya],* i chetr. I un pedaso de פרשה *[parasha]* en רשי *[Rashi].* Este *melammed* era el mas kruel de todos los del *t"t.* Este sinyor se yamava .ח. מ. צ, *[H[am] M. S.],* era de talya *orta* i godro, era peludo komo Esav. Kuando vinia la manyana a su ofisyo en el enverano, el se avriya la pechadura ise desnudava, se kitava los *mintanes* i el bonete, i los pyezes deznudos ke golian a guezmo de נבלה *[nevela].* Se aremangava las pyernas fina al djinoyo i los brasos fina el kovdo, yeno de kaveyos ke paresian komo unas espinotas. **[18a]** La pechadura yena de pyelo i los ojos komo unas *chanakas.* Los *talmidim* ke echavan una ojada sovre el, se les asemejavan al מלאך המות *[malah a-maveth].* El tomava en su mano un nyervo o una verga de *kizildjik* ise asentava en un *postekyi.*

Kuando le empesavan a echarles la פרשה *[parasha],* el bushkava achake para ir aharvando a los *talmidim.* Ande mas, kuando algun padre mandava alguna kesha por su ijo, el kitava la *falaka* del armaryo, i la aro[n]java en el varandado del *t"t* de un kavo fina el otro, i azia un ruido de truenos.

Los *talmidim,* a esta *dubara,* les tomava frio i kalor, pensando a ken les va akayer la esfuerta. Estonses, el *haham* azia desenyas a los monitores ke tomaran a el ninio i ke lo echaran en basho i le metian la *falaka,* abashava el komo un leon i trinkando los dyentes komo un tigre. I empesava a darle kon krueldad en los pyezes asta una kuenta kele paresia a el *munasup,* 50, 80, o 100 dadas. Despues ke lo levantavan al ninio, non se pudia detener en pyes delas fushkas ke se le azian.

El אכזר *[ahzar],* por mas krueldad, le metia un monitor de kada lado porke lo estuvyeran kaminando, koryendo por el varandado entero, i el ninio sufria mas muncho delas dadas ke le dyo.

Enfin, desta esfuerte kayo akorruto sovre unos mansevikos ke non pudyeron mas sufrirlo: 3 de eyos fueron i se izyeron turkos. En mizmo tyempo, tomo i ami a azerme lo propyo de los otros. Yo, syendo guerfano, me akeshi kon mi sinyora madre, dizyendo ke non la puedo somportar mas esta vida. Mi sinyora madre mando a yamarlo a este si. *haham* ile **[18b]** dyo la kesha, dizyendole ake non me aharvara mas. El respondyo en trinkando los dyentes el proverbo [en Ladino] ke "la letra, kon sangre entra", me tomo por el braso i me yevo al *t"t*. En asentandome al banko, el tomo la *falaka* komo de uzo, i echandome los ojos sovre mi, i menazandome kon su kavesa de toro, i aro[n]jo la *falaka* komo de uzo. Yo, ya entendi ke la *sehora* ya la iva echar sovre mi. Echi un bolo i me fui komo una agila. El, mando detras de mi 8 a 10 mansevikos ake me aferraran, ma sus esforsos fueron inutiles. Yo, me fui ala kaza de mi sinyora vava lakuala era la madre de mi sinyor padre, la kuala bivia, i ke morava djunto kon su ija la grande la kuala se yamava Bula Miryam de *h'* Yusef Ezrati.

Mi sinyora vava, vyendome tanto espan[ta]do, i la kara demudada, kaji dezmayado, eya me abraso, me bezo, syendo yo era el uniko ke aviya kedado del fruto de su ijo. Me demando la kavza de esta fuyida. Yo le konti detayadamente todas mis sufriensas. Eya devista se vistyo *kyurdi* i maraman, i ami me desho en guardya kon mi sinyora tia, i se vino ala kaza de mi si. madre kon gritos i guayas, dizyendole, "esta rama me kedo, i esto keresh ke se pyedra? Ke ansi, devista de este *melammed* kruelo, kitaldo". I ansi fue ke me pasaron ala meza de גמרא די ברכות *[gemara de berakhoth]*. Ai fue ke topi un poko de *raatlik*. Ma por dezgrasya, kedi krudo de embezar el *arba' ve-'esrim* komo se deve. Este ombre fue la kavza de salir yo עם ארץ *['am ares]*. Estonses, yo era amante de saver kozas de eskrituras santas. Non topava livros de ke meldar, otro **[19a]** ke unas *gemarikas* en ladino. Tomi ameldar el livriko del הדני [אלדד] {דעד}*{da'ath}* *[Eldad a-Dani]*, la broshura de el בן סירה [Ben Sira], una *gemarika* de Yosef el dela Reyna. Todo esto ke meldi fueron para mi handradjos i kankaravias.

Estonses, vinyeron los primeros portestantes en Saloniko, i trusheron miles de livros de *arba' ve-'esrim* de 2 kolonas la pajina, eskrito en *lashon* i en ladino. I tomi a meldar de mi para mi por el *lashon* i el ladino, i fui entendyendo todo loke me era fasil a entender. Ma algunas kozas delos נביאים *nevi'im* me kedavan por entenderlas. En *konusheando* kon los portestantes ke vinyeron me avansi un poko en el *arba' ve-'esrim*, ma iyo ya me konosko keso *'am aares* enfrente de los savyos, i ke estudyaron byen en la lingua santa. Dunkue, estos krueles *melammedim* fueron la kavza de kedar los elevos inyorantes, ke los de mi edad ke salyeron inyorantes. Yo ya me konto por el mas savyo de eyos, kijendo dizir kela negra kondukta delos *melammedim* fue la kavza de kedar todos inyorantes.

Kapitolo 13

La landra

Ya dishimos ke syendo yo kedi guerfano de padre a la edad de 5 a 6 anyos, i de madre de 15 a 16 anyos, kon un ermaniko *sakat*. Vyendome dezramado de mis paryentes, dishe entre mi, si non yo para mi, kyen para mi? (Avoth 1:14), i bushki de aprontar mi mantenimyento. Me entri en la estampa, en el ofisyo de mi padre, ke dainda estava **[19b]** el empyegado ke kedo despues dela muerte de mi padre, travajando en la estamparia kon 2 מסדרים *[mesadderim]*, i un moso para dar tinta. En este tyempo, la letra ya se avia echo muncho vyeja, kije vazyarla de muevo kon los *kalupes* i matridjas ke ya tenia, i empesi a la ovra. Ma mi maestro, non kijendome embezar los puntos ke se tenian demenester para kada matridja, estuve kaji 2 mezes vazyandolas asta ke eskapi de vazyar las letras. Ma si komo me mankava el soplo, non salyo la letra a dover. Estonses yo, vyendo ke por kavza de non embezarme mi maestros los puntos ke se tenian de menester por ke salyera la letra buena, lo echi a mi maestro dela estamparia.

En este tyempo, me dyo a travajar el si. *Haham, h"r Rabbenu* Gatenyo su livro a ke lo estampara, el livro מחושקים כסף *[Mehoshkim Kesef]*. I syendo empeso la landra de [5]597 al [5]598 [1837-1838], sobrevyó esta peste a un grado muy alto de muertos al dia.

Ma el *haham*, espantandose de esta negra hazinura, non sea ke se muryera, i le kedava {el} el livro por en medyo, el kontinuo a darme manuskrito por ke se eskapara el livro. I pude mantenerme, אפילו *[afillú]* en tyempo de landra. Ma desgrasyada mente ke el livro se eskapo kon esta letra vazyada sin חשבון *[heshbon]*.

En tanto, los ke me vian en tyempo de landra travajar se maraviavan en dizyendo, "un manseviko de 17 anyos ke estuvyera travajando sin eskatimarse de su vida". I ke todo el mundo kedaron de sus echos, todos los *charshis* serrados, la midad del puevlo fuyidos **[20a]** en sivdades ajenas, los firidos estavan muryendosen a syenes kada dia, i yo morava en una kamareta kon mi ermaniko, solos, ma non azia kuento delos espantos ke tenian la djente de los שטנים *[satanim]*, delos danyadores, delos *karakandjos*; de todas estas, yo non tuve dingun espanto, ni menos lo meti en memorya.

Estonses, yevavan una idea falsa la djente ke los pekados del ombre los tenian eskritos enriva de la frente, i ke en vyendolos, el שטן *[satan]* por la kaye, les aro[n]djava la landre, i los firia, i les kavzava la muerte. Munchos de estos fanatikos se tapavan la frente kon un *yemini* por ke non los vyera el guerko la eskritura desus frentes. Los ombres de onze la ora ke se enserravan en kaza, i tapavan las ventanas kon kozas pretas, komian i se echavan de las 12 [7 PM], sin luz porke non se aparara el guerko por la ventana i vyera ke ay djente adyentro.

Mi ermana la sigunda, tenyendo en el vizindado un firido de landra, se vino a mi kaza. El marido, si komo era ombre kaminante, tenia armas, las enkolgo en una pared dela *uda*. Yo, kijendo matar a los gatos porke se ivan a la kaza delos atakados i vinian a la kaza de los limpyos, i atakavan i akea kaza tambyen, i yo tomi una arma delas de mi kunyado, i la inchi kon *barut*, i *sachma*, i me suvi {a la} alatarasa, i vide un gato en el tejado de mi vizino ke era תלמיד חכם *[talmid haham]*, ize fuego i lo mati a el gato. Debasho de este tejado avia una mujer ke estava paryendo. A la boz de el *tufek*, eya paryo a una kriatura, syendo ya la trazera dolor. El *haham* se aparo por el *perde* de mi kaza i me enheremo. I yo, se lo torni **[20b]** atras de un modo en terminos suzyos, el kual , furyozo, sin pensar, i el me lo torno de mezmo.

De vista, el se fue ande el *Haham* si. *Rav, h"r* Shaul, ile konto el fato entero. Devista, me mando a yamar, demandandome porke esto echando el dia entero *fishekes*, i esto espantando a el mundo. Yo le respondi ke non es[t]ava tirando por mi gusto, otro ke por azer bondad a el vizindado por ke non se atake alguna kaza de muevo. Estonses, me disho, "na, ke una mujer estava paryendo i paryo del myedo dela boz del *tufek*". Yo le respondi ke i esto es una bondad, ke la mujer paryo presto! El *haham* demando ke le kitara al gato del tejado por ke se va guzanear del sol. Yo topi una vara, me suvi a su tejado i {se} selo aro[n]ji a su *chardak*.

Avlaremos agora de esta hazinura de landra ke espesya era. Los medikos de estonses dizian ke esta hazinura es un moshkito salido de las suzyedades de unas ranas delas baras ke ay en los kampos de el Habesh (Indyas), i ke la djente de estos lugares la *kulanean* komo *kulanean* en Evropa los frios. I los viyajadores de estos lugares vinian al Edjipto, i atakavan al Edjipto. I de Edjipto, se atako la Turkiya, syendo ke estonses non konosian en Turkiya koza de kuarentina. Ma la Evropa tenia en sus frontyeras *lazaretes* para el ke vinia de la Turkiya ilos metia ai, i despues los deshava entrar.

Kuando le dyeron el prenchipato a Mehmed Ali Pasha, la Evropa izo un tratado kon Mehmed Ali Pasha a ke izyera una kuarentina 3 dias antes del Edjipto porke los viajadores del Habesh non podyeran entrar en el Edjipto sin azer la kuarentina (40 dias). **[21a]** I asta muestros dias, esta kuarentina egziste. En este modo, se pudo abandonar esta hazinura de el mundo.

Oy ke eskrivo{s} ya ay 3 anyos ke esta hazinura se abandono, ke antes de este tyempo en la Turkiya se aparesiya kada 15, 20, 25 anyos. I kuando se aparesiya en la Turkiya dava una temor a todo el mundo syendo se arravdonavan en la anyada ke vinia dita hazinura, en kada sivdad se ahazinavan miles de personas adyentro de 3 mezes del enverano. Yo era estonses en el [5]598 [1838] era aedado de 18 anyos, ma non konosi de estos espantos ke tenian la djente.

En este tyempo, se atak{a}[o] mi ermana la grande ke morava en mi kaza, sin tener yo dingun avizo de eya. En akel tyempo, kuando alguno kaiva hazino, kalia ke yamaran algun mediko espesyal ke konosia byen la natura de esta hazinura. El se yamava *h'* Yaakov Haten. Asu lado, avia una persona empyegado del קולל *[Kolel],* i se yamava *h"r* Moshe Ezrati, era un tio de mi kunyado. Kuando los fui a yamar, los trushe por una puertizika sekreta, al mediko djunto kon Moshe Ezrati. El le apalpo en los lugares ke ésta landra salia, ke era en 3 lugares, los kualos son: en la garganta, debacho la keshada, i debasho del lado, i debasho de las íngles un tolondro en forma de un pipiniko.

Ma este mediko era tan kapache ke konosia esta firida si era de bivir o de murir. La firida de mi ermana era livyana, non era tanto grave. El tio de mi kunyado por non desturvarlo i kitarlo de gaste, le disho ke la enk{r}uvriera la koza porke non se supyera. El mediko le dyo unos inguentes ke le fueron fregando **[21b]** en esta firida. I ansi fue ke en manko de 10 dias, la firida se desparesyo.

Mi kaza, era el *dosheme* {era} mesmo kon la kaye. Las noches vinian los כלבים *[kelavim]* i azian una rebuelta. Mi ermana kontava ke kada noche vinian los שדים *[shedim]* i derrokavan el *kaldirim* dela kaye. Yo, ke non kreia en estos handrajos, salia kada manyana en la kaye i via ke non se salyo ninguna pyedra de su lugar. Mi ermana me kombido a ke me echara en su kamareta djunto kon su ermaniko, syendo yo tenia una kamareta en resparte. Yo le refuzi, ma mi ermaniko, sintyendo los espantos ke tenia mi ermana, me ovligo a yevarmos la kama adyentro desu kamareta en un *kyenar* respartido. Entre la noche, empesi a sintir un ruido en la kaye ke paresia en verdad dezazer el *kaldirim.* Yo alevanti la kavesa i miri por una fendriz dela puertizika sekreta, i avia un lunar muy klaro, atini ke era una partida de perros, una madre kon sus *yavrikos,* ke estavan ai *engreendosen,* i era un gueso ke tenian, ke uno lo keria, i el otro lo keria, i esto era el sonete de el *kaldirim!* Yo tomi una toyaka ke tenia en mi lado i avri la puerta sin azer dinguna rebuelta. Sali a la kaye i le di una buena palicha i fuyeron unos por aki i otros por ai. I tomi el gueso i lo truche adyentro de kaza, i serri la puerta.

Mi ermana i mi kunyado, ke sintyeron la rebuelta de la kaye, se empesaron arankar los kaveyos. De el espanto ke tomo mi ermana, le echaron un grano siego en la espalda ke lo yamavan karvonko del kual se gormo sus pekados. Yo les mostri el gueso i les dishe, "na el *dikyel* ke arankan las pyedras de el *kaldirim,* i ke a **[22a]** los guerkos ya les di una buena leksyon porke non vengan mas por aki".

En el tyempo de esta hazinura, avia de 30 a 40 guardyanes i 15 a 20 mujeres vyejas guardyanas. I avia un kortijo kon una partida de kazas de el *kolel,* ke ai estavan aparejados kuando los yamavan por algun firido. I ya avia un guardian *bashi* ke el mandava en la kaza de el firido a una mujer kon ombres, i 2 ombres kon una mujer a la kaza del firido un ombre alto, grodo, royo. En tyempo bueno, era pintor, *(boyadji).* Kuando el mediko le dava algun *[haber]* ke en tala kaza se topa algun firido, i[v]a el i azia vazyar la kaza de todas sus paryentes, i se salian afuera i los mandava en algun lugar separato, i se deznudavan los vistidos, i se vistian ropas limpias, i azian en este lugar 10 dias de kuarentina. I kedava la kaza entera kon todos los byenes en poder de estos guardyanes komo si fueran eyos mizmos los patrones, i eran sirvidos en gaste de el patron de la kaza. La manyana, les mandava el dezayuno, a medyo sus buen armorzo, i la noche lo mezmo. I un *altilik* de djornal por [kada] uno ke era el guardyan *bashi* ke kovrava. El *raki* les iva kon *binlikes,* el vino era kon baril. Si el hazino se muria, lo yevavan al muerto a בית החיים *[beth a-hayyim],* i kedava la kaza serrada 40 dias. En los 5 por syen delos firidos ke kedavan bivos estavan los guardyanes ai komyendo i bevyendo i emborrachandose. Al dia de 41, se lo yevavan en el hazino a el banyo, i eyos *beraber.* I todas las ropas las echavan en mojo por un dia o dos, i las lavavan byen. Estonses tornavan todos los paryentes en kaza. **[22b]** Kuando a los firidos ke murian de esta hazinura, o ke algunos matavan los guardyanes, era un kavzo de esta hazinura ke les vinia una fyevre tan huerte ke perdian sus konsensyas, i se alevantavan komo los barraganes i azian estrasos en la kaza. Los guardyanes, kijendo estar en sus postos emborrachandosen, lo tomavan a el hazino, lo echavan en su kama, lo atabafavan kon una kolcha, i se asentavan kada uno por una parte de la kolcha fin ke se le tomava al *suluk* de el hazino, i mueria.

Akontesyo una dezgrasya estonses ke una muchacha se firyo i le metyeron 2 guardyanas i un guardyan. La muchacha era muy ermoza, indimas en la kayentura se le izyeron sus karas komo la roza. El guardyan, borracho, se enflamo i bushko de dezonorar a la muchacha. Ma si komo la mosa onesta, i ensima de su hazinura i de la kayentura fuerte no somportava, non se desho dezonorar. El guardyan, vyendo ke non reusho a su negro eskopo, la atabafo kon la kolcha; esto fue la kavza de su muerte! Este guardyan mando a las 2 guardyanas a ke lavaran las ropas, i kumplyo su mala echa despues dela muerte de la muchacha. Las guardyanas abarrontaron lo ke este maldicho ombre izo, se lo komunikaron al guardyan *bashi,* i devista fue i se lo disho a el si. *Rav, h"r* Shaul esta mala echa. El si. *rav* akojo una partida delos *hahamim* i delos *gevirim* i se fueron a *t"t.* Mandaron 2 guardyanes, los forsudos, i aferraron a este asasino, i lo trusheron a *t"t.* Lo izyeron *istindak,* i atorgo su mala echa kon dizyendo ke estava borracho. Lo echaron en basho de el kortijo del *t"t,* i le metyeron la *falaka,* i le dyeron 500 palos asta ke lo desharon **[23a]** *bayileado.* Lo tomaron los 2 guardyanes, i lo yevaron a la prezyon delos guardyanes ke es de בר מינן *[bar minnan],* lo echaron en una gruta, i non supe ke fue de el.

Este fato non es kontado de dinguno otro ke lo vide yo kon mi ojo. Era un ombre ke vistia *djubben* i *entari,* i era syego de un ojo, i se yamava ש. מ. ט. *Ham [S. M. T].* En supyendo este fato eskandalozo el puevlo, non se fiavan mas las famiyas en deshar a los firidos solos en mano de los guardyanes. En kavzo de algun atako, se kedavan el padre o la madre para asigurar a sus keridos kon un guardyan o dos, i ke en este modo pudyeron salvar a munchos de sus paryentés de la muerte.

Kapitolo 14

Nizam Askyeri

Despues dela matansa delos djanisares ke se izo en At Meydan, Sultan Mahmut el Sigundo fue un ombre tan savyo i tan korajozo. El tenia un korason de leon komo ya es alavado en las estoryas de todos reyes. El fue kapache de tomar de su parte a Ala [Agha] Pasha ke era el kapo de todos los djanisares, ko{s}[n] sus prometas kele izo el Sultan. El lo konvensyo i akonsejo a el *yenicheri* entero ke eran 40 mil almas dela *kishla* de Estanbol en At Meydan para traerles una repuesta de el Sultan satisfazyente. Ala [Agha] Pasha se fue ande el Sultan. En myentres, vistyo 20 mil almas de *sultuk* i pantalon, i los armo de fuziles i apronto 2 baterias de tiros, la una de la una entrada dela kaleja de At Meydan, i la bateria de la otra entrada dela kaleja, i 10 mil detras de kada bateria. **[23b]** Dela otra parte, ke es la mar, armo todos los navios de gerra, i ke ala prima sinyal avrieran fuego delas bokas delos tiros. Vinyendo Ala [Agha] Pasha, se suvyo en un lugar alto, i les respondyo, "el Sultan non tyene menester de dar kuento a dinguno. El, komo kapo de la nasyon, el save rijir muy byen su imperyo".

En sintyendo esta repuesta, los djanisares echaron todos en una un grito de vengansa, non supyendo ke las entradas de At Meydan estavan embutidas de *has askeri*. Eyos se dirijeron para la *kishla* para tomar las armas, enkontraron kon el fuego delos tiros i los *krushumes* de los *tufekes*. I eyos se tornaron de la parte dela mar por topar sus fuyidas, enkontraron kon los tiros delos navios de gerra ke toparon la muerte 40 mil almas adyentro de 2 oras ke se izo una estera de muertos en At Meydan. Eskapandose esta shéna, mando i derroko todos los *odjakes* i *kapis* ande los *yenicheris* azian las sedutas.

Despues de un poko de repozo de las armas, el kito *tellales* i la bandyera santa kon *bolukes* de *nizames* armados ake avrieran todos sus magazenes, sus butikas, a ke estuvyeran trankuilos en sus echos, i mando *askyeres* vistidos a la moda evropea en todas las grandes sivdades, i ke desbarasaran a todo el *yenicheri* ke se topava en todo modo de lugar.

En Saloniko, mando de 8 a 10 *tabures* de *askyer*, i fueron aferrando a todo el ke apartenia a el *yenicheri* i los aprezava en *Beyaz Kule*, i kada noche matavan de 10 a 15, sigun era la porsyon ke aferravan el dia. I en kada 1 ke matavan, echavan un tiro. En este modo, se savia en Saloniko la kuenta de los matados de la noche.

[24a] Por esta razon, la yamavan de vyejo a esta torre *Kanli Kule*, asta tyempo ke suvyo a el trono muestro soverano, Sultan Hamid Sigundo, i dyo orden a ke por endelantre la yamen *Beyaz Kule*. Devista yamaron una partida de enkaladores, i la enkalaron entera, i la izyeron una palomba blanka komo la ven oy.

Kuando vinyeron estos askyeres en Saloniko kon los kapos rijidores, en sus kaveseras un *kaymakam*, un *emir alay*, i un *alay emini*, *binbashi*, *yüzbashi*, todos eyos vistidos de uniforma de *sirma* de klavedon. Estos altos funksyonaryos tomaron kada uno un *konak* por sus kuentos. Esto fue el empesijo de el repozo de todos los puevlos.

Estos altos funksyonaryos dainda non vistian kamiza a la franka. Eyos kijendose vistir a uzo evropeo, eyos demandaron a un syerto *Ham* Daniel Andjel, ke su gruta de *Karı Pazar* era el asyento de estos funksyonaryos, le demandaron a el ke les perkurara de tomarles kamizas a la franka. El asavento kyen vendia de estas kamizas, i non topo, syendo estonses inda non avia makyinas. I los frankos ke vistian eran todas echas de la mano de mi si. madre, ke este ofisyo fue er{a}[e]dado de su madre, i de su si. vava. Supyendo *Ham* Daniel ke era menester de yamar a mi si. madre, porke les izyera a kada uno una duzena de kamizas, bushko de yevar a mi si. madre ande estos sinyores. I mi si. madre le respondyo ke eya non iva en kaza de turko, otro ke todo el ke kere ke venga en kaza, i le tomava mezura, i se las kuzia. Este si. *Ham* Daniel demando a komo era la kamiza de echura por una. I respondyo ke a todos los konsolos i merkaderes les toma un *altilik* de echura por kamiza. *Ham* Daniel le respondyo ke el tomava por korrederia 100 por 100 delo ke les desmersava a estos sinyores.

[24b] Mi si. madre le respondyo, "va byen, si me pagan a 2 *altilikes,* tomá el uno vos". Este si. le disho, "yo vos vo a traer aki 3 personas porke les agash a una duzena a kada uno". Mi si. madre penso ke es 3 personas ke van avinir, ma kuando sintyo de el sonido delos kavayeros, ke kada uno de eyos tenia 20 soldados de detras deyos, armados i suvidos a kavayo, se incheron las kalejas, yenas de toda esta djente. Por mijor dizir ke las kalejas de mi kaza eran kalejikas, syendo por la una parte tenia 3 pikos de anchura, i la otra 2. Echando una ojada por la ventana, a la vista de los vistidos en*sirmados* i las espadas enkolgando, devista enserro a mis 3 ermanas mosas en una kamareta. Entraron los 3 grandes i 4 a 5 *binbashis* kon eyos, non tenia ni menos siyas por asentarlos, fue kostrata de tomar de el vizindado i asentarlos todos eyos, altos, puerpuedos, kuvyertos en la *sirmá.* Sinyor Daniel non era manko de eyos. Era gordo abastante, alto, una *shemle* de seda en la kavesa, ent[a]ri de *shamaladja, djubben* de *shali, kushak* de Tarabuluz. Mando a el *charshi* a sus mosos a ke trusheran *top*es de *muabethane.* Trusheron de 40 a 50 *top*es de esta ropa para ke les izyera una duzena a kada uno. En vyendo la ropa, mi si. madre le disho ke el presyo ke demando non le konvyene, syendo esta ropa es muy dura para kuzirse. *Ham* Daniel le acheto a 3 *altilikes* por tomar la mitad el, syendo los funksyonaryos non savian ni dos ni tres, solo lo ke les dizia el, syendo la kasha de *Chilibi* Menahem estava avyerta para todo modo de *pusula* ke le mandavan. Mi si. madre les tomo mezura de kada uno delas ropas ke eskojyeron, i kitava מעשר *[ma'aser]* de kada duzena un *anteri* para mi, ke de estas 10 duzenas me aparto para mi kazamyento 2 *antaris,* **[25a]** 5 *mintanes,* 5 djaketas. Devista ke se fueron, mi si. madre kon sus 3 ijas, i 3 disheplas otras arp{e}aron la mano, i de dyentro de un mez eskaparon 8 duzenas de kamizas. El dia ke se eskaparon, vinyeron estos 3 sinyores i se amezuraron kada uno una kamiza, i el resto las empakaron i las mandaron a sus kazas. Trusheron una rida yena de *altilikes,* i le pagaron {i le pagaron} a mi si. madre. Ala buelta, torno si. Daniel a tomar su mitad. Mi si. madre le empeso a azer *djefa.* El le respondyo ke, " non es de vos solo ke tomo mitad, es אפילו *[afillú]* akel ke karrea arena para la *kishla,* le tomo la mitad". De este modo, este ombre se izo milyonestro. Ma ke provecho, ke non kedo nombransa ni deel, ni de su byen, syendo tuvo 3 ijos, i todos eyos muryeron sin tener ijos. El chiko solamente bive en ירושלים *[Yerushalayim],* ma sin tener ijos. I ya es aedado *chirka* 70 anyos.

Kapitolo 15

El fuego de [5]600 [1839]

Prima noche de ראש השנה *[Rosh a-Shana],* 2 la ora [9 PM] estando kada uno i una en su kaza, sintimos 2 kolpos de kanon anonsyando[mo]s fuego. Este fuego salyo de *Papuchchilar Hani* i tomo de 4 partes. El enséndyo, ke se vino asta *Kari Pazar,* i arodeo todos los *charshis* en una flama, i se fue por *[H]amza Bey,* i kemo todo el kuartyer franko asta la Puerta de el Vardar, se atorno por la Torre de la Marina, i kemo fina la plasa i el kuartyer de עץ החיים *[Es a-Hayyim],* kemo la karneseria, todo esto se izo *tarla,* asta ke vino ala קהלה *[keilla]* de Aragon. Los *haverim* de dita *keilla,* vyendo ke ya se va a kemar, derrokaron todas, todas las kazas ke avian a el deredor de la קהלה *[keilla].* En este modo, pudyeron salvar la קהלה *[keilla].* Enfin, se puede dizir

[25b] ke *chirka* medyo Saloniko se yevo las flamas de el fuego, kaji mas muncho terreno de el fuego de [5]650, [1890] ke yo, salyendo a el dia a ver a el fuego de la *kyoshe* de el *tidjaret* vyejo, se via la Puerta de el Vardar, sin dingun entrompyeso. Boltando de kara ala mar, se vian la mar i las naves. En verdad ke fue este fuego muy grande, ma non era de fraguas ke abitavan el puevlo, syendo lo{s} mas muncho fue *charshis*; i el kuartyer franko, era kada kaza ke kontenia una guerta i un kortijo muy largo. Estonses, inda non avia kompanyias de sigurita en muestra sivdad, i kedaron אפילו *[afillú]* algunos rikos sin sus byenes i averes.

A kontinuar (2)[4]

La kitada del Rav Matalon

En este anyo, los חכמים *[hahamim]* estavan envailes de algunas kozas ke azia el *Rav* Matalon a su plazer, i eyos, el kontraryo. Ma kuando vino la fin de desbrochar, fue ande es ke *h"r* Yeoshua Modiano, se le muryo la mujer. Syendo un riko potente i savyo, i ke inda estava en la flor de el bivir, bushko de tomar una mujer a su plazer. Entre tantas mujeres ke le trusheron, el eskojo una ermoza i non tanto aedada, i de buena משפחה *[mishpaha],* se despozo kon eya.

Tomo avizo el *Rav* Matalon de este echo i mando a dizirle ke non puedia tomar a esta mujer, syendo eya es otomana i él era italyano. En paryendo esta mujer, los ijos se van a pasar a la bandyera italyana. Dunke, por esta razon el non puedia tomar a esta mujer.

H"r Yeoshua, kualo kon su rikeza i su sensya, i ke era uno delos grandes de la sivdad, ezistyo para tomar a esta mujer. El *rav* le mando a dizir ke el non dava orden a ke le dyeran קדושין *[kiddushim]* kon esta mujer. **[26a]** I si en kavzo non eskucha, el daria avizo al *hukyumat.*

Estonses, vyendose amenazado *h"r* Yeoshua, mando djente

ande el *rav* a ke se *desvacheara* de este kapricho, i ke le akometyeran una partida de moneda. El demando ke kyeria tantos i kuantos. *H"r* Yeoshua, en tal de kontentar su dezeo i alkansar a esta mujer, el mando la moneda demandada i se kazo kon esta sinyora.

Estonses, si komo el *Rav, h"r* Avraam Gatenyo i el *Rav, h"r* David Yosef pasavan las oras kon *h"r* Yeoshua, en sus konversasyones se avryo la kuestyon del fato de el *Rav* Matalon. Eyos ke estavan enflamados de antes delas echas de antes non konvenivles para un *rav,* se asentaron en una asamblea djeneral los *hahamim* kon los *gevirim* i dechidyeron delo kitar de su posto. Mandaron 2 *talmide hahamim* grandes de nombrado de todos los *gevirim* dizyendole ke non es rekonosido mas por *rav.* En vyendose el *rav* akulpado, el les aro[n]djo el *firman* ke tenia de el governo de gran rabino.

Kapitolo No. 16

Los Kazamyentos

En mi tyempo, los kazamyentos se azian de un modo tan eskuro ke kuando despozavan algun ijo o alguna ija, se azia el echo a plazer de padre i madre, el novyo i la novya non se konosian, ni menos se vian del tyempo ke despozavan, otro ke kuando kazavan, syendo en este entervalo non pasava el novyo por la kaye de la kaza de la novya. A mi, kuando me despozaron, mi ermana i mi kunyado me disheron, "ya te despozimos", sin konoser yo, ni menos, al padre de la novya.

Vinyendo el tyempo de el kazamyento, ma sin entender para ke servia mi novya, me imajinava ke era para azer **[26b]** kolada, i para azer komidas, o ke mirara los echos de kaza{s} El dia de mi kazamyento, las mujeres izyeron todos los aparejos menesterozos. I ora 9 [4 PM], veo ke vyenen mis paryentés i mis ermanas byen vistidas. Eyos, despues de pokos puntos se fueron a traer a mi novya. En sus retorno, veo vinir una kuantita de mujeres ke non las konosko, entre eyas mis ermanas i una medya mujer i medya ombre, komo la serena de la mar. Pregunti a mis amigos, "ande esta mi novya"? Eyos me apuntaron kon {kon} el dedo a la ke estava en medyo de mis ermanas. Yo dishe en-tremi enkantado, "esto es por novya"? Non asemeja el kustum, ni a mosa, ni a mujer, syendo en su kavesa yevava {en su kavesa} un bonetiko tan chiko de estofa enkolgando vetas de bril, un velo enkastonado de *sirma*. I byen! El vistido de mujer era un sayo, i *anteri*, i mestas, i kalsado amariyo. Es esto novya? A esta vista, me se embrolyo el meoyo. Aun non era tan fea la vista, ma kon estos brutos artes me se asemejo a la serena de la mar. "Pasensya", dishe entre mi. Me disheron ke le echara konfites. Yo tanto *shashireado* estava ke los arro[n]ji ande me vino.

Ala suvida de la eskalera ya avia una vyeja kon un pedaso de sharope kolorado duro ke, apenas suvyendo la novya, se la metyo en la boka, i la novya lo echo por un lado dela keshada ke paresiya un guevo ke tenia en la boka. Ami me paresyo ke tenia la kara auflada, i sus karas eskorchadas de el pilador ke le izyeron el dia de antes. Enfin, paresia alevantada de una hazinura muy fuerte.

Entre esto, vinyeron mi djente, me vistyeron un *antari* de
[27a] kotne de Brusa, una *djubbe* de panyo albo i una toka byen asentada, ya se entyende byen a ke asemejava yo kon esta *memma* en mi kavesa, sin barva, i sin mustacho. Me izyeron aparar a el espejo, echi el ojo i me vide tan bruto ke eskupi al espejo. Me yevaron a la קהילה *[keilla]* i kantaron el קדיש *[kaddish]* i la קדושה *[kedusha]*, ma ami me estava paresyendo ke me estavan azyendo צידוק הדין *[sidduk a-din]*.

Kuando arivimos a kaza, empesaron otra vez a karpir los *paytanim*, i me disheron ke le metyera el anio a la novya. Me mostraron un dedo salido debasho el velo, i yo enklavi akeya *halka* en akel *trabizan*. Los חזנים *[hazzanim]* disheron los שבעה ברכות *[shiv'a [sic] berahoth]* ke asemejavan alas קינות de ט״ב *[kinoth]* de *[tish'a be-av]*, i mos entrimos. Despues me tornaron adyentro otra ves, i me izyeron bezar la mano de mi ermana ke estava asentada por madre de novyo, i mi kunyado por padre de novyo; al kunyado de la novya syendo el padre non se topava en Saloniko, i la madrasta de mi novya ke eya me dyo 5 rubyes de bezadura de mano. Despues, empesaron akantar las tanyedoras, 2 mujeres vyejas kon sus panderos en la mano kada uno el *boy* de una basina, kon 3 sonajes de *tenekye.*

Estonses, empesaron a salir a baylar, enprimero 2 mujeres vyejas, i despues kada una *sira* a pares.

Entre este tyempo, ya estuvyeron ordenando las mezas, ma a el novyo kon su djente mos asentaron a komer de prima. Antes de esto, mos entraron ami i mi novya por avlarmos, ma non a avlar solamente, komo me enkomendaron, dizirle "buenas noches", i darle un poko de *raki,* ma ke eya non lo risivyo! Yo melo bevi todo, ile echi en la alda unos kuantos konfites kon un dukado adyentro, i mos salimos afuera.

[27b] Devista, ke avri la puerta, me tomaron mis {a} parientés, i bezavan , i abrasavan komo uno ke vyene dela gerra i retorna bivo i salvo.

Me asentaron a la meza. Despues ke ya komimos i bevimos, me yevaron a echar ke en myentres ke estavamos komyendo, seyevaron las mujeres a la novya, i la yevaron a echar, kyen tanyendo, i kyen baylando, i algunas vyejas se entiznaron las karas ke asemejavan a las brushas, se le metian delantre la novya kon la alguenga de afuera. La deznudaron, i la estiraron a la kama, tapada kon unas kortinas, ma a la novya non le dyeron a komer ke ansi era el uzo.

Vinyendo a mi, me tomaron de la meza i me yevaron entre 2 personas ensima de sus ombros, i ivan kantando יַקְרִיבֶ(י)נּוּ, *[yakrivennu,* macho sano lo ayegara (Leviticus 1:3, 10)], kon los siryos ensendidos asta la kamareta dela novya. Los ke me yevavan en sus ombros me kijeron entrar adyentro sin abasharme, la puerta era bashika, me dan kon fuersa una kavesada en el portal de la puerta. En akel tyempo, avian unos goznos por enkolgar los תפילין *[tefillin].* Este gozno me se da en el meoyo i me se aze un tolondro el *boy* de un guevo. Tomaron mi djente un *beshlik* i una rida, i me ataron el turujon.

Despues, me deznudaron i me metyeron una toka blanka de un maraman ke paresiya un *mulla*. La djente se retiraron dela kamareta en echandome la yevadura por afuera komo akeyos kondenados a prezyon fuerte.

En echandome a la kama, echi el ojo i vide una mujer echada kon las karas emboladas, kon el pilador del dia de antes ke paresia una hazina de virguela. Eya desu parte, vyendome ami kon akeya toka blanka i una shakekera ke me avian atado tan apretente kedimos, tanto yo, komo eya, **[28a]** komo unos aperkantados. Ami me se asemejo ke eya era una komadre i a eya le paresyo ke era yo algun *imam* ke vino de la Mekka.

Keridos meldadores! Ya vos puedesh imajinar en el negro estado ke mos topavamos, tanto yo komo eya. Yo non pude kitar ni una chika palavra de mi boka de la pasyon dela dada ke me dyeron en la frente, ande mas vyendo a mi novya tan bruta, embolada las karas komo una figura ke vyene de kamino, kemada del sol. Eya por su kuento non tyene el dirito de avlar antes ke le avle el novyo de antes, ide mas ke le esta paresyendo ke tyene echado a su lado un *hafis,* eya pensa ke non se avlar el espanyol; en turko, eya non save, me kere demandar agua. Ansi les enkomendavan a las novyas, la prima palavra ke deve de avlar la novya a el novyo es de demandarle agua. Non tyene kara de me ver en este estado. Dizime, sinyores leedores, komo se kaza topandome en esta grande estrecha?

En fin, akea noche la pasimos de una hazinura de tifo tanto yo komo eya.

Ala manyana, mos despertaron i toparon las kozas sin regla. En pasando una ora, veo ke trayen una mujer vistida de *fes* i *kófya* byen amezurada, tenida por 2 lados, i las tanyederas echando unos bramidos, i la azen asentar a la novya ami lado.

Yo tomi apensar ke me keria matar de mi para mi, ma non topi ke muerte era *munasip,* darles a mi ermana i mi kunyado en ke estrechura negra me metyeron. Ma me apasensyava kon dizyendo *Allah kerim,* en pasando los dias dela fyesta muy angustyozos.

Kuando sali dela חופה *[huppa]*, me fui enel ofisyo por ganar **[28b]** el mantenimyento para mi, i para mi mujer, (i ermaniko ke desho mi padre. Lo desho en la tripa de mi madre; me se muryo ala edad de 17 anyos de hazinura de mal de pyedra).

En tanto lazdrando i kansando, pude reuchir abasteser los gastes menesterozos para mi famiya. Ma entre "te disho" i "me disho", al anyo ya mos izimos patron de una ija. Alos 3 anyos de kazado, mo se izo 2 ijas, al de 5, un ijo, son 3. Al de syete, otro, se azen 4.

En este entervalo, se asembro la holera grande. Fuimos ovligados de fuirmos de la sivdad i mos fuimos, yo kon otro un amigo djunto i muestras famiyas i tomimos una *uda* en Orundjik. La holera empeso kon muncha fortaleza a *karar* ke se ivan muryendo asyentos el dia.

En la fortaleza dela epidemia, se aferro el *ayaktash* ke mos fuimos *baraber*. Fin 5 oras, el se desbaraso. Yo, vyendome atornado de 4 kriaturas en el kampo, dishe entre mi, "non ay mijor de tornar a la sivdad". Mos alevantimos, yo i mi mujer mos karreimos i mos vinimos a kaza. Al otro dia, fui ala plasa por alguna koza de komanya i non vide del 5 por 100 del povlado ke avian en la sivdad, i por ande pasavan 3 ivan karreando muertos, komo los karneros dela *kasapana*. Yo non ize otro ke inchir un bokal de *raki*, i tomi una ave, la degoyi i la yevi en kaza. Dishe un *"shu"*, *"bu"*, i inchi unas kuantas dramas de *raki*, i me las bevi komo agua, i me fui akompanyar a los muertos.

Al otro dia, me *endjideyo* un frio fuerte, i me echi kon una kayentura muy huerte. En tanto se **[29a]** aferro un ijiko kon la holera, se muere i se lo yevan sin tener dingun avizo. Yo, al otro dia vyendo el mediko ke ya sudi, me ordeno él kinino. Yo le pregunti a mi mujer ande estava mi ijiko. Eya me respondyo porke non izyera rebuelta, "lo pasi a la otra kamareta". Estando en estas avlas, se aferra el otro adyentro de 2 oras, i se embarka i este.

Agora kedimos kon las 2 ijas solo, i kon mal en peyor pasimos la anyada angustyoza. En amaynando la holera, se atorno el puevlo a la sivdad, i kada uno i una mos fuimos amirar al mal i al byen.

Al otro anyo, paryo mi mujer una ija. La *fakira*, vyendo ke pedriyo 2 ijos de una i non los pudo kovrar, selo tomo muncho a korason, non kijendo ezmerar su vida enfrente los ijos, eya mal rijida, non se pudo alevantar dela kama de parida. Este aranko le kavzo la muerte. Estonses me kazi kon una mosa por non tomar ni bivda, ni kita.

(1) a kontinuar [5]

Kapitolo 17

La Muerte de el רב ח"ר שאול, [*Rav h"r* Shaul]

Komo ya lo dishimos de antes, ke el *Rav, h"r* Shaul se izo distinguir de mucho tyempo antes por un ombre santo, i ke azia maraviyas, todo el puevlo en djeneral tenian muncho temor deel. Kuando ayego ala edad avansada kaji de 88 anyos, vino el tyempo de su muerte. Kuando kayo hazino, todo el puevlo kreian ke este ombre non devia murirse. Ma kuando apezgo su hazinura, los dias i las noches non mankava partida deel puevlo de ir surve{r}yandolo. Un dia a oras de tadre, ke ya kedo de bivir, el puevlo entero vinyeron a yorar i a endechar, las kayes yenas asta el *meydan* de Lube. Estuvyeron la noche entera **[29b]** asentados en basho kon los livros de ט"ב *[Tisha be-Av]*, ken meldando la איכה *[Eha]*, kyen las קינות *[Kinoth]*. Al dia, munchos de eyos kedaron en תענית *[Ta'anith]*. I fueron akompanyarlo toda la djuderia, kompanyas, kompanyas de מלמדים *[melammedim]* kantando las קינות *[kinoth]* i 32 חזנים *[hazzanim]* kon sus מזמרים *[mezammerim]*, kantando el חיזון *[hizzun]*. I esta לויה *[levaya]* turo fina la tadre. El dia entero non uvo avyerto non butikas, non grutas, non *charshis*, ni menos plasas, otro ke todos serrados, i todas las *ummoth* kedavan enkantados de la seremonia funebre ke se le izo a este ombre, syendo era konosido de todas la אומות *[ummoth]*. I ke kuando algun גוי *[goy]* tenia alguna litiga kon djidyo, non se iva a djuzgar, ni a *metropolit,* ni ala aotorita lokala, otro ke ande el *Rav, h"r* Shaul. El kitava konténtes a todos. Asta la muerte de este ombre uvo temor entre el puevlo de la otorita relidjyoza.

Despues los grandes de la komunita nombraron a el רב ח"ר אשר ז"ל *[Rav, h"r* Asher *z"l]* por gran rabino, i a *h"r* Hananyà Saporta por רב הזקן *[rav a-Zaken]*.

El primer kolpo ke kijo dar *h"r* Asher fue el echo del זנות *[zenuth]*. El metyo unos kuantos surveyadores por las kayes de las זונות *[zonoth]* por ve{n}[r] kyen entrava i salia en las kazas mal afamadas, i fueron trayendo raportos de kada uno i uno. Los yamava en su prezensya, i sigun el pekado ke el les topava, les azia el משפט *[mishpat]*, a kyen davan palos dyentro de *t"t*, a kyen davan מלקות *[malkuth]*. Entre esta djente, vyeron salir a un ombre de la kaza de un grego ke en su manseves se kontava komo תלמיד חכם *[talmid haham]*, i era de buena famiya. I non premetyendolo las chirkostansas de kontinuar a meldar, el salyo al *charshi*, i se izo korredor de un merkader—de un grego—ke ya es savido en los dias de *yorti* delos gregos, el ke yama por el nombre del *yorti*. Por enshemplo, **[30a]** *ayos Vasil* todo el ke se yama *Vasil* aze fyesta akel dia, i vyenen a vijitarlo todos los paryentes i konosidos. Este ombre ke dishimos, ke se izo korredor de este merkader i ke se yamava מ. ג. [M. G.], fue a vijitar a su ámo, i vyendolo los surveyadores entrar i salir de dita kaza, dyeron raporto a el *Rav, h"r* Asher. El le demando, ke bushkava a entrar en esta kaza de grego. El ombre le respondyo ke el non tenia menester de dar kuento a dinguno de su entrada i de su salida. A esta repuesta ke non se la esperava, el *rav* se aravyo i lo maltrato por el koraje ke tuvo a responderle de tal modo. El ombre era muy korajozo, indi mas ke era savido de Ley; el ensistyo e[n] su komportamyento. Non se desho muncho esperar el *rav,* mando i lo metyo en prezo. Estando en la prezyon, disho a algunos de eyos unas palavras ensultantes. Fueron i se lo komunikaron a el *rav.* El se enfuryo muncho, i mando un *takrir* a la Puerta ande era la otorita, dizyendo, esta persona *din ve ima{m}[n] {soydu} [sövdü] ve haham bashinin namusuna dokundu,* [{se rovo} [ensulto] a la ley {i al imam} [i a la fey], i toko a la onor del hahambashi], devista ke lo kiten a barrir kon los *prangadjis* por la kaye kon kadena en los pyes i una *yufta* en la pechadura. I lo sir{i}kulurearon por todas las kayes. A la vista de este eskandalo, el puevlo se revolto muncho i se aflosho un poko el fanatizmo.

Otro kolpo kijo dar ande es ke un *haham* de Sheres, nombrado *h"r* ש. ח. [Sh. H[am]] tuvo un djuzgo de 2 personas. Tuvo djuzgado el *Rav, h"r* Asher a 2 Shereslis, i en indo en Sheres, estas 2 personas lo trusheron el djuzgo ande este si. *haham.* El sudéto si. djuzgo areves del *Rav h"r* Asher, i vino a su konosensya el djuzgo ke djuzgaron en Sheres.

El *Rav, h"r* Asher, kijendo mostrar su enfluensa por azerle **[30b]** בזיון *[bizzayon]* a este *haham,* bushko de parte de la otorita por trayerlo en Saloniko. Ma este si. *haham* non era menos savyo ke el en la relidjyon, ma ke non era riko komo el.

Estonses, Sheres dependia de Saloniko, ma los Shereslis tanto amor ke le tenian a este *haham,* eyos se armaron de selo i se fueron 2 personas enfluentes a Kostantinopla. Eyos izyeron el diavlo en 4, i gastaron suma de moneda, i reusheron a azer la komunita de Sheres endepen{t}[d]yente de Saloniko, i non lo desharon vinir a Saloniko a si. *haham.*

Otro un fato akontesyo en Saloniko de ke un djúzgo ke kortaron בית דין *[beth din]* de תלמוד תורה *[Talmud Tora].* El kondenado fue i se lo izo saver a el *Rav, h"r* Asher. En supyendo del fato, djuzgó a la kontra. Estonses, lo mandaron apretar a el kondenado a ke ovedesyera lo ke djuzgaron eyos. Este ombre mando a dizir ke, "non konosko la ley vuestra, si non la Ley de el si. *Rav, h"r* Asher". El kapo de בית דין *[beth din]* se yamava *h"r*.ש. פ [Sh. P.].

Era un savyo delos grandes, kontados de Saloniko. Por la ozadia ke tuvo el שמש *[shammash]* deel *Rav, h"r* Asher de avlar kontra este *Haham, h"r* ש. פ. [Sh. P.], mando a su שמש *[shammash]*, i lo enheremo a el שמש *[shammash]* deel *Rav, h"r* Asher. I se fue a la ישיבה *[yeshiva]* de Alkalay, ke ai se topavan todos los savyos, i se los konto a sus kolegas el fato entero. Eyos se metyeron en kolora kontra el *Rav, h"r* אשר [Asher].

Si komo el se kontenia en su sensya, masimamente en su rikeza, el keria sorpasar a todos los savyos ke avian en la sivdad. Ma esta seryedad kavzo una rebuelta entre grandes i chikos de la sivdad, i esto fue la kavza de azerse un partido grande ke se yamavan los מימונים *[memunim]*.

Kapitolo 18

Los ממונים [*Memunim*]

[31a] Una partida de manseveria izyeron una adjunta por peskuzar i saver las reglas dela komunita. Eyos toparon unas kontrayedades en los rijos dela komunita, ande es la prima de eyos, ke el rovo dela gabela dela karne era de un modo tan negro ke izo enflamar mas muncho a la manseveria. I es ke la gabela, la merkavan uno de los גבירים *[gevirim]* kada anyo; la otra, la tomava otro גיביר *[gevir]*. En kada anyo era חוזר חלילה *[hozer halila]*, el propyo era de 32,000 o 34,000 sigun les paresia a eyos. El ke merkava la gabela akea anyada ya estava asentado de rodeos, syendo ya avia de ganar para pan i para pitas. Los mansevos mandaron a yamar 2 karneseros delos grandes i les demandaron kuantas בהמות *[beemoth]* degoyavan en el anyo. Eyos respondyeron, "de 7,500 a 8,000". I rijia la gabela por kada kavesa de בהמה *[beema]* a 30 *gassim*. Estonses, en vyendo la manseveria la suma grande de la gabela ke entrava, se sobrevyaron mas muncho. Tomaron a egzaminar la gabela del vino i la gabela del kezo, i vyeron ke es una suma grande de entrada ke ay en la komunita, i los proves van enguayando i esklamando por la kaye. I non ay kyen los oyga. Estonses, empesaron a echar gritos por la kaye el puevlo entero demandando a ke se izyera un konsilyo en muestra sivdad. Estonses, un mansevo yamado ד. ב. [D. B]. este fue קול מבשר מבשר ואומר [*kol mevasser mevasser ve-omer,* la boz del pregonero pregona i dize]. Tomaron en la mano las kozas minudas i se prontaron dos חכמים *[hahamim]* i los metyeron komo רבנים *[rabbanim].* El uno se yamava *h"r.*ש. מ. [Sh. M.], el otro, *h"r.*ר.ש. [R. Sh.], i empesaron a tomar a los kezeros en la mano, ke esta gabela del kezo **[31b]** era para ביקור חולים *[bikkur holim],* ke la entrada era 40,000 a 50,000 gr. a el anyo. I el resto era, toma tu i dalo a ברוך *[Baruh].* Esta anyada de los *memunim* rijó 110,000 gr. Enfin tomaron שוחטים *[shohatim]* i se asaventaron de 2 שוחטים *[shohatim] kachakes* ke non tenian חזקה *[hazaka],* ke les rijia a los שוחטים *[shohatim]* 160,000 gr. el anyo. Estonses disheron los *memunim,* komo vyene aser kelos שוחטים *[shohatim]* tomen 160,000 gr. i la gabela dela karne ke tome 35,000? Estonses, i akel anyo uvo *boldjelik* en el kodrero, i estavan komyendo las אומות *[ummoth]* a syen gr. la oka, i los djidyos a 6.20, i empesaron a esklamar los djidyos, dizyendo, porke ke sea ke las *ummoth* [a] 100 gr., i los djidyos a 6.20. En pujando ensima del 100 gr., 50 gr. por kodrero ke le vyene 10 gr. por oka, sea 3 *gassim,* estos 3 1/2 demazyado ande estan? I los ke avian aparte dela gabela de la komunita avian gabelikas sekretas. Estonses, izyeron por eskrito una proklamasyon en buena regla: "esta yamada a el puevlo en dandoles a saver las mankuras i las dezreglas ke ay en muestra sivdad". I perkuraron de echar enbasho la חזקה *[hazaka]* de los שוחטים *[shohatim],* i las gabelikas sekretas, i de formar un konsilyo por el avenir para meter en regla todas estas entradas ke estan pedridas. De este modo, pudyeron tomar los ממונים *[memunim]* a sus lado djente kompetente. En vyendo todo esto, el partido del si. *Rav, h"r* Asher, ke sus enfluensas se aflosho, bushkaron un mezo por enrezyar sus fuersas. Eyos lo akonsejaron a el si. *rav* a ke dyera su demisyon, pensando ke el puevlo entero se ivan a alevantar kontra los ממונים *[memunim],* i masimamente en Estambol ke tenian partido de eyos i el si. *rav*. Eyos non lo ivan **[32a]** a deshar a dar la demisyon.

Estonses, tenia ke azer una kondisyon dizyendo ke si le kitan un *firman* de la Puerta para kastigar el a su pareser, finke {ke} se *ka[ri]shtireara* la otorita.

Malgrado todos estos penseryos, el *Kaymakam* de Estambol le acheto de vista i vino la envitasyon[6] a vista, puvlikada en el Djurnal ישראלית *[Yisraelith]*. De vista ke se supo esta notisya, se incheron todos de limunyo. El puevlo del si. *rav* izyeron un reklamo a Konstantinopoli dizyendo ke, "non lo desahamos salir ike tornaran atras la demisyon". El *Kaymakam* les respondyo ke kalia ke el *rav* mezmo mandara una eskrita de repintisyon. I ansi fue ke el mando a dizir ke, "el puevlo non me estan deshando bivir yo. Por kontentar a el puevlo, demándo atras mi demisyon". I ansi fue ke kedo en su estado, ma flósho. I estonses, se formo un konsilyo, i empeso a azer munchas reformas, asta ke bivyo si. שאול מודיאנו [Shaul Modiano], syendo era él prezidente. Despues dela muerte deel si., el konsilyo le kedo por notar, ke oy es una forma ke kedo.

Las entradas son munchas, ma las salidas son mas munchas, i las sedutas son muy raras. I ke de kuanto se formo el konsilyo, ni fina agora non uvo kitar un rezokonto porke sepan el puevlo ande se esta konsumyendo tanta moneda. Ke por dita razon kuando echan votos para formar konsilyo muevo, non mandan ni de el kuento delos envitos, visto el deskonto de los ke entran en el konsilyo muevo por rijir, veremos fina kuando se van a konsintir a areglar los echos de la komunita komo se deve! דור הולך ודור בא והארץ לעולם עומדת [*dor ole ve-dor ba, ve-a-ares le-'olam 'omedeth*, djenerasyon va i djenerasyon vyene, ma la tyerra para syempre se sostyene (Eccl. 1:4)]. Munchas vezes *La Epoka*[7] esklama sovre esta kuestyon, ma fue קול קורא במדבר [*kol kore ba-midbar*, una boz pregona en el dezyerto (Isaiah 40:3)].

Kapitolo 19

Las Eskolas i la קופה די חסד עולם [*Kuppa de Hesed 'Olam*]

[32b] En muestra sivdad 40 anyos antes reynava la inyoransa entre muestros korelidjyonaryos. El pasyonozo i enfatigavle si. Moizé Alatini, de bendicha memorya, pensando de trayer a la sivilizasyon a el puevlo Salonikyoto, el enjunto kon si. Shelomo Fernandes i el *Rav, h"r* Avraam Gatenyo, *z"l*, izyeron unas kuantas sedutas i pensaron de konkriar una קופה *[kuppa]* ke le dyeron por nombre חסד עולם *[hesed 'olam]* de un modo a ke todos los djidyos bankyeres i merkaderes ke tomaran parte a esta קופה *[kuppa].*

Estonses, izyeron una asamblea djeneral de toda la aristokrasia de la sivdad en kaza de el si. *Rav, h"r* Asher Kovo, נ״ע, *[n"'E,* su repozo en Gan 'Eden], i konvinyeron 24 פ(י)קידים *[pekidim],* si. Alatini i si. Shelomo Fernandes, prezidentes, el *Rav, h"r* Asher, prezidente onoraryo, el *Rav, h"r* Avraam Gatenyo, sekretaryo. I izyeron una taksa en las merkansias de entrada i de salida, i izyeron afirmar a todos los merkaderes de Saloniko. I por ke non se les supyera la[s] entradas i salidas de kada merkader, metyeron una kasha serrada i siyada por ke echaran po{k}[r] un burako de la kasha sus taksas. I kada 2 mezes, miravan sus *defteres,* ilos mandavan a kombidar alos merkader[es]. Vinyendo, ya echavan kada uno i uno por el burako de la kasha el empórto de sus taksas sin ke supyeran de uno a otro las salidas i las entradas. Kuando se eskapava la {a}kojeta, se avria la kasha, se arekojia toda la moneda de la entrada, i se echavan en una bolsa, i se metian en la kasha de si. Fernandes. Esta קופה *[kuppa]* se estabilyo en los unos kuantos anyos antes ke se konkriara la Aliansa *Yisraelith* de Paris.

[33a] Lo primero ke tomaron en mano fue el meldado delas kriaturas de תלמוד תורהה *[talmud Tora]* ke fina estonses era muy deploravle el embezamyento de los elevos de *t"t.* Les izyeron semanada alos מלמדיה *[melammedim]* para ke se pudyeran mantener. Eyos eran 26 מלמדים *[melammedim],* los izyeron apar apar, ke {ke} en myentres ke el uno akojia los *talmidim* kada manyana, el otro ke los estuvyera arisivyendolos i aresentandolos. I taksaron las oras de el meldado de la manyana fina la medyo dia, i de medyo dia para la tadre, iles dyeron enstruksyon a los *melammedim* en ke manera ke fuera el metodo de el meldado.

Despues, miraron las entradas de ביקור חולים *[bikkur holim].* Eyos konkriaron unas entradas muevas en desparte de la gabela del kezo, i dela azeyte, i de el salado, por ke pudyeran abasteser a los gastes de el menester de *bikkur holim.* Metyeron en paga—de 2 medikos ke avia—metyeron 8 porke non sufrieran los proves.

Despues, tomaron el echo de konkriar eskolas de ninyos i de ninyas, syendo estonses los *talmide hahamim* tomaron a murmurear en dizyendo ke, "en las eskolas non ameldar en linguas ajenas, ke mozotros non las konosemos". Si. Alatini fue kostreto de kitar un *firman* del Governo Emperyal kon dizyendo ke todo djidyo ke puede ayudar a la ovra de las eskolas tyenen el ovligo de dar sus konkorso masimamente. Los *talmide hahamim,* i a sus kavesera el gran rabino, deven de ayudar a los entremetedores de dita ovra de las eskolas por el embezamyento de las linguas profanas i la lingua de el pais. Este *firman* fue meldado en prezensya de la asamblea djeneral i de los *hahamim* de dirito. En el anyo de [5]617 [1856], se formo la prima eskola de ninyos **[33b]** kon 60 elevos pagantes, i 40 *gratis,* i trusheron un maestro de Paris ke se yamava Musyu Li{t}[p]man, un ombre tan entelidjente i savyo, tanto de muestra relidjyon, komo en la lingua franseza. El era un puerpo rezyo, yeno de salud.

Ma, si komo muestros ijos estavan embezados a el barbarismo, eyos lo izyeron sufrir, i le dyeron muncho ataganto. El estuvo dos anyos i medyo en muestra sivdad ke por 3 anyos era el kontrato, i paso 6 mezes kon la hazinura seventeria. El doktor si. Alatini i sus kolegas izyeron munchos esforsos para lo salvar.

Vyendo ke era inutile en muestra sivdad de sanarse de su hazinura, le pagaron sus 3 anyadas, i lo mandaron a su sivdad.

Despues de tanta pena i fatiga de el anturadjo, si. Alatini ke kompozo kon tanta sudor i tanta pena el *t"t*, i el ביקור חולים *[bikkur holim]* i la eskola, muestros sinyores de Saloniko en rekompensa a sus buenos servisyos por la bondad ke izo a la populasyon djudia, eyos bushkaron de azerle un komploto, asta ke fue kostreto de dar su demisyon. El izo estampar una proklamasyon i la izo espartir a todo modo de persona, dando a saver la pena i fatiga ke tuvo el, i el ovligo ke tyene el ombre de azer byen kon sus korelidjyonaryos. I ke tyene el poder de azerlo i non lo aze, tyene el pekado sovre su kavesa.

En retirandose [el] i dando esta demisyon, munchos de muestra komunita fueron a rogarle a ke retirara su demisyon, ma el ensistyo a no retirar esta demisyon syendo era un ombre ke el "si" era "si", i el "non" era "non" syempre! Muestra sivdad, syempre tuvimos el negro *mazzal* ke non tura lo bueno muncho, ke este buen ombre, si non tenia tantas fatigas, el iva a kontinuar a azer munchas reformas nuevas en muestra komunita, ke fina agora, ya tuvyeramos un eshpital a el uzo Evropeo, ke esto yevava en su memorya de azer. Ma el negro *mazzal* de la provaya fue ke se izyeron de guerko a azerlo fuir por algunas personas de negro komporto.

[34a] Dishimos de las penas i fatigas ke tuvo este ombre de byen. Diremos algunas de estas fatigas i de el komploto.

Yo konosi algunas de eyas. I es ke, los ke metian ijos en la eskola de los poderozos, ke estavan embezados a tener a sus ijos en *t"t* o en alguna חברה *[hevra]* partikolara, eyos estavan embezados a pagar a los *melammedim* una chika paga de 4-5 gr. la semana por kada uno. Ma, en entrando a sus ijos en las eskolas, eyos fueron presyados por sus poderes kada uno sigun sus fuersas. Les izyeron la taksa los פקידים *[pekidim]* i taksaron el presyo de sus pagas en 3 kategorias:

Prima, una lira turka al mes por su ijo. Sigunda, medya lira; i tersera, un kuarto de lira al mes. Ma, kuando alguno tenia de 2 a 3 ijos, la paga de prima klase era por el sigundo de sigunda klase, i por el tersero, tersya klase, kijendo dizir ke un poederozo ke tenia 3 ijos a la eskola, el mas riko pagava una lira i tres kuartos al mes por sus 3 ijos. Vengamos a la sigunda klase, por el primo pagava medya lira, i por los otros dos, a un kuarto al mez.

Tersya kategoria, pagavan a un kuarto de lira por kada ijo.

Los padres ke estavan uzados a pagar un *altilik* a el mes por sus ijos, esta taksa de la eskola se les izo muy godra.

Ma las primeras mezadas fueron pagandolas regolar. Fina el primo anyo, ya empesaron a kedar *baka{h}ya*. El sigundo anyo, se izo muy godra **[34b]** la *baka{h}ya*. Los "abonados" merkaderes de la קופה חסד עולם *[kuppa hesed 'olam]* empesaron a falsar de echar a la kasha loke era sus diritos, asta ke vino el echo ke un merkader grande echo un *yuzlik* falso. Ma si komo era en prezensya de 4 פקידים *[pekidim]*, el sonete de la pyesa ke kayo se sintyo muncho klaro, i era el trazero de los vinidores.

Syendo ya era tadre, me izyeron avrir la kasha i este pedaso de metal estava enriva de toda la moneda ke avia en la kasha. Yo se los amostri i le[s] dishe, "na, el pedaso ke sintitesh kayer por el burako. Eyos vyeron ke era falsa"!

El si. *Haham, h"r* Avraam Gatenyo fue, me yamo para un *kyenar*, i me demando si yo pudia deskuvrir de kyen era este pedaso de moneda. Yo le dishe ke ya selo puedo topar. Si. Alatini me demando en ke manera lo puedia yo deskuvrir. Yo le dishe ke vo a azer un mezo ke non lo sepa el merkader, syendo este pedaso era mandado de el merkader por mano de un moso dela gruta a ke lo echara en dita kasha. Me fui ande este empyegado de el merkader i le dishe, "sepas ke akel pedaso ke echatesh a la kasha, mira a ver de kyen lo tomates, ke es falso". El ombre lo tomo i me lo torno por un bueno.

Estonses, el si. *haham* i si. Alatini, ke ya me konosian por ombre kapache, ke konosia el mundo entero, ke[n] era djusto i kyen era falso, komo ya les tuve echo la preva en otras okazyones, estonses vyeron dela poka entrada ke entrava en la kasha, vyeron el afloshamyento de el puevlo, i izyeron una asamblea para inovarla de muevo. Ma ke no esta ves reusheron a traer en kamino derecho a el puevlo de Saloniko, visto ke en poko **[35a]** tyempo deskayo la entrada a una mizerya.

De otra parte, los pagamyentos delos padres delos elevos delas eskolas estavan atrasando sus pagas. Vyendo ke la kasha de la eskola ya vino a su fin, no pudyendo pagar los grandes gastes menesterozos dela eskola, me disho un dia si. Alatini a [ke] les dishera de su nombrado a akeyos ke atrazavan sus pagas, i ke les dyera a entender ke era menester ke pagaran sus devdas. Yo fui a 2 vezes la semana en kada uno i uno azyendoles deskorsos. A un kon todo, eyos ivan echando oras. Entre estos padres, uvo un ombre ke tenia 3 ijos a la eskola ke ya devia 3 bimestres de todos 3 ijos. Fui ande el porke me pagara al menos la mitad, i despues de tyempo la otra mitad. Topandose adyentro la gruta un socho de si. Alatini el kual era uno de los 24 פקידים *[pekidim]*, me enkorajo, i le empesi a demandar kon dulsor de nombrado de si. Alatini, kreendo ke en topandose dito si. en prezensya, se iva averguensar, i me iva apagar.

Non vos puedesh imajinar mi deskoraje en vyendo ke antes ke avlara al merkader, avryo este si. deputado, i empeso a ensultarme, dizyendome ke, "vos, vash atagantando al mundo kon la *arká* de si. Alatini! I kada uno tyene su *merak* en sus echos, i vos vinish en los dias de vapor ke kada uno tyene su korespondensya de dia de vyernes, ke tyenen ke pagar sus kambyos. Ma, si. Alatini non tyene este penseryo de los merkaderes! Ke ansi, anda en la buena ora"!

Ya se entyende byen ke estas palavras duras de este si. a tan korajozo ke era yo, en akea ora me ize komo una estatua de marmol. I yo me torni a mi echo.

[35b] El si. socho tornando a su gruta, le avlo por mi a si. Alatini ke, "este *tahsildar* esta azyendo muncha dezonor a su nombre, i azyendo *tadjis* a los merkaderes ke se les enklava en la *yaka* en las oras ke estan embarasados, ke ansi le disho, i ke trokara *tahsildar*, i ke me dyera{s} keshas porke non los atagante tanto a los merkaderes". Si. Alatini, ke era un ombre de muncha pasensya, konosyendo a su socho ke era mal avlador, de otra parte ke ami ya me tenia prevado muchas vezes ke fui fiel a sus servisyos, devista me mando a bushkar kon 3-4 empyegados de su gruta. Ala fin, me toparon, i me mandaron a la kaza de si. Alatini, i non en su gruta. Yo devista fui i lo topi en su kabineto sekreto. El kijo prevarme i en ves por saver la verdad. El me tomo kon *fyaka* a demandarme deke non esto kaminando en el rekavdo a dover, syendo el si. kashero *h"r* Moshe ben Veniste, נ"ע, *[n"'E,* su repozo en Gan 'Eden], me mando a dizir ke en la kasha non se topa moneda, ilos *aylikes* kyeren ser pagados a los maestros i empyegados dela eskola, i vos non le avesh yevado moneda. Yo le respondi ke non este apensar ke ya esto azyendo mi dover, ma ke los merkadores me van echando de una semana para la otra. I ala fin, non me pagan! Ke ke le aga yo? El me disho, "parese ke non le dizish de mi nombrado". "Es verdad, si. ke en vezes les digo, en vezes, no, por non tomar su nombre por *masha"*.

El me demando, "kuando dio los *kochanes* delos ke deven"? Yo los tenia en buena regla al סדר דילה אלפא ביתא *[seder* dela *alpha bethá].* Kayo ke en el primo devdor era el si. ande me paso la shena, el kual ya devia 3 bimestres, ke kyere dizir 18 *aylikes* de sus ijos. Si. Alatini non kijo mas por otros, ke ya entendyo el *muzevvirlik* ke le vendyeron por mi.

[36a] El me disho solamente, "ya entendi, andavos a la buena ora, i tene kudyado de arekavdar ". Yo sali de ai *sheshireado* komo un pato, non kijendo azerlo tomarse *merak.* Por dita razon, non le konti el fato ke me paso unas kuantas oras antes. Me fui derechamente ande el si. *Haham, h"r* Avraam i le konti todo el fato, i le rogi a ke risivyera mi demisyon, syendo yo estava pedriendo 3 tantos de la mezada ke tomava. El si. *haham* me afalago en dizyendome ke si. Alatini me tenia muncho *nazar* ke non estuvyera apensar ke ya me konose por ombre fiel.

El dia de vyernes, fui ande si. Alatini a demandarle ke *hizmet* kyeria. El me disho ke fuera ande el si. *haham* i ke le dishera a ke ora tenia ke vinir en su kaza, i ansi fue.

En sus konversasyones, le disho el si. *haham* ke ח' סעדי [*Ham* Sa'adi] estava muy enfasy[ad]o de las kozas ke le pasan, i a el non se los puede dizir. I le konto el fato ke yo keria dar la demisyon. Si. Alatini le respondyo, "yo ya esto satisfecho i lo tengo munchas vezes prevado, ke ni una vez le tengo topado falsia en el. I yo konosko a mi socho ke syempre le plazyo de avlar mal por uno i por otro, אפילו *[afillú]* por mi mezmo, ke esto es su natura".

En otra okazyon, yo supe ke bushkavan de azer un komploto por azer deskayer la enfluensa ke tenia en muestra sivdad s. Alatini, i el mas kuryozo de todos era su socho.

Este sekreto komploto fui yo i se lo komuniki a el si. *haham*, i non a el si. Alatini, syendo ke yo via todo su ardor de este buen ombre por la pasyon ke tenia por sus korelidjonaryos.

[36b] Un dia el si. *haham* se lo deskuvryo a el si. Alatini, el kual non pudo mas somportar las endjustisyas ke pasavan entre sus kolegas, i el zelo ke tenian ensima de el. Penso estonses de retirarse i dar su demisyon aregla. Todo[s] los kuentos de las eskolas, i de *bikkur holim*, de entradas i salidas, i izo estas por una chircular, i la espartyo a todo el mundo por ke vyeran todo el travajo ke se izo en estos 5 anyos.

Yamandome un dia en su kaza, entrandome en una kamareta, i me izo asentar en dandome pendola, tinta i papel. I me la izo kopyar en diktandome del italyano, azyendolo en letra espanyola[8].

En eskrivyendo esta chircular, dyentro delas palavras de esta eskrita, avia un paragrafo monstrando kuanta pena i lazerya tuvo el para konkria[r] entradas para el *Talmud Tora*, i Bikkur *Holim*, i las eskolas. I kuanto el puevlo fue desovedesyente , i perkuraron de derrokar todos los simyentos delo ke tuvo asementado. Mas despues de lo dicho. Agora, del komploto ke bushkaron de azerle.

Estonses, yo detuve la mano de eskrivir. I el me demando, "porke non kontinuash a eskrivir"? Yo le respondi ke, "algun dia me van a enforkar por la oreja, supyendo ke yo deskuvri dito komploto. Eyos van a bushkar algun achake para me azer mal kualkyer dia".

Si. Alatini me dyo su palavra de om[b]re ke él may me desharia tokar la unya. I yo le ize su komando i se los estampi en sekreto ke non lo supyeron dinguno. I los yevi guadrados en mi kasha fin ke me komando ke los espartyera. Primo dela [semana] de Medyanos de Pesah, me yamo imedyo la lesensya a ke espartyera todos los mil chirkolares djunto kon un **[37a]** rezokonto. I despues de una ora, fueron a rogarle la komisyon de *bikkur holim* a ke non se retirara de eyos, syendo ke kon la favor suya, estava el echo kaminando bueno. El les respondyo ke, "de la komisyon de *bikkur holim* non esto deskontente, i si en kavzo su prezensya sera menesteroza, el empleara todas sus fuersas por non deshar deskayer el ביקור חולים *[bikkur holim]* dela provaya"!

Despues de un poko tyempo, el tuvo menester de azer un viaje en Evropa. I la noche ke al dia iva a partir se adjuntaron todos los ermanos i ijos en una meza, i tuvo la bondad de rekomandarme a eyos ke en kavzo de menester, de protejarme. I ansi fue. Despues de poko tyempo ke ya estava en el viyaje el si. doktor i kavalyer, vino una *irade* de Kostantinopla a ke todo modo de estampador era menester ke tuvyera una lesensya de el governo para ke pudyera estampar.

Yo, en non savyendo la rekomendasyon, me adresi a un ombre de azer byen ke era muncho amigo mio, el si. Emanuel ben Rubi, el kual era muncho entrado entre los si. Alatinis i Fernandes, i le konti ke non puedo estampar sin tener *emtia* de estampa. El non me desho eskapar de avlar, i me yevo en prezensya de los ermanos de si. Alatini, i les konto el fato. I devista, eyos me dyeron una karta para Chilibi Avraam ben Zonana, dizyendole ke izyera todo lo posivle a ke me izyeran kitar un *emtia*. Estonses, fue ke me disho si. Emanuel ben Rubi ke yo ya estava rekomendado antes ke partyera si. Alatini, syendo el se topo akea noche en el pranso.

I otra karta ke tomi del si. *Rav, h"r* Asher, *n"'E,* [su repozo en Gan 'Eden], para el si. *Rav* Avig{a}dor de Kostan i parti de vista por la kapitala. I prezenti mis kartas aki i ai. Eyos me prometyeron ke non estuvyera apensar ke fin pokos dias ya me ivan akitar el *emtia*. I ansi fue.

Kapitolo 20

El fuego de Iskilich

[37b] Kaji en el anyo [5]617, [1857], en anonsyando unos tiros de fuego ke salyo en el kuartyer franko, en una kaza de un merkader, fin ke fueron los ayudos, el fuego avia tomado grandes proporsyones. Despues de 2-3 kazas otras, era la kaza de el si. merkader Iskilich el kual estava azyendo, en resparte de sus merkansias, azia la kontrabanda en sekreto deel *barut,* i alkanso a tener debasho de su magazen *chirka* 500 bariles de *barut,* i los vendia a los ajenos a las eskondidas.

Ma el non abitava esta kaza, syendo estava en kampanya. El korredor ke tenia el si. י. ב. ש. [Y. B. Sh.], vyendo ke esta kaza ya se va akemar, koryo presto a el lugar, i avryo el buro, i tomo toda la moneda ke se topava adyentro, i se la yevo a kaza, sin ser visto de dinguno. Despues de 15-20 minutos, se aferro la dita kaza a un ke estavan azyendo munchos esforsos, tanto los pompyeros, komo los de las *kandjas,* si[n] saver ke debasho el magazen avia *barut.* En kayendo la *bina* kemando ensima de el magazen, se aferraron de una todos los bariles de *barut,* i izo una eksplozyon terrivle ke alevanto toda la *bina* kemando asta las nuves, i kayo en las kazas delos lados i en las naves, i barkos de la mar. Tanto fue el *parlad*eamyento ke se sintyo el sonete fina 2 oras de kamino, a *karar* ke se avryo el terreno de este lugar, i se izo komo una mar, i arro[n]djo a todos los ayudantes en el fuego, i mato una suma de djente ke kedaron debasho las ruinas. Los ke kedaron bivos empesaron a fuir de una manera ke paresian lokos. Muncha djente, del sonete kayeron en basho, ilos ke ivan koryendo, los estavan trespizando, syendo eran mas de 2,000 almas ke estavan mirando en el fuego, i kedaron mas muncho matados del trespizamyento de los ke mato el fuego!

[38a] Akea noche fue una desgrasya ke non uvo may: i todo el puevlo en una guayatina, kyen por los ijos, kyen por los maridos, kyen por sus famiyas.

Al dia, fueron trayendo a el תלמוד תורה *[Talmud Tora]* todos los matados, i era una endecha grande de ver a sus keridos muertos i trespizados de esta katastrofa. I fue un limunyo grande en djeneral. El si. Iskilich fue aferrado i aprezado, ma si. Alatini empleo todas sus fuersas , i kon la fuersa de la moneda, el fue desparesido delas manos ke ya lo avian kondenado para enforkarlo. I non suspyeron el mundo ke modo fue fuido de las manos de la otorita. I despues de tyempo, se supo ke estava en una de las sivdades de Evropa ke de ayi non lo pudyeron tomar. Ma el si. korredor י. ב. ש. [Y. B. Sh.] se kedo kon toda la moneda, sin puederle dizir dinguno nada. Parese ke fue alguna suma grandisima ke esta persona alkanso a tomar, syendo ke despues de poko tyempo se supo la rikeza de este ombre i la avi[a] estado *kulaneando* kon los mushos enshutos עד היום *['ad a-yom].*

Yo, ke nunka en mis dias ke non sali aver fuego, syendo fui akavidado, ma akea noche fui ovligado de ir a este fuego, non para verlo, otro ke syendo era serka dela kaza de si. Shelomo Fernandes. Fui a ayudar por desbarasarle el *konak* i meterlo adyentro la gruta, syendo era él prezidente dela *kuppa hesed 'olam.* Esta fue la kavza ke me topi adyentro este *konak*, en este fuego. Ma adyentro de el *konak,* i non afuera, i de el sonete dela fortaleza de el *parlade*amyento, se meneo el *konak,* i non kedo ni un vidro en las ventanas. Yo, sintyendo los gritos i las guayas delos firidos, i los trespizados, bushki de fuyirme por una puerta sekreta, i sali a la *kyoshe* de Malta. I yo koryendo, me entri por el *Charshi* de los *Tellales,* i me vine en kaza. Mi mujer, ke ya me estava asperando, mos metimos a yorar, i uno, i otro, **[38b]** sin saver la matansa asta ande arivo.

A la manyana, supimos toda la desgrasya entera en konosyendo unos kuantos amigos ke fueron matados de los tizones de fuego i de los trespizados.

Kapitolo 21[9]

La Vinida de S. M. El Sultan Abdul Medjid

La vinida de Su Maestad, el Sultan Abdul Medjid en Saloniko diya de myerkoles, 25 tammuz, anyo de 5619, [27 July 1859]. Kuando tuvo la entisyon el Sultan de salir aviajar, 20 dias antes desu partensya mando una *irade* al Pasha de aki dizyendo ke en todo modo de eskala de la Turkia se dyo orden de preparar i aki, en Saloniko lo esteso.
La prima koza ke izyeron fue ke dela eskala dela Marina fina el Saray del Pasha fueron kortando todos los *shaynishes,* asta ke alimpyaron todas las kayes i empesaron amobiliar algunos lugares de buena ropa, *de-aynu:*
1. El Saray del Pasha,
2. El *konak* i el *choshk* de la guerta de Yusuf Pasha,
3. El *konak* dela Torre dela *Tabahane.* I se izo una mueva eskala enfrente de la *dita* Torre para la mar,
4. La *Djami* de la Santa Sofiya le izyeron ariva un lugar para el Sultan, para kuando verna a azer la orasyon de medyo dia de vyernes,
5. La kaza de si. Daryo Alatini, *ay"a,* [el Dyo ke lo guadre, *amen*] para el kuniado del Sultan, Kapitan Mehmet Ali Pasha. **[39a]**
6. La kaza de si. Shelomo Fernandes, *ay"a,* [el Dyo ke lo guadre, *amen*], para el *Ser Askyer Pasha.* I aprontaron de todos los *eznafes* ke apartaran 2 dias para limpyar el kamino de la Puerta Mueva para la *mevlane* i el kamino de Orundjik i Besh Chinar, ilos notaron.

La eskala grande dela Marina la adovaron, i al kavo de *dita* eskala, izyeron una buena eskalera komo de kaza de 8 pikos de anchura, i prontaron un *pastav* de panyo londje, para el dia ke arivara el Sultan, tapar la eskalera i toda la eskala fina latyerra del {Misir} Misir Charshi. Despues, el Pasha de aki mando por eskrito atodos los kapos de nasyones *[milletes]* ake aprontaran a todas las kriaturas delas eskolas, i los eskolaryos, i ke los vistan todo de ropa blanka. I izo *nizam*, i ke les enbezen algunos kantes buenos para el dia ke arivara el Sultan de salir arisivirlo kon todos los kapos i grandes delas nasyones byen vistidos.

I ke por todas las noches ke restara el Sultan en muestras sivdad de avrir i *duzudear* todas las butikas delos *charshis* kon buenas asendeduras, i lo propyo por todas las fronteras delas kazas ke esten kon luzes fina 4 a 5 [11 a 12 PM] de la noche. I ansi, ke todos se prontaron.

Estonses, se akojero{s}[n] si. Alatini i si. Fernandes i los 24 *pekidim* en kaza del si. *rav* i me enkargaron a mi por el kante ke les embezara a los elevos, ke non manki de azerles un kante en el *mekam* de *adjem* i otro en *huzzam* kon mi nombre en presipyo de los *batim*, i otro uno en *mekam rasti* ke fue apropyado para el akompanyamyento en Espanyol komo ya esta eskrito mas ariva. I 3 dias antes de arivar el Sultan en muestra sivdad, arivaron en muestro porto 10 navios de gerra, i el dia de myerkoles demanyana del 25 *tammuz* [5]619, [27 July 1859], arivo el Sultan kon 6 **[39b]** vapores de gerra, djunto i su ermano Aziz Efendi, i 3 ijos, i su kuniado, Kapitan Mehmet Ali Pasha, i el *Ser Askyer*, Riza Pasha.

I de vista ke ankoro, salyo Riza Pasha kon muncha furya atyerra para ver los lugares ke tuvyeron mobiliados de antes ke los vijito. I de vista, torno al vapor del Sultan, i le dyo asaver ke lugar *munasup* para su apozada sera el *choshk* de Yusuf Pasha. En el *choshk* dela guerta para él propyo i para su ermano kon los ijos al *haremlik*, i *disharilik* del dito *konak* de Yusuf Pasha i su kuniado, Kapitan Pasha, ande si. Daryo Alatini, i por Riza Pasha, ande si. Shelomo Fernandes, i resto desu djente en diversos otros lugares.

I entre estos, todos los kapos de nasyones kon sus akompanyados i las kriaturas delas eskolas ya abasharon de sus lugares, se fueron azyendo paradas, paradas, ke empesaron, *de-aynu,* dela punta dela eskala fina la entrada de *Misir Charshi.* Todos los muzikantes i toda la Guardya Emperyal de 2 partes izyeron una kaleja, i del presipyo de *Misir Charshi* fina el kavo delos soldados dela sivdad de 2 partes parados. I los chikos delas eskolas turkas kon sus [h]odjas parados en el kampo dela oria dela mar, i del kavo de *Misir Charshi* fina la Puerta dela Marina. De una parte estuvyeron los veskovos gregos kon sus akompanyados, i dela otra parte, 50 kriaturas i 50 mosikos gregos vistidos de blanko ke los ninyos tenian en sus manos a una rama vedre, i las ninyas a un masiko de rozas para kuando pasara el Sultan echarselos delantre.

I despues, adyentro dela sivdad, dela Puerta de la Marina fina el *Zibil* del Komercho, estuvyeron parados los 70 mansevikos djidyos, byen vistidos de blanko al *nizam,* byen peynados kon sus *fezes* pretas de *medjidie* byen aformoziguados. I kada uno, una kokarda korolada en su pecho metida. I todos, de maneras blankas **[40a]** en sus manos, i kada uno un papel de kolores en sus manos para kantar la ora ke pasara el Sultan.

I de la otra parte, unas 200 kriaturas byen vistidas ala turka para responder אמן, *[amen],* de loke tenian ke dizir los de enfrente. I *morenu a-rav* Asher Kovo parado kon sus akompanyados delantre deel *Zibil* del Komercho. I dela punta dela eskala fina el lugar ke tenia ke ir el Sultan, todos los kaminos inchidos de arena.

Ansi ke ala ora 4 dela manyana [11 AM] salyo el Sultan de su vapor kon una barka buena mobiliada ke Kapitan Pasha detenia el *dumen,* i todas las naves i vapores bandireados byen de kolores. I deel punto ke salyo deel vapor fina la eskala, fueron tirando de todas las naves i vapores, i las *fortezas* fina ke pizo la eskala. I el Sultan non pizo sovre el panyo ke avian echado enbasho, otro ke por la parte ke estava avyerta fina el *Binek Tashi.* I *bineyo* sovre su kavayo ke avian prontado i empesaron las muzikas atanyer i akantar, todas las kriaturas ke era una koza muy ermoza de ver i oyir.

El pasar dela djente fue: primero el *vidjuh* de Saloniko, despues

Yusuf Pasha kon el Pasha Komandante dela ora, Mehmet Ali Pasha, i Riza Pasha, i resto de su djente, i 5 kavayos del Sultan byen mobiliados de kuanta buena djoya ay, ke non se puedia kalkolar su *valuta.* I despues, chirka 100 personas de panyo korolado sus vistidos, kon espaletas i koronas en sus kavesas, kon unas plumas de kolores ariva. I detras delos ditos, paso el Sultan kon su korona enbirlantada i *sorguch* en su kavesa. De detras, pasaron el ermano kon sus 3 ijos kon koronas de briyantes en sus kavesas. I ando el Sultan sigun dishimos en el *choshk* de la guerta de Yusuf Pasha, i su ermano i los 3 ijos, en el *konak* del dito si. Mehmet Ali Pasha, **[40b]** en kaza de si. Daryo Alatini, i Riza Pasha en kaza de de si. Shelomo Fernandes, kon sus saltanates en las puertas dela kaye. I el Sultan, repozando una ora, de vista partyo para la Puerta Mueva akavayo i entro por una puerta ala Torre de la Tabahane, i salyo por la otra sin restar. I de ayi, se fue a *Besh Chinar* ke ya tenian sus *chadires* aprontados por el, i su ermano kon sus ijos. I estuvo *chirca* 2 oras en *Besh Chinar*, i torno al *konak* de Yusuf Pasha ke komyo dela noche. I pasando medya ora dela noche, se fue torna akavayo a *Besh Chinar*. I su ermano kon sus ijos restaron el dia en *Besh Chinar* kon la noche. El kamino dela Puerta Mueva fina *Besh Chinar* estava echo komo una kaleja, todo asendido de flamas a kolores i de la Torre de la *Tabahane*, i todas las naves i vapores empesaron a echar *avai fichek* de kolores. I toda la sivdad ensendida de artifisyos ke era una koza muy ermoza de verse. En el tyempo todo ke resto en *Besh Chinar*, iva dando ordenes asus *muabendjis* ke vinian akavayo adyentro la sivdad entre avrir i serrar el ojo, i estuvo en akel lugar asta las 4 [11 PM] dela noche, i torno a karosa adurmir asu *konak*. El sigundo dia, djueves del 26 *tammuz* [July 28], despues de komer del medyo diya, a las 6 [1 PM], partyo para la kampanya de si. Abot [Abbott] de Orundjik a karosa de dos kavayos *kulaneandola* kon su mano sin kochas. I arivando en dito lugar, kamino todas las montanyas de Orundjik, i despues entro en la kampanya de si. Abot [Abbott] ke estava byen preparada sigun dishimos kon panyo en basho en la entrada, i non pizo sovre el panyo otro ke por los lados ke estuvo kaji un kuarto de ora. I ansi ke de vista se torno a su *konak* de Yusuf Pasha kon la propya karosa *kulaneandola* el propyo.

I despues de aver repozado kaji medya ora en su *konak,* partyo torna kon karosa para *Besh Chinar* ke ayi komyo dela noche i resto **[41a]** fina 4 dela noche [11 PM] en *Besh Chinar* komo la noche de antes kon las ensendeduras i los *avai fichekes,* i partyo para durmir al *konak* de Yusuf Pasha. I dela tadre de djueves del 26 *tammuz* [July, 28] mando avizo al *Vali* de aki, Sait Pasha, por eskrito kombidando a todos los *mishlishes* i kapos de nasyones i a los konsolos ke se aprontaran para dia de vyernes del 27 *tammuz* [July 29] a la ora 8 del dia [3 PM] para emprezentarse en *Besh Chinar* al Sultan. I dia de vyernes, la ora 4 [11 AM] salyo de su *konak* akompanyado de su djente komo el dia del arivo para la orasyon del medyo dia ala *djami* de Aya Sofya, en el lugar ke le tuvyeron prontado de antes byen mobleado, i paso kon vistido de uniforma. I despues de aver eskapado la orasyon, salyo dela *djami* i se kito el vistido de uniforma i se vistyo simplemente, i se suvyo a su karosa de 2 kavayos, *kulaneandola* el propyo. Se fue por la Puerta Mueva para *Besh Chinar* en su *chadir* de panyo korolado, avyerto de todas las partes. I detras de su *chadir,* avian diversos *chadires* prontados para los kombidados. I empesaron a vinir todos en dito lugar. I el Sultan se metyo en pyes en su *chadir* delantre la puerta, ke su kara dava para la sivdad. I delantre de dito *chadir,* estavan parados los soldados i las muzikas emperyales, ma sin sonar. I el kapitan, Mehmet Ali Pasha, i Riza Pasha, i sus *muabendjis* i otros 4 *vizires,* ke son: Ismail, *Ser Askyer Bashi* de Monastir, Abdi Vali Pasha de Monastir, Sait Pasha, governador de Saloniko, i Yusuf Pasha. I de vista, dyo orden a sus *muabendjis* ake empesaran a aprezentar a los kombidados:

1. Los 4 Pashas ke son, Ismail Pasha de Monastir, Abdi Vali Pasha de Monastir, Sait Vali Pasha de Saloniko i Yusuf Pasha.
2. El gran *mishlish* de Saloniko.
3. La djustisya kriminal. **[41b]**
4. El veskovo de Saloniko kon 3 merkaderes gregos i los veskovos

delas *kazás* de Saloniko, i le dyeron a el Sultan un kavesal byen lavorado delas ninyas dela eskola de aki de valor de 4 a 5 mil groshes. I lo risivyo.

5. La komisyon delos ~~estabilisis~~ estabilis de aki.

6. *Tidjaret Mishlishi.*

7. Los konsolos Franses, Inglez, *Nemse*, Ruso, Toskano, Olandez, kon un papel byen eskrito, rengransyandolo desu buen vinido del Sultan en Saloniko, ke se lo meldo el konsolo Ruso.

8. מורינו הרב ח״ר אשר קובו [Morenu a-*Rav, h"r* Asher Kovo], ח״ר משה ן' ויניסטי [*h"r* Moshe [Be]n Veniste] i sinko merkaderes, los kualos son, si. שלום האקים [Shalom Hakim], si. יצחק משה טיאנו [Yishak Moshe Tiano], si. יצחק יאושע מודיאנו [Yishak Yeoshua Modiano], si. שאול מודיאנו [Shaul Modiano], i el si. יעקב משה מזרחי [Yaakov Moshe Mizrahi].

9. Los *beyes* de *rutbelis* de Chika Klase ke todos estos fueron reprezentados deun *muabendji* del Sultan. I a todos fue avlando a 5 byervos menesterozos a kada uno de su *maslaat,* i en kada avla del Sultan non avia responder otro ke una *temenna.*

I kuando *morenu a-rav* kon su djente fueron reprezentados del *Ser Askyer, Riza Pasha,* ke de vista ke los reprezento, izyeron una *temenna,* i le disho Riza Pasha, "el es el *Hahambashi*". I el respondyo ke izo muncho *has.* Despues demando por los otros kye[n] son, i disho ke son los grandes dela nasyon. Respondyo el Sultan ke izo muncho *has* de todos, i les enkomendo ke miren a la provaya. I devista salyo Riza Pasha dizyendole ke syendo los ditos non konosen la lingua vuestra, izyeron *vekyil* a vuestro esklavo para dizirvos ke de dia i de noche non mankan de azer *duva* por vos i por vuestro reynado. I respondyo el Sultan de buena gana, ke izo muncho *has,* i se tornaron atras.

[42a] I despues de todo esto, se retiro la muzika sonando i se fueron kada uno a su lugar. I restó el Sultan kon su djente asta las 3 de la noche [10 PM] en *Besh Chinar,* ke ayi komyo i se izo el *djumbush* de las noches pasadas.

El propyo dia ala tadre, mando Sait Vali Pasha, governador de Saloniko por eskrito a todas las nasyones i *mishlishes* ake se apronten para el sigundo dia de shabbath del 28 *tammuz* [July

30], para akompanyar a la partensya del Sultan kon todos los chikos komo el dia del arivo. I ansi se izo.

Dia de shabbath demanyana, ke ya se prontaron toda la djente, aparados en sus lugares ke avian estado el dia del arivo ike el Sultan ya estava de pronta partensya, kon todos los pashas, esperando afuera de el *konak* de Yusuf Pasha.

En akel punto, se desho de vinir Riza *Ser Askyer Pasha* kon si. Shelomo Fernandes i si. Moshe Alatini, i de vista los reprezento a el Sultan en su kamareta en pyes, ke por 2 puntos non se avlo, i despues si. Alatini i si. Fernandes rengrasyaron a el Sultan desu buena vinida en Saloniko, el kual respondyo ke izo muncho *has* de los ditos.

I despues, respondyo Riza Pasha: "Sinyor, estos 2 sinyores son los ke vos avli ayer ke syempre estan mirando en el byen de la sivdad sin dingun enteres". I torna respondyo el Sultan ke izo muncho *has*.

Estonses, si. Fernandes avrio su boka kon ditas palavras, "Sinyor, a vuestro esklavo Riza Pasha le dimos una eskrita para kuando tenesh gusto ke vola aga ver". I respondyo el Sultan kon una avla en franses, ke "ésta sivdad prosperara muncho". Kon todo esto paso, se detuvo el Sultan de 10 a 12 puntos, sigun dishimos, ke toda la djente esperando afuera en el ojo del sol. I de vista ke salyeron si. Fernandes i si. Alatini, partyo el Sultan **[42b]** akavayo para la eskala dela Marina, akompanyado desu djente, komo el propyo dia del arivo.

Ala ora 12 [7 AM] dela manyana, se embarko asu vapor kon muncho *saltanat* i fueron tirando delas forteresas, i de las naves i delos vapores, fina ke entro en su vapor. I estuvo en el porto fina las 5 del dia [12 noon], i partyo *le-shalom*. I de muevo tiraron delas forteresas i delas naves i delos vapores i parese ke estu[vo] kontente dela sivdad i *Besh Chinar*, syendo ke de aki partyo para *Shio*, ke non restó en este lugar mas ke 6 oras, i partyo para Kostan.

I aki desho de paras alas 3 nasyones ke son turka, grega i djidia a 20,000 groshes akada eskola, en desparte otros 65,000 groshes de *sedaka* para los *hodjas* i todos los proves ke a los djidyos toko de parte 26,000, i alos gregos se les dyo en resparte por prezente del kavesal ke le tuvyeron dado en *Besh Chinar* de parte delas ninyas, 5,000 groshes en *beshlik.*

A parte, dyo algunos prezentes ke son: al Vali, Sait Pasha de aki, una tabakyera de tabako ermoza, i otra a Mehmet Pasha de *Tophane,* i unas 10 oras de pecho a los patrones de kazas ke en las kualas estuvyeron apozados alguna djente de su deredor.

Despues dela partensya del Sultan, tomaron la porsyon dela moneda ke desho alos djidyos i la kuala kayo en mano del *rav* i de el *kolel.* Eyos izyeron la espartisyon a sus buen pareser. I ami, por el mi *zahmet* ke tuve por ordenar los kantes i azerles *meshk* a los ninyos, ke estuve 20 dias eskojendo 100 mansevikos i azyendoles *meshk,* me taksaron 500 gr. I 2 ayudantes ke tuve allado de mi, les dyeron a 150 gr. a kada uno. Esta resefta de la espartidura, se la mostraron a si. Alatini en **[43a]** ke me apartaron 500 gr., se aravyo en dizyendo ke, "este ombre ke izo 3 kantes agradavles, i estuvo 20 dias azyendoles *meshk* alos ninyos, es muncho poko". Estonses disheron deme adjustar otros 300 groshes, ma el ensistyo, i disho ke me dyeran 1,500 gr.

Ma ke provecho! Ke fue menester de gastar otros mil gr. de mi pecho para me melizinar de tanta lazerya i fatiga ke tuve. Kayi en kama un mez entero. Por tanto ke me dyeron a enbivir las kriaturas para trayerlos en un punto ke todo el mundo estuvyeron kontentes, i toda mi lazerya fue aplodida de grandes i chikos en djeneral.

Kapitolo 21

[43b] Los 2 Kazamyentos

Despues de un anyo dela vinidura del Sultan Abdul Medjid en Saloniko, uvyeron 2 fyestas grandes. La primera fue la fyesta de la ija de si. Shelomo Fernandes kon el ijo del ermano, si. David.

La novya, sinyorita Ortensya kon si. Djon Fernandes, ke komo este briyo de fyesta asta este tyempo non se tyene visto, syendo si. Shelomo era konsolo Toskano. I tuvo la shans de toparse en muestro porto navios de gerra fransezes. Fueron envitados el amiral i los komandantes de todas las frigatas, todo el korpo konsular, el governador djeneral kon los altos fonksyonaryos, el si. *Rav,* H[am] Asher kon el si *Haham, h"r* Avraam Gatenyo, firmadores de la *ketubba,* el *metropolit* kon la komunita grega, i toda la aristokrasia djudia. En fin, todos los altos fonksyonaryos vistidos de uniforma, komo el korpo konsular i los de las frigatas fransezas, ke dava un gusto de ver los parados ke eran de dos partes soldados. I de la puerta de la kaza de si. Shelomo asta la kaza del novyo, estava en basho kuvyerto de panyo korolado, ke por ayi iva apasar la novya. 30 mansevikos vistidos blanko kon las kokardas en los pechos kantando, la muzika dela frigata franseza adelantre la novya ivan sonando. En fin, una seremonia ke non se alkansa a azerlo kon moneda, otro ke kon *mazzal.*

Estonses, fueron los primeros bilyetos ke me estamparon *yaldizlis.*

En el kortijo, estavan las mezas aparejadas i kuvyerta de tela, echa komo una *sukka.* Todo el menester dela meza era de plata fina aparejada para el pranso de la noche. **[44a]** La sigunda fyesta fue despues de pokas semanas, el kazamyento de el ijo [de] el si. *Rav, h"r* Asher, el kual se yama Hayyimachi kon la ija del si. *Haham, h"r* Yakovachi Kovo, yerno del si. *rav.* I en esta fyesta *anke* non uvo koza de grande, syendo non se uzava dainda en las fyestas delos *hahamim,* ma a las vezes de 10 *paytanim* kon 30 mansevikos kantando el *peshrev* de שוש תשיש, *[sos tasis],* de nuevo de la kaza dela novya asta la kaza del novyo. Adelantre la novya, todos estos kantadores ivan kantando kon muncha grasya.

Lo propyo a el akompanyamyento de la *keilla.* I en tornando dela *keilla* en kaza, trusheron a el novyo kon kantes en *ebrayko.*

I en esta fyesta uvo munchos altos fonksyonaryos ke vinyeron a tomar a el si. *rav* i los קדושין *[kiddushin]* i שבעה ברכות *[shiv'a [sic] berahoth]* se kantaron kon un kante muevo apropyado de antes i echo *meshk* a los muchachikos.

A la noche, se dyo un *pranso* para 120 mujeres ke kon las luzes a muchidumbre, i las djoyas ke yevavan en sus kavesas las mujeres dava una vista ekstraordinarya, ke al menos entre todas estas kavesas de mujeres salia de 10 a 12 okas de perleria.

A la sigunda noche ke fueron kombidados los ombres, fue ordenada la meza komo la prima noche, i uvyeron otros 120 kombidados. Todos de la prima *klase* de Saloniko. I se paso la nochada fina el dia kon kantes i algunas *shakas* por azer riir de el si. *rav.*

Kapitolo 22

La Aliansa Israelita de Paris

[44b] Despues dela demisyon dada de el prezidente si. Alatini, los djidyos de Saloniko se vyeron ovligados de mandar a sus ijos a las eskolas, ma la eskola primera ya se avia dezecha, i el direktor ya se avia [ido] a su lugar. Estos sinyores, {vyendosen} [se vyeron] repentido[s] de lo ke non afavoresyeron a si. Alatini delas echas buenas ke les azia i vyendo el fruto ke dyo dyentro de 3 anyos la eskola de los ninyos.

El primo elevo de dita eskola ke es Musyu Shalem avrio una eskolika kon 20/25 elevos i empeso a lavorar. Otro un elevo sigundo dela dita eskola, yamado [Be]n Ardut, i este avrio una eskolika kon unos kuantos elevos. I este empeso adar los presipyos dela lingua franseza.

Myentres este tyempo, vino en Saloniko un maestro dela lingua franseza, (ma non me akodro el nombre), el reverendo *h"r* Yeuda Nehama izo un komitato, i avrio una eskola kon dito maestro en tomando una kaza grande i arekojeron chirka 100 elevos, todos pagantes. I unos 30 elevos enternos kon buena paga. I areglaron una eskola en tomando otros maestros ayudantes i Musyu Shalem maestro dela lingua ebrayka, despyegandoselas en fransez. Esta eskola en el presipyo empeso a kaminar bueno, ma despues de poko tyempo, empeso a koshear. Entre estas anyadas, se formo en Paris la Aliansa Israelita. El eskopo de esta Aliansa es por aklarar a los djidyos del Oryente i su program es de espandir la lingua franseza, i la lingua de el pais, i la lingua ebrayka. **[45a]** I kitaron en estampa unos chirkulares i mandaron a todas las sivdades del Oryente, en demas en la sivdad de Saloniko i akompanyados kon una karta al reverendo *h"r* Yeuda Nehama dandole a saver a ke izyera aderentes por tomar parte en esta Aliansa. El reverendo *h"r* Yeuda Nehama izo todos sus esforsos para alkansar una suma de abonados para la Aliansa de Paris, la kuala era el presyo de 6 frankos al anyo.

Ma el non pudo alkansar a una suma de abonados sufichentes. Eskrivyo estonses una karta a la Aliansa de Paris, dandoles a saver ke para alkansar sus eskopos era menester de mandar a rogar a si. Alatini a ke el se entremetyera en esta ovra, i dandole a saver ke de anyos antes, la idea de este ombre fue la kategoria dela Aliansa de Paris.

Estonses, la Aliansa de Paris i el Prezidente, Musyu Kremyo, ke era el avokato de prima klasa de Paris, le eskrivyeron a si. Alatini en unos terminos ke fue ovligado si. Alatini de atorgarles, i su dezeo ya era esto.

Estonses, izo una asamblea djeneral, i dechidyeron de kitar unos chirkolares envitando a todo el puevlo de la sivdad a ke se abonaran a dita sosyeta kada uno a su rango. El mas minimo fue ke pago 12 frankos delos kualos los 6 frankos para Paris, i los otros 6 los echavan en una kasha separata para la ovra dela eskola dela Aliansa.

Estonses, pudo rekojer chirka 250 abonados i syempre fue kresyendo i non desminguando.

La Aliansa de Paris prometyo de su parte de mandar un direktor kapache kon ayudarles una paga anual a dito direktor, i el resto ke pagaran dela sivdad. **[45b]** Estonses, azyendo kalkolo delas entradas delos elevos pagantes i un ayudo dela komunita i konkriando unas entradas para dita eskola, se metyeron ala ovra en adjuntandose kon el 24 deputados. I tomaron 2 kazas grandes alkiladas, una para eskola de ijos, i una para ijas.

I la Aliansa antes de mandar al direktor, mandaron un delegado de nombre si. Kazes, el kual egzamino a todos los elevos pagantes i *gratis* i izo una nota kon los nombres de kada elevo para kada klase i klase. Despues de pokos dias, mandaron el direktor, el kual se yamava Musyu Maks. En vinyendo, Musyu Maks metyo a kada elevo a su lugar.

En verdad ke la talya de este direktor non era un ombre alto, ma su kapachita era uno de los raros direktores ke topan en las eskolas del Oryente. Ma si komo despues de 4 o 5 anyos muryo el direktor de la eskola de Paris, mandaron a yamarlo por darle este posto. En su lugar, mandaron a si. Yisrael Dannon por direktor, el kual dirijo la eskola 15 anyos. Malgrado todos los esfuersos echos, las entradas non abastesian a los gastes.

En este entervalo, vino en Saloniko el filantropo rey dela *sedaka* i de bendicha memorya, el Baron Hirsh a egzaminar los kaminos de fyerro i pozo en kaza de si. Alatini. Despues de dezayunar, se fueron djuntos kon si. Karlo a la estasyon, i 2 otras personas, kon un treno espesyal fueron asta Yuvyeli [Gevgelya], i tornaron a medyo dia a pransar ande si. Alatini.

En la konversasyon del pranso, se avlo de las eskolas, **[46a]** i de el defisito de kada anyo. El demando kon ke se tapa este defisito? Le respondyo si. Alatini ke, "si tenia unas eskolas merkadas, en non pagando la *kyira* de 200/300 liras al anyo, se tapava este defisito".

El demando kuanto era menester para estos 2 estabilisimyentos. Respondyo si. Alatini ke kaji kon syen mil frankos se pudia merkar 2 lugares ke prevalyera para eskolas. El respondyo ke, "agan una suskripsyon los poderozos de la sivdad, i el resto adjusto yo".

En indose de Saloniko, el filantropo Baron de Hirsh, si. Alatini non se detadro de azer una asamblea djeneral de todos los poderozos de Saloniko. Ala kavesera, el se eskrivyo por 400 liras. Si. Shaul Modiano, ke su uzo era de dar la mitad de si. Alatini en todas las suskripsyones, se eskrivyo por 200 liras. Despues, se eskrivyeron los Sayas, los Tianos, los Alhasi[d]s, i echet. i echet. I se incho la suma de 45,000 frankos, i mandaron la nota al Baron de Hirsh, el kual metyo debacho 55,000 mil frankos, ke se izo la suma de 100,000. En vinyendo esta moneda en una kasha, se merko la kaza espasyoza i larga por 2,200 liras para eskola de ijos, i la kaza del si. doktor Palombo kon vasto kampo. I en una partida de el kortijo, fraguo unos aziles para eskola de ijas. I en un kanton de este kortijo, fraguaron un lugar de 3 a 4 kamaretas para morada dela direktricha, ke asta el tyempo ke eskrivimos, las eskolas van kaminando en buena regla.

Malgrado todo esto ke dishimos, aki van entrando kada anyo donasyones tanto de defuntos komo de fyestas. Aun kon todo, ay defisito.

Sintimos ke una karta fue adresada ala Baronesa de parte **[46b]** [de] si. Alatini. La Baronesa mando a demandar una nota de las kozas ke mankan en la sivdad de Saloniko por estar al koryente.

Si. Alatini le dyo a saver todas las kozas {ke} mankas ke faltan en Saloniko. I dela mizerya ke egziste entre la numeroza provaya, i de un eshpital tan menesterozo en muestra sivdad.

La Baronesa, vyendo detayadamente lo ke le eskrivyo si. Karlo, eya se apresuro de vista de mandar 10 mil fr. por espartirlos entre la provaya. I esta moneda vino en un tyempo menesterozo, en *'Erev* de *Pesah,* ke se aprovecharon tantas menesterozas famiyas de onor, ke las bindisyones de toda esta djente suvan al syelo, i ke la Providensya le alarge las vidas a esta reyna de la *sedaka.* Eya prometyo a si. Karlo Alatini ke mas despues tenia ke mandar un delegado, konfiante suyo, ake egzamine loke ay de azer en esta sivdad. Asta oy ke eskrivimos, esperamos kon despasensya a este delegado. Tenemos la esperansa ke en vinyendo este delegado, el komunikara ala Baronesa toda la mankida ke vera kon sus ojos ke ay de azer en Saloniko, i kreemos ke se fraguara un eshpital tan menesterozo.

I puede ser ke ara tapar el defisito delas eskolas ke asta oy esta avyerto, i chirka de 30 mil frankos, i ke por endelantre ara la Baronesa.

Por desgrasya, ay 6 mezes ke muryo este andjel del syelo ke non bive mas por muestra dezventura. Eya tuvo mandado 20,000 frankos para 3 dispenserias i 200,000 fr. para la fragua de un eshpital, en prometyendo de mandar kada anyo 30,000 frankos para los gastes menesterozos, i 60,000 frankos para la fragua del *Talmud Tora a-Gadol,* ma los eredadores anularon las subvansyones.

Kapitolo 23

La Estamparia de Si. Danielucho

[47a] Ya dishimos de antes dela krevita de Chilibi Menahem Faradji. Esta krevita fue la kavza de arastar la otra una komandita kela diridjia el si. Behorachi Shaki, el kual tenia muncha relasyon kon los merkaderes de Vyena. El tenia de aver de un merkader de Vyena una suma grande de moneda. Dito merkader empatronava una estamparia. Si. Shaki non pudyendole tomar toda la devda de este merkader, le tomo en paga dita estamparia, i la trusho en Saloniko, la kuala era kumplida en todos los materyales, komo 20 *kalupes* kon sus matrises, 2 prensas a mano i 500 plakas de materyas para vazyar letra, etch., etch.

Kuando vino la krevita de Chilibi Menahem, el ijo chiko si. Danielucho, vyendose desramado, el tomo todos estos *alates,* i los trasporto en otro lugar, tomando un pedaso de terreno a *kyira,* fraguo una *baraka* muy grande, i yamo a 2 empiegados ke tenia mi si. padre, i aresento las makinas en dito lugar. I empesaron a vazyar letra de todo modo de artikolo, Rashi de punto 8, 10, 12; de mezmo מרובע *[merubba']* de todos los puntos, i supo *kandirear* a 3 merkaderes i un *talmid haham,* los kualos poseian moneda, i otro un *haham* ke era merkader en livros. Les mostro una nota de todos los livros ke non se topavan kon presyo alto, los kualos en estampandose de muevo, vinian a kostar muncho barato, i se ganava 80 por 100 en ditos livros, komo el *Zoar*, los *Tikkunim*, el *Hok le-Yisrael*, el *Sefer a-Berith* en Ladino, i se izyeron sochos. El metyo por kapital la estamparia, i los otros sochos metyeron la moneda menesteroza.

Ma non izyeron kalkolo ke esto ke valian karos, era **[47b]** kuando non se topavan, i los meldadores de estos livros eran pokos.

Eyos izyeron el kalkolo dela ganansya i echaron a miles, i non avian merkadores ni de 5 por syen. En este modo fueron depozitando los 95 por 100 en un magazen ke lo tomaron a *kyira*, i lo fueron *istifando*. Ma el si. Danielucho, myentres este tyempo, a mezura ke ivan estampando i guadrando la moneda ke entrava delo ke se vendia, el la iva empleando en buen modo, en indiyanas godras i vino vyejo. En este modo, fue pasando 4 a 5 anyos. En fin, los ovradores de dita estamparia empesaron a kitar el lavoro suzyo. El se aravyo kon eyos, i perkuro de entrarme a mi por direktor por ke adovara las mankidás del travajo. Ma, yo ke tenia un kuniado grande ke lo estimava komo padre, non me desho salir de mi lavoro i ir adovar lavoro de otros. En tanto, yo vazyi de 30 a 40 mil letras de Rashi, i tomi a lavorarles en mi estamparia a una partida de pligos de זוהר *[Zoa]r* kon un presyo ke me konvino a mi. Estonses, vyendo el travajo limpyo, ke yo les estava kitando, entro una baraja kon los sochos ke le estuvyeron dando la moneda i izyeron un bilanso detodo el djíro ke se izo en estos kuantos anyos, i vyeron ke el si. Danielucho ya se komyo 2 tantos dela estamparia ke avia metido por *sermé*. I de toda la entrada, non avia ni un soldo en kasha, solamente los livros ke restaron: de kualos mil, i de kualos 1500, de 8 a 10 artikolos de livros. Bushkaron de venderlos en groso, non toparon a venderlos ni a el 20 por 100 ke les kostava. En fin, le tomaron la estamparia de su mano kon todos los materyales i se la vendyeron a el reverendo, *h"r* Yeuda Nehama por nada. El sudéto si. tomo un *m[a]sd[o]ri* i fraguo una **[48a]** *baraka* en un *kyenar* de su kortijo. Ma, las prensas non las pudo asentar, ni uvo ken las *kulaneria*. Si. Nehama me tomo por socho. Yo, visto la baratura del koste dela estamparia, i kijendo kitar un entrompyeso, kijendo dizir, "enfrente de mi vino, non vendas vinagre", i lavori chirka un anyo, ma yo kovrava el lavoro. Ala vez, vido ke ganansya non avia, fue kostreto de me vender ila otra mitad, i me desbarasi de este konkorrente.

La *Masá*

Si. Danielucho, vyendose desbarasado de la estamparia, el konfeso a una otra persona, patron de *kaza* de fabrikar מצה *[masá]* i venderla a *oka,* echa i buena. Es verdad ke esta idea merese ser alavada, syendo ke akel tyempo era tanto fuerte el echo dela *masá,* ke kada uno se *desvacheava* de su vida fin ke traiva la *masá* en kaza, *de-aynu* ke estonses eran los ke fabrikavan *masá* era 20 fornos ke avian avyertos para el ke traiva el sako de semola ke merkavan deel molino i los depozitavan en una kamareta de estos ornos. I era ke ivan vinyendo sakos de los בעלי בתים, *[ba'ale batim],* i los depozitavan en este lugar. I anke se les pagava una taksa por *oka* dela *masá* a los orneros, ma era kon fogera, ke kada uno keria tener la *masá* en kaza un dia antes. Anke estavan lavorando de dia i de noche, non abastesian a kontentar a todos, i era kon akometer paras a los lavoradores, a las muchachikas, a la ornera por ke tomara su semola una ora antes de otros. I era menester de yevar lenya, **[48b]** i azeyte para los *kandiles,* i *raki* para los mosos. I a medya noche, vinir a yamar a el patron de la semola, sea kon luvya, i nyeve, i tinyevla kalia ke uvyera una persona de la famiya para estar surveyando, ke si en kavzo non avia persona kuando azian la *masá,* apenas vinia la mitad dela *masá* en kaza.

Avia otra kategoria de djente ke komian "mundado", los kualos tenian mas muncha pena delo ke kontimos a kavza de el fanatizmo. I era ke merkavan trigo, lo traivan en kaza, i yamavan a el vizindado, se akojian de 10 a 12 mujeres i estavan mundando el trigo a grano, a grano, non sea ke se topara algun grano de sevada. I despues, lo yevavan al molino, i yevavan savanas limpyas, i despues ke lo muelian, inchian los sakos, ilos traivan en kaza, i ya [aviya] djente sernedores ke ivan de kaza en kaza, i se asentavan en el varandado 3 personas: uno kitava a el polvo a parte, otro la semola, otro el salvado ke a penas de 100 *okas* de trigo, kedavan 50 okas de semola.

Lo mandavan en el orno i tomavan dopya paga porke se kyeria eskaldado todos los *alates* menesterozos para fabrikar la *masá.*

Ya entyenden muestros meldadores kuanta pena i fatiga kostava este pedaso de torta. Ma, kuando se vido el primer anyo *masá* echa i buena vender a *oka,* se les avriyo los ojos a el puevlo entero. A el otro anyo, se avrieron otros 4 ornos ke vendian a *oka.*

I kuando si. Alatini estabilio este molino a makyina, se serraron todos los molinos a kavayo. I los orneros ya merkan *azir* la semola del magazen de si. Alatini, i la fabrikan por sus kuentos, i la venden a *oka.*

[49a] I anke kostára un grosh mas la *oka,* el *raatlik* ke tenemos, ke la ora ke kere ir la persona merkar *masá,* ya la topa *azir,* vale la pena.

Kijendo dizir ke esta membrasyon desho si. Danielucho Faradji.

Kapitolo 24

La Seremoniya del ל״ג לעומר [*Lag la-'Omer*] ila Estamparia de גמילות חסדים, [*Gemiluth Hasadim*]

Antes 40 anyos, la noche de ל״ג לעומר *[Lag la-'Omer],* algunos בעלי בתים, *[ba'ale batim]* de muestra sivdad azian una nochada de fyesta, i kombidavan algunos de sus paryentés, i kombidavan de 8 a 10 *talmide hahamim,* ke la yamavan הלולא, *[illula]* de Ribbi

Shimon. Meldavan una partida del *Zoar*, i despues era pranso, i estavan asta el dia komyendo i bevyendo i kantando. Non mankavan ke a el dia, azian otros lo mezmo.

Supito, se izo una idea un *sobadji.* Por apanyar moneda, azia de la tadre en el ק"ק ארא‎גון *[k"k Aragon]* un *derush* por las sirkostansas de Ribbi Shimon. I egzajerava unos kuentos maraviozos ke los oidores lo tomavan por siguro lo ke estava dizyendo este *darshan.* I en demas, aparejavan de la tadre diversos siryos, yevando unas etiketas el nombre de Ribbi Shimon, el nombre de Ribbi Elazar, i sus *haverim,* i los rendia el por la ensendedura de kada uno. I vido ke dyo buen rezultado. Tomo azer kada noche de los *yarsayates,* komo la nochada de Ribbi Meir i de Moshe Rabbenu, i etch. I empeso a profitar buena moneda.

Despues enventó otro un envénto. Izo unas kashikas de *tenekye,* siadas kon un burakito en riva, i una etiketa estampada ensima la kashika, dizyendo "por el *zahuth* de Ribbi Shimon". Despues de asender todas las kandelas, empesavan todos a una bos el *pizmon* de *bar Yohay,* despues el *pizmon* de יה רבון עלם ועלמיא, *[Yah Ribbon 'alam ve-'alemayya,*[10] *Yah,* Sinyor del mundo i de los mundos]. **[49b]** En la otra, el *zahuth* de Ribbi Meir; en la otra, por el *zahuth* de Moshe Rabbenu. I las enkolgo en kada pilar dela *keilla,* i kada uno delos ke azian la orasyon dela manyana, echavan en ditos *kutis* lo ke tenian de gusto. El avria kada mes estos *kutis* i topava ala ברכה, *[beraha]* del Dyo.

El les *darsava* kada shabbath, {i} i se akojian una mása de puevlo inyorante, i les estava kontando מעשׂיות, *[ma'asiyyoth]* de diversos akontesimyentos; i kuando vinia *shabbath* de *Purim,* i les kontava el echo de *Aman* en una egzajerasyon ke azia riir a el puevlo entero. I kada kuento ke kontava, savia azer diversas bozes komo akel *kara yoz.* Azia ande el *shekerdji* un puerpo de *alfinik,* i la enkolgava en medyo dela *keilla* en figura de Aman, i lo atavan kon un espa[n]go, ke kuando vinia akontar el echo ke fue enforkado, tomavan este espa[n]go i iva travando, i todo el puevlo djuntos kon el ivan gritando, *isa! isa! isa!* Lo suvian i lo abashavan fin ke lo davan en basho i lo azian pedasos. Este eskandalo se azia delantre el היכל הקדש, *[ehal a-kodesh],* en un lugar santo ke [en] este lugar se azen las orasyones para el Dyo. I muestros pastores non se konsintyeron de esta negra echa, asta ke la gazeta *La Epoka* salyo a esklamar en dizyendo ke, en esta seremoniya si se topan algunos de otras *ummoth* ke toman a pensar loke esto es, i lo toman por el Hristos. Estonses, el *kaymakam efendi* defendyo este eskandalo de azer.

En myentres este tyempo, los *hahamim* se empesaron a selar de sintir ke el puevlo ya lo yaman *h"r* a este personal, i empesaron a murmurear. Ke izo este konfesador para tapar las bokas delos mumureantes? La tadre de *Lag la-'Omer,* kombido de 40 a 50 *talmide hahamim,* i les dyo ke meldáran a 2 salmos de *teillim* a kada uno, fin ke se *bitireavan;* **[50a]** i despues ke meldáran un pedaso de *zoar* por las chirkostansas. I arodeo el עגול *['iggul]* de la *keilla* entera kon unas farbalás de papeles de kolor.

I despues de *minha* i *arvith,* tomaron a kantar komo de uzo, espartia moneda komo a los *dayyanim* a 2 *altilikes;* a los sigundaryos, a un *altilik;* enfin, a los mas chikos, a un *beshlik.* Estonses, izo serrar las bokas delos murmureantes.

I por azerse mas byen kyerer i enventar otra entrada mueva, el nomino una komisyon a la kuala les envento de azer mil kashikas de *tenekye* semejante a las de la *keilla,* i las despartyo a los בעלי, בתים *[baale batim]* para ke echaran un *metalik* por alma kada semana, i en kavzo de algun *kyefsizlik* o algun parimyento, ke echaran lo ke les plazia.

En fin, kada mez, iva de kaza en kaza i avria las kashikas kon una yavizika, i las vazyava en una bolsa grande, i despues ke kitava su porsyon de esta bolsa, la yevava ande el kashero de la komisyon, i kontavan la moneda ke re[ko]jia kada mes, i kovrava 20 por 100 por su lazerya.

En este modo, se izo el una buena pozisyon, i kada anyo, vinia a la estamparia, i le estampava 1500 etiketas para apegar a las kashikas.

En el entervalo de 4 a 5 anyos, uvyeron otros ke savian *darsar* semejante. Eyos izyeron en kada *keilla* i *keilla* esta seremoniya, vinyeron a la estamparia, estamparon i eyos semejantes etiketas.

En alkansandolo a saver este si. dicho ariva, se fue a la komisyon, dizyendo ke ya mos salyeron konkorrentes para azer lo mezmo de mozotros, i se va aflakar muestra entrada.

Me mandaron a yamar a mi i me demandaron, "porke izitesh a otros loke estamos azyendo a guestra estamparia"?

[50b] Yo les respondi ke, "la estamparia mia non es apropriyada para un *perat,* todo modo de *mushteri* ke vyene, le devo de estampar yo". Me defendi kategorikamente.

El si. konfesador de todos estos echos les disho ke en el echo dela estamparia ay muncho ke ganar. En un dia, se puede ganar 200 *groshes,* ke un dia le enkomenda las etiketas, i al otro me las da, i me toma 200 *gr.* de mi, non kyere dicho en otros lavores. Syendo ke en la kasha ya ay moneda, se puede avrir una estamparia i se puede ganar otro un tanto. Ala komisyon les agrado la sena.

La estamparia de גמילות חסדים, *[gemiluth hasadim]*

El si. kashero, ke nunka estuvo de buena umor kon mi, el akonsejo a la komisyon de azer una estamparia, syendo ke paras ya avia en la kasha sin lazrar, i sin sudar. Eyos eskrivyeron a Vyena, i trusheron una partida de letras de *rashi,* diversos karakteres de letra *merubba,* i tomaron una *uda* a *kyira* en *papuchilar hani,* i tomaron a primo *mesadder* ke tenia en mi estamparia i merkaron una makyina de un grego ke le avian abandonado la estamparia suya.

El estrenamyento de esta estamparia

En akel tyempo, un merkader iva a kazar un ijo, se alevantaron la komisyon i el si. kashero, se fueron ande el merkader a ke les dyera los bilyetos a estampar a el estrenamyento de la estamparia.

Este merkader era konsensyozo, i les respondyo ke, "yo non kero ser primer konkorrente para un patron de familya. Demas ke los bilyetos para mi non se yama nada otro ke el ke los dirije. H[am] Sa'adi, ke es el ke rije las fyestas, non me vyene a la fyesta mia en estampando los bilyetos a guestra estamparia". El se defendyo kon muncho koraje ke non les puedia azer **[51a]** sus demanda.

En fin, estos se tornaron en vazio, i pedrieron el koraje, i non fueron mas en dingun modo de fyesta a demandar los bilyetos, ama empesaron a azerme konkorrensya en otros travajos.

Ma ala fin de 2 a 3 anyos, mirando un bilanso, eyos vyeron ke non basta ke non sale el enteres de la moneda, tambyen ke sale un defisit, i la *fira* ke esta dando los materyeles. Estonses, fueron ovligados de abandonar la estamparia. I un anyo o dos fueron kostretos de pagar la *kyira* dela *uda* serrada. Estonses, bushkaron de la vender i non toparon kyen la merkára!

En konversasyon kon un amigo, dizyendo, "ke izyeran esta estamparia"? El les respondyo אם מזרע היהודים מרדכי, לא תוכל לו כי נפול תפול לפניו, [*im mi-zera' a-Yeudim Mordehay, lo tuhal lo, ki nafol tippol lefanav,* si de *semen* de los Djudyos Mordehay, non podras a el, si no ke kaer kaeras delantre de el, (Esther, 6:13)], mirando aver de vendersela a H[am] Saadi, si la kyere. Eyos le dyeron la libertad a este amigo a ke me la prometyera. El amigo me vino a vijitar, syendo yo estava alevantado de *kyefsis.* Me izo la oferta a ke merkára la estamparia. Yo le di la libertad ke si la topava a merkarmela por tantas liras , ke la tomára.

I se fue a la komisyon. En *chalisheando,* la merko por 46 liras, la kuala kostava 160 liras.

Ma ke se izo de la entrada de todas las kashikas i de las 46 liras ke vendyeron la estamparia? En ke tripa se entro esta moneda? *Sual haram!*

Kapitolo 25

De aki se empesa mi estorya partikolar

[51b] Ya tuve dicho de antes, por estar siguro de mi avenir, me alivyani un poko del travajo dela estamparia, i deshi en mi lugar a un empyegado miyo, i yo manyana, medyo dia, i tadre surveyava la estamparia komo direktor, i tomi el ofisyo del kante. I si komo la bos me ayudava para este ofisyo, era *sevda* ke tenia. Un dia, avyendome sintido kantar el maestro ke avia estonses en muestra sivdad, el kual se yamava *h"r* Aaron Barzilay, el me yamo i me disho, "syendo tyenes una buena grasya, ven a el *meshk,* i embezaras munchos *pizmonim* ke ami, me tuvo embezado tu si. papu ke el kual era el primo delos kantadores".

Estonses, arekoji 5 a 6 amigos, un poko grasyozos, i me los yevi a el *meshk,* i empesi a embezar *pizmonim* de todo modo de *mekam,* asta ke ya tomi la fama por todo Saloniko. I non avia *ziafet* o fyesta ke yo non fuera yamado por kantar, syendo antes de mi non avia en este ofisyo kantadores pertenesyentes i savidos en kantes ebraykos, i lo mezmo en turko.

Solamente, mi si. maestro, ke era kumplido solamente en kantes ebrayko[s], ma ya tenia su ofisyo, ke era shastre, i era el primo maestro en este ofisyo delos ke se topavan en Saloniko en korte i en kustura. El tuvo muncha amor de embezarme todo lo ke savia, asta ke me embezo todos los kantes de las *tefilloth* de *yamim noraim,* i me yevava en su *keilla* por ke le ayudara a kantar los *pizmo[ni]m* de estas orasyones, syendo el era el *mezammer* de la *keilla* נוה שלום *[Neve Shalom],* el kual los tuvo embezado de un syerto Estambolli ke se yamava *h"r* Yaakov Kamhi.

[52a] En este tyempo, el si. maestro, djunto yo i mis kolegas, renovi[mos] el kante deel *t"t,* ke kanta kada manyana de shabbath, ke esto ya era uzo de vyejo, ma avia vinido en un grado muy basho, syendo todos los kantadores ya eran vyejos.

Kuando estabili una partida de mansevos de 20 kantadores ke tomo un briyo, asta ke ya vinian djente kada manyana de shabbath a sintir de el kavo de la sivdad.

I asta ke mozotros viniamos a el kante, se topavan en *t"t* mas de 2000 almas. I syendo mi maestro ya se avia empesado a envyejeser, vyendo ke yo ya era kapache, me dyo la libertad de azer el *taksim* para empesar el *fasil.* Yo tuve a merkar un livro del *Rav* Najjar ke en el kual en el kavo de kada *bakkasha* ay unos *pesukim* konvenivles a la *bakkasha.*

Yo, los kantava estos *pesukim* komo un *son taksim.* En este livro ay para kada shabbath, en su *parasha,* ay unos *pesukim* ke konvyenen por *taksim.* I yo, les azia el *taksim* kon estos *pesukim,* i en el *mekam* del *fasil* ke ivamos akantar. Despues, i se azia un *fasil* de 10 a 12 pedasos entre *peshrefes, bestes, semayis* ke tomavan mas de una ora el kante. En fin ke yo tomi la direksyon de maestro, ma el maestro tenia 2 ijos, i empesaron a selarse de mi, syendo el puevlo todos me amavan, i tenia el paso a delantre, ma eyos non tenian la fuersa de kantar komo mi. Tambyen, amava muncho la sensya de la poezia, non solamente en ebrayko, ma la mas muncha parte en espanyol. I en las fyestas, yo les azia unos brindis a kada uno komo le pertenesia. I en kada okazyon, azia una partida de *bentes* en las chirkostansas ke se prezentavan, komo en el estrenamyento de el arreglamyento de el *t"t,* una poezia konvenivle. No mankaron i algunas romansas.

[52b] Despues, tomi a azer un livriko de poezias por *purim* [11]komo ya egziste asta oy en poder de los abitantes de Saloniko, ke les fue agradavle a todo el puevlo asta oy. Tambyen, a la vinidura de su Maestad, el Sultan Abdul Medjid, ize 3 kantes, 2 en *leshon a-kodesh,* i uno en espanyol para su partensya, las palavras i el son kompuestos mios. Estonses, tomi el paso muy largo en este ofisyo, ma הקנאה והתאוה [והכבוד] מוציאין את האדם מן העולם, [*a-kina vea-taava [vea-kavod] mosiin eth a-adam min a-'olam,* el selo i el dezeyo [i la onra] kitan a el ombre de el mundo, (Avoth

4:21)].

En tanto, non era solo en el kantar ke tomi paso largo, tambyen ke en kada *kuppa* i socheta ke se estabilia en muestra sivdad, era yamado yo por diridjirlos.

La prima fue en la *kuppa* de *hesed 'olam*, sigunda en el *tahsi[l]darlik* de las eskolas ke se estabilyeron estonses. Despues a la vinidura deel Sultan, me dyeron la karga de azerles *meshk* a los ninyos i de areglarlos, i de apararlos, prontos para el kante dela entrada dela sivdad. I vyendo la buena reushida, grandes i chikos, me rengrasyaron. Ma i en esta chirkostansa, el selo de algunos non mankaron, i bushkaron de presigirme. I si komo era protejado de si. Alatini, i de el *Rav, h"r* Asher, i de el *Rav, h"r* Avraam Gatenyo, non me podian *djinidar*. Asta ke vino unas okasyones ke les toko en los entereses de algunos ke non les agrado nunka lo djusto, ni menos la verdad.

Kuando se estabiliyo la *Socheta de Byen Azer*, la manseveria de esta socheta eran todos enfluentes, bushkaron de enderechar los rijos de muestra sivdad, komo ya lo tuvimos dicho de antes, los kualos bushkaron de afavoreser la gabella de el vino i de la karne, i chetera.

Eyos vyeron ke la paga de los *shohatim* era 5 tantos de la entrada de la gabella de la karne. Estonses, kitaron una **[53a]** proklamasyon azyendo una yamada a el puevlo. Esta chirkolar me la dyeron en mi mano por ke la fuera afirmada de todos los grandes. Mis kontraryos me sospecharon ke era yo el ke les dava konsejo a los deputados de dita socheta. I empesaron mas a enrezyar la inimistad sovre mi persona.

Ya dishimos de antes ke esta chirkolar izo una sensasyon entre todo el puevlo. I mas despues salyo la [כיתה] *kitta* delos *memunim.*

En uno delos viajes ke tuve echo en Kostan fue en akel tyempo ke dyo la demisyon el si. *Rav, h"r* Asher. En este tyempo, se topava en Kostan un sinyor paryente de eyos, i enfluente Selanikli, ma era un kontraryo de eyos ke non tenian nunka buenas relasyones kon eyos.

El izo una karta para el *Kaymakam* de Estambol a ke le

achetara en la demisyon, ma yo non supe nada de esta demisyon. Me yamo este sinyor i me dyo la karta a ke la yevara ande el *Kaymakam,* sin saver, ni menos lo ke kontenia adyentro. Al dia de vyernes, ke aparesyo el *Djurnal* [ישראיליטה] *Yisraelita,* mi amigo, chilibi Yehezkel Gabbay, me izo saver la demisyon, ke yo kedi enkantado de este fato.

Ma me entro el sospecho ke la karta ke me dyo a yevar este sinyor non fuera la kavza de el acheto. Pasando una semana, vide en la *Gazeta* [איזראאילית] *Izraelith* ke la demisyon torno atras.

Este sinyor, vyendo ke la demisyon torno atras, [i] pensando ke en indo a Selanik yo—syendo era muncho entrado en la kaza de el sr. *Rav, h"r* Asher—non sea ke le iva a kontar las kozas ke paso entre el i los grandes de Estambol, i ke non sospecharan a el, mandó una karta a el si. *rav* dandole a saver ke *Ham* Sa'adi fue la kazva de azer achetar la demisyon; **[53b]** dunkue non sea ke lo risivan mas en su kaza, syendo fue un *muzevvir* para el.

En tornando yo a Selanik, apenas despues de entrar en mi kaza, fui a saludar a el si. *rav.* Ya vide kon el agror ke me risivyo, le demandi, ke es la kavza de el yelor. El me respondyo lo ke le eskrivia la karta.

Yo me defendi kategorikamente, en dizyendole, "komo puede ser ke yo so en esto komo un בן בית, *[ben bayith],* a ke aga una falsia semejante? Demas, kyen yo en Kostan para azer achetar una demisyon de un *rav*? Yo so un ombre ordinaryo, sin tener relasyon kon dingunos delos Estambollis".

"En tanto, si me dize kyen es el ke mando dita karta, puede ser le deskuvrire alguna koza". El me respondyo ke, el eskrividor disho ke, non te demos a saver su nombre.

Estonses le dishe, "kale ke sea alguna persona basha i manko demi, ande se espanto ke sepa yo su nombre".

I me respondyo ke, "ya es un otro grande". Estonses yo le dishe, "syendo ke ya es un ombre grande, ke le emporta si se su nombre"? En esta konversasyon, se topo ai i el si. Yaakov Kapuano ke el kual ombre de konsensya, i mirandosen kon el sr. *rav* de parte a parte, el le disho a el si. *rav* ke, "yo lo tengo por siguro ke esto es un *muzevvirlik* de el si. ke konosimos, i yo konosko a si. Sa'adi ke non es ombre de azer semejantes absurdidades".

El si. *rav* me respondyo ke, "yo ya me *kandireo* de tus avlas, ma va date a entender kon Hayyimucho i *kandirealo*". En topando a Hayyimucho, i le demandi eksplikasyones de esta karta. El non se desho ni eskapar de avlar, ke salto komo un leon en dizyendo ke ,"todo lo ke dize la karta es verdad, i vos sosh el kulpavle".

Yo bushki de defenderme, ma fue inútile ke tomara una **[54a]** de mis palavras en konsiderasyon. I de estonses i en delantre tomó una aborresyon sovre mi, i bushkava syempre a vengarse. Despues de este tyempo, salyo el echo de la chirkolar. El izo un komploto kon unos kuantos ke ya bushkavan de *djinidiarme* en metyendosen de akordo kon todos los *shohatim*, i estabilyeron una sochyeta kon dar un grosh de *medjidie* al mes kon el eskopo de azer bondades alos sochos en kavzo de menester. I en poko tyempo, rekojeron una armada de 400 a 500 personas en esta sochyeta entre eyos: la partida rabbinika i una partida grande de *bragalis*.

Lo primo ke tomaron en mano fue de konkriar un *Beledie* Djudayko, i tomaron un *vezne* kon *dramas,* i ir apezar las dramas de todos los *matrapases*. A kyen topavan las dramas manko, le tomavan un *beshlik* de *djeza* por drama.

Despues, izyeron de 5 a 10 *bolukes* de estos *bragalis,* i en kada *boluk* un hahamiko. I kada shabbath, se espartian unos en kada puerta de sivdad, otros en las *kavanes*. I en kada mansevo ke pasava, le estavan eskarvando los *djepes,* i en kyen topavan paras, o *tutun* ensima, eyos se lo tomavan, i lo *aharvavan;* i alos ke topavan en los kafes, lo mezmo. I dyeron una pavor entre los mansevikos ke non se puedia imajinar.

Ansi fue ke empesaron a profitar muy bueno, i empesaron a kaminar kon muncha ozadia. Ma les iva reushendo, syendo el puevlo djidyo de estonses era muy flosho, ande mas ke vian bolar la bandyera santa enfrente deyos. En vyendosen ke sus plano les va reushendo, bushkaron de vinir a sus eskopo verdadero de aflakar a la sochyeta de Byen Azer, ke esto es la baza prensipala.

Komo ya lo dishimos, eyos bushkaron de echar una red a mis **[54b]** pyes, ma non topavan el enstrumento. Ke ke agan? Tomaron por enstrumento para mi de atakar a mi ijo kon algun pekado. I kon este mezo, akuzarme, i ami tambyen.

Non topando ni esto, eyos alkilaron un prove kon unas kuantas paras a ke dyera *'eduth* ke ami ijo lo vido fumar en dia de shabbath. I ansi fue ke a el dia de alhad, 9 *iyyar 5634* [26 April 1874], izyeron una asamblea de toda la *hahamaya,* i kombidaron a todos los mansevos, los mas berbantes de sus sochos. Los akojeron en kaza desu eminensya, ke paresiya una trupa de revoltados. Ma, ni el si. *rav,* ni el [דלת העם] *deleth a-'am,* non pensaron ke todo sus eskopos era por mi, otro ke empesaron a *malshinar* a otros en primero: kyen paso sus komandos ke fueron ala *kavane,* kyen ke le toparon paras ensima, o *tutun,* a kyen ke lo vyeron entrar en gazinos publikos.

Bi-helal, atakaron ami ijo kon este pekado ke va adar *'eduth* ke lo vido fumar el dia de antes.

Por ke djuzgen muestros meldadores si son verdaderas mis palavras, o si fue por alkansar el dezeo de sus eskopo, les vo [azer] una remarka ke kualunke sea, lo puede espyegar. I es ke kuando mandan a yamar a mi ijo, non es dinguna maraviya, ma ke antes de yamarlo a el, me mandaron a bushkar a mi. Si es verdad ke mi ijo peko, ke me bushkaron a mi? Ma, a la verdad es ke ami me kerian i non ami ijo, syendo ke si bushkaron a mi ijo, es por kasarme a mi!!!

I me mandaron a yamar ami antes de mi ijo, ma yo non lo pensi, ni manko me paso por idea de esta konfafa ke eyos la kerian meter en ezekusyon. I por mas preva, ke fue este *'eduth* en falso: prima es ke el *'ed* era un ombre pedrido, el es un *hammal* de la mas basha klasa, a tanto ke el kamina deskalso en dias de frio, i va komyendo por las kayes komo las בהמות *[beemoth];* anke tyene muncha moneda, el es arepudyado desus kolegas. **[55a]** Ma esto non emporta, syendo eyos non puedian topar ombre onesto porke dyera semejante testimonyansa falsa.

Otra preva mas sakra es ke una kombinasyon ke en este dia

de shabbath del 8 *iyyar* 5634, [25 April, 1874], mi ijo ke non se topava adyentro la sivdad. I es ke una kompanya delas mas altas famiyas kijeron divertirsen en una kampanya de Orundjik. I el dia de djueves, yamaron a un *lokandadji* konosido i le enkomendaron a ke gizara todo lo ke era menester para un pranso de 20 personas. El *lokandadji,* despues de azer todo el aparejo menesterozo, syendo amigo i mezmo paryente, le rogo a mi ijo porke se fuera kon el en este pranso, porke le fuera un ayudo de kamaryer por sirvir la meza de esta alta sinyoria.

Mi ijo non le refuzo, i partyo djunto kon el *lokandadji,* i sus mosos, i las kargas de komanya dia de vyernes de el 7 *iyyar,* ke arivaron a la kampanya a la ora 9 [4 PM]. I asta la ora 11 [6 PM], izyeron todos los aparejos para el dezayuno dela manyana, i para el armorzo del medyo dia, i tornaron noche de *al-had* a la 4 1/2 [11 1/2 PM] en Saloniko.

Todo esto, non pudyendolo saver los ke kijeron atakar ami ijo i ami onor, mos mandan a yamar para kitar a lus sus prodjeto. Mozotros, non pensando de todo al plano ke formaron esta djente, fuimos devista i mos prezentimos delantre la asamblea de todos los si. *hahamim.*

El si. *rav* tomo la palavra i disho, "savesh ke guestro ijo es akulpado de azer un pekado ke la Ley de משה, [Moshe] molo akavido de non ensender lumbre en shabbath"? Yo le respondi, " Si., kuando fue echo este pekado"? El me respondyo, "ayer". I yo le demandi, "ande fue echo este pekado, adyentro la sivdad o afuera la sivdad"? El me respondyo ke el *'eduth* lo vido fumar en una *kavane* de Saloniko.

Kuando me asiguri ke es dyentro de Saloniko, le demandi a este *'eduth,* "si en kavzo le mostro kualmente ke es falso kon prevas **[55b]** ke se satisfachan toda la senyoria, ke va a ser la ley de este falsador"? El me respondyo ke se le aze la penalita ke merese vuestro ijo si sera en verdad akulpado. Yo les respondi, "va byen".

Les respondi yo, "ke salga el *'ed* en *meydan?* ויצא העגל הזה ויפתח ה' את פי האתון [*va-yese a-'egel a-ze,* i salyo el bezero el este (Ex.32:24) *va-yiftah A' eth pi a-athon,* i avriyo A' a la boka de la azna (Nu.

22:28)]. El respondyo loke le metyeron en la boka, dizyendo ke el vido echar el sigaro en basho dela ventana de la *kavane* tala. Estonses, ize mandar a yamar a el *lokandadji* i 3 mosos, i los pari a el djuzgo.

Eyos respondyeron ke, חיים סעדי הלוי, *[Hayyim Sa'adi a-Levi]* estava kon mozotros de dia de vyernes, la ora en 8 [3 PM] fin a las 4 a 5 [11 PM to 12 AM] de noche de alhad (tadre de shabbath) en la *kule* de Orundjik, sirvyendo alas famiyas de Alatini, de Fernandes, i de Matalon. El si. *Rav* Kovo i el si. *Rav* Gatenyo, el *Rav* Arditi, el *Rav* Nahmias i todos los *dayyanim* non tenian la mas chika idea ke todos—akea masa de *hahamikos* ke estava parados enfrente—eran ke estavan asperando el mas chiko senyal para azer estrasos en mi i mi ijo, afin de azermos pedrer dela egzistensya delos bivos, ni menos mozotros puedriamos saverlo ke ya era la konfafa dechidida para esto, ike mizmo esta socheta fue enteramente fondada kon este eskopo.

El si. *rav,* en sintyendo a los 4 *'edim* ke trushe, ya se satisfezo. Esta djente, vyendo ke el plano de eyos ke komponyeron, se fue a montes, uno de entre eyos *shirilan takumu, pilpila harrifa,* kijo azer una observasyon, i avrio su boka, i tomo la palavra en alevantandose en pyes, dizyendoles a los *'edim* muestros, "savesh ke mozotros vamos a trayer *'edim* kualmente ke Hayyim Sa'adi a-Levi se topava ayer en Saloniko. I en vinyendo, i estos *'edim,* vozotros sosh falso[s] i tenesh ke somportar, i vozotros lo mezmo de el kulpado"? **[56a]** En verdad, yo non puedo nyegar en vyendo a este *hahamiko* empesar alevantarse delantre de tanta senyoria, tomarse la libertad i la ozadia de avlar semejante.

Yo, de vista ya entendi ke este *satan* kere embrolyar a los *'edim* miyos. Estonses, miri ke *munasup* de muerte topar para este desgrasyado? Ma non topi otro ke me alevanti en pyes kon muncha *fyaka,* i le dishe a este *hahamiko* bendicho, בסמן טוב *[be-siman tov],* si. *dayyan!* I me bolti para los si. *rabbanim* en disyendoles, "Sinyores!!! Me premetan dizirles a ke le agan un lugar para este muevo *dayyan*". I dishe a el, בכווד״, *[be-havod],* si. *dayyan* muevo, estas remarkas las azen a los ke eyos tyenen el dirito i non un sempliche *haham*."

Si. meldadores!

Vos puedo djurar por lo mas santo ke todo esto ke vos entretuve non uvo la mas chika palavra ke yo dishe en esta asamblea, syendo ke de los ke se topavan prezentes en esta shena lamas parte biven a inda i pueden dar *'eduth* delantre el Dyo i dela djente.

Mi korason se adolorya i mi puerpo se dezmenuda{n}, mis pyernas i mis brasos estan kon esta *bamya*. Es[t]ando eskriviendo esta estorya ke despues de 9 anyos yo la akumplo, en akodrandome akel dia eskuro, akel dia maldicho, akel dia ke non aparesyera el sol, o alomanko estuvyera *hazino* i non me topara en esta angustya. I mezmo rogo a el Dyo, mis keridos non se topen en semejante desgrasya, יאבד יום אולד בו, [*yovad yom ivvaled bo,* se depyedra dia ke fui nasido en el (Job 3:3)].

En supito, se sintyo un ruido fuerte entre todos los asistyentes del komitato de la dita sochyeta de la egzekusyon, ke non se savian de los gritos de uno a el otro, loke dizian. Ma una bos salyo de entre eyos i grito, "daldos, mataldos, a el padre i al ijo, O Dyo"!

[56b] Todos los sochos, sin saver ni entender, mos empesaron a *harvar* kon tanta krueldad ke mozotros i los ke eran de muestro partido, non topavamos ke modo salir de sus manos. Los ke mos kerian protejar eran, i eyos, *aharvados.*

Mozotros, fin salir de la puerta de el kortijo medyos muertos, i asta vinir a la puerta de kaza, se akojeron otras 500 personas, mas i mas, i los ke ivan vinyendo, sintyendo los gritos, "daldes, por *kavod* del Dyo!", ke i akeyos se azian de guerko. En fin, mos akompanyaron, *aharvandomos* a mi, i ami ijo, i a otros dyez amigos ke i los kualos tuvyeron la mezma eshuerte, *aharvando* sin piyadad. Esto alkanso a azyer ke si demandavan de uno a el otro, "ke es la kavza de esta vengansa", el otro le respondyo, "kyen save? Mozotros, por *kavod* de el Dyo lo estamos azyendo"! Ke por un mirakolo kedimos bivos! Non les basto ni kon esto. Entraron dyentro de mi kaza, rompyeron todos los *djames,* espejos, me rovaron ropa, el kovre. En este entervalo, koryeron unos kuantos turkos, i mezmo jandarmes. Ma por dezgrasya, todo fue en vano, syendo ke eyos se kontavan uno por syen.

En fin, yo, por eskapar a mi alma, non miri las almas de mi famiya, me tripi por una ventana de la kozina, i sali en el *chardak* de el vizino, deskalso i deskavenyado, akompanyado de algunos sochos de la sochyeta de Byen Azer, pude reushir a alkansar la gruta de si. Alatini, i topi el abrigo. En este mezmo punto, ya tomaron avizo de esta triste shena los deputados de la sochyeta de Byen Azer. Eyos kerian azer una buena operasyon, ma si komo si. Alatini tuvo avizo de esto, los izo arepozar, dizyendoles ke el ya iva a tomar satisfaksyon de esta katastrofa.

Syendo si. Alatini era syempre de sangre yelada, ya entendyo ke en esta ora puede akonteser desgrasyas de una parte **[57a]** i de otra.

En akel momento, disho si. Alatini de mandar un mesadjero ande si. *rav* dizyendo, "ke koza es este solevantamyento del puevlo, unas echas ke aziamos burla de los turkos en tyempo del *yeni cheri,* agora akeos afeos los eredimos los djidyos? En un tyempo ke muestro soverano *Sultan* izo *kanunames,* i non les p{ro}[er]mete a dinguno de djuzgar, otro ke alos tribunales kompuestos de parte del governo".

A estas palavras ke mando a dizir si. Alatini a el si. *rav,* se afalagaron el komitato de la *socheta* de Byen Azer por las oras. Komo ya lo dishimos de antes, ke si. Alatini era de korason tyerno, el bushkava syempre de afalagar las kozas, i non deshava engrandeser la inimistad unos kon los otros. De otra parte, si komo el era ombre umano, i verdadero, non tenia la mas chika idea ke fuera *mesherikero,* el mesajero ke mando. Ma por dezgrasya, se topo ai un ombre ke el kual disho ke el azia este mandado; i de vista fue i lo izo.

Ma en ke manera? Echo ashufre por un kavo i *katran* por la otra, (esto ya era su natura de syempre). El trusho una repuesta favoravle en dizyendo ke el si. *rav* non tuvo parte en este echo, i ke devista de su *shelihuth,* el *rav* ya mando a su *shaliah* a esparzir a el puevlo. Ma despues desu *shelihuth,* se fue ande eyos i ensendyo el ashufre i el *katran,* i los aresendyo en buen modo. I eyos ke ya lo bushkavan, se asentaron de muevo a azer un plano para eskombrar la verdad.

Ma para akreditarsen kon el puevlo ke era djusto loke eyos estavan aparejando para azer, eyos fueron puvlikando, kuanta mintira i falsia pudyeron topar por ke el mundo se *kandirearan.* Prima, fueron dizyendo ke yo i mi ijo ensultimos a toda la *hahamayya* en sus fachas. Sigunda, ke tokimos en *kavod* de la Ley. **[57b]** Tersya, ke este ombre esta avriendo los ojos de el puevlo por boltarlos las ideas en los gozos de este mundo. En akea noche mezma, se metyeron de akordo todos los *shirilanes,* i tomaron kada uno su misyon para el dia. I la manyana, se akojeron todos eyos. Lo primero ke tomaron, fue de espartirsen los *charshis,* indo de gruta en gruta, i de butika en butika, apregonando, מי לה' אליי, [*mi l-A', elay,* ken por A', a mi, (Exodus 32:26)], todo el ke בשם ישראל, *[be-shem Yisrael,* kon nombre de Yisrael], ke se vayan a al *t"t a-gadol!* A los *hahamim,* los kombidaron para el *k"k* Ashkenaz, i ansi izyeron.

Todos los merkaderes, chikos i grandes, ivan indo a *bolukes,* a *bolukes,* koryendo sin saver el motivo de esta yamada debasho la santa bandyera. Kuando ya vyeron ke el *t"t* i el *k"k* Ashkenaz ya estavan embutidos de djente, mandaron un koreo a la *keila* de los ashkenazim, i vinyeron todos los *hahamim* a el *t"t a-gadol.*

Los kitaron a todos los ninyos en medyo de el kortijo del *t"t,* i izyeron traer alas mitrayozas i 13 *shofaroth,* כנגד 13 מדות רחמים, *[ke-neged 13 middoth rahamim,* eskuentra de las 13 *middoth* de piadades] i empesaron, komo de uzo, kon el *ehal* avyerto a echar en fila los kolpes, i alevantavan una sinyal ake gritaran todos los ninyos אמן, *amen.* Kuando sintian boz de kuerno rechuflan, ke se sintia las bozes asta lugar leshos, ke se estremesian los guesos. I tomaron a meldar el salmo de 109, en echando los ojos en blanko, i vertyendo lagrimas falsas para mostrar a el puevlo su *hanefuth.*

Despues de toda esta triste seremoniya relidjoza, eyos se fueron en un lugar propyado, i kitaron un papel de unas kondisyones aboresivles, eskrito en לש"ה, *[leshon a-kodesh,* la lingua de santedad], i lo izyeron afirmar de todos los asistyente[s], tanto los *hahamim,* komo el puevlo, sin entender, ni estudyar todo lo kontenido. Fueron afirmando a la papa syega, a *karar* un tio—ermano de la madre de mi mujer—i un sovrino se afirmaron en este maldicho papel dela egzekusyon de la Edad Medya. Ma uvo de 4 a 5 *hahamim* de alta klasa ke non **[58a]** kijeron afirmarsen, dando por repuesta ke eyos non afirman una setensya por matar almas inosentes.

En esta karta, kontyene algunos *bentes* muy floshos, ke kual una persona de konsensya ke la melda, las topa muy endjustas. En rezumido, puedo dar deloke meldó en esta karta un amigo mio. I es, prima, ke dingun בעל ישראל, *[ba'al Yisrael,* patron de kaza djudyo] me puede dar שלום, *[shalom].* Todo ombre *be-shem Yisrael,* [kon nombre de Yisrael] non me puede dar a ganar, *afillú peruta ketanna,* [*afillú* un grosh chiko]. Dingun djidyo puede meldar, non kere dicho, ninguna koza ke sale de mi estamparia. Ma ke ni livros relidjyozos son *asur* de meldarlos, "non le pueden dar bilyetos de fyesta a estampar, non lo pueden tomar por kombidador, etchetre", i todo el ke bushkara de azer la mas chika favor a esta famiya es *'avaryan.* En fin, todos somos *hayyavim* להשמיד להרוג ולאבד את כל ..... הטף, [*le-ashmid la-arog ule-abbed eth kol ..... a-taf,* por destruir, por matar ipor depedrer a toda ..... famiya (Esther 3:13)], הרי זה משובח [*aré ze meshubbah,* de syerto, ésto alavado].

Ma todo esto se izo sin konsentimyento del si. *rav* i de los otros *rabbanim.* I ningun djidyo non puede kumpli[r] *minyan* kon mi. I de estonses ke non vo ala *keila.*

En esta barana ke se izo la manyana non estuvyeron kontentes, syendo uvo una kombinasyon ke en akel tyempo, estuvyeron las luvyas demandadas. Ordenaron devista un *selihoth* para la ora 9 [4PM], i pregoneros salyeron, ke todo *be-shem Yisrael* devian vinir a *t"t a-gadol* por rogar a el Dyo a ke mandara luvyas. A la ora fiksada, serraron todos sus negosyos, i se fueron a la *t"t,* estando azyendo orasyon por la luvya. Se alevanto un *shaliah* de Lembe[r]g kon los ojos a la banda, i disho, s.! si komo so *shaliah* de Tiverya, i tengo la lesensya de *enheremar* en nombrado de los si. *hahamim* de esta sivdad, agora yo vengo a *enheremar* ברשות בית דין של מעלה ומטה, [*bi-reshuth beth din shel ma'la u-matta*[12], kon lesensya del *beth din* de ariva i de abasho] a el *'avaryan* Sa'adi Levi i a toda su famiya.

Estas palavras dizyendo וארובות השמים נ{מל}[פת]חו [*va-arubboth a-shamayim ni{mlá}[ftá]hu*[13], i finyestras de los syelos fueron avyertas (Genesis 7:11)], **[58b]** ma ke esta luvya fue en akel anyo komo si kayera delos syelos אש וגפרית ורוח זלעפות, [*esh ve-gofrith ve-ruah zil'afoth,* fuego i ashufre i vento de ardedores (Psalm 11:6)], ke non salyo ni para asimyente. A el otro dia, toda esta shena ke paso, ni kon esto estuvyeron kontentes.

Eyos izyeron un *takrir* para el *Vali* a ke me aprezara, syendo ensulti a el חכם *[Haham] Bashi.* De vista, le mandaron un avokato sin diploma.

[Este avokato, syendo estuvo aprezado por kavza de su fuyida en los *istindakes* ke le izyeron, embezo un poko la lingua, i tomo por ofisyo la avokasiya. Fue de akeyo ke le konfiyo su defensa].[14]

En akel mezmo punto, tomo 10 *zapties* en mandandolos a mi kaza por aprezar ami i a mi ijo. Estuvyeron todo el dia bushkando por kuanta *musandara* ay i non ay, i en los magazenes! I otros 250 djidyos de los *sofus*, los kualos eran todos eskojidos (*illet-i kyimuru).* Enfin, non topado nada, se tornaron todos komo los.......

[Toda esta rebuelta i seremonia ke izyeron, pensaron en sus imajinasyon ke yo, o de el espanto, o de la merikia, me iva a muerir al dia. Ma yo ize *istinaf.* Egzaminando el tribunal, les paresyo *munasup* por azer una *musaade* a los fanatikos, dyeron una setensya de 31 anyo. Ma yo me adresi a la kasasyon i tomi por avokato el malah, Refael el kual les [prezento] dokumentos i vino todo *vazli.* Estonses, dyo una setensya de 31 anyo. Ya pasaron 28, mankan 3. Despues *Allah kerim*!][15]

Toda esta rebuelta fue en oyidos de s. Alatini. I los deputados dela socheta de Byen Azer se prezentaron ande el, supyendo todo por apunto. El se estremesyo de sintir, non topo otro remedyo por las oras, otro ke yamar a su kashero, Shemuel Ben Rubi, i konsinyarme en su mano a ke me yevara en su kaza, (syendo este s. tyene una alavada fragua en *Chaush Manastir*), a ke me guadrara por unos kuantos dias, syendo se espanto ke en esta ida, non bolára almas i non se afirme el refran ke dizen, *ben kah u-ven kah,* guay dela ija de Yiftah (Judges 11:31-35).

En tanto, yo fui yevado a la kaza de dito s., i fui tratado komo si fuera un konde de parte su noble famiya. Ma, el *arlilik* ke non me fayaron, i supyendo ande esto enserrado, non puedian, a dingun presyo de ayi kitarme, solamente a mi ijo, lo pudyeron meter en mano, ma eyos non kerian otro ke a mi.

Ma, el s. kavalyer, supyendo la buyisyon del fanatizmo ke sobrevyó **[59a]** muncho, kijo echar aguas para amatar el fuego. El le enkomendo a su kashero ke la noche de myerkoles ke me yevara ande el *bim bashi,* i ke me konsinyara en su poder, en dizyendole, "[A]latin[i] *baziryan* te saluda, i te entrega en tu mano a este ombre asta ke él te mande a dizir ke lo soltes, el kual es el ke mandates a bushkar por *emir* del *Haham Bashi".*

El s. Shemuel Ben Rubi, en anonsyandome esta novita, devista le acheti a irme la ora 2 [9 PM] dela noche. Yamo a su kamaryer, en sendyo un *fener* kon 2 *parmachetas,* i mos fuimos todos 3 komo ke mos ivamos a ir a alguna fyesta. I me konsinyo en mano del *bim bashi,* el kual me izo asentar en su *uda* i fui byen tratado.

I se torno el s. Ben Rubi, i fue avizarselo a el s. *rav,* kualmente s. Alatini ya le izo su veluntad. Ma s. *rav* non tanto maraviyado kuanto el izo, syendo ke el i la deputasyon era ke ivan djugando este rolo de teatro. I el s. *rav* non se entereso tanto; ilas kozas ke ivan pasando non le azian saver.

Ma s. Ben Rubi de su parte les djugo, i el, su rolo, komo muestros meldadores ya lo konosen byen. El tuvo dicho ke s. Alatini ya les izo su veluntad, ma ke fin manyana, la ora 8 [3 PM], aspera de kitarlo. Esta dicha de s. Ben Rubi les fue komo un golpe de fuzil, syendo el yevarme en prezo de s. Ben Rubi non fueron plazyentes, syendo este aprezar de parte de s. Alatini es komo una onor para mi; i eyos kerian mandarme kon dezonor kon 10 *zapties* i 500 personas detras akompanyando komo un ombre kondenado para la muerte, de mas, la dicha de s. Ben Rubi ke "fin la manyana, la ora ocho, manden a kitarlo".

A la manyana, izyeron un *kibbus* grande, i dyeron i tomaron, i dechidyeron de avizarle a s. Alatini kon unas patranyas **[59b]** ke al otro diya ivan a azer mezos de mekitar de prezo. Ma el fue tokado de non azer su palavra, non risivyo kon kara a la deputasyon. Eyos, vyendosen ke non fueron risividos byen, al otro dia dechidyeron de kitarme. Enformado de esto, un korero me vyene anonsyandome ke non sea ke salyera sin konsentimyento de s. Alatini. Ala ora en 9 [4 PM], me mandaron a yamar de el *idare mishlishi,* dizyendome ke, "el *Haham Bashi* ya emprezento tu pekado, i te damos la libertad de salir".

Yo les respondi kualmente non fui nunka pekador a el *Haham Bashi,* ni ke el me tuvo aprezado, otro ke por el komando de s. Alatini fui mandado kon un ombre, empyegado suyo. Ma si keresh, ke mande s. Alatini su ombre komo kuando el me mando, i salire de vista. El *mishlish,* sintyendo mi repuesta razonivle, me mando a mi lugar.

El ombre ke fue mandado por kitarme yevo la repuesta ande eyos, kon sal i pimyenta i limon, los kualos, en sintyendo esto, se incheron de ravya, i toparon para echar mas kulpas sovre mi, dizyendo, non so dinyo para salir por dicho muestro, para azer kreer al mundo ke "el non fue aprezado de muestra parte".

El diya de vyernes, vino s. Alatini ande el *Vali Pasha,* dizyendole ke una persona ke vos tuve mandado kon un empyegado mio, la ora 11 [6 PM] mándo a akel propyo ke lo konsigno, se lo entregash en su mano kon un *zaptie* ke los akompanye fin a su kaza. El *Pasha* le respondyo ke el *Haham Bashi* ya mando ayer a una persona ke lo kitara. Ma el, non kijo salir, dizyendo ke el non es aprezado desu eminensya.

El kavalyer le respondyo, verdad es ke yo lo aprezi por kontentar a el s. *rav,* ma si komo espantado de algun presigimyento muevo, non kijo salirse sin mandarle yo mi **[60a]** persona. Estonses, le disho el *Pasha,* ya tuve risivido enformasyones de parte el konsolo inglez, i del konsolo italyano, i ya le mándo un raporto a el *Haham Bashi* sovre este echo.

Enfin, la ora onze [6 PM], se apresuro s. Ben Rubi ande el *bim bashi,* i me izo kitar, akompanyado de un *zaptie.* Mos fuimos a kaza del s. Ben Rubi, asta dia de lunes de manyana. En tanto non mankimos, ni mankaremos de rogar a el Dyo por las vidas de este djentil ombre i de su noble famiya, ke la kuala non es manka djeneroza ke su onorado marido; por su alta karidad de djente umana, ke en akeas oras i otras, fueron para mi unos andjeles protejadores.

Antes de afinar el kuento, daremos a saver a muestros leedores la pasensya del djenerozo i filantropo kavalyer. En este entervalo ke estuvo azyendo el byen azedor, estuvo gerreando kon 2 partidos. A el uno, los estuvo akonsejando denon arepudyarsen dela djente en este echo, dizyendoles, "non saves ke todo el puevlo basho esta sodjefto al partido rabbiniko? Es menester de darles a entender kon muncha pasensya i kon delikadeza para trayerlos a la razon". Al otro partido, dandoles a entender ke a el puevlo se kere giado komo el tyempo lo demanda, i non kon esta fortaleza. En fin, en tantas vezes ke los tuvo yamado en su kaza a los ke fue menester, bushkando de arandjar la koza, en la ultima vez le disheron ke kalia ke tomara la pena i ke fuera ande su eminensya, i ke ayi se eskapara todo. El byen aventurado kon su korason de pichon les disho, si es por esto, ke non kede la koza; yo, vo yo mezmo.

Ma antes de ir, mando 2 personas onoradas adelantre, a s. Avramucho Mizrahi i s. Moshe Shaltiel ke despues de tanta pena, le trusheron por repuesta ke en indo, la koza era **[60b]** eskapada.

Ke ansi fue. El gloriozo, dinyo de alavasyones, se fue ande su eminensya, i en pokas palavras, el reusho, ma si komo mis kontraryos non kerian afinar el echo, porke seles *bozeava* todo el plano kompuesto de eyos. Estonses, por satisfazer a s. Alatini, izyeron una koza, i se asentaron a el lado de su eminensya, i dyeron una התרה, *[attara]* a la moda. Ma s. Alatini, ke non savia de estas ערמות, *['aramoth],* kedo muy kontente de verlos meldar i meneandosen, le paresyo ke ya vensyo una gerra.

El se alevanto gustozo i rengrasyandolos porla onor kele izyeron, i se fue devista a su posto.

En el punto, yamo a s. Ben Rubi, dizyendole, "manyana, kuando abashas, trayes a s. Sa'adi kon ti *beraber*, syendo ya lo ize emprezentar sin estar el ombre en prezensya de eyos". Ma de muncho respekto non le respondyo, otro ke lo rengrasyo por su fatiga.

Ala noche, s. Ben Rubi me trusho la novita. Yo ya entendi kelo enganyaron, ma ke modo se dize a un andjel de el Dyo ke lo enganyaron? Esto le puede kavzar alguna merikia por mi kavza; i un s., ke yo non lo meresko a ke el se enteresára en mi dezgrasya. En fin, toda la noche non me entro esfuenyo, pensando si le dire ke lo enganyaron, o me kedare kayado. Pensando ke manyana non selo diga otro, non savia en ke determinarme. Al dia, abashimos en djunto kon s. Ben Rubi, i me prezento delantre de el. El estava alegre i sonriyendose, komo ke tenia el relumbror de el Dyo sovre sus karas.

En primero, el me tomo akonsejar mas mijor de un padre, dizyendome ke es menester de kaminar por endelantre kon muncha delikadeza: "Yo vos asiguro ke ya se eskapo todo, i salid i mirad guestro echo komo de antes, i non estesh apensar mas". **[61a]** Yo non topava ke responder, otro ke, "se lo rengrásyo muncho por la bondad ke me izo". Ma, non tuve el koraje de eksprimirle mis sintimyentos kon terminos bastante{s} sufichentes. Yo sali de su prezensya kon las lagrimas en los ojos; non fue otro ke topar kon s. Avramucho i kontarle todo lo [ke] paso. El me disho ke ya va a tomar la pena por asaventarse ke modo fue este echo burlozo. Ala tadre, se fueron en djunto kon s. Moshe Shaltiel en la kaza del si. ..... Eyos demandaron, ke modo de *shaka* fue esta de enganyar a s. Alatini, darle התרה, *[attara],* sin trayer a el ombre de delantre?

El respondyo, "mosotros ya los satisfazimos a s. Moizé! Ke *karishtereash* muncho"? "Byen", le disheron, "s. Alatini non tyene menester de satisfezarse, el kere la koza ke sea eskapada i non deshada medya kruda, i medya {kruda} [kocha]". Eyos disheron ke el ya estuvo kontente kon lo ke vido. Eyos dyeron i tomaron en la koza, i vyeron ke todo fue kankaravias, syendo el papel afirmado de vengansa kuando non se arazgo, todo lo ke navigo el enfatigavle fue pedrido. El respondyo ke, "fue solo por perdonarlo, ma por la setensya ke se dyo por este ombre, non se balda nunka". Eyos respondyeron, ke el ombre non tenia demenester התרה, *[attara]*, syendo el non rekonosyo nunka חרם, *[herem]*. Dunke "es por modre ke vozotros bushkatesh vengansa". [syendo[16] el s. *rav* Hayyim Gatenyo lo akonsejo ke non tenia *attara*, "i si en kavzo lo kerej, ami ya me sovran munchas *attaroth* ke yo non la *kulaneare*, la dare ke vistir].

Vyendo ke sus palavras non izyeron efeto, devista se retiraron, i fueron se lo komunikaron a s. Alatini.... Tornamos a lo deantes [de] esta triste shena, se espandyo el ruido entre todas las nasyones, i todo el ke supo este fato, eskroshea dyentes. El konsolo inglez i el konsolo italyano adresaron sus keshas a el governador, dizyendo ke le traya una mankansa a su onor i su fonksyon deshar akometer semejantes aktos eskandalozos de parte el kapo relidjyozo ke puedia trayer unas konseguensas sangrientes, **[61b]** i la responsabilidad kaye a la otoridad.

A estos raportos delos 2 konsolos i de otros altos personajes, el *Vali Pasha* devista mando a su eminensya un *takrir* en unos terminos muy pikantes. En mezmo tyempo, amenazandolo ke si en kavzo se syente de oy i endelantre semejante, la responsabilidad kaye imedyatamente a el. De mas, tokante a estos *softas* ke forman una espesya de *belediye*, si son aparesidos, eyos seran apenados, syendo el governo ya estabilio un *belediye*, i les dyo sus leyes i sus priviledjos por administrar su fonksyonamyento. En fin, "a este ombre ke tuvitesh aprezado de ser akuzado por pekador, yo tomi enformasyones ke es inosente, solamente ke el kual es un liberal ke es kontra tu veluntad. En este punto, mánda a kitarlo porke non te sea alguna dezonor".

A vista de este *takrir*, fue loke me mando a kitar, ma ke yo non kije salir, komo ya lo dishe deantes. De ayi ver la inimistad, syendo seles derroko el plano ke avian avyerto un negosyo kon ir pezando las dr[amas] i tomando de *djeza* un *beshlik* por dr[ama] manko.

Vengamos a el echo miyo. Despues ke sali de ande s. Alatini, me fui a mi kaza, ma non puedia azer dingun echo, syendo el ofisyo me lo izyeron *batal*, la estamparia se serro, syendo non deshavan vinir a dinguno a estampar ninguna koza.

Una semana paso, un mez, i 2 mezes, estó mantenyendo mi famiya de 12 almas delas pokas paras ke tuve esparanyado de antes. Ma los fanatikos lo tenian por siguro ke en poko tyempo yo me tenia ke murir, kualo por sus vanas kreensas de su ekstraordinaryo *herem* ke eyos lo izyeron kon tanta *saltanat,* i kualo por el *merak* ke tenia en vyendome abandonado demi echo, i demas la estamparia serrada. **[62a]** Por mas negro, los bilyetos delas fyestas los azian estampar en otra estamparia foresta. Sus eskopo fue de pedre[r] la egzistensya de mi i mi famiya, i azer una vengansa mortal. Ma fue ala kontra, komo dize el proverbyo המה יבנו ואני {ה}א[ה]רס, [*emma yivnu va-ani {e}e[e]ros,* eyos fraguaran, i Yo derrokare (Mal. 1:4)]. Dunke, eyos pensavan, "por una koza o por otra, se va a murir i echar el myedo entre el puevlo, i restabilir sus enfluensa relidjyoza".

Mal grado todos sus penseryos, la providensya non les desho kumplir sus dezeos. Prima, por el penseryo de el *herem,* ke non me paso ni por idea. Kuanto por el *mazon,* enkorajado de mi inosensya, i partikolarmente de los aklarados amigos, non me estava tanto desespera[n]do. Komo ansi fue, ke el primo ke me se aparesyo, fue el s. Hayyim Faradji, avokato *enos* vinido de *Shirin.* El sigundo, fue el s. Ezra Nigrin. En este mezmo tyempo, me trusho un travajo de Yanina, el kual eran unas *gemarikas* de *perek* ladinadas en grego, i este ombre me se izo un *malah.* A esta djente, les kédo a dever las buendades ke me izyeron.

El s. avokato, el me trusho un livriko de la socheta mueva ke se estabilyo en Shirin. I me dyeron a estampar una estorya mueva entitolada *el matador enkuvyerto,* i otra, *la pasyon de el djugo* la manseveria del *serk dezentim, [cercle des intimes]* ke ainda oy non olvído sus rekonosensya a estos braves mansevos.

Ma, ni los 2, ni los 22, no abastan para los 32, vyendo el mi negro avenir ke me pude traer de ir eskripando de mi chiko kapital.

Ditos mansevos me akonsejaron si savia traer un *emtia* por estabilir un djurnal. Yo pensando al *usul* para kitar un *firman,* era emposivle syendo era menester ke el *Vali Pasha* lo izyera *tasdik* del *Haham Bashi* la *arzuhal* ke le iva a echar. **[62b]** Ya entendes[h], s. leedores, en akel tyempo ke ivan bushkando ke, el ke les traiya algun *haber* negro por mi, le davan gran *bakshish.* Non kere dicho de dar *{t}[d]avetname* de su parte porke yo estabilire gazeta ke en akel tyempo, si de sus manos les vinia, kerian abandonar la gazeta de Vyena, *el Nasyonal de Kostan*, ke tantos artikolos puvlikaron kontra eyos por este fato mio.

Esto era siguro ke en lugar de byen me iva a kavzar mas mal.

Estonses, non tuve otra *chare* ke de ir ande el enfatigavle, mi byen azedor. Yo me prezenti un dia ande el, enkorajado de mi amigo, s. Ben Rubi, ile konti toda mi pasadia. El me sintyo kon {kon} muncha atansyon. I otra, ya estava afrontado de el djugo ke le izyeron por mi kavza. El non kijo mas entremeterse por non komprometer su onor kon semejante djente.

I ya entendyo ke mi rovina estava muy serka, i si komo el era muy piadozo, el me enkorajo a ke la renovara la estamparia, i ke izyera trayer letras turkas, latinas i gregas.

Kuanto a paras, non estesh a pensar. Yo le dishe ke me se topavan unos kuantos fondos, ma non bastavan, ni menos para el gaste menesterozo. El non me desho venderlos, otro ke se los dyera a su kashero a guadrar. Yo non topava en ke terminos rengrasyarlo. De mas, el me dyo una eskrita desu mano de rekomandasyon para un amigo suyo de Kostan , a ke estuvyera en mi favor por kitar un *firman* para la gazeta, i otra karta para otro amigo de Vyena a ke me dyera todo los materyales menesterozos por la estamparia. Yo de vista parti por Kostan.

Arivando a Kostan , me prezenti ande s. Tiano, le konsinyi la letra de s. Alatini. En akel punto, mando a yamar **[63a]** a el s. Gabbay, ile disho ke "este echo de ti lo kero en sekretamente, a todo presyo". I si komo este sinyor Gabbay ya era mi entimo amigo, el respondyo ke non mankara de azer todo lo posivle.

En akel dia mezmo, me reprezento ande el *kaymakam efendi* el kual me izo muncha onor. El me izo asentar, me izo traer *kave.* En verdad, por la primera vez ke yo vide un kapo de relidjyon tan entelidjente i tan umilde.

En fin, el s. Gabbay le dyo a entender toda mi estorya. I ke el

s. *Rav* Gatenyo syempre estuvo en mi favor, i a kontra de todos los ke bushkaron mi rovina. El me demando si tenia alguna letra de su parte, i yo se la mostri de vista. Despues de meldarla, el le dyo la lesensya a s. Gabbay a ke izyera todo lo posivle.

A el otro dia, me yevo kon el a *Baba Alili [Bab-ı Âli]*, i me prezento delantre un ombre ke el ya lo konosia ke mezo esta persona se azia estos echos, el kual me demando la salud de un amigo Selanikli, ke si le savia trayer alguna letra de este amigo djidyo. Yo le respondi, kon muncho plazer, basta ke sea mi amigo, pensando non sea algunos delos kontrayadores mios. El me dyo palavra ke en trayendo una karta de dita persona, el iva a emplear toda su fuersa de azerme kitar el *firman,* sin ser menester deranshear a dinguno.

Estonses, me kedi enkantado ke por ayi se deskuzga todo lo teshido. Ma i kuanta mi alegria fue kuando sinti ke este amigo era mi ijo, syendo kuando le demandi el adreso, i me disho, *kyetabtchi* Hayyim. Estonses, le dishe ke, "este ombre es mi ijo"! Devista ke sintyo ke este amigo suyo ~~era~~ es mi ijo, devista salto en alto i me disho, ke el devista se iva a meter a la *idjra.* **[63b]** I izo lo ke izo, dyentro de 3 semanas me izo mandar el *firman* asta Saloniko.

Meldando dita estorya, puedresh entender las kombinasyones ke aze trayer el Dyo a un ombre inosente.

Agora, ternan muestros meldadores una demanda emportante dizyendo, "ke modo vyene a ke tanta djente esten tanto kontraryos? Entre eyos, non manka djente de konsensya a tener este *karar* de inimistad i de azer una vengansa mortal en una famiya numeroza, bushkan[do] de pedrerles el pan i presigirlos asta depedrer su membrasyon"?

Keridos meldadores!

Non vos manka razon si azesh esta demanda, ma ke la persona toma satisfaksyon sigun es la rasa umana. Ma kuando una persona syente ke su amigo lo ensulto, o ke le izo algun danyo, i non se lo deklaro, a este ombre, se le aze una raiz de inimistad sin ke salga de su korason nunkua, komo lo tuvo s. Hayyimucho. Todos estos ke me persigyeron asta la muerte, kada uno i uno tyene su razon, ma de otra parte yo tenia la razon i non eyos.

[דהיינו] *de-aynu,* ke esto es: Prima, es ke los unos se imajinan ke yo fui el kavzante de azerles achetar la demisyon de el s. *rav.* Sigunda, es ke en tyempo de *la socheta* de Byen Azer, y[o] era el ke les dava detalyos a la komisyon, i ke iva akojendo *sochos,* ke era kontra eyos, ma si eyos pensavan ke yo era un empyegado, i kalia azer mi misyon kon derechedad, ma ke a eyos non les konvenia, yo non kulpava nada.

Kuanto a los otros, la razon ke tyenen non la pueden dizir, ni eyos propyos, syendo es muncha verguensoza. Syendo kuando eran eyos kombidados en algunas fyestas, **[64a]** les paresia ke era por eyos solos, i kerian estarsen el dia i la noche en fila estar komyendo i bevyendo.

Ma el patron de la fyesta non les puedia dizir, "andavos", otro ke me lo deshava ami a ke bushkara mezos porke se fueran, syendo yo, komo mensyonado [kombidador] dela fyesta, azia molde por afinar la סעודה, *[se'uda],* porke kerian aprontar la meza para otros kombidados. Esto les era kontra sus *kyefes.* Eyos murmureavan entre eyos, kon ensultos, dizyendo ke era yo el kavzador de *bozear* la meza.

Otra razon ay ke en vezes tomavan a platikar algunas דרשות, *[derashoth],* kon גמטרייות, *[gematriyoth],* muy dezmodradas. I syendo yo non puedia detenerme en frente de loke non somporta la konsensya, selos dezazia kon alguna repuesta, i ke era aroves del *pasuk.* Estonses, eyos non topavan de ke muerte matarme, ma non me puedian azer nada.

Toda estas kozas i otras munchas se fueron adjuntando en sus korasones, ila inimistad la tenian fraguada asta ke toparon la ora favoravle para eyos. Ensistyeron por topar la fin, ma el Dyo delos syelos penso lo aroves desus penseryos.

Komo dize el proverbyo רבות מחשבות בלב איש ועצת ה' היא תקום, *[rabboth mahashavoth be-lev ish, va-'asath A', i takum,* munchos son los pensamyentos en el korason del ombre, ma el konsejo de A' es el ke se afirma (Proverbs 19:21)].

Parese ke el todo poderozo non pudo somportar mas, El les

metyo en korason de ensistir en sus kapricho de azer una semejante *dubara* ekstraordinarya, ke *afillú* vyejos non tuvyeron visto azer en kozas mas emportante[s] komo lo ke izyeron en mi personal.

Syendo ke fin a este tyempo, el puevlo se guadravan de non risivir la boz de esta arma vyeja, ma en vyendo los {k}[g]rupos i mitralyozas i kon tantas miles de djente i tantas miles de kriaturas respondyendo אמן, *amen,* kuando sintiyan boz de kuerno ke chuflan (Neh. 4:12), **[64b]** i 13 שופרות, *[shofaroth],* (ma uno de estos 13 era mio ke abandono a los 12), i meldaron el Salmo de 109, yeno de maldisyones i en sima de mi puerpo non izo dingun efeto, ni en dinguno delos de mi famiya. Me echaron una *yulle,* se las bolti atras. Esto les dyo el koraje, mizmo alos fanatikos, dizyendo ke esta arma ya paso la moda, non tyene dinguna valor. I eyos mezmos de estonses asta oy non la *kulanean* mas. I mas mijor dizir, non les kedo mas de dita arma, syendo vazyaron la *kyula* entera ande mi, i ke ya entendyeron eyos ke era un pishtol sin *trapandja* ke tenian en sus manos, i ivan mostrandola a todos. Ma agora ke ya lo supyeron todo el puevlo ke era una arma ke non tyene dinguna valor, non la mostraron mas, komo dize el turko, *takya dushtu, kyel yoruldu,* [le kayo la takya, se le vido la kalavasa].

Por oras, *chok shukyur* por el dia ke me tópo! Ike me tópo endispuesto, azyendo esta estorya, bendigo a el Dyo ke por mi *sebeb* salvaron todo el puevlo de esta lepra ke ainda reynava en Saloniko. Aun ke tanto mal pensaron eyos de traer sovre mi i sovre mi famiya, perdono i non rogo ni menos en orasyon al Dyo por ke se vengara de todos mis kontraryos, otro ke rogo syempre a el Dyo a ke El los perdone i El ke les bolte el korason para byen אמן, *[amen].* Solamente, ami i mis ijos ke non se olvide אמן, *[amen].*

Kapitolo 26

La Estamparia עץ חיים, [*Es Hayyim*]

Non toparon mas *munasup* de azer, vyendosen muncha moneda en la kasha, estabilieron una esta[m]paria yamada עץ חיים, *[Es Hayyim]*, por azerme la konkorensya. Los primeros materyales ke trusheron, en dezbarkandolos del vapor a el komercho, les kayo la kasha a la mar. Ma ke provecho, syendo ya estava asigurada. Kon la moneda dela sigurita mandaron i fondaron de muevo materyales. I ay 28 anyos ke egziste esta estamparia. I se tyenen engrutido en esta estamparia de 500 a 600 liras, syendo los direktores de esta estamparia non konosen este ofisyo, i la estan dirijendo los ovradores. En el presipyo, estamparon livros de *hahamim* ke non dan dingun provecho. Despues tomaron otros travajos, i algunas kozas minudas. I lo ke egziste asta agora es por ke non es paras de pecho de uno, otro ke son paras de todos los sochos.

Non topando mas para azerme la konkorensya, estabriyeron una gazeta kon nombre El Avenir, ma esto non turara muncho tyempo, espero en el Dyo.[17]

Kapitolo 27

[65a] El Kostum de Ombre i de Mujeres i de Mosas

Los ombres se vistian de 4 modos. Algunos yevavan *kalpak* kon *djubbe*, i *antari*. Los otros, ke era la mas porsyon de Saloniko, yevavan bonete. El *esnaf adami* yevava toka asentada a *tarzi* de bonete, ma era kon *fes*. Los bragalis yevavan toka retorsida.

En Shabbath, esta kategoria de djente yevavan *djubbe* de panyo *kirmis* i de panyo *mavi*, el *dolan* entero de *shirit aladjali*. En la *djubbe kirmis* davan blu, en la *djubbe* blu davan *kirmis*.

La manseveria de esta djente, en semana yevavan bragas de lana, en Shabbath, *shalvar*. En vyerno, *shalvar kui*, en verano, *shalvar* blanko i *mintan* blanko ke non abastesia una hase para un *shalvar*. I los yamavan vistidos de "arroz *koladji*". Despues de tyempo, la djente grande se kitaron el *kalpak*, se metyeron *shemle* de seda blu *kyenarli*. La sigunda klase, en semana toka asentada, en *Shabbath*, bonete por *kavod* de *Shabbath*.

I despues de tyempo, troko la moda, i la manseveria se vistyo a la franka, asta este tyempo ke eskrivimos. Los bragalis trokaron moda tambyen, kualos empesaron a vistir a la franka, kualos *djubbe* i *antari*, ma la *djubbe*, kyen la yeva echada a el ombro, kyen debasho el lado, i komyendo pipitas por las kayes. Mas de 25 anyos, los bonetes kedaron entre los *hahamim*. El resto de el puevlo, todos por todos kon *fes*, i algunos mansevikos trokaron moda, los kualos sin ser frankos, se visten chapeo.

[65b] El Kostum delas Mujeres de Tyempo Vyejo

Muncho pokas yevavan en sus kavesas *halibis*. Esta *halibi* era de una espesya de *karapusa* de ropa de seda, lavradas. En el *kyenar* de dita *karapus[a]* era de una tantela estrecha de *sirma*, i klavedon. Ensima de esta *karapusa* avian unos kuantos plumajes. En tyempo de fyestas, se metian *chichekes* de diamantes en la kavesa, ma poko tyempo turo esta moda.

Las ke vinian de *Yeni Sheir* [Larisa] o de Estanbol yevavan en sus kavesas *tarbushes*. Este *tarbush* era en figura de una tovajika chika de ropa de vejetal. El *kyenar* entero de *katife* blu, i estas lo propyo ke en las fyestas se metian *çhichek* de diamantes. Estas mujeres eran muy raras en Saloniko. I despues de poko tyempo troko esta moda.

Muestras mujeres de Saloniko vistian mezmo loke visten oy, ke es *fes* i *kofya,* sayo, i *entari.* Loke troko es ke yevavan *mestas* i sapatos amariyos, i agora yevan estivlas o *kunduryas.* En fyestas, yevan manias de oro i *yardan* de oro. Ay poko tyempo ke troko la moda del *yardan,* i yevan *yardan* de perla i un tokado *yedek* de perla. Ma de vyejo, en las puntas del *yedek* yevavan enkolgando unos orejales de pyedras valutozas, i poko tyempo despues estos orejales non los *kulanearon.*

En tyempo vyejo, kuando la mujer salia a la kaye, vistia un *kyurdi* ensamarrado de panyo *kirmis.* La samarra de adyentro era de *pondekyi.* Por afuera, era un *prevaz* de un *zera* de anchura de su samarra, i se kuvijavan la kavesa kon un maramar blanko ke paresian unas andjelas. Despues de tyempo, troko i esta moda ke en lugar de *kyurdis,* yevan *kirimes* de seda o de lana, ensamarrados de *samur.* Kuanto a las *kofyas,* non troko, solamente ke el *boy,* ke en tyempo vyejo era la *kofya* kantidad de un metro, i agora son muncho mas kurtas. Tambyen los *fezes* ke yevan en las *kofyas,* estonses era kantidad de una tavla, i lo kual agora son muncho mas chikos. **[66a]** De poko tyempo, {en} va trokando la moda ke el 25% delas mujeres ya visten a la franka. Non kyere dicho ke ilas mosas ke estan oy kazando, las mas munchas {munchas} ya estan vistyendo este modo.

Las mosas en tyempo antiguo vistian mesmo al uzo delas Vlahas. En la kavesa, yevavan una *fes* komo una *takyika* kuvrida kon *pishkul mavi* de seda i detenida kon una barvera. I la kaveyera sela azian trensas ke paresian unos *shiritikos.* I a la punta delas trensas, deshavan un *pishkuliko* de kaveyos a kada uno i uno. El vistir era de una ropa de *basma,* un fostan a la vez, ke era de 2 a 3 telas de anchura i una fermele estrecha komo un kontush, i kuando salian a la kaye, se metian una *djubbe* de panyo, muy estrecha a el uzo Vlaho. El bel era muy estrecho i las mangas eran estrechas kantidad ke non les vinia la mania al braso. I las faldas de abasho avian espati de seda blanka mizmo i los *yartimaches* ke era kantidad de un piko avyerto. La kavesa se kuvrian kon un djal ke la una punta de adelantre, i la otra se la echavan ensima los ombros, uzo adjeno. Las *kunduryas* ke yevavan era apena[s] ke la kara tapava los dedos del pye solo.

Kapitolo 28

Los Kazamyentos del Tyempo Vyejo

Ilas novyas, las traivan kon vistido de mujer, sayo, i *antari,* i *mestas,* i sapatos amariyos. En la kavesa les metian un *kalpakito* de *sirma*—ke lo yamavan *findjan*—komo una *mishtrapa,* i un velo, el *kyenar* de *sirma.* Ocho dias antes, davan alvorada, el dia de antes de yevarla a el banyo, vinia una djudia kon un *tendjeriko* chiko adyentro un pedaso de *termentina* ke lo yamavan pelador. Se metia delantre a la novya i le estava echando pedasos de este **[66b]** pelador en la frente, i en las karas, mezmo debasho delas sejas. Despues ke ya se lo apegavan byen i davan un travon kon muncha fuersa, i se lo arankavan, i la novya se estremesia dela pasyon. Guay de akea novya ke tenia el kuero delgado, le salia la sangre debasho el kuero. A algunas se les auflava las karas ke paresian sudadas de la virguela. I kuando la traivan ala kaza de el novyo, sin konoserla de antes, a la prima vista, le paresia ke era avirguelada. A la suvida dela eskalera, ya estava pronta una mujer vyeja dela paryentez kon un pedaso de sharope duro, la bezava de kara i kara a la novya, i le metia un pedaso de dito sharope de 15 a 20 *dr.* en la boka, i la asentavan a la novya a el *talamo* kon akel trujon de la una parte dela kara ke non era el uzo de komerselo, otro ke selo dirrityera de suyo en la boka. Al novyo, lo vistian i lo asentavan en algun *chardak* enfrente de la puerta de el kortijo ke por ayi va a entrar la novya. Le metian un maraman a la kavesa arapada, el kual era lavrado kon filos de bril, i *pishkules* ke paresia un{o} *imam* vinido de Afganistan.

Despues, para yevarlo a la *keila* kon sus paryentes, le kitavan el maraman i le metian un bonete, i *djubben*. En vinyendo en kaza, kantavan los *shiv'a berahoth* delantre la novya i el novyo. Despues, los asentavan a los konsuegros uno por kada lado; i el novyo, lo alevantavan i le davan a bezar las manos del padre i del konsuegro i dela madre i de la konsuegra, ke la kuala le dava un dukado de regalo. I al novyo, yevavan en otra kamareta afirmar la *ketubba;* i a la novya, kitavan a baylar kon 2 tanyederas vyejas. Myentres se azia de noche, al novyo asentavan en una meza kon sus amigos i sus paryentes, myentres a la novya la yevavan, tanyendo i kantando kantigas de amores, a la kamareta dela kama. La asentavan en una mezika delantre kon un plato de konfites i una ridomika de 2 vazos de *raki*. I al novyo yevavan adyentro, **[67a]** ke yamavan esto el avlar. I le seravan la puerta por afuera, i se asentava el novyo allado de eya. I inchia un vaziko de *raki* i le azia la onor a la novya. La novya alevantava la kavesa en sinyos ke non keria. El novyo vyendo ala novya yena de briles, el vaziko se lo echava él avante i tomava un punyado de konfites kon el prezente se los echava en la alda, i se salia afuera. Entravan las mujeres en un *boluk*, i la tomavan a la novya i la kitavan a fuera, tanyendo i kantando. La asentavan en el varandado, myentre el novyo kon sus amigos se asentavan en una meza respartada, komian i bevian, i la novya kedava en *ta'anith*. La tomavan a la novya sin komer, i la yevavan a echar kon kantes de amores ke sinyifikava konsejos para la novya la kuala dizia, "estos empesijos, madre mia, disheme un konsejo komo are kon el amor primero? El me ama i yo lo kyero". "Ija mia, teneldo en palavras kela nochada kyere seer pasada". I al novyo, lo yevavan kantando *pizmones*, i lo alevantavan komo alevantan a el *hathan*, i lo entravan adyentro, i lo desmudavan, i lo echavan, i se salian todos afuera. El novyo entrankava la puerta por adyentro, i del resto ya se entyende.

Kapitolo 29

[67b] El Rijo de el Komer en las Fyestas

Los pransos en las fyestas se empesavan de este modo. El dia delos קדושין, *[kiddushin]*, despues ke el novyo vinia del banyo kon sus amigos, metian una meza i se asentavan de 20 a 30 amigos, asigun era los amigos ke tenia. La komida era pishkado, i karne, i arroz, i frutas. Mezmo era i la noche de el enserro, meza de ombres i meza de mujeres. Ala otra noche, eran los kombidados ke se yamava la nochada de el konsuegro, ke vinian todos los kombidados dela parte del novyo i dela parte de la novya.

Dia de *shabbath*, lo esteso. Noche de *alhad*, lo mezmo, i entre la boda non mankavan algunos *ziafetes* en resparte.

El dia de el peshe, azian meza de *talmide hahamim* ke komian i bevian, i les davan *aspaka*.

Estonses, las kamaretas de 50 anyos antes eran de 8 a 10 metros de grandura alomenos, la sofa era de 4 metros *doshedeada* kon *mindeles* i *yastikes*. Las mezas eran kon *sinis* de kovre. El masero arodeado de un *peshkir* de kaji 7 a 8 metros, esto era por tovajas. En esta sofa ke dishimos, se metia 3 mezas. En los *minderes* se asentavan algunos, i los *yastikes* era ke se asentavan por sia. I era de 2 a 3 vazos en la meza, i unas kuantas kucharas de palo para komer arroz i una ridoma preta de 1000 a 2000 *[dramas]*, ke la tomava uno de la meza entre sus *pachas*, i le iva echando vino a kyen paresia al detenedor de la ridoma. Metian una kuna de peshe en medyo la meza. I de ai, ivan komyendo todos kon las manos. I despues, metian un tayero grande de karne kon *zarzavat*. El ke metia la mano primero, tomava dela karne lo *mevuhar*, el sigundo, el tersyo, lo ke kedava, i el resto, chupavan los guesos. I despues, una komida de aves, el ke tenia braso mas elguengo, akel aferrava el pedaso mijor, los ke non alkansavan, kedavan kon un gueso en la mano.

[68a] Despues, vinia el arroz ke apenas dava un buyor ke kedavan los granos komo *sachmas*. El arroz vinia en una supyera grande, kuvyerto de asukar i kanela, ke non se via arroz. I kuando se komia lo de ensima, ya avia aparejado 2 platos de asukar i kanela para ir espolvoreando. El ke tenia meoyo, se guadrava de antes una kuchara en su alda, el ke non alkansava kuchara, tomava un gueso dela paila de la ave por kuchara; el ke non alkansava ni esto era forsado de azer la mano kuchara.

Se entyende ke la mitad del arroz, medyo krudo i medyo kocho, les kaivan en las barvas, syendo estonses *kulaneavan* barvas elguengas, i anke el ke tenia la barva preta, se le azia blanka delos granos de ke le kaiyan en sima.

I despues de la komida, kitavan a el novyo a baylar kon alguno de sus amigos, i despues salian todos los kombidados a par a par.

Los tanyedores eran un kombidador i un tanyedor separato, i estavan kantando en los bayles lo ke les vinia en la boka, ke eran 3 bayles: son de baylar, son de saltar i *chichek avasi*. Myentres los bayles, los ke estavan en las mezas, i eskapandose el vino dela ridoma preta, avian de eyos buenos chufladores de vino, tomavan a djugar a la morra, i el ke pedria, mandava i tomava un kantaro de vino, i estavan bevyendo sin ku{a}[e]nta. Kuando se eskapavan los bayles, tomavan a azer kozas de *shakas*, kyen se metia una *samarra* arrovez, kyen tomava una savaná blanka i se metia en la kavesa una óya yena de agua, i se vinia a djugar ande el kombidador ke el kual yevava bonete grande. Ilos בעלי דינים, *[ba'ale dinim]*, empesavan a gritar: tu me deves, yo non te devo; tu me dishites, yo non te dishe. Alfin, era ke el ke yevava la savana kon el *tendjere* de agua en la kavesa tapada, se abokava para el s. *haham*, para le dizir al oido alguna palavra, i le vazyava el *tendjere* ensima el s. *haham* sin ke se depedriera gota, i lo azia *trushi*, de ariva asta basho. **[68b]** I todos los kombidados estavan azyendo atansyon a el djuzgo ke los kualos ya estavan borrachos pedridos.

I la[s] mujeres ke ya avian eskapado de komer se entravan a la sala kon la novya, para ver esta shena, se metian todos en una riza. Se metian el novyo i la novya a riir, esto era por משׂמח חתן וכלה, [*mesammeah hathan ve-halla,* alegrar al novyo i a la novya].

Despues, tomavan 2 personas i se asentavan en basho, uno enfrente de otro, i les atavan las *pachas* una kon otra, i las manos una kon otra, i empesavan a meter adyentro los *yastikes* asta ke se les tomavan el *suluk*. Esto lo yamavan nave ke enkargar. Despues ke ya azian la rema entre los 2 atados, salia uno por kapitan, i dizia ke, esta nave va azer avaria. Kale ke se de demuevo un *kalafat*. Traian 2 almirezes kon las manos, i les empesavan amartiar, i tomavan a kantar komo los marineros ke el *kalafatchi* dizia, *ya isa!* I los kombidados respondian al yámo.

Estos eran los kombites i las *shakas* de tyempo vyejo. Todo el tino delos antiguos era en komer i bever, syendo estonses non avia lusos en las kazas, apenas se topava una velika en la ventana i 5 a 6 sias de tornero, *donadeava* la kaza, i un espejiko enkachado ke apenas se via la kavesa dela persona ke se keria mirar. El vistir era una *dolama* de panyo en semana, i lo mezmo en shabbath, ke las kualas kedavan de ירושה, *[yerusha],* para los ijos.

Dunke, lo poko ke ganavan ya les bastava para komer i bever.

Kapitolo 30

[69a] Las Shambashugas

De tyempo vyejo, la primera melizina ke davan para el hazino era ke le echavan en la boka de el alma de 15 a 20 sambashugas o por ke estava kalado, o por ke tuvyese alguna dolor en la boka del alma i en kualunke myembro de el kuerpo. I non avia kaza sin tener una ridoma de 25 a 30 sambashugas depozitadas para ora de menester. Kualunke ke tuvyese alguna dolor, komo dishimos ande ke fuese, ya le echavan sambashugas devista.

La mas parte del puevlo, salyendo *Pesah* ke lo yamavan primavera, se echavan a basho de 10 a 15 sambashugas para trokar la sangre. I es verdad ke la hazinura de almoranas non egzistia tanto komo agora.

Estonses avian de 8 a 10 personas ke se mantenian de este negosyo. S. Abot [Abbott], topandose en Londra en su manseves, supo ke las sambashugas valian un *shilin* la una, i ke eran mandadas de Saloniko. El savia ke se vendian a 2 un *metalik* en muestra sivdad; el penso de tomar este negosyo por primer.

En su tornada por Kostan, supo kitar un *firman* i la izo *meri* la sambashuga. Este *meri* lo tomo el por una kuantita de anyos.

En vinyendo en Saloniko, izo azer proíbito a estos ke traivan las sambashugas, los tomo el por empiegados ke toda la sambashuga devian trae[r]sela a el.

I empeso a azer una furtuna ekstraordinarya en embiando botas yenas a la Eoropa. Estonses metyo por *bekchis,* en las baras ke salen ditas sambashugas, a una djente dela mas negra espesya, asta ke vinyeron a echar a un ombre adyentro la bara ke ai fue su muerte.

Estos *bekchis* era{s}[n] djente asasinos de la montanya, i ke el les azia dar *ray,* i los tomava por *kavazes.* I tuvo merkado [un terreno] en Orundjik tan **[69b]** grande, i de muncha arvoleria, i fraguo una kampanya.

En el sigundo viaje ke izo a Londra, ke ya estava rikishishimo, se namoro de una muchacha ke era kativada de la gerra ke tuvyeron los inglezes, i kijo merkarla para el. Ma el respondyo a su amo, ke "si el la tenia ke vender a alguno, ke fuera kon kondisyon ke la tomara por mujer i non por mantenuta".

Esta muchacha era vinida de *soy* de djidyo. Estonses se la vendyo a el s. Djon [John] Abot [Abbott] kon esta kondisyon ke la tomara por mujer. I el se kontento, i la tomo por mujer komo la ley de estonses. Ise la trusho a Saloniko, la kuala era una muchacha tan ermoza, sin dinguna makula, i le nasyeron de eya un ijo i una ija. Despues fraguo en Malta, ande es agora el *han* de Lombardo, un *konak* muy ermozo, i en el kortijo, se fraguo 4 a 5 grutas por el.

Pasando unos kuantos anyos, el la aborresyo a esta mujer, i empeso a tomar mantenutas, syendo era amador de munchas mujeres. I el tenia un ombre ke lo tomo a su lado por peshkador de mujeres a la ke le dava el ojo, kuento de moneda non azia en mal de akontentar su dezeo.

I akada una de eyas les tomava una kaza en esparte kon sus servisyales, i kuando le plazia, se yevava a alguna de eyas en la kampanya de Orundjik para kontentar su pasyon, syendo non tenia otro penseryo ke esto.

El se fue anch[e]ando en el komercho, i se izo el primer bankyer de Saloniko. I tomo tanta enfluensa ke todo loke keria el azia. Estonses, la mujer primera se kesho ande el konsolato inglez, el kual yamo a s. Abbott dizyendole ke la ley ingleza non da amano a deshar a su mujer. El ensistyo a non kererla mas konoser por mujer. Si komo ya dishimos ke era ombre de muncha enfluensa, non le pudo el konsolo torser el braso.

El konsolo eskrivyo a Ingiltera kontando todo el fato. I le mandaron una setensya de el governo ke kalia ovedeser a el **[70a]** konsolo a todo loke le komandava.

En tanto, el konsolo lo ovligo a ke le tomara una kaza para eya respartada kon sus servisyalas i un moso para ke le trushera todo loke eya demandava. I le izo una mezada sufichente. Este sinyor, non pudyendo somportar loke el konsolo le ovligo, eskrivyo a Londra munchas kontraydades por el konsolo, i lo izo sufrir a el konsolo asta ke le kavzo la muerte.

Ma el konsolo era un ombre muy bueno i djusto, i todo loke le izo somportar este ombre, le dyo el Dyo un ijo tan kapache ke pudo tomar la venganza de este sinyor.

El lo izo sufrir en el tyempo ke estuvo en kama echado para murir, syendo ya dishimos en el fuego de Iskilichi, ke le kemo la kaza i las grutas, i los *defteres*, i todo. Tomo a litigar kon el ermano, s. Bab [Bob] Abot [Abbott], en dizyendo ke non era el su socho, syendo non avia prevas porke todos los dokumentos se avian kemado en el fuego.

El ermano izo trayer de Londra 2 avokatos de prima klase en pagandoles 10 liras el dia a kada uno, i los gastes de viaje en esparte.

En vinyendo en Saloniko i egzaminando el echo, i vyeron ke el ermano tenia la razon.

I syendo el ermano era ekonomikó, non gastava la moneda komo s. Djon, se tomo lo efetivo. I syendo la trávida de s. Djon era ekstraordinarya, i un *konak* ke fraguo a pyedra, ke oy es de la banka otomana, en el kual gasto chirka 10 milyones de frankos, ke fue gastando la moneda en azer i dezazer la fragua ke turo 15 anyos fin ke se eskapo. I los echos le fueron indo para *píso,* kedo adever a Londra una suma grande de liras.

Estonses, lo izyeron perkurador a el konsolo—s. Blint [Blunt], el ijo de el konsolo ke izo sufrir i le tomo la vengansa—a ke el se empatronara de el byen ke le avia kedado, i ke se lo vendyera en *mezat*.

El konsolo kito *tellal* ke todo el ke keria merkar ropas valutozas ke **[70b]** vinyera en el *konak* ke es ai dela banka. I ivan vinyendo kada dia merkaderes, i el *tellal altiriando* i el s. sinyando dela kama las ropas ke se le estavan vendyendo, syendo le kostavan los ojos dela kara. I vendyo el konsolo asta la ultima koza ke avia en la kaza, i lo izo todo en moneda. Estonses, el ijo de este s. vino en Saloniko por tomar alguna koza de erensya. Ma topo las kashkas, porke i todas las kazas ke tenian las mantenutas, las kito afuera i las vendyo. I en la kampanya de Orundjik ke tenia tantos miles de *chichekes* alavados, ilas estatuas ke avia metido en dita guerta, todo se lo vendyo a *yok paasina* en prezensya de el *hazino,* i muryo kon ansya i sospiro. Esta fue la vengansa de lo ke le izo sufrir a el padre. Este konsolo ay mas de 25 anyos ke esta en muestra sivdad, i syempre fue un ombre derecho i bueno ke se komporto kon todo el mundo. El es un byen azedor, i tan umilde ke kon la mas chika kriatura el se desha kerer. I agora, partyo para Amerika por ambasador.

Kapitolo 31

Los Moradores en el Mes de *Nisan*

Antes 40 anyos, los moradores trokavan kazas en el mez de *Nisan*. Los s. *hahamim*, djunto el *Rav, h"r* אשר, [Asher], *n"'E,* [su repozo en Gan 'Eden], pensando el *sa'ar* ke yevavan los moradores en este tyempo, syendo era en salida de invyerno, i el gaste ke tenian demenester para la Paskua, bushkaron de aremedyar este echo.

I izyeron una הסכמה, *[askama]* a ke los moradores enveche de trokar kaza en *Nisan,* ke se trokaran en *Ellul.*

Sovre esto, uvo munchos debates, ma ala fin reusheron. Porke kuando era en *Nisan,* era 15 dias de valor para la Paskua, i kedavan munchos moradores sin kaza asta dia de *kal hamira*. I izyeron el trokamyento de kaza en *Ellul.*

Los patrones non achetavan, syendo ke kuando vinia Pesah, se aremedyavan delas *kiras,* i los ovligaron a ke kovraran kuanto era de djusto de *Nisan* asta *Ellul.*

[71a] Estonses, kitaron unas chirkolares ke dingun patron non puede forsar a su morador a ke le page la anyada entera, solamente de *Nisan* asta *Ellul.*

Esta mezma chirkolar me la dyeron ami a ke la apregonara en Shabbath en *t"t* en el mez de *Adar.*

En esta regla se esta kaminando fin a este tyempo.

Kapitolo 32

La Matansa de los Konsolos del 6 Madjo 1876

Vyernes la tadre de el 5 koryente, el treno de Uskup arivando, trusho en muestra sivdad una muchacha bulgara kijendo azerse turka, i vistida a la turka para apareserse a *hukyumat.* Apenas abashava a la estasyon, rogo alos *zapties* ke estavan prezentes ke la yevaran devista a el *hukyumat* por darles asaver su determinasyon. Apenas ke izyeron pokos pasos ke una kantidad de mansevos gregos, ke ya estavan avizados, bushkaron de tomar a la muchacha de sus manos i la metyeron en una karosa, kelos kualos le kitaron el *yashmak* i el *feredje* en prezensya de todos los asistyentes. I los *zapties* ke se topavan en poko numero non pudyeron empidir la koza. I los turkos ke se topavan en las *kavanes,* syendo era *hiderelez,* kedaron maraviyados i dezplazyentes de ver todo este páso.

A la otra manyana, ke fue *shabbath,* la ora 5 [12 PM] a la turka, el puevlo turko, i *arnautes,* i *yabandjis* ke se topavan en muestra sivdad, fueron a reklamar de el *hukyumat* ke la muchacha kere azerse turka, ke la trusheran a el *hukyumat*, i ke le preguntaran en ke ley keria kedarse, o turka, o kristyana.

El *hukyumat* respondyo ke esta echa ya se estavan mirando eyos. A esta repuesta, todo el puevlo se akojeron a *Saatli Djami.* El Vali vyendo toda esta rebuelta, i ke el demas antes ya estava bushkando **[71b]** de meter mano a la muchacha, ma dezgrasyadamente non se pudo embezar en ke lugar estava eskondida.

Estonses el Pasha mando de 5 a 6 personas onoradas a ke afalagaran a akeos akojidos en la *Djami,* a ke se fueran kada uno a su echo.

Syendo el i su *mishlish* ya estavan okupandosen, eyos respondyeron ke, {ke} non se tenian ke ir de akel lugar sin tomar a la muchacha. En tanto, el s. Sarito Abbott, konsolo de Almanya, i el s. Jul Mulen, konsolo de Fransya, indo ande el Pasha por prekurar de adovar las kozas, ma dezgrasyadamente, eyos se fueron derecho a la *djami,* ande estuvyeron akojidos todo el puevlo kon la esperansa, paresyendoles de trankuilizar los espritos ezaltados, en ke en el kamino seles tuvo akavidado ke non era ora ke se aparesyeran en akea rebuelta. Ma eyos non kijeron kreer la koza tanto apretada, kontinuaron sus kaminos, i se entraron en la *djami,* en medyo de todo el puevlo.

El *Vali Pasha* de su parte, supyendo ke los konsolos entraron en la *djami,* se alevanto devista, el kon todo su *mishlish,* i se fueron a la *djami* porke non akontesyera algun *tazvirat.* Apena ke entro el *Vali Pasha,* se alevantaron todo el puevlo en una, dizyendo ke en kualunke modo kerian empatronarsen dela muchacha i la ivan a tomar por fuersa. El Vali ke vido la koza muy serya, el kon su *mishlish,* empesaron a rogar a los konsolos a ke izyeran trayer a la muchacha, syendo la koza estava byen embrolyada. Ma eyos respondyeron ke si komo la muchacha estava eskondida, era muncho dificile para toparse, ma ke eyos ya estavan prekurando para toparla. Entanto, los turkos pedrieron la pasenya, i empesaron a gritar de muevo ke si non traivan a la muchacha, eyos non deshavan salir de sus manos alos konsolos.

Atanto ke vyeron los konsolos ke la koza estava muncho fuerte, eskrivyeron bilyetos premurozos ake entregaran a la muchacha en sus poderes, syendo estavan eyos en grande perikolo. Ma dezgrasyadamente, las repuestas tadraron, i azyendose tadre, los turkos se echaron ensima de los konsolos, rompyeron las ventanas de fyerro, entraron en la kamara ande se topava el Vali, i **[72a]** el *mishlish,* i los konsolos, i kon grandisima furya, empesaron aharvarlos kon los fyerros ke kitaron delas ventanas, syendo non avia *askyer* bastante ke puedia defender a el puevlo. Los dos konsolos dezgrasyadamente desharon la vida i kedaron viktimas de el furor deel puevlo. I en ke la prezensya del *Vali* ke estava prekurando de defenderlos, ma non pudo valer nada. Los sinyores del *mishlish* fueron tambyen aharvados, el *Vali* mezmo fue maltratado. El *Alay Bey* risivyo munchos golpes de aharvasyon, un *yuz bashi* tanto fue la lenya ke le dyeron, ke lo echaron en la kama, a munchos *zapties* firyeron.

En loke akontesyo estos dezastres, la muchacha ya vinia konsinyada, ma por dezgrasya fue muncho tadre.

Diversos golpes de revolver i de pishtol estuvyeron echando en el ayre. Despues de esto, kada uno se torno a su lugar. Las 2 kalavrinas fueron transportadas noche de *alhad*, el konsolo de Alemanya a su kaza, i el de Fransya a las monakas katolikas.

El *Vali Pasha* telegrafó a Monastir a ke mandaran devista *askyer* por estar siguros de alguna rebuelta.

Alhad la ora 5 a 6 [10 AM to 11 AM], empesaron a vinir *askyer* de lugar serka, a la tadre trusho el treno de Eskopya chirka mil *askyeres*. Muestra sivdad se topava estonses enteramente serrada, guardias numerozas kaminavan por las kayes, ma despues de estas mezuras, esperavan ke tuvyera su lugar.

La sivdad entera estava adoloryada de akeas krueles dezgrasyas ke akontesyeron, i todas las nasyones tomaron biva parte de akeos limunyos. En el entervalo de 3 dias, empesaron a vinir naves de gerra de syertas potensyas. I martes demanyana, arivo la nave Golua, la kuala trusho adyentro el viche-amiral fransez.

En akel mezmo dia, ala una ora turka [8 AM], una grande kantidad de guardyas sirkolaron en muestra sivdad, i la metian a grande seguridad. En el *molo* se topava una grande kantidad de enfanteria i de kavaleria ke formaron un kordon en buenisima regla. El puevlo non savia ake **[72b]** iva atribuir tanto aparejo, tala fue la sekretina de las adjuntas i de el djuzgo. Una ora despues, en medyo de un gran repozo i kayades, sesh personas delos emprezyonados los mas kulpantes, se vido trayer deel *kapan* turko, i en mezmo tyempo los amirales i fonksyonaryos ajenos, akompanyados de muestro *Vali Pasha*, abasharon de la korveta, se entravan dela oria deel molo en diversas barkas, i en manko de medya ora, se vido ezeguir la pena de sesh asasinadores kulpantes, promotores dela mala echa.

Despues de azerles la *idjra,* saludos ofisyales kontraka[m]byaron, entre eyas, fregatas fransezas i alemanas i turkas, i kada uno torno a su repozo i a su echo.

A la ora 11 a 12 [6 PM to 7 PM], transportaron los kadavres a el eshpital, i a la manyana fueron yevados a sus fuesas.

Dia de myerkoles, fueron kombidados todos los myembros delos *mishlishes,* i los *muhtares* de ir al *konak,* metyendosen en rango todos los fonksyonaryos, entre en medyo de eyos su e{n}kselensya, el *Vali Pasha.* Eshref Pasha izo un deskorso muy manyifiko, dando a saver delos djuzgos ke se izyeron kon muncha atansyon i kon provas de testimonyos valivles.

Diya de shabbath deel 26 koryente, kon muevos avizos, el fue anonsyado ke el resto de los kulpantes tenian ke se[r] apenados sigun sus kulpas. I asiguró a el puevlo ke non tuvyeran el mas minimo espanto.

Mozotros non dubitimos ke su ekselensya, Eshref Pasha iva a kontinuar el repozo komo de antes, ike todo, sin dubyo se iva a olvidar tan presto.

Ma mos desplazyo bastante dela pedrita de estas 2 viktimas ke eran unas bravas i dinyas personas, las kualas se desparesyeron a la flor de sus edad. I de el resto, la populasyon de muestra sivdad, tuvyendo dado syempre provas de ermandad entre mozotros, i de kualunke relidjyon sea. Dunkue, esperavamos ke las desgrasyas akontesidas non enflueran syerto a trokar o a aminguar los muevos sintimyentos de ermandad.

[73a] Los Funerales delos Konsolos Aleman i Fransez

Djueves a la tadre deel 18 koryente, en las paredes se meldaron los avizos delos funerales delos konsolos fransez i aleman ke devien tener lugar a el otro dia de manyana.

El primo, tuvo lugar a la ora 6 i el sigundo era 8 ala franka. Al vyernes demanyana, al esklareser, vimos ke grandes kompanyas de soldados se paravan en todas las kayes. En kada *kyoshe* ke dava el pasaje para el *djadde,* avian kordones de soldados ke defendian el pasaje, de modo ke el puevlo kon muncha pena pudo arivar en las kayes por las kualas los defontos ivan a ser pasados.

Ala ora 10:30 ala turka dela manyana [5:30 AM], vimos a su ekselensya, el *Vali Pasha,* akompanyado de Vahan *efendi, mushtesar* de el *hakyim,* komo tambyen todos los konsolos i los delegados fransezes i prusyanos kon *terdjumanes.* Todos en uniforma se rendyeron a la eskala, ande esperaron el dezbarko deel viche-amiral fransez. I ala onze [6 AM], ala turka, vinyeron en grande akompanyamyento delos *askyeres* turkos adelantre i detras, kompanyas de soldados de kada nasyon ke fueron dezbarkados delas naves, djunto todos los viche-amirales i komandantes, i ofisyeres de kada nave ke se topo en muestro porto. I todos djuntos, se rendyeron a la kyeza katolika.

La klisya estava kuvrida de una gran kantidad de bandyeras i de aparejos de luyto.

Todos los notavles de Saloniko de todas las nasyones estuvyeron asperando el s. *rav a-gadol, h"r* Avraam Gatenyo, akompanyado de los reprezentantes de muestra komunita, de dyes *hahamim* i una kantidad de mansevos de luto. I el metropolit efendi, akompanyado delos reprezentantes de la komunita grega, tambyen de su parte vinian en la kyeza. I a la puerta, los dos kapos se enkontraron i saludandosen, entraron djuntos. La seremonia funevre adyentro la klisa turo chirka medya ora, i despues el konvolyo entero se metyo a kamino.

Es emposivle de vos dar a entender esta vista funerala ke azia atristar **[73b]** kualunke, i azia movimyentos de empresyon.

Tres rangos de soldados turkos kaminavan adelantre i detras el *Vali,* djunto Vahan efendi, i el amiral turko. Despues vinian todos los soldados de todas las potensyas, kon los *tufekes* de boka abasho, i kaminaron kon gran repozo i regla. Despues vinia el metropolit efendi, i despues los katolikos pretes, ke despues de eyos, vinia el funeral ke lo tenian los marineros fransezes, i despues todos los konsolos, viche-amirales, komandantes, ofisyeres de todas las naves ke se topavan en muestro porto, djunto los delegados fransezes i prusyanos, el s. *rav* kon sus reprezentantes, i despues todos los notavles de la sivdad. Todos vistidos de luyto, i se serrava kon grandes filas de turkos. El konvolyo funevre salyo dela klisa i tomo el kamino dela banka otomana, torno por la kaye del teatro, i torno por la kaye maestra. Despues, tomo de muevo el kamino del[a] *djadde* del *charshi* ke se fueron derechamente a la eskala, ande los esperavan diversos ofisyeres fransezes kon una barka entera *donadeada* de luyto ande la kasha funevre fue depozitada, akompanyada de 2 pretes katolikos, apartenyentes a las naves fransezas. Ke apenas la barka funevre empeso akaminar, ke una gran kantidad de golpes de kanon se sintyo de todas las fregatas, fin ke la kasha fue depozitada a bordo de la fregata Golua. Entanto, toda la kompanya ke ivan detras se enkaminaron devista para la kyeza grega mueva, yamada San Nikola por azer las onores meresidas a el konsolo aleman, ande fue echa la sheremonia relidjyoza de una, en manko de un[a] ora salyeron de la kyeza, i se metyeron en kamino. Adelantre vinian los soldados komo de antes, despues el *Vali* kon Vahan efendi i el amiral turko, el s. *rav* kon todo su seguita, i despues vinian los pretes gregos, i despues marineros alemanes, ke los kualos yevavan la kasha funevre, i despues los sinyores reprezentantes komo de antes. El konvolyo se enkamino por las mas mijores kayes, i anchas, fin el Metropolit onde el defonto fue enterrado.

[74a] En akel punto tambyen, los sonidos de la artileria se sintyeron, i las bandyeras ke estava[n] abasho en senyal de luyto fueron alevantadas.

Todo se paso kon la mas grande trankuilidad i repozo grasyas a las buenas i savyas mezuras ke su ekselensya, Eshref pasha tomo de antes.

Kapitolo 33

La Gerra de la Turkia kon la Rusia

Despues dela katastrofa dela matansa delos konsolos, la Eoropa topo la ora en alevantandole unas kuestyones a la Turkia, las kualas le demandavan unas reformas por asigurar la vida de todos los kristyanos, masima[me]nte la Rusia ke ala kuala se le derroko todo el plano de el rolo ke estava djugando el s. Inyatef kon Sultan Aziz, el kual estava derrokando a el governo en azyendo unos gastes tan terrivles, ke kada anyo azia mas de un milyo{s}[n] de liras de oro [de] gastes, asta ke dizian las gazetas ke 40 karosas al anyo trayiva de Evropa, tan valutozas ke arivo una de entre eyas ke kosto syen mil liras. Demas, tenia palasyos, yenos de mujeres, asta a mil i syen mujeres se mantenian i se governavan dela kasha deel governo. La *validé,* la madre, le azia kumplir todos sus dezeos, asta ke la *vukyela* era e[n]lasa, non lo pudyeron mas sufrir. El trokava la *vukyela* kada dia por la razon ke non le atorgavan a el de trokar la ley ke avia de vyejo, ke el grande dela famiya reyne detras de el rey muerto. El keria tener un partido a ke le firmaran una *masbata* a ke su ijo, Yusuf Izzeddin, ke enreynara despues deel. Ma el *Sheh ul Islam* non le premetia de azer su kapricho, i los ministros estavan kon la ley del *Sheh ul Islam.*

[74b] El se aravyava kon sus ministros i los azia *azil,* i metia otros en sus lugares por ver kualos eran ke le ivan atorgar su kapricho. Ma ni unos, ni otros, non estavan de su idea. De este *merak,* el se *childereyo* de su meoyo, i estuvo azyendo unas kozas ke non son konvenivles para un rey, rijidor detodo el puevlo.

El se avia determinado asta vender Kostantinople a la Rusia i estabilir su reynado en Bagdad, se metyo en relasyones kon el embashador ruso, yamado S. Inyatef.

Los ministros i el *Sheh ul Islam* i toda la *ulama* se metyeron de akordo para estituirlo i enreynar a el princhipe Murat en su lugar. I ansi fue. Eyos se aparejaron todo el menester, i metyeron todas las naves de gerra *vizavi* kon el palasyo de el rey; dela parte de tyerra metyeron 2 batalyones a la kavesera un pasha, todos armados. I a medya noche, fue un pasha kon un *firman* en la mano, firmado dela *vukyela* entera, i de Sultan Murat, i una *fetva* del *Sheh ul Islam.*

Kuando batyeron a la puerta dela kamareta ke estava echado, el se desperto i se metyo en kolorá.

Demando, ken tyene la ozadia en esta ora de desturvarlo? Le respondyeron ke era el embashador Inyatef ke vino por una koza premuroza ke vino. Estonses, travo el *tel* de la puerta i se avrio. Avriendose la puerta, el pasha le meldo el *firman* i la *fetva* de el *Sheh ul Islam.*

En oyendo ditas palavras, se aravyo dezgrazyadamente i perkuro de dar orden a la guardya emperyal, ma eyos ya estavan de akordo kon los ministros de antes. El *pasha* ke le yevo el *firman* i la *fetva* le disho, "s., es inútile de azer dingun modo de esforso, aparavos por la ventana de parte de tyerra i de parte de mar, i veresh ke todo ya esta echo en regla".

I aparandose por una ventana por ver de mar i de otra de parte **[75a]** de tyerra, i vido ke todo estava eskapado. Estonses, se estremesyo i se alevanto de su kama, i lo vistyeron.

Izyeron yamar a la *valide* i ala *sultana* i lo metyeron en un *kaik.* I a la *validé* i la reyna en otro, i los yevaron a el palasyo de Sarayburnu. A kada uno, un apartamento aparte, i a su ijo Yusuf Izzeddin un otro apartamento, porke non tuvyeran relasyones uno kon otro, i buenas guardyas arodeando el lugar.

En akea mezma noche, trusheron a Sultan Murat a el palasyo i lo asentaron en el trono de el rey.

A la manyana, primer dia de שבועות, *[Shavu'oth]*, deel anyo, empesaron a tirar delas forteresas 101 tiro anonsyando el enreynamyento de Sultan Murat. En sintyendo esta novita, todo el puevlo de Estambol yevavan pintados en sus karas la alegria i el gozo, konosyendo el karakter de Sultan Murat ke era konsensyozo i pasensyozo, i ke konosia la politika dela Evropa. Ya savian ke el iva meter al reynado en orden.

Despues de dos dias, se sintyo ke Sultan Aziz se burako kon una tijera la vena del braso ise vazyo las sangres ikedo de bivir. Estonses, trusheron 9 dotores delos mas [reputados] i egzaminaron la koza i afirmaron de komun akodro ke Sultan Aziz fue matado el propyo, syendo ke ilos medikos ya estavan de akodro kon los ministros. Mas despues, se supo la verdad de esta matansa.

El governo Ruso, supyendo toda esta shena, entendyo ke todo su plano sele derrroko, i entendyo ke los turkos non son tan bovos. La Rusia izo alevantar a todos los vasales, a la Servia, a la Bulgaria, i a la Rumania, alevantando unas kuestyones i una revol{v}usyon en la Bosnia Erzegovina. Ma muy presto, la Turkia la metyo a la razon. Despues kito a la Servia enfrente, i a esta chika potensya, lemostro ké valia, ke en pokos dias, le izo unos estrasos ke la armada turka ya via empesado el kamino de Belogrado.

[75b] Estonses, la Serbia demando un armistisyo ke el governo turko selo akordo, i le izyeron la pas kon la Evropa, en rogandole a la Turkia a ke le dyera atras todos los lugares ke le avia tomado, syendo avia kedado muy chika. I fue el djeneral Abdul Kyerim Pasha el ke vensyo esta gerra. Los Ungarezos, amigos dela Turkia, le mandaron a Abdul Kyerim Pasha una espada en briyantes en rekompensa de su bravura.

La Rusia mando una chirkolar alas sesh grandes potensyas en dizyendoles ke el keria salvar a todos sus ermanos kristyanos, i el le keria avrirle gerra a la Turkia sin ningun enteres por su kuento. Estonses, mando un ultimatom a la Turkia, dizyendole ke le avrira la gerra.

El governo turko mando a Abdul Kyerim Pasha, komandante detoda la armada para tapar las orias del Danubyo, syendo ke la Rusia por parte de tyerra non puedia atakar a la Turkia. Estonses, Abdul Kyerim Pasha en la kavesera de toda la armada se paso a Ruschuk por non deshar pasar *askyer* ruso por las aguas de el Danubyo.

Ma Inyatef, ke konosia la natura de Abdul Kyerim Pasha, disho a su governo ke para este personaje es muncho *kolay*, kon un punyado de rublas de oro lo konvensia. I ansi fue ke la Rusia izo unos pontes de kueros de bufano kon muncho artifisyo, i los empeso a echar en el Danubyo para pasar su armada.

Una noche ke empesaron a la ovra, los *Kara Anlis* le vinyeron a dizir a Abdul Kyerim pasha loke pasava. Ma el estando borracho delas rublas de oro, les respondyo ke non tenian ozadia de pizar la tyerra turka. Ma la Rusia en akea noche paso syen mil almas, i se empeso la gerra kon muncha fortaleza. I kaminaron fina la sivdad de Plevna ke ai se topava el djeneral Osman Pasha, komandante de una partida de la armada. **[76a]** El, vyendose enfrente de tantos miles de rusos, izo una bravura. En una noche eskura, avrio las bokaduras de todos los kanones, i mato 10 mil almas de los rusos.

Ma los rusos, tuvyendo la fuersa 10 tantos mas ke Osman Pasha, syendo ya se topo vazio de todo modo de *muimat* i de provizyones de boka, mando avizo i non le dyeron repuesta, syendo i eyos estavan borrachos de el oro departe dela Rusia, i los *askyeres* rusos izyeron bloko a Osman Pasha kon sus *askyeres*, i non tuvo lugar por fuirse.

El fue kostreto de entregarse, el i su armada ke non pueda resistir de{l} enfrente de tantos milyones rusos, i se entrego, el i su armada, en poder deel kual komo kativos. El kual [komanante Ruso], de su parte, le izo una reverensya a Osman Pasha komo barragan ke fue, i lo risivyo kalorozamente a el i su armada ilos mando en una sivdad serkana.

I la Rusia empeso akaminar sin dingun espanto, asta ke vino en San Estefano [Yeshilköy, serka del aeroporto de Estanbol].

La Ingiltera, vyendo ke la Rusia ya se esta indo {el} kon pantuflas adyentro de Kostantinopoli, le echo 6 naves de gerra a la mar de una parte, i de la otra, i amenazandola ke si el dava un paso mas adelantre de ande estava, todo su *askyer* ivan a ser muertos de parte de los de las frigates. La Rusia entendyo ke non podia rezistir enfrente dela Ingiltera, i se kedo en San Estefano, kon toda su armada. La Turkia, vyendosen en perikolo ke la amenazava, mando sus delegados a San Estefanos, i serraron la pas kon la Rusia en unas kondisyones muy dezagreavles, ma a kondisyon ke tenian ke djuzgar la Evropa si estas kondisyones eran djustas o no.

La Rusia se sotometyo a esta trazera kondisyon, syendo la[s] otras 6 potensyas non lo izyeron visto estas kondisyones djuzgarlas entre los dos, kalia djuzgarlas i eyos.

[76b] Estonses, se adjuntaron en kongreso en Berlino, i mandaron delegados delas 6 potensyas, i un delegado dela Turkia, i areglaron las kondisyones a lo ke djuzgaron eyos ke era de djusto, i metyeron los limitos delos lugares ke le ivan adar a la Bulgaria, kon un princhipato i el princhipe ke ivan a meter devia de ser al plazer dela Turkia i dela Rusia. I se prezentaron munchos kandidatos por princhipes, ma la Rusia non acheto a dinguno de eyos, syendo la opinyon dela Rusia era otra, ke keria meter un princhipato desu parte. Ma los bulgaros vyendo ke non se ivan a yamar Bulgaria, otro ke Rusia, eyos bulgaros, se eskojeron por princhipe a Aleksandro de Batemberg, sin rekonoserlo la Rusia por princhipe. En el tyempo ke estava por princhipe, el sufria de todas las 2 partes, si de la Rusia, si de los Bulgaros, i fue ovligado de deshar su posto, i irse a su patria. Despues, eskojeron a el princhipe Ferdinando ke ni a este lo kijo rekonoser la Rusia. Ma este ultimo, por ser rekonosido dela Rusia, *vaftizo* a el ijo, i lo izo ortodokso, ke esto era la demanda de la Rusia, ke keria ke el princhipe fuera ortodokso. Este modo, fue rekonosido por princhipe dela Rusia i dela Turkia. La Turkia desu parte, vyendo ke este princhipe es umilde i ovedesyente, lo izo governador djeneral de la *Rumelia* oryental.

La Gerra del 17 Avril 189{9}[7]

En el Kongreso de Berlino, ovligaron a la Turkia a ke le dyera la Tesalia a la Grechya en pagandole en ratas syen milyones de frankos; i la Turkia le izyeron los *sinires* en la *harta* delas sivdades dela Tesalia ke le tenian ke dar, i ansi fue. Ma despues de poko tyempo, la Grechya le demando otras dos sivdades para ke se le adovara los *sinires*. I kon esta *vesile*, non pago la devda. Non basta ni esto, ke fue levantando en kada poko tyempo a los kristyanos dela Kanea, i azyendole kostar a el **[77a]** governo turko un *kusur* de moneda en kada vez ke se alevantavan. I asta este mezmo tyempo ke eskrivimos ke eyos kerian adjuntar el Girit entero a la Grechya. El governo turko se adreso a las 6 potensyas, eyas deklararon ke les dyera unas reformas suffichentes a ke trokaran sus opinyon, i ke estuvyeran soto la podestania otomana, i se izo el kontratado.

La Turkia, pensando ke ya se eskapo la kuestyon, retiro sus trupas de la Kanea.

Kuando la Grechya vido ke la armada turka se retiro de la Kanea, mando eya de 4 a 5 batalyones, i se revoltaron de muevo. Las grandes potensyas fueron ovligadas de mandar kada una de 2 a 3 navios de gerra para azer akedar alos revoltados.

Ma sin provecho ke kada [dia] ave uvido shenas sangrientes.

La Grechya desu parte parese ke ya avia 8 a 10 anyos ke se estava preparando para azerle una gerra a la Turkia. Esta ultima, estuvo atagantando al governo turko kon ir kitando dia [de] kada dia *bolukes* de ensurdjentes.

La Turkia, vyendo esto, pedrio la pasensya, i mando a Edhem Pasha kon una armada fuerte i munchos komandantes kon sus trupas en la frontyera turko-elena.

En sima de todo esto, los revoltados bushkavan de empatronarsen de Preveze i de Yanina, ma los komandantes kon sus trupas les dyeron buena leksyon i les izyeron tomar la fuida, deshando sus *sinires* atras. Las trupas regolares dela Grechya, kijendo ayudar a estos brigandes, orden fue dado a Edhem Pasha a ke les defendyera i los presigyera. Estonses se deklaro la gerra avyertamente entre la Turkia i la Grechya.

Edhem Pasha, syendo un ombre enstruido de el arte militar i konosyendo la *harta* deel mundo entero byen estudyada, dyo orden a los komandantes en ke modo ke se rijeran i ke kamino ke tomaran. I los soldados, enflamados salyeron kon una bravura de leones, i kon fuersa **[77b]** de sus baterias i sus bayonetas, non tadravan a tomar sus *istihkyames* ilas sivdades ande estavan enserrados en deshando munchos matados i tomando munchos kativos i miles de kashas de kartushas, i lo mezmo de *tufekes* i tiros. Vista la *harta* delos lugares ke tomaron los turkos tan fuertes komo Chataldja, i Vlestino, i Dimo[ti]ko, i Djemre se vido la bravura de los soldados turkos kon ke ardor eyos g{a}[e]rrean por amor dela ley i la patria.

Tambyen, se vido ke la Providensya les ayudo, syendo fue una gerra endjusta departe la Grechya. Eyos toparon la endjustisya en pedriendo la Tesalia entera, i deshandola en mano delos turkos, i kon ke anchura de soldados i moneda se izo esta gerra tan bravamente, i en ke estrechura se topava estonses el governo eleno i su rey ke non esta topando mezos para mantener sus trupas. I vyendose amenazado de parte la Alemanya por sus devdas vyejas ke devia, i la endemnidad ke la estan ovligando las potensyas, se estan revoltando los abitantes kontra los deputados delas kamaras i kontra su rey. Las gazetas de estos dias dize[n] ke el rey Jeorje i su famiya i el eredador van a deshar sus postos, se van a ir a Danimarka ande el rey, su padre.

Dunke, la gerra apena un mes turo, i dekuando se proklamo el armistisyo, ya ay 3 mezes, i las kondisyones dela pas non estan eskapadas. Veremos asta kuando se va a determinar la pas.

Kapitolo 40[18]

[78a] La Entrada i la Kitadura de el Rabbanuth a el Rav Haribbi Avraam Gatenyo

En el anyo [5]635 [1874], en el mes de Tevet muryo el *Rav, h"r* Asher. Despues de unos kuantos dias, el konsilyo nomino por *rabbanim* a 3 de los grandes, a el *Rav, h"r* Avraam Gatenyo, primo, a el *Rav, h"r* Mair Nahmias, sigundo, i *h"r* Shemuelachi Arditi.

Estonses, los grandes dela sivdad bushkaron de azer reformas, i entre las reformas, bushkaron de non echar pechas otro kon las entradas delas gabelas. El *Rav, h"r* Avraam, konosyendo las entradas i salidas de muestro *kolel,* vido ke non abastavan las entradas para las salidas. Por apiadar munchos proves, el ensistyo ke esta reforma non la achetava. Ma si komo los grandes bushkavan sus enteresos i non el delos proves, eyos se determinaron de kitarlo de su posto. Mandaron al gran rabbinato de Kostan dizyendo ke el *Rav, h"r* Avraam esta vinyendo muncho kontra a los enteres[os] deel *kolel,* i ke kitára una *irade* por el posto de gran rabbino pasára a *h"r* Shemuelachi Arditi.

Estonses, el *kolel* gasto un *kusur* de moneda, i izo traer un *firman* embiado de el gran rabbinato de Kostan por mano de su *kyaya,* Jak Gabbay Efendi. I lo trusho kon una *saltanat,* i le fue muncho ensulto a el *Rav, h"r* Avraam Gatenyo, syendo de antes los *gevirim* se adjuntaron en kaza deel *Rav, h"r* Mair. Travaron a sus lados unos kuantos delos *hahamim* i les izyeron afirmar en un papel ke el *Rav, h"r* Avraam non es rekonosido por gran rabbino, syendo antes de azer esta *mazbata,* ivan embiando koreos ande el *rav, h"r* Avraam en ke achetara lo ke dezean eyos. I el les respondia, el puevlo ke me eskojeron por gran rabbino, masimamente ke la karga dela provaya kaiva a el. "Dunke, yo a los djidyos non se los puedo vender, syendo non me los vendyeron eyos ami".

Yo me akodro kon mis ojos dever un milagro ke la tadre ultima ke ivan afirmar esta *basmata,* mandaron un koreo ande el **[78b]** *Rav, h"r* Avraam, dizyendole ke esta tadre es la fin dela *bazmata;* ke ansi, si acheta, byen; tanto ke non, ya es *bitmish!* "I yo, de esta tadre en delantre non vengo mas por aki".

El s. *rav* le respondyo, "kon la ayuda deel Dyo, ke non venresh mas por aki"! I este koreo era un grande de la Asamblea i paryente deel *Rav, h"r* Avraam. El fue a la Asamblea i les dyo la ultima palavra, i fue la fin dela dechizyon.

Este sinyor koreo i paryente, despues de eskaparse la dechizyon, se fue a su kaza, se echo *hazino* ke non turo mas de ocho dias. Estonses se afirmo la palavra deel s. *rav* ke disho, "kon la ayuda deel Dyo kenon verneresh mas por aki".

Despues de un poko de tyempo, empesaron otros 2 a 3 de sus kolegas a desbarasarse de este mundo. Vyendo el resto este triste milagro, empesaron a estremesersen, i empesaron a mandar kada uno ande el s. *rav* ke si puedia ser de risivirlos por risivir un perdon de su parte. El *Rav, h"r* Avraam, si komo era un ombre muy umilde, non les refuzo a dingunos. I fueron vinyendo a uno, a uno, tanto delos *talmide hahamim,* komo los *gevirim,* a demandarle el perdon. I el los perdonava, en dizyendoles, "yo vos perdono, kon ke delos syelos vos perdonen".

Entanto, les kedo negras sinyales en todos sus korasones.

Despues de su muerte de el *Rav, h"r* Avraam, el ijo *h"r* Shemuel, mirando todos los papeles ke kedaron eskritos de su propya mano, topo un papel de serka tyempo antes de su muerte, el kual era un bilanso tan prechizamente eskrito ke de munchos anyos antes, el fue *apotropos* i kashero dela *kuppa* de *yethomim* i *almanoth.* I lo dyo en estampado, i kito 500 egzemplaryos, i los espartyo a todo el puevlo.

En vyendo este bilanso, el mundo kedaron enkantados de maravia. Lo ke iva mas de maraviar es ke una *almana* le trusho 100 groshes **[79a]** a ke se los rijera el. Esta *almana* le dyo su nombre i el nombre de el marido. Pasando 30 anyos, estos 100 gr. se izyeron 600, syendo esta *almana* non tuvo ijos, non uvo kyen reklamara. Un dia kele vinyeron 2 *ba'ale dinim* i le nombraron dela alkunya deel marido ke tenia *maraza* kon el. En sintyendo el *haham* la alkunya deel marido dela bivda kele desho los 100 groshes, el kual era un paryente, le disho el s. *rav* a esta persona, "mandame a este ombre ke me estas nombrando, ke tengo unas paras para darle". Este, devista fue i le dyo avizo a el ombre, el kual le demando deel eredador, "si me das a mi 25 por 100, yo te amostro ande tyenes paras para tomar". El kual, en sintyendo, le akometyo loke demando. Devista, selo yevo ande el *Rav, h"r* Avraam, i le izo *istindak,* i supo ke era un ijo de akel ombre ke muryo sin ijos. Le disho a el *sofer* a ke izyera una risivida, i ke tomara su moneda. I ansi fue. Le amostro a este ombre loke le rijo los 100 groshes, i le dyo la moneda en la mano adyentro una bolsa.

En salyendo a la kaye, el ke le dyo la novitá le reklamo los 25 por 100, i les entro pleyto entre eyos, syendo non keria dar su prometa.

El *shammash* deel s. *haham* ke salyo akea ora dela puerta, vyendo el pleyto, entro ande el s. *haham* i le dyo a saver loke se pasava en la kaye, ke devista los yamo adyentro i le disho a el eredador ke kon *behoth* non le puedia dar nada.

Otro un fato semejante uvo ke una mujer de 40 anyos antes le entrego unas paras a el s. *haham*, i non se supo fina el tyempo ke salyo el bilanso akyen apartenia estas paras. Se kito pregon por todas las *keilloth* i por *t"t*, i non se topo eredador. Los *gevirim* toparon de djusto ke esta moneda, syendo non avia eredador, a ke se empleara esta moneda para estampar el livro sigundo de על הכסף, *'al a-kesef.*

Estonses, los *gevirim* empesaron a azer *vidduy* por el eskandalo kele izyeron a el s. *haham*, i fueron ensima de su tomba, i le demandaron **[79b]** מחילה, *[mehila].*

Kuando *h"r* Shemuelachi se vido solo por *rav a-kolel*, empeso a komandar a los grandes dela sivdad a ke todos los rijos se los dyeran a saver a el. Los *gevirim* non se denyaron dele dar asaver nada, i empeso *baraza* entre eyos. En este tyempo, los *gevirim* le demandavan ke unas butikas ke avian en *Kari Pazar*, las kualas apartenian a una mujer, la kuala las izo *ekdesh* para la *yeshiva* dela puerta del *t"t* ke avia estonses. En semana, se azian las orasyones dela manyana ke se azian en *t"t*. Eskapando, suvian en dita *yeshiva* por sintir alguna leksyon, la kuala es enriva de *asara batlanim*. I syendo el *t"t* se izo *batal* de dizir *tefilloth* la manyana, i el *haham* ke les meldava leksyones muryo, i la *yeshiva* kedo *batal*. Dunke, este *ekdesh* apartyene a el *kolel*, i las butikas deven de pasar al *kolel*. Ma si komo el *Rav*, *h"r* Shemuelachi era *apotropos* de uno delos desendyentes deel *haham* dela *yeshiva*, yamado Nissim, el non acheto a esta demanda, sino ke mando a su *kyaya* kon la mujer de este desendyente a

[dar] *ikrar* al *hukyumat* en dizyendo ke esta mujer es nyeta de akea vyeja, patrona de estas butikas. Eya lo azia el regalo a el marido de azerlo *ikrar* ensima deel, i paso el *ikrar* ensima deel marido akel *{haluhoṭ} [halukkoth]* de Nissim.

Supyendo el kual dela fasfecha sekreta ke izo el *rav*, bushkaron delo kitar desu posto. Mandaron a el gran rabbinato de Kostan. El *rav* mando desu parte karta dandole a saver sigun kijo el a el gran rabbinato. El *rav* de Kostan les mando una karta a el Konsilyo a ke se dezvachearan dela demanda.

En verdad ke los *gevirim* se dezvacharon dela demanda, ma kedaron syempre merikiados kon el asta el dia desu muerte.

I despues dela muerte deel *Rav, h"r* Mair Nahmias, le izyeron dar el posto a *h"r* Yakovachi Kovo ke es un ombre ke konosyo echos de merkansia, i kon su entelijensa, el supo ganar la amistad de todos los dirijadores del Konsilyo. I tomo el titolo de *Kaymakam* i prezidente onoraryo de el Konsilio. I asta oy, el es el rijidor de todos los echos de muestra sivdad.

Kapitolo 41

[80a] El fuego de 5650 [1890]

En el 13 Ellul de [5]650 [29 August 1890], en una butika de *raki* estavan arefinando *raki*, se aferro el techo dela butika i komuniko kon las deel allado, i si komo el ayre era tan fuerte, se esparzyo en el kuartyer entero. I las flamas tanto bolantes ke fue atakando a los otros kuartyeres. I los pompyeros non pudyeron atabafarlo, syendo era de munchas partes las flamas. Se espandyo dela plaseta asta el *Ahche Medjid*, i deel *Ahche Medjid* asta la oria dela mar, ke destruyo tantos palasyos i tantos *kyavgires* fraguados de poko tyempo. I toda la provaya, loke alkansavan a arekojer desus ropas ande la yevavan, ai se kemava, i kedaron chirka 2 mil famiyas de proves en el aver, ke semejante fuego dezastrozo non tyede avido en muestra [sivdad]. I tambyen uvo 2 personas ke fueron la prea de las flamas, un vyejo i un mansevo. I las kazas dela provaya non estavan asiguradas dinguna de eyas.

Ma, las kazas, *enos* fraguadas, i ke los patrones eran poderozos, tenian asigurado tanto la kaza komo el moble. Entre todas las siguritas, suvia la suma de 125,000 liras. Estonses las kompanyias de sigurita mandaron sus delegados i pagaron a kada uno i uno asta la ultima para.

En tanto, algunos adjentes de sigurita izyeron una buena furtuna ke los asigurados ental de tomar la moneda, les deshavan un tanto por syen. Algunos se kontentavan inveche deliras esterlinas, tomavan napoleones. Despues de poko tyempo, tuvyendo avizo las kompanyias de sigurita de esto, alevantaron las adjensias de esta djente, i los reprezentaron a otra djente mas konfidentes. Ke de este fuego i endelantre non ay ke fraguo kaza sin empenyarse a la sigurita. I deel tyempo de el fuego, asta oy ke eskrivimos ke ya ay 3 anyos, non se ave fraguado el 20 por syen de lo kemado. Ma lo ke se esta fraguando lo mas es *kyavgir* i *yarim kyavgir.*

[80b] I el *beledie* izo unas *hartas* tan ermozas para las fraguas kelas izyeron *hanes, hanes*. I las kayes anchas ke la prima es de 20 pikos de anchura, la kuala es deel molo fina *Arnaut Furnu*, i en medyo de esta kaye, izyeron un *lagum* para la mar muy rezyo, i izyeron un *marsh pye [marche pied]* de dos partes a 2 metros de anchura de unas pyedras grandes ke asta [oy] ya estan eskapando, i ya empesaron en medyo la kaye de estas mezmas pyedras a azer el *kaldirim.* I en los kyenares de las 2 partes, plantaron arvolikos, i ke entre 5 a 6 anyos, esta kaye va a ser un *bulevar* muy riko, ke la djente lo van tomar este lugar por pasear. I tambyen, ay kalejas ke son de 16 pikos, i las mas estrechas son de 12 pikos, ke en fraguandosen estos lugares, almenos en el entervalo de 20 a 25 anyos, todo esto kemado va aser la ermozura de [la] sivdad.

Ma por oras, deskayen el presyo delos terrenos ala mitad delo ke valian al prensipyo. La kavza de esto es de non aver paras en el *esnaf adami*. Non kyere dicho en la provaya. I el presyo delas kyiras deskayo de 20 a 25 por syen manko deloke era.

Kapitolo 42

[81a] El Levante de Kasandra

Me olvidi de kontar el echo de la *tabya* de Kasandra, syendo era muy chiko ke apenas tenia 8 anyos. Estonses, se alevantaron los gregos de Kasandra. Estonses, non aviya *nizam askyeri,* era ke kuando avia una gerra, mandavan avizo a toda la tyerra, dizyendo ke vinyeran a defender la patria. Devista, el grande del *yenicheri* metia en kada *han* eskrivanos i un *daul* kon klar[i]netas i la bandyera, i sin muncho esperar, los turkos de kada kazal se armavan asta los dyentes kon *pishtoles* i *yataganes,* espadas, karabinas, i entravan en los *hanes,* se azian eskrivir i metian *on bashis, yuzbashis, bin bashis.* Kuando se inchian un *tabur,* devista les davan munisyones i partian kon muncha alegriya, syendo esperavan de tornar kon muchos obdjetos i moneda del *chapul* ke ivan azer. Kuando partyeron para Kasandra, izyeron mil estrasos kyen se traian mansevos o muchachas por esklavos; de vista, los azian *sunnet.* A las muchachas, las tomavan por mujeres, i los mansevikos les embezavan a tanyer diversos estrumentos.

Yo tuve kuantas vezes de tener ami lado de estos esklavos a tanyer kon eyos en los *konakes* en *chiflikes* de AbduRahman bey, ke las eredo de su padre Ahmet bey, syendo el era el kapo de la armada de Kasandra.

En esta gerra fue ke se fraguo la *tabya* delantre *Beth a-Hayyim* de los djidyos. Los fraguadores les vino *kolay* de tomar todas las pyedras de ensima los muertos, syendo estas *kevuroth* eran de los primeros djidyos ke vinyeron de la Espanya. Estavan serka dela *tabya* ke estavan fraguando, ke por dita razon non se topo la data de los primeros savyos **[81b]** ke vinyeron a estabilirsen en Saloniko. Non les basto kon yevarsen las pyedras de ensima los muertos, sinon kada diya kalia ke fueran unos djidyos a *angarya* a karear tyerra kon *torbas*, ocho diyas ke se toparon todos los *charshis* serrados, syendo era kon *adjile* la fragua dela *tabya*, non aviya apartasyo[n] de vyejo i mansevo, grandes i chikos, *hahamim*. Todos kalia ke fueran a karyar tyerra.

Estonses, al *toran h"r* Shelomo Mordoh, *'a.a.*, [paz sovre el], selo yevaron ala gerra. Me kontaron ke este s. era muy savyo en la *tehuna*. Una noche, la ora ke lo izo despertar a Ahmet bey en dizyendole ke esta era la ora de venser al inimigo. I ansi fue ke tanyeron las trompetas, i se alevantaron todos komo los leones, i izyeron una matansa muy sangriyente. I los ke kedaron, kualos dyeron i kayeron, kualos selos tomaron por esklavos. De esta batalya fue ke se eskapo la gerra. Ma non se olvidaron los grandes del s. *h"r* Shelomo i les dyeron munchos regalos, i lo respektavan komo ombre santo. Kada anyo, merkavan un kalendaryo los beyes de dito sinyor en turko. Los ke tuvyeron korespondensya kon eyos eran djente grande. 3 de eyos gregos, matados a golpo de espada: *Arhoadiko*, i s. Menekshe i s. Polardos. De estonses tomaron grande espanto los gregos.

[Epilogo]

[82a] Despues de el 9 Iyyar [5]634 [26 April 1874] de la katastrofa, fue algunos selozos de ver el adelantamyento de mis echos, bushkaron de vengarsen. Ma la Providensya no desho kumplir sus deseos. Yo me glorifiko fin oy ke eskrivo, ke es en anyo de [5]662, [1902], kijendo dizir ke ay 28 anyos de estonses asta oy. Yo me di al ofisyo de la estamparia i lavori kon grasyas a los muchos ayudos de el filantropo kavalyer, Moizé Alatini, נ"ע, i a los buenos konsejos de el s. *Rav*, *h"r* Avraam Gatenyo, yo progresi syempre en mis echos.

En el entrevalo de estos 28 anyos, yo parvine a kazar 9 ijas i 3 ijos. Enrekesi mi estamparia, fragui mi kaza sin tener menester ayuda de dinguno, otro ke de mi lavoro. I a los ke bushkaron mi mal, המה {ק}[כ]רעו ונָפלו ואנחנו קמנו {ונדודעת} [ונתעודד], [*emma kare'u va-nafalu va-anahnu kamnu ve-nith'odad,* eyos se arodeyaron i kayeron, i nos, nos alevantamos i nos aderezamos, (Psalm 20:9)].

En el korso de estos 28 anyos, mi puerpo somporto diversas *hazinuras* de las kualas yo kedi salvo, estando syempre sotometido a la veluntad de el Dyo.

De los persegidores, ya pasaron ala tomba i ya les perdono, solamente son pokos. I [los otros] kuando me enkuentran, me saludan, ma si byen amargamente de despero, syendo non les ize preva de murirme. I kuando alguno muere, los ke kedaron, temblan de espanto, porke se van apokando sus kolegas.[19]

De los persegidores, pasaron ala tomba i yo les perdono, solamente son pokos. I [los otros] kuando me enkuentran, me saludan, i si byen amargamente de despero, syendo no les ize preva de murirme. I kuando algun[o muere] de los ke kedaron, temblan de espanto, porke se van apokando sus kolegas. **[82b]**

[96a] Dita poezia es echa por s. Sa'adi a-Levi, b"v por el dia dela partensya de su Maestad Abdul Medjid Han ke partyo de Saloniko por Konstantinopoli en dia de Shabbath el 28 *Tammuz, Shenath* 5619 en *Mekam* de *Rast*

1. Alavad al Dyo, el puevlo eskojido,
ke mos vino el Rey bueno i kumplido.
Un ombre tan savyo i muy entendido,
arijos de el Dyo santo salyo de su nido.
Biva, biva el Rey, sea byen venido.
2. *Besiman tov* sea kon buena vinidura,
esta alegria mos sea de tura.
En sus dias buenos tenemos artura,
por *zahuth* de el Rey es muy meresido. *Biva, biva*
3. Gran sinyor se nombra i ansi se yama,
entre los reynados, grande es su fama.
I a su povlado mucho el los ama,

kon korason bueno i kon gran sentido. *Biva, biva*
4. Dia de myerkoles, ora dos del dia,
turkos i kristyanos i la djuderia,
mos tomimos todos gusto i alegria.
Kon bozes kantimos, i kon gran sonido. *Biva, biva*
5. Allah ay grande, izo este Rey djigante,
nunka tal se vido, es koza de enkante.
Orasyon agamos al Dyo de avante,
ke mos biva el Rey ke de el Dyo es metido. *Biva, biva*
6. Vida muncha tenga, el Dyo lo enprezente,
ke aga buendades i ke mos kontente.
En sus inimigos su mano pueste,
i en su espada sea byen valido. *Biva, biva*
7. *Zahuth* gran tuvimos todo su puevlo,
de morar en tyerra de este reynado.
Syerto ke el Dyo santo lo aze amado,
en ver ke muy byen mos ave rijido. *Biva, biva*
8. *Hodesh Tammuz* fue kuando el Rey mos vino,
lo izimos fyesta todo el turkino.
Muestra bindisyon suva de kontino,
Dyo de los syelos es muestro kerido. *Biva, biva*
9. Ternemos bondad en sus dias buenos,
syempre sus trezoros ke los tenga yenos.
Mos biva el syen anyos, non menos,
syendo esto es muy byen konvenido. *Biva, biva*
10. Yamemos al Dyo grande i poderozo,
ke este *malhuth* syempre este en repozo.
Biva muestro Rey, syempre korajozo,
por el mundo entero sea enfloresido. *Biva, biva*
11. *Kavod* a el Rey agamos en djunto,
kon mucho plazer i kon mucho gusto.
Syendo muestro Rey, en todo djusto,
porke sus mersedes muchas aven sido. *Biva, biva*
12. Los reyes otomanos, syempre buenos fueron,
kon el *rahamanuth* eyos se rijeron.
Syerto de los syelos byen ke mos kijeron,

por este *zahuth* syempre aven vensido. *Biva, biva*
13. **[96b]** Miremos, ermanos, azer orasyones,
kale bindizirlo todas las nasyones.
Por bondad de el Rey, muestras intisyones,
delantre el Dyo alto sea risivido. *Biva, biva*
14. *Nam* grande tomimos kuando el Rey mos vino,
ermozo de vista, alto komo un pino.
Ayer, púvliko entero metimos en tino,
beraha dizyendo todo el ke lo vido. *Biva, biva*
15. Sultan Abdul Medjid es un Rey ermozo,
i konvino al reyno, ke es muy piadozo.
Syempre esté kontente kon gusto i gozo,
syempre su *mazzal* lo tenga suvido.
Mos biva el Rey, sea byen vinido,
vaya en buen ora kon su buen partido. *Biva, biva*
16. Suvenir desho el Rey gloryozo,
Abdul es su nombre, *Medjid*, el orozo.
Devemos yamar al Dyo poderozo,
yeve al monarka presto asu nido. *Biva, biva*

[Mi Ultima Rogativa][20]

Mi ultima rogativa ke (es) ago amis ijos es de estampar esta e storya, temprano o tadre, kon todos los modos a non pasar mi enkomendansa sea en muestra estamparia, sea en Vyena o en Beogrado kon guadrar kopya en otro livro, i adovando algunas frazas i algunos byervos difisiles de turko o de *leshon a-kodesh.* Adjuntando a esta estorya la djura de Purim, entrá[d] todo kon letra de *Rashi.* I pues todas las poezias ke topash en [el] sakito sin falta, i seresh bindichos, i ternesh *aslaha* i *beraha* ande .....resh, *amen.* Sa'adi a-Levi

Notes

[1] Based on a date in the margin.

[2] Y. F. for Yaakov Fernandes.

[3] For Aramaic אַלְפָא בֵּיתָא, the alphabet.

[4] Continuation missing in manuscript.

[5] Continuation missing in manuscript.

[6] Marginal note in the manuscript has *la demisyon,* the resignation.

[7] *La Epoka,* Ladino newspaper founded by Sa'adi.

[8] *En letra espanyola, i. e.* in the cursive alphabet called *soletreo.*

[9] Even though there was already a chapter 21, Sa'adi must have felt that the visit of Sultan Abdul Medjid deserved a separate chapter number with a title. He squeezed it in his shaky handwriting immediately after chapter 20, creating a duplication.

[10] Title of the famous *piyyut* by Israel Najjara from Damascus sung on Friday nights in both Sephardic and Ashkenazic synagogues.

[11] In a letter he wrote to Binyamin Rafael ben Yosef, the editor of *Shire Yisrael be-Eres ha-Kedem, (Istanbul 1926, pp. 481-3)* Rabbi Abraham Dannon calls these Jewish "small poetry books" by their Turkish name *djonk*. Apparently, these were well-known by that name among Jewish circles. The full text of that letter is reproduced in I. Jerusalmi, *The Song of Songs in the Targumic Tradition, (Cincinnati 1993).* See also *djonk* in the Glossary.

[12] This statement is couched in the language of the *kal nidré* recited on the evening service of the Day of Atonement.

[13] Sa'adi has *nimlahu* (a *hapax legomenon* in Isaiah 51:6), "they dissipated" instead of *niftahu*, "they broke open".

[14] This barely legible paragraph appears at the end of the page with an asterisk indicating its location here.

[15] This barely legible paragraph appears at the right side of the page with a circle indicating its location here.

[16] The next two lines, from "syendo el si. *Rav*.... la dare ke vistir" have been added by Sa'adi to the bottom of the page in the manuscript. Here they have been incorporated into this text.

[17] This sentence appears on the right margin of page 64b. It has been moved here where it belongs logically. On the left side of the chapter heading, there is a later addition of a sentence with an illegible word that mentions "El {Koryer} [Koreo] de Viena".

[18] Chapter 33 is followed by chapter 40!

[19] The following paragraph in a different handwriting is a repetition.

[20] Transliteration of addition between pp. 27b and 28a.

Glossary

*Abbreviations**

abr.	abbreviation
ar.	Arabic
aram.	Aramaic
coll.	collective
engl.	English
fr.	French
gr.	Greek
it.	Italian
lad.	Ladino
lat.	Latin
Ne.	Nehama
old. sp.	Old Spanish
ott.	Ottoman
pers.	Persian
pl.	plural
port.	Portuguese
prob.	probably
Rd.	Redhouse
sp.	Spanish
syn.	synonym
tr.	Turkish

* For ease in usage, most entries are exactly as they appear in the text.

Ladino/Hebrew/Turkish-English Glossary

A

aaz	*'azl* > *aaz,* spelled אאז, dismiss from office, see *azil*
abarrontar	for *abarrotar,* to preserve, secure (evidence)
abasho	below •*abasho de:* less than; approximately
aborreser	to abhor, hate
achake	also *achak,* sp. *achaque,*pretext •*kon el achake ke:* under the pretext that, Ne. 5b
achetar	it. *accetare,* to accept
adjem	ott. عجم, *acem,* name of a Turkish musical mode
adjente	it. *agente,* agent, agency
adjile	ott. عجله, *acele,* hurry •*kon adjile:* in a hurry
adjunta	it. *agiunta,* gathering, council, committee •*adjuntas i djuzgo:* court sessions and sentencing
adjuntar	to join •*adjuntar byervos:* to combine Hebrew consonants with vowels to create words •*embezar a adjuntar:* learn to read
adovada	translation of מְתֻקָּן, adorned •*trusho un kavayo byen adovado:* he brought an exquisitely adorned horse
adyentro	also *dyentro,* inside
aer	for *ayer,* yesterday
afalagar	to comfort, calm down
afamado	famed •*kazas mal afamadas:* houses of ill-repute
afavoreser	sp. *favorecer,* to favor; support

aferrar	to catch, grab
afillú	אֲפִלּוּ, *afillú,* even if
afinar	from *fin,* to bring to an end, conclude
afíto	a happening •*se le izo un afíto:* he had an episode
aftara	see *haftara*
Agha	tr. *Ağa,* Agha title of a Janissary officer, •*Ağa* (or *Ala*) *Paşa:* title of Janissary head with the rank of a Vizier, Rd. 18a
agora	now (occurs once as *a* + *gora*)
agror	sourness •*agror ke me resivyo:* (sour) cold reception he gave me
aharvar	to beat, strike •*aharvasyon* (made up word): beating •*golpes de aharvasyon:* (blows) waves of beating
Ahche Medjid	for *Akçe Mescid,* place named after a White Mosque
ahir	pers. *âhûr,* a stable
ahnasath orhim	see *hakhnasath orhim*
ahzar	אַכְזָר, *ahzar,* cruel; a cruel person
ainda	see *inda*
akavar	from *kavo,* end, to finish •*akavado*, finished
akedar	from *kédo,* quiet, to quiet down, stop
akojer	to gather, collect
akometer	to commit; pledge, promise
akorruto	often, Ne. 21c, Rc. 9
akulpar	to blame
akumplir	to complete, wrap up
Ala	see *Agha*
aladjali	tr. *alacalı,* multicolored; striped
'alam	aram. עָלַם, *'alam,* world, in עָלַם וְעָלְמַיָּא, *'alam ve-'alemayya,* eternity of eternities, borrowed from a poem by Israel Najjara
alat	ott. آلت, *âlet, âlât,* tools; also, "pots & pans"
Alay Bey	tr. *Alay Beyi,* commander of the gendarmes, Rd. 44b
alay emini	tr. *alay emini,* paymaster of a regiment, Rd. 44b

albo white

alevantar to raise •*alevantar el nombre en vida:* "raising", i.e.naming a new-born after a living relative, a custom totally shunned by Ashkenazim

alfinik sp. *alfeñique,* sugar paste •*alfinikado:* a light cookie that melts in the mouth, Ne. 26c

alhad aram. חַד בְּשַׁבָּא, *had be-shabba,* FIRST (day) of the week, Sunday. Note that the Arabic word for Sunday is يوم الواحد , *yawm al-wahid,* rather than *al-had!* •*noche de alhad:* Saturday night •*tadre de alhad:* Sunday evening

alkunya ar. الكنيه, *al-kunya,* sp. *alcuña,* tr. *künye,* patro nymic; last name

Allah *Allah;* God •*Allah kerim:* God is gracious

almaná אַלְמָנָה, *almana,* widow

almirez ar. المهراس, *al-mihrâs,* mortar and pestle

almoranas αἱμορροΐδες, hemorrhoids, (ar. is *basur)*

alpha betha aram. אַלְפָא בֵּיתָא, *alpha betha,* alphabet •*'al seder alpha betha:* alphabetically arranged

alsar to raise

altilik tr. *altı,* six (piaster piece), Rd. 53b

altiriando tr. *arttırmak,* to increase; bid (at an auction)

alvorada dawn; family celebration to display the bride's trousseau, Ne. 32c

Aman see *Haman*

amanazar same as *amenazar*, to threaten

'am ha-ares עַם־הָאָרֶץ, *'am ha-ares,* "people-of-the-land", ignoramus

andar (as a verb) to go; (as a noun) an apartment •*andar de ariva:* upper apartment, Ne. 38aII

ande where •*ande mas:* moreover, furthermore

angarya *ἀγγαρεία,* tr. *angarya,* forced labor, Ne. 38b

ánke it. *anche,* also; even if

ankoro it. *ancora*, anchor

anteri tr. *entari,* loose robe

apalpar to touch; examine by the feel, Ne. 41b

apanyar	to catch, also, "to gather, pick up" (extra profit)
apar	pair •*a par, a par:* by pairs, two by two
apareser	to appear •*si son aparesidos:* if they come into the open
aperkantado	subjected to a *prekante,* exorcism, exorcised
apotropos	ἐπίτροπος, אַפּוֹטרוֹפּוֹס, manager
aprekantado	see *aperkantado*
apretada	pressing, squeezed; critical
aprezentar	for *prezentar,* to introduce
'aramoth	pl. of עָרְמָה, *orma,* guile, trickery, deception, craftiness
arba'a	אַרְבָּעָה, *arba'a,* four •*arba'a ve-'esrim:* the 24 books of the Jewish biblical canon, the Jewish Bible also known as *TaNaKh*
aré	azeré
arepozado	from *repózo,* rested, relaxed
arepudyar	to repudiate, dismiss, dodge
aresentar	translating הוֹשִׁיב, *hoshiv,* to settle
arhoadiko	ἀρχιδιάκονος, archdeacon
arká	tr. *arka,* backing •*kon la arká de:* with the backing of
arlilik	tr. *ağırlık,* heaviness; seriousness, frustration, Ne. 48b
armorzo	*emordium,* take a bite, sp. *almuerzo*, lunch, Ne. 31b
arnaut	tr. *Arnavut;* Albanian
arodear	to go around
aro[n]djar	(also *aro[n]jar)* to cast, throw •*arodjarse:* to launch oneself
aro[n]jar	see *aro[n]djar*
arravdonar	to cause great damage, ravage, Ne. 49c
arreglamyento	arranging; remodeling, Ne. 51a
arremedyarse	to draw support, be helped
arreventar	to burst •*arreventar la fyel:* to burst the bile; scare to death, Ne. 55b
arroz	rice •*arroz koladji:* rice "starcher"

arp(e)ar	prob. for *arpar,* to scratch, tear to tatters; speed up
artifisyo	workmanship •*artifisyo de makinas:* the use of machines •*kon ke artifisyo:* with what ruse •*asendida de artifisyos:* lit up with fireworks •*kon muncho artifisyo:* with lots of ingenuity
arvith	עַרְבִית, *'arvith,* evening service
arzuhal	ott. عرضحال, *arzuhâl,* "presentation of a sit uation", petition; application •*echar un arzuhal:* submit a petition
asamarrado	from *samarra,* covered with fur
asara	עֲשָׂרָה, *'asara,* ten, (fem. numeral used with masc. nouns)
asaventarse	הִתְיַדַּע, *hithyadda',* get information; be aware, acquainted; inquire, Ne. 59a
asembro	to take root, establish itself
asementar	to sow; create •*asementar simyente:* to sow a seed, suggest an initiative, Ne. 60a
asentar	to sit •*asentar un kante:* compose a song •*asen taron en el trono:* inaugurate a Sultan *(cülûs)*
ashufre	sulfur
ashugar	from ar. الشّوار, *aš-šawār,* sp. *ajuar,* trousseau, Ne. 65b
asimyente	see *simyente,* seed, Ne. 61c
askama	see *haskama*
askyer	tr. *asker,* soldier
asolapado	for *asolado,* isolated; scarcely populated, Ne. 62c
aspaka	see *haspaka*
asperar	to wait, Ne. 63c.
asur	אָסוּר, *asur,* forbidden
asta	sp. *hasta,* until; as long as
at	tr. *at,* horse, •*At Meydan,* Hippodrome
ataganto	sp. *atragantar,* to choke; bother
atakarse	be afflicted with disease, specifically tuberculosis
atinar	from *tino,* pay attention
attara	see *hattara*

avai	ott. هوائي, *havâî,* aerial •*avai fishek:* fireworks
avaria	it. *avaria,* damage at sea
'avaryan	aram. עֲבַרְיָן, *'avaryan,* sinner
aventador	fan
avirguelada	suffering from *virguela* or chicken-pox, Ne. 593c
avokasiya	sp. *abogacia,* instead of Lad. *avokateria,* profes sion of a lawyer
avokato	it. *avvocato,* lawyer
ayaktash	tr. *ayaktaş* friend, companion, Ne. 71b, Rd. 101b
aylikes	tr. *aylık,* monthly salaries
ayuda	help •*kon la ayuda deel Dyo:* with God's help
azarado	sp. *acerado,* fortified like steel •*vino azarado:* old wine fortified with iron filings
azil	ott. عزل, *'azl* > *aaz,* אאז, •*azer azil:* dismiss from office, fire
azilo	shelter; kindergarten, Ne. 74b •*azilo para eskola de ijas:* kindergarten for girls
azir	ott. حاضر, *hazır,* ready; •*merkan azir:* they buy ready-made
az[l]	ott. عزل, *'azl* > *aaz,* אאז, dismiss from office, fire
azyer	for *azer,* to do; cause (in factitives)

B

ba'al	בַּעַל, *ba'al,* owner; master •*ba'al a-bayith:* head of family; sponsor, host •*baale batim:* heads of households •*ba'ale dinim:* litigants, contestants •*ba'al Yisrael:* a Jewish adult
bab	aram. בָּבָא, *bava,* ott. باب , *bâb,* gate, door; chapter •*Bâb-ı Âli:* Sublime Porte or seat of the Ottoman government in Istanbul
BabaAlili	tr. mistake for *Bâb-ı Âli*, see *bab* above
baka(h)ya	ott. بقايا, *bakaya,* remnant; arrears
bakkashoth	בַּקָּשׁוֹת, *bakkashoth,* petitions, supplications recited before the morning prayers

bakshish	pers. بخشش, *bahşiş,* tip; *baksheesh*; gift
baldar	from ar. بَطَّلَ, *battala,* sp. *baldar,* abolish, annul
baldirin	tr. *baldır,* calf of the leg, Ne. 78a
bamya	tr. *bamya,* okra •*esta bamya:* this unfortunate situation; this "pickle" or "nonsense"
bandyera	it. *bandiera* •bandyera santa: the "holy flag"
banyarse	take a bath •*banyarse en la sudor:* be drenched in sweat
bara	swamp, Ne. 79c
baraber	tr. *beraber,* together
baraja	fight, quarrel, misunderstanding, Ne. 79c
baraka	it. *baracca,* hut, shed
barana	turmoil •*en esta barana:* during this upheaval
baraza	see *baraja*
bar minnan	aram. בַּר מִנַּן, *bar minnan, afuera de mozotros,* far from us, God forbid
barut	pers. بارود, *bārūd,* gunpowder
barvera	from *barva,* strap placed under the chin
bashi	tr. *başı,* head-of- •*hahambashi:* chief rabbi
basma	tr. *basma,* printed fabric
basmata	tr., see *mazbata*
basho	low; short •*a basho de:* at least
batal	ott. بطّال, *battal,* idle
batim	בָּתִּים, *batim,* pl. of בַּיִת, *bayith*, household; stanza (in poetry)
batlan	בַּטְלָן, *batlan,* idle person •*'asara batlanim:* a *minyan* or group of ten Jews who spend most of their time in the synagogue and get their livelihood from the congregational *kuppa* in order to be free to study *Tora* and perform commandments *(misvoth)*: "What is a large city? Anyone that has ten *batlanim*", (Megilla I:3)
bayileado	tr. *bayılmak* fainted
bazarya	from *bazar,* market •*chufletes de bazarya:* cheap whistles

bazbilik — probably from *bashibozuk(luk),* irregular soldier; unruliness, Rd. 139a

baziryan — pers. بازرگان, *bezirgân/bazirgân,* merchant; title used for a Jewish merchant, Rd. 170a

bazmata — see *mazbata*

be-Av — בְּאָב, *be-Av,* during the month of *Av* (August)

be(h)ema — בְּהֵמָה, *be(h)ema,* animal

be-havod — בְּכָבוֹד, *be-havod,* with/for the honor •*be-havod, sinyor:* please, Sir

behoth — בְּכוֹת, *behoth,* crying •*kon behoth:* with weeping, by insisting, unfortunately

bekchi — tr. *bekçi,* night watchman; guard

bel — tr. *bel,* waist

beledie — or *belediye,* ott. بلديّه, *belediyye,* municipality; city council

ben — בֵּן, *ben,* son •*ben bayith:* familiar with, intimate

benish — judicial robe with wide sleeves worn by rabbinic judges, Ne. 87a

bent — tr. *bent,* paragraph, Rd. 156a

beraha — בְּרָכָה, *beraha,* blessing

berbante — it. *birbante,* rogue, rascal

berber — it. *barbiere*, tr. *berber,* barber

besh — tr. *beş,* five • *Besh Chinar:* Five Plane Trees (place name)

be-shem — בְּשֵׁם־, *be-shem,* in the name of..., on behalf of...

beshlik — tr. *beşlik,* five piaster coin

beste — pers. بسته, *beste*, the words of a musical composition

betha — aram. בֵּיתָא, *bethá,* second letter of the Semitic alphabet, see *alpha betha*

beth- — construct of בַּיִת, *bayith,* house •*beth-din:* rabbinic tribunal •*beth ha-hayyim* cemetery

beyaz — tr. white, *Beyaz Kule,* White Tower

beyes — pl. of tr. *bey,* high placed individuals in Ottoman hierarchy

bi-helal — בִּכְלָל, *bi-helal,* see *kelal*

bikkur	בִּקּוּר, *bikkur,* inquire •*bikkur holim:* look after the sick; fund for the sick
bin/bim	tr. *bin,* thousand •*bimbashi/binbashi:* army Major
bina	ott. بنا, *binâ,* building, not to confuse with the Hebrew word בִּינָה, understanding
binek tashi	tr. *binek taşı,* horse block
bineyo	tr. *binmek,* to mount a horse
binlikes	tr. *binlik,* large bottles holding 1000 *drams*
bi-reshuth	בִּרְשׁוּת-, *bi-reshuth,* with the permission-of-
bir	tr. *bir,* one •*bir verirsan, ikyi sayarum:* if you give me one, I shall count it as two, *i. e.* two for the price of one
bitireavan	tr. *bitirmek,* they finished
bitmish!	tr. *bitmiş,* finished • *ya es bitmish:* it is over!
bizzayon	בִּזָּיוֹן, *bizzayon,* shame, disgrace; insult •*bizzayon ha-Tora:* dishonoring the Tora
boka	mouth •*boka de el alma: epigastrium* or pit of the stomach, Ne. 94a
blanko	white •*echando los ojos en blanko:* showing the white of one's eyes; fainting; in an ecstatic mood, Ne. 91c
boldjelik	tr. *bolca + lık,* abundance
bólo	from *bolar,* flight
boluk	tr. *bölük*, company (milit.) •*bolukes, bolukes:* in groups (and groups)
boy	tr. *boy,* size
boyadji	tr. *boyacı,* painter
bozear	tr. *bozmak,* to spoil
bragali	sp.-it. + tr. *braga, braca,* breeches •*bragali:* breech-wearing riffraff, lower-class individual, Ne. 99a
bramido	from *bramar,* roar •*bramido:* roaring in anger, Ne. 99a
brave	prob. after the fr. *brave,* rather than the sp. or it. *bravo,* brave
bril	gold/silver thread, tinsel

brindis	sp. *brindis,* salute, toast, Ne. 100a
broshura	fr. *brochure,* pamphlet, booklet
brusha	witch, Ne. 100a
bu	tr. *bu,* this •*dishe un shu bu:* I said this and that
bufano	sp.-it. *bufalo,* water buffalo, (tr. *manda),* Ne.100c
bulevar	fr. *boulevard,* boulevard
burlozo	funny, strange, ridiculous
butika	ἀποθήκη, sp. *botica,* store
buyisyon	made up noun from *buyir*, boiling, seething
byenaventurado	אַשְׁרֵי־, happy, most fortunate

Ch

chadir	tr. *çadır,* umbrella; tent
chalgi	tr. *çalgı,* musical entertainment (with instruments),band
chalisheando	tr. *çalışmak,* to work, work hard; try
chanaka	tr. *çanak,* bowl
chapul	tr. *çapul,* to plunder, pillage, loot, Rd. 240a
chardak	tr. *çardak,* trellis, porch, awning
chare	pers.-tr. چاره, *çare,* way, means
charshi	tr. *çarşı,* market
chevere	tr. *çevre*, circle; noose •*çevere de oro:* a gold noose
chichek	tr. *çiçek,* flower •*chichek avasi:* name of a melody
chiflik	tr. *çiflik,* farm
childereyo	tr. *çıldırmak,* to go crazy •*childereyo de su meoyo:* he went out of his mind
chilibi	lat. *caelebs,* celibate; tr. *çelebi,* gentleman, well-educated; title of the leader of the *Mevlevî* order; title of respect for men, even non-Muslims •*Chelebon:* man's name among Turkish Sepharadim.
chirka	lat.-it. *circa,* approximately
chirkolar	it. *circolare,* circular letter, notice, flyer

choshk tr. *köşk,* mansion

chuflan sounding, blowing •*kuerno ke chuflan:* the blowing of the *shofar* (horn)

chuflar to whistle •*chuflador de vino:* one who holds well his wine

D

dada from *dar,* "given", a blow (that is inflicted)

dainda see *inda*

dar to give, The verb *dar* is used to recast the Hebrew *hiphil* into Ladino, such as *dar a saver,* to inform; *dar a entender,* to explain •*dar a mano:* permit

darsar דָרַשׁ, *darash,* to preach a sermon

darshan דַּרְשָׁן, *darshan,* preacher

daul tr. *davul,* drum

davadji ott. دعواجى , *dâvâcı,* plaintiff •*tengo un davadji:* I have a plaintiff

[d]avetname see *tavetname*

dayre ott. دائره, *daire,* circle; office

dayyan דַּיָּן, *dayyan,* judge

de "by" introducing the author after a passive verb •*protejado de sinyor Alatini:* protected by Mr. Alatini

de-aynu aram. דְּהַיְינוּ, *de-(h)aynu,* that is...

defter διφθέριον, tanned leather, ott. دفتر, notebook

defyende probably for "defende", forbids

deleth דֶּלֶת, *deleth,* door, gate •*deleth ha-am:* people's council

delikadeza delicate •*kon delikadeza:* delicately, carefully

demas moreover; furthermore

demudada changed; strange; unusual

deputasyon body of deputies; delegation

deranshear fr. *déranger* for *deranjear,* to bother, upset

derisha דְּרִישָׁה, *derisha,* see *hakira u-derisha*

derush דְּרוּשׁ, *derush,* rabbinic exposition; talk; sermon

desbarasar	get rid of •*se desbaraso,* he expired
desbrochar	to unbutton; be frustrated; come to a head
desfriasyon	from *frio,* cooling; shivers
deshar	let; allow; leave; happen • *se desho de vinir:* he happened to come •*deshar a su mujer:* to divorce one's wife
deskavenyarse	(from *kaveyo*) bare one's head
deskuzir	to unstitch, come apart •*ke se deskuzga el teshido:* that the (fabric) plan gets undone
deskyere	see *teskyere*
deslindarse	from *lindo,* charming •*deslindarse:* to be disenchanted, Ne. 128c
desmayado	fainted
desnyegar	to deny •*eya se desnyego de todo lo ke le estavan dizyendo:* she denied everything she was told
desparte	beside •*en desparte:* aside from, in addition to, Ne. 130a
desramar	to sever, uproot, Ne. 132a
desvacheava	tr. *vazgeçmek*, to give up; abandon
desvaynada	drawn out •*kon la espada desvaynada:* with a drawn out sword
dezazer	to undo; tear down, destroy •*dezazer el korason:* get upset
dezmenudar	to be reduced to small pieces, crushed, Ne. 129b
dezmizeryado	miserable looking
dikyel	for tr. *diken,* thorn, main cause
din	דִּין, *din,* judgment •*ba'al din:* litigant
dirito	it. *diritto,* right
disharilik	tr. *dışarılık*, area "outside" the *haremlik* reserved for the men
disheme	for *dizeme,* tell me
divre-	דִּבְרֵי־, *divré-*, words-of- •*divre hahamim:* words of the rabbis, rabbinic rulings and enactments as opposed to biblical injunctions
djadde	ott. جادّه, *cadde:* main street; avenue
djal	prob. fr. for *châle,* shawl

djam	tr. *cam,* glass; window
djami	ott. جامع, *câmi,* mosque •*Saatli Djami:* name of a mosque which apparently had a clock
a djanim!	tr. *canım,* O, my dear soul! Come on!
djanisar	see *yenicheri*
djastre	see *shastre*
djefa	ott. 'جفا, *cefâ,* suffering, grief
djemido	groan, moan, wail
djemulamyento	for *djemilamyento,* a chorus of *djemidos*
djep	tr. *cep,* pocket
djeza	ott. 'جزا, *cezâ,* penalty, punishment; fine
djidia	for *Djudia*
djinediarme	for *indjidarme,* tr. *incitmek,* to hurt, harm
djiro	it. *giro,* turn over
djonk	pers.-tr. جونك, cönk, a manuscript collection of folk poems, Rd. 232a •the *livriko de poezias* mentioned on p. **[52b]** is probably a *djonk* of *Koplas de Purim*
djornal	it. *giornal[iero],* daily (pay)
djubbe	also *djubben*, ott. جبّه, *cübbe*, robe or coat with full sleeves and long skirts
djudia	Jewish woman; •*la djudia:* servant, maid
djueves	for *djugeves,* Thursday
djumbush	pers.-tr. جنبش, *cünbüş/cümbüş,* merrymaking, reveling
djurnal	newspaper
dolan	tr. *dolan,* edge
dolama	tr. *dolama,* a wrap, Rd. 308a
donadear	tr. *donatmak,* to decorate, ornate
dor	דּוֹר, generation •*dor ole ve-dor ba:* one generation goes, another comes
doshedear	tr. *döşemek,* to furnish
dosheme	tr. *döşeme,* floor, pavement
dover	(for *dever*) to owe •*adover:* as due, expected
drama	δραξμὴ, tr. *dirhem,* unit of weight

dubara	pers.-tr. دوباره, intrigue, noise •*dubara ekstraordinarya:* unusual outrage, scandal, Ne. 147b
dumen	it. *timone,* tr. *dümen,* rudder, Rd. 317b
dunke	it. *dunque,* therefore
dushtu	tr. *düştü,* has fallen
duva	ott. دعا, *duâ,* prayer
duzudear	tr. *düzeltmek,* straighten up; decorate
dyentro	it. *dentro,* within
dyeron	they gave •*dyeron i tomaron:* they discussed

E

ebrayko	it. *ebraico*, Hebrew
echar	throw; lie down; utter a word; introduce to; invest •*echar arzuhal:* submit a petition •*echar sambashugas:* to apply leeches •*echar pecha:* to impose a tax •*echar haramoth:* to issue excommunications
eche	also *echetra*, it. *etc.*
edim	עֵדִים, *'edim,* spelled phonetically אידים, witnesses
'eduth	עֵדוּת, *'eduth,* testimony, also used for "witness" •*dar eduth:* testify
efendi	αὐθέντης, an autocrat, tr. *efendi,* person of means; master; Sir; title given to a variety of officials in the Ottoman empire.
efetivo, lo	it. *effettivo,* cash
eguardo	fr. *égard,* •*a su eguardo:* in regard to his opinion, on his account
Eha	אֵיכָה, Book of Lamentations
ehal	הֵיכָל, temple; palace •*ehal a-kodesh:* Holy Ark
egzekusyon	execution •*sochyeta de egzekusyon:* a bunch of executioners
ekdesh	see *hekdesh*
ekonomikó	οἰκονομικὸς, economic; tight with money, frugal

el aya — הַהוּא גַּבְרָא, that man or "I", for the masculine, *(Gittin 55b)* and *eya aya*, הַהִיא אִתְּתָא, that woman or "I", for the feminine are somewhat similar to "yours truly thinks," for "I think," in English. It is also curious that in Talmudic Aramaic forms like these may apply either to the speaker or to the interlocutor. (See Margolis, *Lehrbuch der aramäischen Sprache des babylonischen Talmuds,* p.70)

elguenga — long, elongated, extending, Ne. 157b

Elul — אֱלוּל, *Elul,* the month of September

embarasado — busy

embarkarse — to sail off; to die

embever — to absorb •*dar a embever:* make suffer, humiliate

embezar — 1. for לָמַד, *lamad,* to learn •*kedi krudo de embezar:* I was left behind in learning
2. for לִמֵּד, *limmed,* to teach •*embezado de un maestro a kantar:* taught to sing by a master

embolado — disoriented; funny looking (due to the *pilador),* Ne. 159b

emir — ott. أمر, *emr, emir,* order •*por emir de:* by the order of

emir alay — pers. for ميرآلاي, tr. *miralay,* colonel

emirname — ott.-pers. امرنامه, *emirnâme,* written order; decree

emmeskarse — for *emmesk[l]arse*, it. *immischiarsi,* interfere, meddle

empakaron — for *empaketaron,* to pack

empatronar — to become an owner; own

empenyarse — to commit oneself, subscribe to an insurance policy, Ne. 161ab

empórto — amount

emprezentar — hand over; forgive a debt

emtia — ott. امتعه, *emti'a,* (pl. of *metâ'*) goods; wares; merchandise •*emtia de estampa:* printing equipment

en — in; used also for *a la, a el* •*mando en Salonik:* he sent to Salonika •*me fui en el ofisyo miyo:* I went back to my work •*la yevi en kaza:* I took it home •*a ke achetara en* (introducing direct object) *la demisyon:* that he accept the resignation

enbivir — enliven; excite
enchusa — see *enkyusa*
endechar — to cry and chant dirges
en demas — see *demas*
endjideyo — tr. *incitmek,* to hurt; be stricken by
enfasyo — for *enfasyado,* annoyed
enfrente — in front of, before; because of
engreendosen — tr. *eğlenmek* for *engleneandosen*, playing, having fun
enguayar — to lament; wail
enhaminado — en + חַמִּין, *enhamminado,* hard-boiled eggs
enherem — חֵרֶם, *herem,* in a state of excommunication •*enheremar:* excommunicate
enkachar — to bind, frame, Ne. 170b
enkalar — to whitewash
enkantado — "under a spell", amazed, perplexed, ambivalent, worried, puzzled
enkaminar — to set out, start walking
enkastonado — it. *incastonare,* to insert, set, (fr. *enchâsser*)
en ke — same as *aun ke,* even though
enklavar — to nail, apply, administer
enkyusa — it. *inchiusa,* cheese pie, Ne. 173c, (*enchusa* in Istanbul)
e[n]lasa — sp. *en* + *laso,* tired, exhausted •*la vukyela era e[n]lasa:* the ministers were sick and tired
enos — pers.-tr. هنوز, *henüz,* not yet; only just
Eoropa — for *Evropa,* Europe
enresparte — same as *endesparte,* in addition to
ensamarrado — see *samarra,* covered in fur
ensanyar — become angry
enséndyo — fire
ensenyar — see *ensanyar*
enserrado — closed; locked up

ensérro	privacy •*noche del ensérro:* first night of conjugal privacy similar to the *yihud* among Ashkenazim
enserró	to lock up, hide
ensirmado	covered with *sirma, q. v.*
ensistyo	he insisted
entari	see *anteri*
enteres	interest (percentage)
entikiado	see *tikia*
entiznar	from *tizon*, blackened with soot
entrankar	from *tranka,* to bolt •*entrankar la puerta:* to bolt a door
entremetedores	intermediaries; proponents
entrompyeso	confusion; obstacle, Ne. 182b •*sin dingun entrompyeso:* unmistakably
envailes	for *enbayles,* up in arms, Ne. 84b
envento	invention; innovation, smart idea, Ne. 183b
envito	invitation
eredad	inheritance
'Erev	עֶרֶב, *'erev,* eve •*'Erev de Pesah:* Passover eve
esfuerte	from *suerte,* fate, destiny, see *eshuerte.* The use of the word אִיספּוּאִירטי, *esfuerte,* in Sa'adi's manuscript displays an unusual tilt toward *fuerte,* strong!
esheth ish	אֵשֶׁת־אִישׁ, *esheth-ish,* a married woman
Eshkenazi	(variant *Ashkenazi*), *Eshkenazi* is a common family name used among people whose ancestors came originally from the lands of the Ashkenazim.
eshuerte	from *suerte,* destiny
eskabuyarse	remove oneself, quit
eskadrunyar	sp. *escudriñar,* to examine, scrutinize, investigate
eskatimar	sp. *escatimar,* to lessen •*eskatimarse de la vida:* to withdraw from normal life, Ne. 188b
eskombrar	sp. *escombrar,* to remove garbage, get rid of, distort
eskopo	it. *scopo,* purpose

eskorchada	burned; scorched
eskripar	sp. *escarpar,* to rasp, scrape •*eskripando de mi chiko kapital:* scraping the bottom of my puny savings
eskriveria	set of writing tools
eskrosher	to gnash teeth •*eskrosher dyentes:* to be upset
eskuro	obscure; dark; bizarre; secret
esnaf	ott. أصناف, *esnâf,* pl. of *sınıf,* class •*esnaf adami:* middle class; artisans
espago	σπάγγος, (*espango* in Istanbul), it. *spago*, string, cord
esparanyar	it. *sparagnare,* to save (money)
espartir	distribute; separate •*espartia una pared:* a wall separated
espati	σπαθὶ, shamrock, Ne. 194b
esperar	to hope (used 4 times) •*esperavan de tornar:* they hoped to come back, Ne. 194c; but also to wait, expect (used 11 times), •*esperando afuera:* waiting outside. In Istanbul, *asperar* and *esperar* are not interchangeable
espinotas	tr. *iskorpit,* scorpion-fish, Ne. 195b
espolvoreado	it. powdered
espyegar	it. *spiegare,* to explain
estabilio	a cross between sp. *estabilecer* & it. *stabilire,* he established •*estabilito:* establishment •*komisyon de los estabilis de aki:* a committee of local inhabitants
estatistika	as in engl. "vital statistics", personal information
estera	mat, carpet
esteso	it. *stesso,* same
estituir	it. *istituire,* to institute; institutionalize
estivla	it. *stivaletto,* ankle boot
estofa	sp. *estofa,* silk fabric
estofado	or *estopado,* stuffed, drenched, Ne. 199a
estraso	vandalism, blackmail, violence, Ne. 199b
estrecha	narrow; impasse

estupando	sp. *estupendo,* stupendous, marvelous, Ne. 201a
ezaltado	it. *esaltato,* exalted, excited
ezeguir	it. *eseguire,* to execute, carry out an order
ezekusyon	execution •*azer la ezekusyon:* start proceedings
ezistyo	should be אינסיסטייו, *ensistyo,* he insisted, rather than אי[ג]זיסטייו, *e[g]zistyo,* he existed!
ezmerar	to polish; take care of, Ne. 192 b
eznafes	see *esnâf*

F

facha	it. *faccia,* face
fakira	ott. فقيره, *fakîre,* poor woman
falaka	ott. فلقه, *falaka,* a staff with a loop of rope let through two holes by which the feet of a culprit are held up for the bastinado, Rd. 359a
falda	it. *falda,* hem
famiya	family •*su famiya:* his wife, his house, דְּבֵיתְהוּ
fanatizmo	fanaticism; extremism; superstition
farbalá	from "furbelow", pleated border •*farbala de papel:* showy paper ornament, Ne. 205b, Rd. 360a
fasfecha	prob. from *farsa fecha,* farce, trick, Ne. 206a
fasil	ott. فصل, *fasıl,* concert program, all in the same *makam*
fato	it. *fatto,* fact
fayar	old sp. for *hallar,* to find
fendriz	sp. *hendrija*, crack, (*indriz* in Istanbul)
fener	φανάρι, tr. *fener,* lantern
feredje	ott. فراجه, *ferace,* coat worn by Ottoman women
fermele	tr. *fermene,* (prob. fr. *parement)* braid used as trimming, Rd. 367b, as in *Fermeneciler,* a section in the Grand Bazar in Istanbul
fes	ott. فس, *fes*, fez
fetva	ott. فتوى, *fetva*, legal opinion issued by a *Mufti*
fila	file, rank •*en fila:* in file; continuously

findjan	pers.-tr. فنجان, *fincan,* coffee cup; head covering shaped like a *findjan*
fira	φύρα, فره, *fire,* loss, wastage; shrinkage
firido de	stricken by
firman	pers.-tr. فرمان, *ferman,* imperial decree •*kitar un firman:* issue, obtain a *firman*
fishekes	tr. *fişek*, cartridges •*echar fishekes:* fire bullets •*avai fishek:* fireworks
fogera	port. *fogueira,* fire •*kon fogera:* urgently, Ne. 214c
foresto	it. *forestiero,* foreign; distant; unfamiliar
franka	*a la franka,* Western style as opposed to *a la turka*
franko	Frank; European; Western
frio	cold •*frios:* to have a cold; shivers
fyaka	it. *fiacca,* lassitude •*me tomo kon fyaka a demandarme:* he started to ask me nonchalantly
furun	φοῦρνος, tr. *fırın,* oven •*Arnaut furnu:* Albanian oven, bakery

G

gabela	sp. *gabela,* a tax on specific food items
garrean	for *gerrean*, they fight
gassim	גַּסִּים, *gassim,* large, Ottoman coins of undetermined value •*por kada kavesa de beema a 30 gassim:* 30 large Ottoman coins per head of cattle
gemara	גְּמָרָא, *gemara,* text of the *Talmud* •*gemara de Berahoth:* Tractate *Berahoth*
gemarika	abbreviated books; small tracts
gematriyoth	γάμμα = τρία, numerical value of a word based on the sum total of its letters
geulla	גְּאֻלָּה, *geulla,* redemption
gevirim	pl. of גְּבִיר, *gevir,* well-to-do person. Depending on context, the Mishnaic Hebrew

	masculine plural גְּבִירִין, *gevirin,* can be sarcastic.
golpe	blow; cannon shot
gormar	גָּרַם, *garam,* cause (suffering) •*gormarse sus pekados:* to atone for one's sins, Ne. 228a
gozno	hook, Ne. 228c
grosh	ott. غوروش, *guruş, kuruş,* piaster worth 40 *paras*
gruta	store; office
guaya	clamor, outcry •*alsar guayas:* raise an outcry
guestro	for *vuestro,* your
guevo	egg •*guevo enhaminado:* hard-boiled egg

H

haber	ott. خبر, *haber,* news, information
hafis	ott. حافظ , *hâfiz:* one who has memorized the Qur'an; a cantor
haftara	הַפְטָרָה, *haftara,* weekly prophetic portion
haham	חָכָם, *haham,* sage; Sephardic rabbi
hahamayya	חֲכָמַיָּא, *hahamayya,* Aramaic type plural of *haham* to create a "collective" with a touch of irony
Haham Bashi	tr. *Hahambaşı,* Head Rabbi, Chief Rabbi
hahamiko	*haham* with a diminutive of endearment, a young, inexperienced *haham*
hakhnasa	הַכְנָסָה, *hahnasa,* bringing in •*hakhnasath orhim* hospitality
hakira	חֲקִירָה, *hakira,* investigation •*hakira u-derisha:* investigation and inquiry
hakyam	prob. for ott. حاكيم, *hâkyim,* judge
halibi	ott. حلبي, *Halebî,* head dress, scarf in the *Haleb,* Aleppo style
halka	ott. حلقه, *halka,* hoop, (wedding) ring
haluhoṭ	for *halukkoth* חֲלוּקוֹת , foundation for the raising and distribution of funds •*halukkoth de Nissim:* the Nissim Foundation, Ne. 249c
ham	חַם, *ham*, shortened form of *haham,* used for ordinary Jews who are not rabbis •*ham Sa'adi*

	ha-Levi: Mr. Sa'adi ha-Levi
Haman	הָמָן, *Haman*
hamira	aram. חֲמִירָא, *hamira,* (passive participle) fermented, leavened •*kal hamira:* "all/any leaven", with reference to the search for leaven on Passover eve •*diya de kal hamira:* day before Passover
hammal	ott. حمّال, *hammal,* porter
han	pers.-tr. خان *han,* commercial building •*hâne:* building unit; apartment
hân	tr. خان *hân,* title given to a Muslim ruler: Abdulmedjid Hân or the Agha Khan
handrajo	from ar. إنضرج , *inḍaraja,* split, sp. *andrajo,* rag; stupidity •*yo no kreiya en estos handrajos:*I gave no credence to that garbage
hanefuth	חֲנֵפוּת, *hanefuth,* (based on חָנֵף), hypocrisy
hanumes	tr. خانم, *hanum/hanım,* Turkish ladies
haremlik	ott. حرملك, *haremlik,* women's apartments
harrifa	aram. חָרִיפָא, *harifa,* sharp; smart •*pilpela harrifa:* hot pepper, a hothead
harshlik	tr. خرجلك, *harçlık,* allowance, pocket-money
harta	χαρτί, ott. خريطه, *harita,* map
harvar	see *aharvar*
has	see *haz*
has	ott. خاص, *haṣ,* special •*has askeri:* special forces
hase	cotton fabric
haskama	הַסְכָּמָה, *haskama,* agreement; rabbinic *imprimatur* •*izyeron una askama:* they issued a rabbinic decree
hasnadar	pers.-ott. خزينه دار, *haznedar.* treasurer
haspaka	הַסְפָּקָה, *haspaka,* providing needs; granting gifts
hathan	חָתָן, *hathan,* groom
hattara	הַתָּרָה, *hattara,* release from a vow; forgiveness •*dar attara:* exonerate •*attara ala moda:* a made-up release
haver	חָבֵר, *haver,* business partner
hayyav	חַיָּב, *hayyav,* duty-bound, obligated

haz	ott. حظ, *haẓ,* pleasure, •*tomar haz:* enjoy
hazaka	חֲזָקָה, *hazaka*, priority; license
hazine	ott. خزينه, *hazine,* treasury
hazino	ar. خزين, *hazîn,* sick; patient •*hazinura:* disease
hazne	ott. خزنه, *hazne* for *hazine,* (protected) container
hazzan	חַזָּן, *hazzan,* cantor
hekdesh	הֶקְדֵּשׁ, *hekdesh,* gift to a synagogue or a pious foundation, endowment
herem	חֵרֶם, *herem,* excommunication •*herem de kol bo:* an all inclusive excommunication
heremoth	for חֲרָמוֹת, *haramoth,* the correct plural of *herem*, excommunication
hesed	חֶסֶד, *hesed,* kindness •*hesed 'olam:* everlasting kindness
heshbon	חֶשְׁבּוֹן, *heshbon,* account •*sin heshbon:* without planning
hevra	חֶבְרָה, *hevra,* partnership; society; congregation
hiderelez	pers.-ott. خدرللز, *hıdrellez,* spring celebration, possibly connected with Elijah (mentioned as *Ilyâs* in the Qur'ân 37:130), occurring 40 days after the spring equinox around May 6, Rd. 479a. For *hidir*, green, see below
hidir	from ar.-ott. خضر, *hadir,* green; vegetation •*hizir/hidir: Hidir,* legendary person who attained immortality by drinking from the *abi hayat,* "Water of Life", Rd. 2a and *hidir,* 482a
hillula	הִלּוּלָה, *hillula,* celebration
hizmet	ott. خدمت, *hizmet,* service
hizzun	חִזּוּן, *hizzun*, trained singing; melody of funeral dirges
hodja	pers.-tr. خواجه, *hoca,* teacher
holera	*χολέρα,* cholera
Hosha'na	הוֹשַׁעְנָא, *hosha'na* (Hosanna), a litany chanted daily during *Sukkoth* at the conclusion of the morning service •*Hosha'na Rabba:* the Great *Hosha'na*

chanted to celebrate the seventh and last day of the festival of *Sukkoth.*
The word הוֹשַׁעְנָא*, hosha'na* which means "save us" is probably an aramaized form of the Hebrew phrase הוֹשִׁיעָה נָּא*, hoshi'anna* found in Psalm 118:25. "Save us" is also the translation used by both the Jewish Publication Society Bible, (Philadelphia 1999) and Da Sola Pool's *Festivals* Prayer Book (New York 1963).

hozer	חוֹזֵר*, hozer*, returning •*hozer halila*: again and again
h"r	*haham ribbi*
Hristos	Χριστὸς, Christ
hukyumat	ott. حكومت, *hükümet,* government; authority
huppa	חֻפָּה*, huppa,* bridal canopy
huzzam	ott. هزّام, *hüzzam,* name of a *makam* or musical mode

I

ia	for *iva,* was going
idare	ott. إداره, *idâre,* management, directing •*idare mishlishi:* executive council
idjra	ott. إجراء, *icrâ,* implementation, carrying out •*meter a la idjra:* start implementing
idle	for idle individual in a community, see *batlan*
iggul	עִגּוּל*, iggul*, circle
ikram	ott. إكرام, *ikram,* displaying courtesy, kindness
ikrar	ott. إكرار, *ikrâr,* declaration, deposition
illet	ott. علّت, *illet,* disease, plague •*illet-i kyemuru:* black plague, "the dregs of society"
illula	see *hillula*
imam	ott. إمام, *imâm,* prayer leader; Muslim scholar
inda	also, *ainda, dainda,* still
indemas	see *demas*
inimas	see *demas*

inútile	it. *inutile,* useless
ipogo[n]dria	ὑποχόνδρια, hypochondria
irade	ott. إراده, *irâde,* imperial decree
isa, isa, isa	tr. *isa, isa,* a command to coordinate the action of a group towards a specific move, "pull", "pull"
Iskilich	unknown family name
Ismirni	Smyrna, *Izmir*
istifando	ott. إستيف, *istîf,* pile; build up inventory
istihkyam	ott. إستحكام, *istihkâm,* fortification
istinaf	ott. إستيناف, *istînâf,* making an appeal
istindak	ott. إستنطاق, *istintâk,* cross-examination, interrogation to establish the truth
iyyar	אִיָּר, *Iyyar*, (second or) eighth month of the Hebrew calendar

K

kabaet	ott. قباحت, *kabahat,* guilt, fault
kachak	tr. *kaçak,* smuggled; illicit
kaddish	קַדִּישׁ, *kaddish*, a doxology in Aramaic recited between the various parts of the liturgy or after a *limmud* session
kafe	coffee-house
kaik	tr. *kayık,* rowboat, *caïque*
kal	Sephardic pronunciation of the Aramaic כָּל, "all", as in *kal nidré* rather than *kol nidré* or *kal hamira* rather than *kol hamira*
kal	for קָהָל, *kahal*, synagogue
kalada	influenza, flu; cold
kalafat	it. *calafato,* minor repair of a boat •*kalafatchi:* caulker, repairer
kalavrina	from "cadaverine", (chemical found in corpses), cadaver, Ne. 261c
kaldirim	tr. *kaldırım,* side-walk
kalpak	tr. *kalpak,* fur cap •*kalpakito,* small *kalpak*

kalupes	ott. قالب, *kalıb/kalıp,* molds; matrices (in printing)
kamaryer	it. *cameriere,* valet, waiter
kam[b]yo	exchange, interest •*ke tyenen ke pagar sus kambyos:* because they have to pay their bills
kaminante	walking •*ombre kaminante:* one who makes the rounds, guard
kamino	road •*kamino de fyerro:* railroad
kande	also *kante,* chant
kandeleria	candles (with collective ending)
kandida	see *kuantita*
kandil	καντήλι, tr. *kandil,* oil-lamp •*azeyte para los kandiles*: oil for the tapers in the oil-lamps
kandirear	tr. *kandırmak,* to convince; mislead •*kandirearse:* be convinced
kandja	tr. *kanca,* hook, grapple •*los de las kandjas:* firemen with grapples
Kanea	Crete
kanistro	κάνιστρον, it. *canestro:* wicker basket
kankaravias	clowning, farce, Ne. 266a
kanli	tr. *kan*, blood •*kanli:* bloody •*Kanli Kule:* Bloody Tower
kanuname	ott. قانوننامه, *kanunnâme:* code of law
kantidad	see *kuantita*
kapan	tr. *kapan,* closed market, such as Unkapan, Ne. 268b. Also, a place of confinement, jail •*se vido traer deel kapan turko:* were seen being brought from jail
kapi	tr. *kapı*, door, entrance to the Janissary barracks
karakandjos	tr. *kara,* black + *kancı,* bloodletter, ghost, Ne. 270b
karapusa	port. *carapuça,* hood, Ne. 271a
karar	1. ott.قرار, *karar,* decision 2. ott.قدر, *kadar,* power; amount •*ke karar de amor:* so much love •*a karar ke se ivan muryendo:* so much so that they were dying

karayoz	tr. *karagöz,* main figure of the Turkish "shadow show", funny fellow
karear	to carry, to move •*karyar tyerra:* to move soil
kari	tr. woman •*Kari Pazar:* market for women
ka[ri]shtirear	tr. *karıştırmak,* mix; interfere
karnesero	butcher
ka[r]nitures	for *garnituras* in Istanbul, trimmings, ornaments
karpir	lament, wail
karvonko	carbuncle, pimple, large boil
karyar	see *karear*
kasapana	tr. *kasaphâne,* butcher shop
kasar	to hunt
kasha	coffer; fund •*kasha publika:* "Community Fund"
kashero	treasurer
katife	ott. قديفه/قطيفه, *kadife,* velvet
kativada	it. *cattivata,* captive, slave
katran	ott. قطران, *katran,* tar
kavane	tr. *kahvehâne,* coffee-house
kavaz/kavas	ott. قوّاس, *kavvas,* archer; bodyguard in attendance on a dignitary or consul
kave	ott. *kahve,* coffee
kaveyera	(from *kaveyo)* hair; coiffure
kavod	כָּבוֹד, *kavod,* honor •*por kavod del Dyo:* for God's sake
kaymakam	ott. قائمقام, *kaymakam,* second in command, acting official; *locum tenens* •*ordu kaymakamı:* lieutenant colonel •*kaymakam efendi:* honorable *kaymakam* referring to the *Av Beth Din* or head of the rabbinic court
kaza	it. *casa,* house, business firm, company, establishment
kazá	ott. قضا', *kazâ,* county
kedusha	קְדוּשָׁה/קְדֻשָּׁה, *kedusha,* holiness
khedive	pers.-ott. خديو, *Hidîv, Khedive,* governor of Egypt, see *prenchipato*
keilla	קְהִילָה/קְהִלָּה, *kehila,* congregation; synagogue

ke kual	for *ke kualmente, q. v.*
kelal	כְּלָל, *kelal,* general rule •*bi-helal:* in general; including
kelaloth	קְלָלוֹת, *kelaloth,* curses •*kelaloth nimrasoth:* uninterrupted curses
kelavim	כְּלָבִים, *kelavim,* dogs
ke-neged	כְּנֶגֶד, *ke-neged,* according to •*ke-neged 13 middoth rahamim:* corresponding to the 13 attributes of mercy
kerim	ott. كريم, *kerîm,* generous; magnificent
ketubba	כְּתֻבָּה, *ketubba,* written marriage contract in Aramaic
kevura	קְבוּרָה, *kevura,* grave
kezo	cheese •*kezero:* cheese vendor
kibbus	קִבּוּץ, *kibbus,* gathering; meeting
kiddush	קִדּוּשׁ, *kiddush,* declaring holy; sanctifying
kiddushin	קִדּוּשִׁין, *kiddushin,* the seven wedding blessings
kinoth	קִינוֹת, *kinoth,* dirges recited on the 9th of *Av*
kippurim	כִּפּוּרִים, *kippurim,* atonements •*Yom a-Kippurim:* Day of Atonement
kira	ott. كرا', *kirâ,* rent
kirim	tr. *kırım,* pleat, Rd. 654b •*kirimes:* fur lined coat, Ne. 286b
kirmis	tr. *kırmızı,* "crimson", red
kishla	tr. *kışla,* barracks
kitta	כִּתָּה, *kitta,* class, group; committee •*kitta delos memunim:* the group of controllers
kiyare	pers.-ott. كار, *kâr,kiyâre* piece sung after a *peshrev*
kizildjik	tr. *kızılcık*, cornelian cherry
kláse	it. *classe* (used 11 times) also gallicized as *klasa* (used 7 times), class
klavedon	filigrane, Ne. 288b
klisya	ἐκκλησία, tr. *kilise,* church
kochan	tr. *koçan,* stub
koche	the name of a carriage, popular in the Hungarian town of Kocz, that spread to all European

	languages. Here, *kocha* is a coachman •*sin kochas:* without coachmen
kodesh	קֹדֶשׁ, *kodesh,* holiness
kofya	elaborate hairdo worn by married Sephardic women, Ne. 289a
kohen	כּוֹהֵן, *kohen,* name of the priests that officiated at the Temple
kokarda	fr. *cocarde,* rosette, boutonniere
kokona	κοκκῶνα, pomegranate seed; •*se alevantaron las kokonas:* (mockingly) the elderly, spoiled women or *kokonas* got up, Ne. 289b
kol	קוֹל, *kol,* voice •*kol mevasser:* the voice of a herald; a proclaiming voice, a rallying point
kóla	κόλλα, starch, •*koladji:* laundryman who does starching •*vistido de arroz koladji:* impeccably dressed in white, starched garments
kolay	tr. *kolay,* easy
kol bo	כָּל־בּוֹ, *kol-bo,* all-in-it, all inclusive, general
kolada	laundry
kolel	כּוֹלֵל, *kolel*, community •*la kasha de el Kolel:* Fund of the Kolel
kolora	anger •*tomarse kolora:* get angry
komadre	midwife
komandita	it. *accomandita,* sp. *comandita,* limited partnership, Ne. 219c
kombidador	organizer of a celebration
kombinasyones	for *afitos,* occurrences
komer	eat, absorb, "take"
komercho	it. *commercio,* customs
komodo	for *ke modo,* how
komponyer	for *komponer,* to put together, arrange
konak	tr. *konak,* mansion, palace
konfafa	plot, scheme, Ne. 297b
konfesó	he divulged a plan, convinced •*konfeso a uno de fabrikar:* he convinced someone to produce •*konfesador:* schemer, contriver, Ne. 297b

konfites	Jordan almonds
konkriar	engender, come about; declare (disease)
konsinyar	to surrender
kontado	counted; well-respected
kontraka[m]byar	it. *contraccambiare,* to exchange; reciprocate
kontratado	contracted agreement, agreement
kontraydades	contrarieties, slanderous statements
kontush	prob. for fr. *contour,* edging
konusheando	tr. *konuşmak,* talking
koreo	courier
korpo	it. *corpo,* body •*korpo konsular:* diplomatic corps
korredor	middle-man, agent, broker
kortar	from גָּזַר, *gazar,* to cut; decide •גְּזַר־דִּין, *gezar-din, kortar djuzgo:* to reach a verdict
kosa	for *koza,* thing, matter
koshear	sp. *cojear*, to limp, stumble, falter
Kostan	abr. for Constantinople, Istanbul
kostar	to cost •*kostar los ojos de la kara:* to cost an arm and a leg
kostreto	it. *costretto,* obligated
kotne	כְּתֹנֶת, *kethoneth,* ott. كتن, *keten,* linen
kovrar	to gain, get back, replace, charge •*kovró unos frios:* he got the shivers
kozina	kitchen
krushun	(pl. *kruşumes),* tr. *kurşun,* lead; bullet
krevita	sp. *quebrar,* to break •*la krevita de Chilibi Menahem:* the bankruptcy of Chilibi Menahem, Ne. 309a
kualmente	it. *qualmente* •*respondi kualmente:* I answered whereby..., Ne. 315b
kuando a	see *kuanto a*
kuantita	it. *quantità,* quantity, amount
kuanto a	as for
kuarta	1 quart
kuartana	(fever occurring every fourth day), malaria,

	Ne. 316a
kueyo	neck
kui	tr. *koyu,* dark (color)
kulanear	tr. *kullanmak,* to use •*kulanean:* they use •*kulanear karosa:* drive a carriage •*kulanear barvas:* accustomed to wear beards •*frios ke los kulaneo munchos mezes:* shivers that lasted many months (strange use of kulanear), Ne. 311b
kulé	tr. *kule,* tower •*Beyaz Kule:* the White Tower
kumple-*minyan*	*person* "countable" in a religious *quorum* or *minyan*
kuna	cradle but also platter, Ne. 312b
kundurya	κόθορνος, later κουντοῦρα, tr. *kundurya,* shoe
kuppa	קֻפָּה, *kuppa,* money-box; fund •*en kada kuppa i socheta:* in every Fund and Organization •*kuppa[th] hesed olam:* welfare society
kurdi	see *yurdi*
kushak	tr. *kuşak,* wide sash
kusur	ott. کسور, *küsur,* left over, balance •*kusur de moneda:* a sum of money
kuti	tr. *kutu,* box
kyatip	ott. کاتب, *kâtib/kâtip*, scribe; secretary
kyavgir	pers.-tr. کارگیر, *kârgîr, kâgîr,* brick building
kyaya	pers.-tr. کاهیا/کیا, *kâhya, kâya,* steward
kyef	tr. کیْف, *keyf, keyif,* pleasure, delight, enjoyment •*kyefsiz:* indisposed; in a bad mood •*kyefsizlik:* indisposition, sickness •*alevantar de kyefsis:* (get up) be healed from a light ailment
kyel	tr. *kel,* bald; baldness
kyeman	pers.-tr. کمان, *kemân,* violin
kyenar	pers.-tr. کنار, *kenâr,* edge •*yamar para un kyenar:* take someone aside •*kyenarli:* with an edge
kyepazelik	tr. کپازه لك, *kepazelik,* shame, scandal
kyetabtchi	ott. کتابجی, *kitapçı,* bookstore owner
kyeza	it. *chiesa,* church
kyimur	aram. גּוּמְרָא, *gumra;* coal. Targum to Lev. 16:12 is

גּוּמְרִין דְּאֶשָּׁא, for גַּחֲלֵי־אֵשׁ, *burning coals*; charcoal

kyira — ott. كراء, *kirâ,* rent

kyoshe — pers.-tr. كوشه, *köşe,* corner

kyula — pers.-tr. كلاه, *külâh,* conical hat or cap •*vazyaron la kyula:* they emptied their arsenal, Ne. 320c

kyurdi — see *yurdi*

L

ladinado — a Hebrew text translated into literal Spanish •*ladinado en grego:* a literal Greek translation using Hebrew letters

lag — made of *lamed* = 30 and *gimal* = 3, a total of 33

Lag la-'Omer — among Sepharadim, the 33rd day **of** the *'Omer.* Ashkenazim call it *Lag ba-'Omer*

lagum — tr. *lağım*, sewer

landre — plague

lashon — לָשׁוֹן, *lashon,* tongue; (the Hebrew) language

lav — לָאו, *lav,* negative commandment

lazaret — ott. نظارت, *nezâret*, it. *lazaretto,* observation area for incoming passengers, Ne. 325a

lazerya — for לַחַץ, *láhaṣ*, hard work

leedor — also, *meldador,* reader

lenya — wood •*dar lenya:* administer a beating

lesensya — permission

le-shalom — לְשָׁלוֹם, *le-shalom,* for *in* peace (Ex. 4:18), peacefully

leshon a-kodesh — לְשׁוֹן־הַקֹּדֶשׁ, *leshon ha-kodesh,* the holy tongue, Hebrew

levante — from *alevantar,* an uprising

levaya — לְוָיָה, *levaya,* funeral procession

Ley — translating the *Persian* דָּת, *dath,* decree, law, *Tora*; religion

limunyo — sadness

locum tenens — see *kaymakam*

lokandadji — ott.-it. from *locanda,* restaurant •*yamaron un*

	lokandadji, they called a caterer
londje	long
lo tavo	לֹא תָבוֹא, *lo tavo,* you shall not enter •*lo tavo el be-tho*: you shall not enter his home
Lube	in *meydan* de Lube: Lube square
luso	it. *lusso,* luxury
luyto, luto	mourning

M

ma'aser	מַעֲשֵׂר, *ma'aser* tenth part or tithe
ma'asiyyoth	מַעֲשִׂיּוֹת, *ma'asiyyoth,* short stories
mabbul	מַבּוּל, *mabbul,* flood; abundantly
maggi'a	מַגִּיעַ, *maggi'a,* touches, is involved •*el era maggi'a:* he was a contact man
mákula	a stain; blemish •*sin dinguna mákula:* unblemished, perfect
makka	מַכָּה, *makka,* plague
ma'la	מַעְלָה, *ma'la,* above
malah	מַלְאָךְ, *malah,* angel •*malah ha-maveth:* angel of death
mallogrado	ill-fated, unlucky •*muryo mallogrado:* he died prematurely
malkuth	מַלְקוּת, *malkuth,* punishment; lashes
malshinar	מַלְשִׁין, *malshin,* to slander, vilify
manera	from *mano,* hand, glove, Ne. 341c
mankansa	deficiency, defect; blemish
mankidá	syn. of *mankura*, lack, missing thing; shortcoming Ne. 343a
mankura	lack, missing thing; shortcoming, mistake, Ne. 343b
mano	hand •*dar a mano:* permit, allow
manseveria	coll. young people
mantenisyon	for *mantenimyento,* sustenance, livelihood
mantenuta	it. *mantenuta,* mistress; kept woman
maraman	or *maramar*, scarf

maraza — ott. معارضه, *muâraza,* quarrel, Ne. 347b; a legal case

maré — aram. מָרֵא, מָר, מוֹר, *mare* or *mar* or *mor*, lord, master; individual

marsh pye — fr. *marchepied,* foot-path

mása — mass; a bunch of

masá — מַצָּה, *maṣṣa,* unleavened bread; *matza*

masbata — see *mazbata*

m[a]sd[o]ri — μάστορης, mason

masero — tablecloth, Ne. 349c

masha — tr. *maşa,* pincers, tongues •*tomar su nombre por masha:* abuse one's name

masiko — bouquet, Ne. 349c

masimamente — it. *massimamente,* maximally; above all, especially

maslaat — ott. مصلحت, *maslahat,* business; rank

matta — מטה, *matta,* below

matrapas — ott. *madrabaz* (uncertain), middleman, swindler, Ne. 351b, Rd.717b

matridja — it. *matrice*, matrix • *vazyar matridjas:* to cast matrices/fonts

matyer — material

mavi — ott. ماوى / مائي, *ma'i/mâvi;* (color of sea- water), blue, Rd. 724a, 738b

may — it. *mai,* ever

maynar — to decrease, lessen, abate, Ne. 351c

mazbata — ott. مضبطه, *mazbata,* official report, legal proposal

mazon — מָזוֹן, *mazon,* food, sustenance

mazzal — מַזָּל, *mazzal,* constellation; luck

medjidiye — ott. مجيديّه, *mecidiye,* coin worth 20 piasters or 1/5 of a gold lira

mehila — מְחִילָה, *mehila,* pardon, forgiveness

mehoram — מְחֹרָם, *mehoram,* under a ban, excommunicated •*mehoram!* cursed!

mehuppah מְהֻפָּךְ, *mehuppah,* upside down, overturned

mekam ott. مقام, for *makam,* musical mode, tune

melammed מְלַמֵּד, *melammed,* teacher

meldado for לִמּוּד, *limmud,* Tora study (also, in memory of a deceased)

meldador also, *leedor,* reader, student

melizina medicine (drugs); *medikeriya:* medicine (science)

membrasyon memory; recollection

memma prob. from ar. ائمّه, *aimma,* the plural of *imâm,* a turban worn by high ranked Muslim, Syrian-Christian and Jewish religious scholars and judges

memunnim מְמֻנִּים, *memunnim,* appointed officials; comptrollers

merak ott. مراق, *merâk,* worry

mereser to be worthy of •*un sinyor ke yo no meresko:* a gentleman that I don't deserve

meri ott. مرعى, *mer'i,* enforced •*izo meri:* make legal, authorize

merikia also *mirikia,* see *merak,* anxiety; curiosity

Merkada redeemed, bought •*Merkada,* (as a proper name)

merubba' מְרֻבָּע, *merubba',* square; •*letra merubba':* square Hebrew letter

mesadder מְסַדֵּר, *mesadder,* organizer; typesetter

mesammeah מְסַמֵּחַ, *mesammeah,* to make rejoice; render happy

mesherikero port. *mexeriquiero,* gossiper, scandal-monger, Ne. 360b

meshk ott. مشق, *meşk,* teaching or practicing Ottoman music or calligraphy

meshkiye ott. مشقيّه, *meshkiyye,* musical exercise

meshubbah מְשֻׁבָּח, *meshubbah,* praiseworthy, famous

mesta tr. *mest,* light, thin soled boot (worn indoors or inside overshoes)

metalik tr. *metelik,* Ottoman coin worth 10 *paras*

metropolit μητροπολίτης bishop •*el Metropolit:* probably the name of a cemetery where a bishop was buried

meuppah see *mehuppah*

mevasser — מְבַשֵּׂר, *mevasser,* bearer of good news •*kol mevasser mevasser ve-omer:* the voice of the herald announces and says

mevlane — pers.-ott. مولويخانه, *mevlevîhâne,* lodge of Mevlevi Dervishes

mevuhar — מְבֻחָר, *mevuhar,* chosen; a choice piece

meydan — tr. ميدان, *meydan,* open space •*salir en meydan:* come out, step forward

mezammer — מְזַמֵּר, *mezammer,* singer of Psalms

mezat — ott. مزاد, *mezad,* auction •*vender en mezat:* sell at an auction

mezo — it. *meso,* means •*por mezo de:* by means of •*azer mezos:* find the means

milletes — aram. מִלְּתָא, *milletha,* ar. مِلَّة, *millet,* any distinct Religious Community within the Ottoman empire, such as the Jewish *millet*, the Muslim *millet*, etc., See *Qur'an* 12:38, where in a reference to his pagan ancestors, Muhammad says: *I have left the "millet" of a people who does not believe in Allah.* Here, as in other qur'anic passages, the word *millet* describes his religion. Similarly, *millet*^{u} *Ibrâhim* means Abraham's religion rather than Abraham's nation!

milyonestro — presumably, multi-millionaire

mindel — or *minder,* ott. مندر, *minder,* cushion to sit on

minha — מִנְחָה, *minha,* afternoon service

mintan — pers.-tr. نيمتن / منتان, *mintan/nîmten,* heavy outer half-shirt

minyan — מִנְיָן, *minyan,* Jewish *quorum* for congregational functions

mirikia — see *merikia*

mishlish — ott. مجلس, *meclis,* assembly, council

mishpaha — מִשְׁפָּחָה, *mishpaha,* family; ancestry, lineage

mishpat — מִשְׁפָּט, *mishpat,* judgment; sentence

mishtrapa — ott. مشربه, *maşrapa,* metal drinking cup; metal mug

Misir	ott. مصر, *Mısır* Egypt •*Misir Charshi:* Egyptian Market
misvat tefilla	מִצְוַת־תְּפִלָּה, *misvath tefilla,* service in honor of the groom after the wedding similar to the Ashkenazi *Aufruf*
mitrayoza	machine-gun •*i mitrayozas,* with machine-guns, Ne. 365b; here a metaphor for the blowing of the *shofar*
mobles	fr. *meubles*, furniture
modre	contracted from *amor de* •*por modre de,* + Past tense: because + Future tense: in order that
molde	means, way •*azer molde:* act within one's means
molo	it. *molo,* pier
monaka	μόναχὴ, nun
monte	mountain •*irse a montes:* go up (in smoke), become unreal
morada	home; housing
morador	dweller; renter, tenant *(kirâcı)*
Móro	Maur: Sicilian Jew. In Salonika, Sicilian Jews were mostly fishermen and were called *Moros,* Ne. 369b
Morpurgo	Famous family name from Northern Italy, originally from the city of Maribor in Slovenia known as Marburg in German
morra	a game for two based on guessing the number of fingers hidden at a given time, Ne. 369c
mosa	maiden; servant
moso	servant; employee
muabendji	ott. مابينجى, *mabeyinci,* court chamberlain
muabethane	pers.-ott. محبتخانه, *muhabbethâne,* a kind of complicated embroidery, Rd. 788b
muhtar	ott. مختار, *muhtar,* elder (of a village)
muimat	ott. مهمات, *mühimmat,* munitions of war, ammunitions

mulla	ar.-ott. مولاّ, *molla,* Muslim scholar
munasip	also *munasup,* ott. مناسب, *münâsip,* appropriate
muncho pokas	a few!
mundado	specially sorted, Ne. 373b
Murteza(n)	ott. مرتضا', pleasing, admired; *Mürtezâ* (male name)
musade	ott. مساعده, *müsaade,* permission; favor; concession
musafir	ott. مسافر, *misâfir,* guest •*a musafir: as* a guest, לְאוֹרֵחַ
musandara	fr. *mansarde,* roof-window; dormer, attic
musellim	ott. مسلّم, *müsellim,* administrative official under a *Vali* authorized to deliver, *(teslîm)*
mushteri	ott. مشترى, *müşteri,* customer
musteshar	ott. مستشار, *müsteşâr,* counsellor
musyu	Ladino pronunciation of fr. *Monsieur*
myedo	fear
muzevvir	ott. مزوّر, *müzevvir,* one who falsifies; a sneek, double dealer, Ne. 375c
muzevvirlik	ott. مزوّرلك, *müzevvirlik,* trickery; tale-telling, Ne. 375c

N

nafe	pers.-tr. نافه, *nâfe,* soft fur from animal's belly, Rd. 860a
nasyon	nation; religious community, see *millet*
natural	natural; customary, usual
na' ve-na'	for נָע וָנָד, *na' ve-nad,* "restless wanderer" said about Cain (Gen. 4:14)
nazar	ott. نظر, *nazar,* look; observation; consideration •*tener muncho nazar:* look with favor, have esteem for
negosyo	it. *negozio,* business, shop
Nemse	tr. نمچه, *Nemçe,* Austria

nerde	1. interrogative *ande* for tr. *nerde, nerede,* where? frequently confused with *nereye,* whither 2. relative *ande* for tr. *nereye,* whither, to where
neve-	נְוֵה־, *neve-,* oasis-of, •*neve shalom,* oasis of peace
neviim	נְבִיאִים, *neviim,* prophets
nevela	נְבֵלָה, *nevela,* carcass; foul, putrid
nimláhu	the word נִמְלָחוּ, *nimláhu* from Isa. 51:6, "though the heavens should *melt away*" is a mistake. The correct word is נִפְתָּחוּ, *niftáhu* as in Gen. 7:11, "the floodgates of the sky *broke open*".
nimrasoth	נִמְרָצוֹת, *nimrasoth,* strong; intense
nizam	ott. نظام, *nizâm*, order •*nizâm askeri:* "new army" introduced by Sultan Mahmud II in 1826 to replace the janissaries. It was called *asâkir-i mansûre-yi Muhammediyye,* the invincible Mohammedan soldiers with emphasis on Islâm. •*vistido al nizam:* wearing a uniform
novita	it. *novità,* news
nuho	נוּחוֹ, his rest •*nuho 'Eden:* may he rest in Paradise
nyervo	nerve; dried beef tendon used as a whip to administer painful lashes, Ne. 387c

O

odjak	tr. *ocak,* hearth; Janissary barracks
ofisyo	trade, profession
oglu	tr. *oğlu,* son-of
oka	ott. اوقه, *okka,* a weight unit
olu	see *oglu*
ombre	man •*este ombre,* this man, "I", see *el aya*
'omer	עֹמֶר, *'omer,* sheaf •*en el Omer:* the period of 7 weeks from *Pesah* to *Shavuoth*
on	tr. *on,* ten •*onbaşı,* corporal
ora	hour •*echar oras:* procrastinate
ordenar	to set (a table)
oria	border, side •*oriya de la mar:* seashore

orta	tr. *orta,* medium
Orundjik	also *Orundjuk,* place name
Osha'na	see *Hosha'na* and *Hosha'na Rabba*
otro ke	in *non...otro ke* for לֹא...אֶלָּא, *lo...ella, ne...que,* not...but /other than, or simply "only" •*ma eyos non kerian otro ke a mi:* but they wanted no one, but me; they wanted *only* me
óya	terra-cotta bowl
ozadia	audacity

P

paásina	pers.-ott. بها/پها, *bahâ/pahâ,* value, price •*yok paasina:* for nothing
pacha	pers.ott. پاچه, *paçe/ paça,* leg •*entre sus pachas:* between his legs
palicha	from *palo,* stick, a blow with a heavy stick
palo	stick; lash
pandero	tambourine
pandja	pers.-ott. پانجار, *pançar*, beet
panyo	woolen cloth
pápa	maybe from *palpa,* to touch, feel •*a la papa syega:* with closed eyes, blindly, Ne. 529a
papuchilar	tr. *papuççular,* shoemakers •*Papuchilar Han:* Shoemakers' Bldg.
pará	pers.-ott. پاره, *para,* smallest Ottoman coin; penny
parar	present; show off
parasha	פָּרָשָׁה, *parasha,* weekly Tora portion
parea	παρέα, group, company
parimyento	from *parir,* childbirth, Ne. 410a
parladeamyento	tr. *parlamak,* explosion
parmacheta	also, *esparmacheta*, candle; matches, Ne. 410c & 194a
parnasim	פַּרְנָסִים, *parnasim,* congregational leaders
paryéntes	parents

paryentés — relatives

pasar — pass; also translating the Hebrew עָבַר, *'avar,* transgress •*pasó lav,* he transgressed a negative command •*paso sus komandos:* he transgressed their orders

paseo — promenade •*lo toman por paseo:* they may take a stroll

pasha — Akkadian *paḫātu,* governor, aram. פֶּחָה, *peha,* governor, ott. پاشا, *paşa,* general; governor •*Pasha efendimis chok yasha,* long live our lord , the governor

páso — same as *pasaje*, occurrence, event •*este páso ke pasó:* this event that occurred

pastav — large piece of broadcloth, red carpet, Rd. 920a

pasuk — פָּסוּק, *pasuk,* biblical verse, pl. *pesukim*

pasyon — hurt, pain

pasyonozo — passionately devoted, enthusiastic, Ne. 417a

Patisha — pers.-ott. پادشاه, *Padishah,* Sovereign, Sultan •*Patishaimis chok yasha:* long live our Sultan

pato — goose

patranyas — cock and bull stories; non-sensical arguments, Ne. 418c

pavor — fear

paytanim — פַּיְטָנִים, *paytanim,* liturgical poets; cantors

pazar — pers.-ott. بازار/پازار, *bâzâr, pâzâr,* market •*pazara yiden:* one that goes to the *bazaar;* a smart alec

pecha — sp. *pecho,* tax •*echar pecha:* to impose a tax, Ne. 420a, Rc. 111

pedrido — lost •*basho pedrido:* a vile individual

pekador — sinner •*pekador al hahambashi:* to sin against the Chief Rabbi

pekidim — פְּקִידִים, *pekidim,* officials, deputies

penalita — it. *penalità,* penalty

penseryo — thought

perat — פְּרָט, *perat,* single thing; individual, private person

perde	pers.-tr. پرده, *perde,* curtain
perek	פֶּרֶק, *perek,* section, chapter, specifically a chapter of *Pirké Avoth*
perikolo	it. *pericolo,* peril; danger
perkurador	for *prokurador,* attorney, agent
però	it. *però*, but. As opposed to Spanish *péro*, this conjunction is rarely used in Ladino where it was probably revived under Italian influence. It occurs only once in the entire manuscript.
personal	from *persona, person,* personally •*este personal: this individual* •en mi personal: *against me, personally*
pertenesyente	belonging; qualified; worthy
peruta	פְּרוּטָה, *peruta,* a coin •*peruta ketanna:* a small coin, "almost nothing"
Pesah	פֶּסַח, *Pesah,* Passover
pesak	aram. פְּסָק, *pesak,* cutting •*pesak din:* cutting/passing judgment, deciding a case
peshe	it. *pesce,* fish
peshkir	pers.-ott. پشكير, *peşkîr,* towel, napkin
peshrev	pers.-ott. پيشرو, *pişrev* or *peşrev,* pl. *peshrefes,* best known Ottoman musical form played as prelude
peskuzar	challenge; try to justify
pesukim	pl. of פָּסוּק, *pasuk*
peyor	for *peor,* worse •*kon mal en peyor:* from bad to worse
pi a-athon	פִּי־הָאָתוֹן, *pi-ha-athon*, the mouth of the she-ass
pikante	stinging; sharp
piko	one *piko* is approximately 75 cm.
pilador	substance used for depilation
pilpila	aram. פִּלְפִּלָא, *pilpila,* pepper •*pilpila harifa:* hot pepper, hot-head, (hot-head from among this sleazy bunch of people)
pipita	pumpkin seed

pishin	pers.-ott. پشين, *peşin,* immediately
pishkado	fish •*dia de el pishkado:* a reference to the fish served on the last of the eighth wedding day, after the bride had leaped over it as a symbol of fertility, Ne. 432b
pishkul	tr. *püskül,* tassel •*pishkuliko:* small tassel
píso	πίσω, backwards •*indo para píso:* falling behind, suffering losses, Ne. 437b
pizmon	פִּזְמוֹן *pizmon,* liturgical poem
platikar	for *pratikar,* rehearse; combine; discuss
pligo	*(de papel)*, a ply of paper or a sheet of paper
poeder	power •*en poeder de:* "in the power of", holding, having
politeza	it. *politezza,* politeness, courtesy
polvo	dust; flour, Ne. 443c
pompyeros	it. *pompieri,* firemen
pondekyi	ποντικός, Pontic—or related to the Black Sea—a furry animal, such as a weasel or a marten
porke	because; in order that •*porke yo estabilire gazeta:* in order for me to establish a newspaper
poseia	for *posedia,* he owned
posek	פּוֹסֵק, *posek,* a respondent in *responsa* literature; adjudicator of law
postekyi	tr. *pösteki*, sheepskin rug to sit on
prangadji	it. *branca,* claw; *pranga,* shackle •*kon los prangadjis ...kon kadena en los pyes:* with shackled prisoners... wearing chains on his feet
pranso	it. *pranzo,* banquet •*pransar:* to have lunch
prechizamente	it. *precisamente,* precisely
pregon	heralded proclamation •*pregonero:* town crier
prenchipato	**it.** *principato,* principality •*dar el prenchipato a* Mehmed Ali Pasha: appoint Mehmed Ali Pasha *khedive, q. v.* (of Egypt)
premeter	for *permeter,* to allow
premurozo	urgent

presigir	for *persigir,* to pursue, persecute
presyado	from *presyo,* price, assessed, appraised
presyador	appraiser of a trousseau •*ser presyado:* to be evaluated
prete	it. *prete,* priest
prevás/prevaz	pers.-ott. پرواز, *pervaz,* edge, frame, Ne. 450b
prima	first; at first
promete	for *permete*
propyo	proper •*lo propyo:* the same
provaya	aram. masc. pl. sf. *-ayya >aya,* used to create the collective *la provaya,* the poor, a poor neighborhood
Puerta	gate; referring also to the Sublime Porte, the seat of government •*Puerta Mueva (YeniKapı):* New Gate
punto	point •*de todo punto:* in every respect
puntada	pneumonia
pusulá	it. *bosolla,* small box for a compass, by extension the small print on the compass •*todo modo de pusula ke le mandavan:* any bill they sent him

R

raatlik	ott. راحتلك, *râhatlık,* quietude; ease
rabbanim	רַבָּנִים, *rabbanim,* the "collectivity" of rabbis
rabbanith	רַבָּנִית, *rabbanith,* rabbi's wife
rabbanuth	רַבָּנוּת, *rabbanuth,* rabbinate, rabbinic tenure
raki	ott. راقى, *rakı,* same as *'arak,* anise flavored alcoholic Turkish drink
rasha'	רָשָׁע, *rasha',* wicked
rashi	acronym for Rabbi Shelomo Yishaki whose commentaries on the Bible and the Talmud are printed in a small size Hebrew type. He is not the inventor of the *Rashi* script.
rasti	pers.-ott. راست, *râst,* name of a musical mode
ráta	installment •*pagar en ratas:* pay in installments,

	Ne. 467a
rav	רַב, *rav,* title of rabbi in Babylon •*rav ha-zaken:* senior rabbi; head of the rabbinic court
ray	ott. رعى, *ra'y,* submission •*azer dar ray:* cause to accept submission, Rd. 950a
red	net
regalada	most cherished •*ija regalada:* only daughter
reklámo	appeal
relidjyozo	religious; observant
relumbrar	illuminate, glow •*relumbrar del Dyo:* God's radiance
rema	oar •*azer la rema:* to row with oars
rendia	he yielded, auctioned off •*los rendia el por la ensendedura:* he auctioned them off for kindling, Ne. 473c-474a
reprezentado	for *prezentado,* introduced
resparte	same as *desparte,* Ne. 477a
respartado	for *despartado,* separate
restaron	remain •*los livros ke restaron:* the left-over, unsold books
retornar	return; revive
reushidá	it. *riuscità,* success
reushir	it. *riuscire,* to succeed
revi'i	רְבִיעִי, *revi'i,* fourth person called to the Tora
rezokonto	it. *resoconto,* financial report, account
ribbi	רִבִּי, *ribbi,* pronunciation of *rabbi* according to the Palestinian as well as the Sephardic traditions
ridoma	bottle
rijir	to rule, administer
ríjo	administration, management; event, occurrence; habit •*mal rijida:* neglected
riza	ott. ردا', *ridâ,* large kerchief, Rd. 959a
rodeo	turn, twist •*asentado de rodeos:* sitting on, involved in deals
royo	red haired
rubi	variation from *rabbi,* elementary school teacher

rubisim	double plural of *rubi*
rubyes	gold coins
Rumelia	tr. *Rumeli,* European Turkey
rutbe	ott. رتبه, *rütbe,* rank •*rutbelis:* people with rank

S

sa'ar	צַעַר, *sa'ar,* worry; fear, hardship
sade	pers.-ott. ساده, *sâde,* simple
Saatli Djami	tr. *Saatlı Câmi,* name of a mosque with a clock
sach kiran	tr. *saçkıran,* for 'αλωπηκία, *alopecia,* loss of hair, leaving bald patches, Ne. 487a
sachma	tr. *saçma,* buckshot, bullet
sadisfaksyon	see *satisfaksyon*
sakat	ott. سقط, *sakat,* handicapped
sal	salt •*kon sal i pimyenta i limon:* well-seasoned, exaggerated
saltanat	ott. سلطنت, *saltanat,* rulership; splendor, pomp, showiness
salvado	bran
salyendo	coming out •*salyendo de Pesah:* at the end of Passover
samarra	tr. *samur,* sable •*samarrado:* covered with fur
samayi	see *semayi*
sambashuga	port. *sanguessuga,* leech; *sandjirguela* from sp. *sanguijuela,* is used in Istanbul
sarraf	ott. صرّاف, *sarraf,* money-changer; banker •*sarrafbashi:* chief banker
sarla	for *saldra,* will get out
satan	שָׂטָן, *satan*, the devil
satisfaksyon	(also *sadisfaksyon)* satisfaction, (satisfactory) explanation
savaná	bedsheet
sayo	cape, Ne. 500a, Rc. 126
sebeb	ott. سبب, *sebeb,* cause, reason; pretext •*por mi sebeb:* because of me

sedaka צְדָקָה, *sedaka,* charity

seder סֵדֶר, *seder,* order, arrangement

Sedes a locality on the outskirts of Salonika

sehora for שְׁחוֹרָה, *shehora,* black (bile), sadness, worry, anger •*tomarse sehora:* to be upset •*echar sehora sovre uno:* blame someone; make someone angry, Ne. 502b

sekolo it. *secolo,* century

sekretina keeping matters in secret, secrecy

Selanikyoto Θεσσαλονικηότης, Thessalonican, Salonican

Selihoth סְלִיחוֹת, *selihoth,* penitentiary prayers

selo jealousy; zeal •*se armaron de selo:* they were moved by extreme zeal

semayi ar.-ott. سماعي, *semâî,* Turkish musical rhythmic pattern

sena meal

sepelear for *pelearse*, fight; argue

ser pers.-ott. سر, *ser,* head •*Ser Askyer Pasha:* commander-in-chief; minister of war

serbes pers.-tr. سربست, *serbest,* free •*serbes, serbes:* in complete freedom

Seres a town about hundred miles East of Salonika

serkdezentim fr. *cercle des intimes,* circle of intimate friends

sermé pers.-ott. سرمايه, *sermaye,* capital, Ne. 508b

serner sift •*sernedor:* "sifter"

servisyal servant

se'uda סְעוּדָה, *se'uda,* meal; festive meal, banquet

sevada barley

sevara סְבָרָה, *sevara,* opinion

sevda pers.-ott. سودا, *sevdâ,* love, passion, *sevdâlı,* in love; an admirer

seventeria δυσέντερος, dysentery

shadetname ott-pers. شهادتنامه, *şehadetnâme,* document of attestation, certificate

shaka tr. *şaka,* joke

shakekera headband for a *shakeka* or migraine headache

shali	tr. *alpaka*
shaliah	שָׁלִיחַ, *shaliah,* messenger; travelling fundraiser
shalom	שָׁלוֹם, *shalom,* peace •*leh le-shalom:* go in peace
shalvar	aram. סַרְבָּל, *sarbal,* pers.-tr. شلوار, *şalvar,* baggy trousers
shamaladja	tr. *Şamalaca,* embroidered red *(alaca)* fabric from Damascus, Ne. 532a
shammash	שַׁמָּשׁ, *shammash* or *sammas,* attendant; beadle
shanish	see *shaynish*
sharki	tr. *şarkı,* song
sharope	from ar. شرب, sp. *jarabe,* homemade sugar candy
shastre	tailor, seamstress •*shastreria:* tailoring
shashireado	tr. *şaşırmak,* confused
Shavu'oth	שָׁבוּעוֹת, *shavu'oth,* along with *Pesah* and *Sukkoth* constitute the 3 pilgrimage festivals
shaynish	pers.-tr. شاهنش, *şahniş*, bay window on an enclosed balcony, Ne. 533a, Rd. 1046a
shedim	שֵׁדִים, *shedim,* male demons; evil spirits
ShehulIslam	ott. شيخ الاسلام, *Şeyhülislâm,* top Muslim dignitary next to the Grand Vizier
shekerdji	tr. *şekerci,* candy-store
shelihuth	שְׁלִיחוּת, *shelihuth,* fund-raising mission
shemle	ott. شمله, *şemle,* wrapper around the head, turban, Rd. 1056a
shena	it. *scena,* scene
sheni	שֵׁנִי, *sheni,* second (person called to the Tora)
sheshireado	see *shashireado*
shetaroth	שְׁטָרוֹת, *shetaroth,* documents
shethi va-'erev	שְׁתִי וָעֵרֶב, *shethi va-'erev.* The notion of *shethi va-'erev* is based on *Leviticus 13:48* as interpreted in *Hullin 109b.* Commonly, it refers to a non-Jewish custom to be avoided.
Shevat	שְׁבָט, *Shevat,* Hebrew month around February
Shevi'i	שְׁבִיעִי, *shevi'i,* seventh •*Shevi'i shel Pesah:* the seventh day of Passover
shilin	shilling

Shio — Χίος, the island of Chios in the Aegean Sea
shire ha-goyim — שִׁירֵי־הַגּוֹיִם, *shire-ha-goyim,* songs of the gentiles
shirilan — tr. *şirlan*, from *şırlağan*, sesame-oil, Rd. 1061-64 •*shirilan takumu:* a bunch of hooligans
Shirin — or *Shirun,* name of a locality
shirit — ott. شريط, *şerit,* ribbon •*shirit aladjali:* striped ribbon •*shiritikos:* tiny ribbons
shiv'á — שִׁבְעָה, *shiv'á,* seven •*shiv'á berahoth,* colloquial for *shév'a berahoth,* the Seven Blessings chanted at weddings •*shiv'á tove a-'ir* also known as *la buena djente:* the Seven Honorable Citizens in a city, known for their impartiality acting as ombudsmen
shofar — שׁוֹפָר, *shofar*, ram's horn
shóhat — for שׁוֹחַד, *shohad,* bribe
shohet — שׁוֹחֵט, ritual slaughterer
shu bu — tr. *şu, bu,* this and that
shukyur — ott. شكر, *şükür,* gratitude, thanks •*chok shukyur*: many thanks (to God)
sidduk — צִדּוּק, *sidduk,* "declaring just" in the expression *sidduk (h)a-din* or "justification of the judgmement" chanted in a burial
sikkum — סִכּוּם, *sikkum,* amount
simman — סִמָּן, *simman,* sign; signal; hint
simyente — seed; basic capital
sinir — σύνορον, *sınır,* border
sini — pers.-ott. سينى, *sinî,* round metal tray, Rd. 1020b
sinyal — signal •*una sinyal, prima sinyal* are both fem. based on the Hebrew *oth* which is fem.
sira — aram. שׁוּרָא, *shura,* line, row •*en sira:* in a row, taking turns
sirma — tr. *sırma,* gold or silver embroidery
siryo — candelabrum
sobadji — tr. *sobacı*, stove-maker
sobrevyarse — become angry, Ne. 518a
sobrevyó — increased, expanded
socheta — also, *sosyeta,* it. *società,* association, company

socho	it. *socio,* associate
sochyeta	see *socheta*
sodjefto	subjected; under the influence of
sofá	small living room
sofer	סוֹפֵר*, scribe,* scribe
softá	*(*σοφιστής, a sophist?*),* tr. *softa,* bigot, fanatic
sofú	tr. *sofu,* pious; observant
soledad	loneliness •*ala soledad,* (with the *lamed* of Hebrew לְבַד) in solitude, alone
solevantamyento	upheaval
son	sound; tune, melody
sonaje	noise maker •*sonaje de teneke:* tin noise maker
sonar	prob. it. *suonare,* play a musical instrument
soplo	breath •*mankar el soplo:* out of breath, lack of basics
sorguch	tr. *sorguç*, crest, aigrette (worn on the head), Rd. 1028a
sos	שׂוֹשׂ*, sos,* rejoicing •*sos tasis:* you shall surely rejoice
soto	it. *sotto,* under •*soto eskrito:* written/mentioned below
soy	tr. *soy,* lineage; family •*soy djidyo:* does not mean "I am Jewish", but "of Jewish descent"
soydear	tr. *soymak,* rob
sual	ott. سؤال, *sual,* question •*sual haram:* asking is forbidden
sudesyo	prob. for *susedyo*, followed, resulted
sudéto	it. *suddetto,* above mentioned
súdito	subject, citizen
sukka	סֻכָּה*, sukka,* booth
sultana	ott. *feminine* of سلطان*, sultan,* here "queen"
sultuk	vest, Ne. 526a
suluk	tr. *soluk,* breath •*tomarse el suluk:* run out of breath, suffocate
sunnet	ott. سنّت *sünnet,* 1. *Sunna* or tradition of the Prophet 2. circumcision

surgun	tr. *sürgün,* exile
surgunluk	tr. *sürgünlük,* banishment
sutlach	tr. *sütlaç,* rice-pudding

T

ta'anith	תַּעֲנִית, *ta'anith,* fasting
tabahane	tr. طباقخانه, *tabakhâne,* tannery
tabur	tr. *tabur,* battalion
tabya	tr. *tabye,* fort; bastion, Rd. 1075b
tadjis	ott. تعجيز, *tâcîz,* causing embarrassment
tahsildar	ott. تحصيلدار, *tahsîldâr,* debt collector •*tahsi[l]darlik:* debt collection
takrir	ott. تقرير, *takrîr,* official note
taksar	to set aside, fix; tax
taksim	ott. تقسيم, *taksîm,* dividing into parts; instrumental improvisation in music •*son taksim:* final *taksim*
takya	tr. *takke, skull-cap* •*takyika:* a small skull-cap
tal a kual	such as, exactly as
talamo	θάλαμος, for חֻפָּה, *huppa,* wedding canopy
talmid	תַּלְמִיד, *talmid,* student •*talmid haham:* disciple of the sages, rabbinic student; scholar; layman with unusual rabbinic knowledge
Talmud	תַּלְמוּד, Talmud, but also "study" •*talmud lomar:* Scripture says •*beth sefer le-talmud Tora:* school for the study of Tora •*Talmud Tora ha-Gadol:* the Great *Talmud Tora*
tantela	fr. *dentelle,* lace
tanyedor	musician
tanyer	play an instrument •*tanyer shofar:* to blow the shofar
tarbush	pers.-tr. طربوش, *tarbuş,* skullcap
tarla	tr. *tarla,* field
tarzi	ott. طرز, *tarz,* mode, manner; style •*a tarzi de:* in the style of

tasdik	ott. تصديق, *tasdîk,* verification; certification; authentication
tash	tr. *taş,* stone
tavetname	ott. دعوتنامه, *dâvetnâme,* invitation
tayero	large, round and shallow platter, Ne. 544b
tazvirât	ott. تزويرات, *tazvîrât,* instigations, Rd.1172b
te'amim	טְעָמִים, *te'amim,* musical markers in the Bible
teblar	for *temblar,* shiver
tefillin	תְּפִלִּין, *tefillin,* phylacteries
tefilloth	תְּפִלּוֹת, *tefilloth,* prayers
tehuna	תְּכוּנָה, *tekhuna,* astronomy
teillim	תְּהִלִּים, *tehillim,* psalms; book of psalms
tehuppar	תְּכֻפַּר, *tehuppar,* will be forgiven
tel	tr. *tel,* wire; bolt (door)
te[m]blamyento	see *terretemblo*
tellal	ott. دلاّل/تلاّل , *dellal/tellal,* herald, towncrier; middleman, broker
temenna	ott. تمنّى, *temenna,* mideastern salute
tendjere	tr. *tencere,* saucepan •*tendjeriko:* small saucepan
tenekye	tr. *teneke,* tin •*kashikas de tenekye:* small tin boxes
terdjuman	ott. ترجمان, *tercüman,* fr. *dragoman,* aram. תַּרְגְּמָנָא, *turgemana,* interpreter; translator •*terdjumanlik:* act as an interpreter
terretemblo	(in spite of *teblar* for *tremblar),* earthquake
termentina	turpentine; wax
teskyere	ott. تذكره, *tezkere,* short written note, *memorandum*
tevá	תֵּבָה, *teva,* lectern in Sephardic synagogues similar to a *bima*
teveth	טֵבֵת, *Teveth,* Hebrew month around January
tevila	טְבִילָה, *tevila,* ritual bath
tidjaret	ott. تجارت, *ticâret,* business ; business court •*tidjaret mishlishi:* Chamber of Commerce
tikia	tuberculosis

tinya	sp. *tiña,* tinea, scald head, scalp ringworm
tish'a	תִּשְׁעָה, *tish'a,* nine •*tish'a be-ab:* ninth of *Av*
Togarma	תּוֹגַרְמָה, *Togarma,* Turkey, based on Gen. 10:3, also a Turkish coin
toka	turban
tokado	elaborate hairdo for married Sephardic women, Ne. 554b
tolondro	contusion, Ne. 555b
toma	take •*toma tu i dalo a Baruh,* Ne. 80c: indiscriminate squandering of funds
top	tr. *top,* bolt
tópa azir	for *tópa hazir,* finds ready, ready-made
Tophane	arsenal The name *Mehmet Pasha de Tophane* is a Ladino translation of the Turkish general known as *Tophaneli Mehmet Pasha.*
toran	unidentified word
torba	tr. *torba,* bag
tórna	for שׁוּב, *shuv,* again
tornero	it. *torna,* lathe, •*tornero:* lathe operator, Ne. 559a
tové-	see *shiv'a*
toyaka	tr. *toyka,* heavy club, cudgel, Rd. 1184a
trabizan	tr. *tırabzan,* railing, banister, Rd. 1175a, Ne. 560c/II
trae	see *trayer*
trapandja	distorted from tr. *tabandja,* gun
trasportar	it. *trasportare,* transport
travida	withdrawal of money, Ne. 564b
travon	violent pull
trayer	to bring •*ke le traya:* that it might bring
trazer	last •*trazer eskalon:* last step •*trazera dolor:* last (contraction)
trensa	braid, Ne. 565a
trimbuk	a torture press
tripi	*triparse*, to climb •*me tripi:* I climbed, Ne. 567a

trujon	see *turujon*
trushi	tr. *turşu,* pickle •*i lo azia trushi:* he drenched him like a pickle; he soaked him from head to toe
t"t	abbreviation for *talmud tora,* Hebrew school
tufek	tr. *tüfek,* gun, rifle
turkuesko	also, *trukuesko, trukesko,* various forms for Turkish
turujon	bump, swelling, Ne. 569c
tutun	tr. *tütün,* tobacco
tyerno	tender, soft •*korason tyerno:* a tender heart, good heart

U

uda	tr. *oda,* room
ulama	ott. عالم,*âlim,* pl. ʻعلما, *ülemâ,* Muslim scholars
ummoth	אֻמּוֹת, *ummoth,* nations; religious communities or *millets*
un/uno	one; same •*de un nombre:* of the same name •*de una:* simultaneously
usul	ott. أصل, *asl,* pl. أصول, *usûl,* root; method, procedure

V

vaftizó	βαφτίζω , he baptized
Vali	ott. والى, *Vâli,* governor
valide	ott. والده, *vâlide,* mother; (queen) mother
Vali Pasha	the Honorable *Vâli*
valuta	it. *valuta,* value
vapor	steamship
Vasil	Βασίλι, the proper name Basil
vava	grandmother
vazli	ott. وضعلى, *vaz'-lı,* with specific clauses
vazyar	for tr. *dökmek,* to empty •*vazyar letra:* cast/pour a printing font

vekyil	ott. وكيل, *vekîl,* agent, representative; proxy
vela	curtain
verdaderiya	(from *verdad)* truthfulness, veracity, Ne. 588b
vesile	ott. وسيله, *vesîle,* pretext
veta	thread •*veta de bril:* silver thread, Ne. 590a
vezne	ott. وزنه, *vezne,* cashier's office; balance gauge, Rd. 1228b
vida	life •*vidas* (based on Hebrew pl.): life
vidduy	וִדּוּי, *vidduy,* confession
vidjuh	ott. وجوه, *vücûh,* faces; important personalities
vilayet	ott. ولايت, *vilâyet,* province governed by a *Vâli*
vinir	to come •*vinir de la mano:* to be able
virguela	chicken pox
vishnada	tr. *vişne,* sour cherry drink
vizavi	fr. *vis-á-vis,* in front of
vizir	ott. وزير, *vezîr,* minister
Vlaho	Vlach
vukyela	ott. 'وكلا, *vükelâ,* pl. of *vekîl,* ministers; the cabinet

Y

yabandji	tr. *yabancı,* stranger, foreigner
Yah Ribbon	יָהּ רִבּוֹן עָלַם, *Yah Ribbon Alam,* first words of a *piyyut* in Aramaic by Rabbi Israel Najjara
yaka	tr. *yaka,* collar
yakrivennu	יַקְרִיבֶנּוּ, *yakrivennu,* "he shall offer it"
yaldizli	tr. *yaldızlı,* gilded
yamim	יָמִים, *yamim,* days •*mi-yamav:* "since his days", since he was born; ever •*yamim noraim:* Days of Awe
yámo	a call •*respondian al yamo:* they answered the call in kind
yapidji	tr. *yapıcı,* builder; handyman
yardan	tr. *gerdan,* necklace

yarim	tr. *yarım,* half, semi •*yarım kyavgir,* half-brick
yarsayat	Yiddish, *Yahrzeit* used in the Balkans, also, *yorsa*
yartimaches	tr. *yırtmaç,* "slit" in a garment
yashan	יָשָׁן, *yashan,* old • *kaal yashan,* Old Synagogue
yashmak	tr. *yaşmak,* veil
yastik	tr. *yastık,* pillow
yatagan	tr. *yatağan,* heavy, curved knife
yavedura	lock
yaver	pers.-tr. ياور, *yâver,* helper, assistant *aide-de-camp*
yavriko	tr. *yavru,* baby; •*yavrikos:*cubs
yedek	tr. *yedek,* substitute
yemini	tr. *yemeni,* cotton head kerchief
yenicheri	pers.-tr. ينيچري, *yeniçeri,* "new soldier", Janissary
yeni chikma	tr. *yeni çıkma,* newly emerged; rookie, inexperienced
yerusha	יְרוּשָׁה, *yerusha,* inheritence
yeshiva	יְשִׁיבָה, *yeshiva,* rabbinic academy, *Yeshiva*
yethomim	יְתוֹמִים, *yethomim,* orphans
yevadura	see *yavedura*
yevar	to carry •*yevar sa'ar:* experience worry, be worried, go through hardship
yok	tr. *yok,* absence; there is not •*yok paasina:* for nothing, almost *gratis*
yom geulla	יוֹם־גְּאֻלָּה, *yom geulla,* day of redemption
yorti	γιορτή, tr. *yortu,* feast day
yufta	tr. *yafta*, placard around the neck describing a crime
yulle	tr. *gülle,* canon ball, bullet
Yumuldjina	for tr. *Gümülcine*
yurdi	tr. *kürdi,* long coat, Ne. 320c •*yurdi chilibi:* gentleman's *yurdi* •*yurdi ensamarrado:* fur lined *yurdi* •*yurdi nafe*: *yurdi* lined with fur from the belly of an animal ,Rd. 860a •*yurdi sade:* plain *yurdi*
yurultu	tr. *gürültü,* noise, uproar

yuz	tr. *yüz,* one hundred •*yuzbashi* for *yüzbaşı,* captain (military)
yuzlik	tr. *yüzlük,* currency worth one hundred (*gurush* or liras), Rd. 1267b

Z

zahmet	ott. زحمت, *zahmet,* effort, trouble
zahuth	זְכוּת, *zahuth,* merit
zaptie	tr. ضبطيّه, *zaptiyye,* gendarme
zarzavat	pers.-tr. سبزوات/زرزوات, *sebzevat/zarzavat,* vegetables
zemiroth	זְמִירוֹת, *zemiroth,* religious poem
zenuth	זְנוּת, *zenuth,* adultery •*zenuth esheth ish:* adultery with a married woman
zera	זֶרַע, *zera',* seed •*una zera de anchura:* the width of a seed
ziafet	ott. ضيافت, *ziyâfet,* banquet
zibil	ott. سبيل, *sebîl,* public fountain with free access to water •*fi sabil-illah,* for the sake of Allah
zo(h)ar	זֹהַר, *Zohar* or Book of Splendor
zonoth	זוֹנוֹת, *zonoth,* prostitutes

Works Consulted

Works Consulted by Editors for Introduction and Annotations

Anastassiadou-Dumont, Méropi. *Salonique, 1830–1912: Une ville ottomane à l'âge des réformes*. Leiden: Brill, 1997.

Baer, Marc. *The Dönme: Jewish Converts, Muslim Revolutionaries, and Secular Turks*. Stanford, CA: Stanford University Press, 2010.

Barkey, Karen. *The Empire of Difference: The Ottomans in Comparative Historical Perspective*. New York: Cambridge University Press, 2008.

Benbassa, Esther, ed. *Haim Nahum: A Sephardic Chief Rabbi in Politics, 1892–1923*. Tuscaloosa: University of Alabama Press, 1995.

———. *Une diaspora sépharade en transition: Istanbul, XIXe–XXe siècle*. Paris: Cerf, 1993.

Benbassa, Esther, and Aron Rodrigue. *Sephardi Jewry: A History of the Judeo-Spanish Community, 14th–20th Centuries*. Berkeley: University of California Press, 2000.

———, eds. *A Sephardi Life in Southeastern Europe: The Autobiography and Journal of Gabriel Arié, 1863–1939*. Seattle: University of Washington Press, 1998.

Ben-Naeh, Yaron. "Hebrew Printing Houses in the Ottoman Empire." In *Jewish Journalism and Printing Houses in the Ottoman Empire and Modern Turkey*, edited by Gad Nassi, 73–96. Istanbul: ISIS, 2001.

Besso, Henry V. *Ladino Books in the Library of Congress; a Bibliography*. Washington: Library of Congress, 1964.

Borovaya, Olga. *Modern Ladino Culture: Press, Belles Lettres and Theater in the Late Ottoman Empire*. Bloomington: Indiana University Press, 2011.

Cohen, Julia Phillips. "Fashioning Imperial Citizens: Sephardi Jews and the Ottoman State, 1856–1912." PhD diss., Stanford University, 2008.

Cohen, Julia Phillips, and Sarah Abrevaya Stein. "Sephardic Scholarly Worlds: Toward a Novel Geography of Modern Jewish History." *Jewish Quarterly Review* 100, no. 3 (2010): 349–84.

Davis, Natalie Zemon. *Women on the Margins: Three Seventeenth-Century Lives*. Cambridge, MA: Harvard University Press, 1995.

Emmanuel, Isaac S. *Matsevot Saloniki: be-Tseruf toledot hayehem shel gedolei kehilah*. Jerusalem: Kiryat-Sefer, 1963.

Faroqhi, Suraiya. *Subjects of the Sultan: Culture and Daily Life in the Ottoman Empire*. London: Tauris, 2000.

Fleischer, Cornell H. *Bureaucrat and Intellectual in the Ottoman Empire: The Historian Mustafa Ali (1541–1600)*. Princeton, NJ: Princeton University Press, 1986.

Fleming, K. E. *Greece—A Jewish History*. Princeton, NJ: Princeton University Press, 2008.

Fortna, Benjamin C. "Education and Autobiography at the End of the Ottoman Empire." *Die Welt des Islams* 14, no. 1 (2001): 1–31.

Franco, Moïse. *Essai sur l'histoire des Israélites de l'Empire Ottoman depuis les origines jusqu'à nos jours*. Paris: Librairie A. Durlacher, 1897.

Gaon, Moshe David. *Ha-'ittonut be-ladino: Bibliyografyah. Shelosh meot 'ittonim*. Jerusalem: Ben Zvi Institute, 1965.

Ginio, Alisa Mehuyas. "La Familia Ginio (Chinillo, Chiniello, Tchenio, Tchnyo, Ginio): de Aragón a Salónica y Jerusalén." *Miscelánea de estudios árabes y hebraicos* 41, no. 2 (1992): 137–49.

Gounaris, Basil. "Salonica." *Review* 16, no. 4 (1993): 499–518.

Guillon, Hélène. "Le Journal de Salonique, un instrument de la modernization d'une communauté juive dans l'empire ottoman (1895-1910)." PhD diss., Ecole Pratique de Hautes Etudes, Paris, 2011.

Jackson, Maureen. *Mixing Musics: Turkish Jewry and the Urban Landscape of a Sacred Song*. Stanford, CA: Stanford University Press, forthcoming.

Jerusalmi, Isaac. *From Ottoman Turkish to Ladino: The Case of Mehmet Sadık Rifat Pasha's Risâle-i Ahlâk and Judge Yehezkel Gabbay's Buen Dotrino. Enlarged Original Texts in Ottoman Turkish and Rashi Scripts, with Face-to-Face Transliterations, Glossaries and an Introduction*. Cincinnati: Ladino Books, 1990. www.stanford.edu/group/mediterranean/seph_project/index.html.

———. *Kanun Name de penas: Letras de muestro sinyor El Rey*. Cincinnati: Sephardic Beth Shalom Congregation and Hebrew Union College, 1975. www.stanford.edu/group/mediterranean/seph_project/index.html.

———. *Reuven Eliyahu Yisrael's traduksyon livre de las poezias ebraikas de Rosh ha-Shana i Kippur, 5670, and the Six Selihoth of the 5682 Edition: Text in Rashi Characters and in Transliteration*. Cincinnati: Ladino Books, 1989. www.stanford.edu/group/mediterranean/seph_project/index.html.

———. *The Selihot of the Sepharadim: Hebrew Text and Ladino Translation of the Vienna 1865 Alschech Edition. Text Enlarged and Transcribed with an Introduction and Ladino-English Glossary of Select Lexical Items*. Cincinnati: Ladino Books, 1990. www.stanford.edu/group/mediterranean/seph_project/index.html.

———. *The Song of Songs in the Targumic Tradition: Vocalized Aramaic Text with Facing English Translation and Ladino Versions*. The Paraphrasis Caldaica, Amsterdam 1664, Avraham Asa, Constantinople 1744, Yerushalmi, Istanbul 1992. Cincinnati: Ladino Books, 1993. www.stanford.edu/group/mediterranean/seph_project/index.html.

Kafadar, Cemal. "Self and Others: The Diary of a Dervish in Seventeenth-Century Istanbul and First-Person Narratives in Ottoman Literature." *Studia Islamica* 69 (1989): 121–50.

Kayserling, Mayer. *Biblioteca Española-Portugueza-Judaica and Other Studies in Ibero-Jewish Bibliography*. New York: Ktav, 1971.

Kerem, Yitzchak. "The Europeanization of the Sephardic Community of Salonika." In *From Iberia to Diaspora: Studies in Sephardic History and Culture*, edited by Yedida K. Stillman and Norman A. Stillman, 58–74. Leyden: Brill, 1999.

Lehmann, Matthias B. *Ladino Rabbinic Literature and Ottoman Sephardic Culture*. Bloomington: Indiana University Press, 2005.

Lévy, Sam. *Salonique à la fin du XIXe siècle*. Istanbul: ISIS, 2000.

Lewis, Bernard. "First-Person Narrative in the Middle East." In *Middle Eastern Lives: The Practice of Biography and Self-Narrative*, edited by Martin Kramer, 20–34. Syracuse: Syracuse University Press, 1991.

Loewenthal, Robyn K., "Elia Carmona's Autobiography: Judeo-Spanish Popular Press and Novel Publishing Milieu in Constantinople, Ottoman Empire, circa 1860–1932." PhD diss., University of Nebraska, 1984.

Lowenthal, Marvin, ed. and trans. *The Memoirs of Glückel of Hameln*. New York: Schocken, 1977.

Maftirim: Türk-Sefarad Sinagog İlahileri. Turkish-Sephardic Synagogue Hymns. Kantes De Sinagoga Turko-Sefardi. Istanbul: Gözlem Gazetecilik Basın ve Yayın, 2009.

Maimon, Salomon. *Solomon Maimon: An Autobiography*. Urbana: University of Illinois Press, 2001.

Mazower, Mark. *Salonica, City of Ghosts: Christians, Muslims, and Jews, 1430–1950*. New York: Alfred A. Knopf, 2005.

Modena, Leone, and Mark R. Cohen. *The Autobiography of a Seventeenth-Century Venetian Rabbi: Leon Modena's Life of Judah*. Princeton, NJ: Princeton University Press, 1988.

Modiano, Mario S. *Ha-mehune Modillano: The Genealogical Story of the Modiano Family from 1570 to Our Days*. Athens: M. Modiano, 2000.

Molho, Michael. *Matsevot Bet ha-ʿalmin shel yehudei Saloniki*. Tel Aviv: Makhon le-heker Yahadut Saloniki, 1974.

———. *Usos y costumbres de los Sefardíes de Salónica*. Madrid: Instituto Arias Montano, 1950.

Molho, Rena. "Les Juifs de Salonique, 1856–1919: Une communauté hors norme." PhD diss., Université de Strasbourg, 1997.

———. *Salonica and Istanbul: Social, Political and Cultural Aspects of Jewish Life*. Istanbul: ISIS, 2005.

Moseley, Marcus. *Being for Myself Alone: Origins of Jewish Autobiography*. Stanford, CA: Stanford University Press, 2006.

Naar, Devin. "Jewish Salonica and the Making of the 'Jerusalem of the Balkans,' 1890-1943." PhD diss., Stanford University, 2011.

Nehama, Joseph. *Dictionnaire du Judéo-espagnol*. Madrid: Instituto Benito Arias Montano, 1977.

———. *Histoire des Israélites de Salonique*. 7 vols. Salonique: Librairie Molho—Communauté Israélite de Thessalonique, 1935–78.

Olgun, İbrahim. "Aynı Kaynakçası." *Türk Dili* 25, no. 246 (1972): 662–82.

Özdemir, Bülent. "Using Consular Reports as Data Source: A Study on the Population of Salonica in the 1840s." In *The Great Ottoman-Turkish Civilization*, edited by Kemal Çiçek, 549–54. Ankara: Yeni Türkiye, 2000.

Pamuk, Şevket. *A Monetary History of the Ottoman Empire*. Cambridge, UK: Cambridge University Press, 2000.

Poids, mesures, monnaies et cours du change dans les principales localités de l'Empire Ottoman à la fin du 19e siècle. Istanbul: ISIS, 2002.

Recanati, David. *Zikhron Saloniki: Gedulatah ve-hurbanah shel Yerushalayim de-Balkan*. 2 vols. Tel Aviv: ha-Va'ad le-hotsaat sefer Kehilat Saloniki, 1972–85.

Rodrigue, Aron. "Abraham de Camondo of Istanbul: The Transformation of Jewish Philanthropy." In *From East to West: Jews in a Changing Europe, 1750–1870*, edited by Frances Malino and David Sorkin, 46–56. Oxford: Blackwell, 1990.

———. *French Jews, Turkish Jews: The Alliance Israélite Universelle and the Politics of Jewish Schooling in Turkey, 1860–1925*. Bloomington: Indiana University Press, 1990.

———. *Guide to Ladino Materials in the Harvard College Library*. Cambridge, MA: Harvard College Library, 1992.

Romero, Elena. *La Creación literaria en lengua sefardí*. Madrid: MAPFRE, 1992.

Rozen, Minna. *The Last Ottoman Century and Beyond: The Jews in Turkey and the Balkans, 1808–1945*. 2 vols. Tel Aviv: Tel Aviv University Goldstein-Goren Diaspora Research Center, 2002.

Seroussi, Edwin. "Musikah osmanit be-kerev yehudei Saloniki." In *Ladinar: Mehkarim ba-sifrut, ba-musikah uva-historyah shel dovre ladino*, edited by Judith Dishon and Shmuel Refael, 79–92. Tel-Aviv: Makhon le-heker Yahadut Saloniki, 1998.

Shandler, Jeffrey. *Awakening Lives: Autobiographies of Jewish Youth in Poland Before the Holocaust*. New Haven, CT: Yale University Press, 2002.

Skolnik, Fred, and Michael Berenbaum, eds. *Encyclopaedia Judaica*. 22 vols. New York: Macmillan, 2007.

Socher, Abraham P. *The Radical Enlightenment of Solomon Maimon: Judaism, Heresy, and Philosophy*. Stanford, CA: Stanford University Press, 2006.

Stanislawski, Michael. *Autobiographical Jews: Essays in Jewish Self-Fashioning*. Seattle: University of Washington Press, 2004.

Stein, Sarah Abrevaya. *Making Jews Modern: The Yiddish and Ladino Press in the Russian and Ottoman Empires*. Bloomington: Indiana University Press, 2004.

Stillman, Norman A. *Sephardi Religious Responses to Modernity*. Luxembourg: Harwood Academic Publishers, 1995.

Swanson, Glen W. "The Ottoman Police." *Journal of Contemporary History* 7, nos. 1–2 (1972): 243–60.

Terzioğlu, Derin. "Man in the Image of God in the Image of the Times: Sufi Self-Narratives and the Diary of Niyazi Mısri (1618–1694)." *Studia Islamica* 94 (2002): 139–65.

Trivellato, Francesca. *The Familiarity of Strangers: The Sephardic Diaspora, Livorno, and Cross-Cultural Trade in the Early Modern Period*. New Haven, CT: Yale University Press, 2009.

Vakalopoulos, Apostolos E. *History of Macedonia, 1354–1833*. Translated by Peter Megann. Thessaloniki: Institute for Balkan Studies, 1973.

Veinstein, Gilles, ed. *Salonique, 1850–1918: La "Ville des Juifs" et le réveil des Balkans*. Série mémoires, no. 12. Paris: Editions Autrement, 1992.

Wengeroff, Pauline. *Memoirs of a Grandmother: Scenes from the Cultural History of the Jews of Russia in the Nineteenth Century*. Translated by Shulamit S. Magnus. Stanford, CA: Stanford University Press, 2010.

Works Consulted by Translator

Asa, Avraham, trans. *Sefer Kitvei ha-Kodesh: Torah Neviim u-Khetuvim ʿim haʿatakah sefaradit*. 2 vols. Vienna: F. Di-Shmid ve-shutafo Y. Bosh, 1841. First published 1739–44 by Yonah Ashkenazi.

Bloch, Oscar, and Walther von Wartburg. *Dictionnaire étymologique de la langue française*. 2nd ed. Paris: Presses Universitaires de France, 1950.

Brown, Francis, S. R. Driver, et al., eds. *A Hebrew and English Lexicon of the Old Testament*. Oxford: Clarendon Press, 1939.

Coromines, Joan. *Diccionario crítico etimológico de la lengua castellana*. Berna: Francke, 1954.

de Biberstein-Kazimirski, Albert. *Dictionnaire arabe-français: Contenant toutes les racines de la langue arabe*. 2 vols. Paris: G.-P. Maisonneuve, 1960.

De Gámez, Tamar, ed. *Simon and Schuster's International Dictionary: English/Spanish—Spanish/English*. New York: Simon and Schuster, 1973.

Devellioğlu, Ferit. *Osmanlıca-Türkçe Ansiklopedik Lûgat: Eski ve Yeni Harflerle*. Ankara: Doğuş Matbaası, 1962.

Diccionario de la lengua española. 18th ed. Madrid: Real Academia Española, 1956.

Even-Shoshan, Avraham. *Ha-milon he-hadash: Otsar shalem shel ha-lashon ha-ʿivrit*. Jerusalem: Kiryat Sefer, 1980.

———. *Konkordantsyah hadashah le-Tora, Neviim, u-Khetuvim: Otsar leshon ha-Mikra-ʿivrit va-aramit*. Jerusalem: Kiryat Sefer, 1980.

Eyüboğlu, İsmet Zeki. *Türk Dilinin Etimoloji Sözlüğü*. Istanbul: Sosyal Yayınlar, 1998.

Glare, P. G. W. *Oxford Latin Dictionary*. Oxford: Clarendon Press, 2000.

Grandsaignes d'Hauterive, Robert. *Dictionnaire des racines des langues européennes*. Paris: Larousse, 1949.

Jastrow, Marcus. *A Dictionary of the Targumim, the Talmud Babli and Yerushalmi, and the Midrashic Literature*. New York: Pardes, 1950.

JPS Hebrew-English Tanakh: The Traditional Hebrew Text and the New JPS Translation. 2nd ed. Philadelphia: Jewish Publication Society, 1999.

Juhasz, Esther, ed. *Sephardi Jews in the Ottoman Empire: Aspects of Material Culture*. Jerusalem: Israel Museum, 1990.

Klein, Ernest. *A Comprehensive Etymological Dictionary of the Hebrew Language for Readers of English*. Jerusalem: Carta, 1987.

Liddell, Henry George, Robert Scott, et al., eds. *A Greek-English Lexicon*. 9th ed. Oxford: Clarendon Press, 1953.

Little, William, H. W. Fowler, et al. *The Oxford Universal Dictionary on Historical Principles*. 3rd ed. Oxford: Clarendon Press, 1955.

Mirambel, André. *Petit dictionnaire français—grec moderne et grec moderne-français*. Paris: G.-P. Maisonneuve, 1960.

Osmanlı'da Yahudi Kiyafetleri. Istanbul: Gözlem, 1999.

Oxford Paravia Italian Dictionary: English-Italian, Italian-English. 2nd ed. Turin: Paravia and Oxford University Press, 2001.

Özön, Mustafa Nihat. *Büyük Osmanlıca-Türkçe Sözlük*. Istanbul: İnkilâp Kitabevi, 1997.

Recuero, Pascual Pascual. *Diccionario básico ladino-español*. Barcelona: Ameller, 1977.

Redhouse, James William. *Redhouse Yeni Türkçe-İngilizce Sözlük*. Istanbul: Redhouse Yayınevi, 1974.

Schauffler, William G. *Divrei Leshon ha-Kodesh o Diksyonaryo de la lingua santa kon la deklarasyon de kada byervo en la lingua Sepharadith*. Istanbul: A. Churchill, 1855.

Stachowski, Stanislaw. *Studien über die arabischen Lehnwörter im Osmanisch-Türkischen*. Wroclaw: Ossolineum, 1975.

Taylor, James L. *A Portuguese-English Dictionary*. Stanford, CA: Stanford University Press, 1958.

Ya'ari, Avraham. *Reshimat sifrei ladino ha-nimtsaim be-vet ha-sefarim ha-leumi veha-universitai b-Irushalayim*. Jerusalem: Hevrah le-hotsaat sefarim 'al yad ha-Universita ha-'Ivri, 1934.

Index

Abbott, Bob. *See* Abot, Bob
Abbott, John. *See* Abot, Djon
Abbott, Sarito. *See* Abot, Sarito
Abdi Vali *Pasha*, 73
Abdul Aziz, Sultan, 128–29
Abdul Hamit II, Sultan, 45
Abdul Kyerim *Pasha* (general), 130
Abdul Medjid, Sultan, 68–76, 142–48
Abdulkerim Nadir *Pasha*, 130n147
Abdur Rahman *Bey*, 140
Abot, Bob, 120
Abot, Djon, 72, 119, 120
Abot, Sarito, 123
acculturation, intra-Jewish, xxiv
Adjiman, Yeoshua, 12
Agha pasha, 44
Ahche Medjid, 138
Ahmed *Bey* (assistant administrator), 30–31
Ahmet *Bey* (army chief), 140
ailments and diseases, lii; alopecia, 19; kidney disease, 24; hemorrhoids, 119; pneumonia, 16–17; tuberculosis, 16–17. *See also* epidemics
Alatini, Dario, 69–71
Alatini, Karlo, 80, 82
Alatini, Moisé, 105. *See also* Alatini, Moizé; Alatini, Moshe; Allatini, Moïse
Alatini, Moizé, 59, 141; and the Alliance, 79, 80; conspiracy against, 64–65; and *Hesed 'Olam* Fund, 59, 62–66; interventions by, 67, 98, 101–5; as Sa'adi's benefactor, 66, 108–9, 141; and sultan's visit, 69, 75–76
Alatini, Moshe, 75. *See also* Alatini, Moisé; Alatini, Moizé; Allatini, Moïse
Aleksandro of Batemberg, 132
a-Levi, Chelebon, 5
a-Levi, Daout (David), lvi
a-Levi, Hayyim Sa'adi (Kitapchi Hayyim), xix, 96–97, 109
a-Levi, Rachel (Carmona), xxxv
a-Levi, *Rav* Moshe, 109
a-Levi, Sa'adi (namesake), 27
a-Levi, Yeuda (Yehuda Halevi; of Spain), 26
Alexander of Battenberg. *See* Aleksandro of Batemberg
al-Hasid family, 81
Alkalay, Yeuda, 25
Alkalay Yeshiva, 25, 56
Allatini, Dario, 69–71
Allatini, Karlo, 80, 82
Allatini, Moïse, xv, 16n31, 104n130; as a Franko, xxiv, xxviii, xxx; interventions by, xix; reform efforts of, xxx-xxxi, 60n73, 92n119. *See also* Alatini, Moisé; Alatini, Moizé; Allatini, Moshe
Allatini, Moshe ben Eliezer. *See* Allatini, Moïse; Alatini, Moisé; Alatini, Moizé; Alatini, Moshe
Alliance Israélite Universelle (AIU), xv, xxv, xxviii, xxxi, xxxii, xxxv, 78–82; and Shelomo Fernandes, 59n72
alvorada, 114
Andjel, Daniel, 45–47
apartment rental, 121–22
Aragon Synagogue, 47, 86

archbishop, 54, 77
Arditi, *Rav* Shemuel (Shemuelachi), 10, 96, 134, 137
Ashkenazi, xxii, xxiii, 5
Ashkenazi, Avraam a-Levi, 5
Ashkenazi, Besalel a-Levi, xlv, 5–8
Ashkenazi, Yeuda a-Levi, 5
Ashkenazim, 19n33. *See also* Ashkenazi
astronomy, 140
auction, 121
authority, xli-xlii
autobiographies, xiii
Avigdor (*Rav*), 66
avlar, 115
Avraam ben Zonana, 66

Bab-i Ali [Sublime Porte—Istanbul], 109
bands (musicians), 70, 71, 73, 74
banking, 12, 33–35, 59, 120
banquets, 34, 77–78
Barzilay, Aaron, 24–25, 90
baskets, 6
bath, public, 18
bazaar, 20
beadles, 27, 36; as messengers, 14, 19, 25, 33–34, 56; as town criers, 18
beards, 50, 117
Ben Ardut, 78
Ben Rubi, Shemuel, 102–5, 108
Ben Sira (*The Wisdom of Ben Sira*), 37
Beraha, *Rav* Moshe, 10
Berlin Congress [1878], 132
Besh Chinar, 69, 71–73, 75
Bible, quotations from: Deuteronomy 24:10, 22; Ecclesiastes 1:4, 59; Esther 3:13, 100; 6:13, 89; Exodus 32:26, 11, 99; 32:34, 96; Genesis 4:14, 35; 7:11, 101; Isaiah 6:7, 19, 21; 40:3, 59; Job 3:3, 97; Leviticus 1:3, 51; Malachi 1:4, 107; Numbers 22:28, 96; Proverbs 19:21, 111; Psalms 11:6, 101; 20:9, 141
Bible, study of, 37
Bibles, printed, 38
Bikkur Holim committee (fund), 57, 60, 61, 65
birth date, knowledge of, 3
Bitola. *See* Monastir
Bloody Tower, 45. See also *Torre Blanka*; White Tower
Blunt, John, 120–21
bribery, 31–32, 48
Bula Miryam, 37
Bulgaria, 130, 132

candles, 11, 14
care for the poor, 57, 60, 74–75, 81–82, 134–35
cats, 39–40
Cazès, David, 80
cemetery, 140
Cercle des Intimes, 108
chamber of commerce, 73
Chataldja, 133
Chavush Manastir, 102
chief rabbi: in Constantinople, *see* Constantinople, and chief rabbinate; in Istanbul, *see* Istanbul, and chief rabbinate; in Salonica, 11, 29, 60, 74, 101–3, 108, 126, 134–35
cigarette case, 76
cigarettes, xxviii, 96
city planning, 139
class distinctions, xxv
class, social, 6, 11, 12, 94, 95, 112–13, 139
clothing and dress, xxxiv-xxxv, 17, 118; European-style uniforms, xxiv, 45–47; fur, 16–18, 112–13, 114, 117; maidens', 114; men's, 112–13; and sultan's visit, 70–71; women's, 17, 49–50, 113–14. *See also* robes
coffee and coffeehouses, xxxvii, 13, 20, 94, 95
collection boxes, 86–88
confessionary prayers, 137
Constantinople, 12, 44, 128, 131; and chief rabbinate, 92, 109, 134–35, 137; imperial decrees from, 49, 60n73, 66, 68, 109–10, 119, 135; as seat of government, 12, 34, 56, 66, 109. *See also* Istanbul
consuls, xlii, 9; funerals of, 125–27; intervention of, 14–15, 23, 103, 106,

120–21; massacre of, 122–24; sultan's visit and, 73, 73, 76
conversion to Islam, 36, 122
correspondence. *See* mail delivery
corruption, 32, 56–59
council, 58–59
counterfeit money, 62
Crémieux, Adolphe, 79
Crete, 132–33
curses, 11, 12, 23, 34
customs, naming of children, 6, 9

dancing, 32, 50–51, 115, 117
Danon, Israel, 80
Danube, 130
dates (calendar), 3
daughters versus sons, 53
day of *El Pishkado*, 23
Days of Awe, 24, 26, 90
death, following a dispute, 135
death by upset, 24
death penalty, 30
delivery, 22
Denmark, 134
depilation, 50–51, 114–15
devil, 39
dietary laws, 122n142
Dimo[ti]ko, 133
diplomats, 76. *See also* consuls
diseases. *See* ailments and diseases
Djemre, 133
Djenyo, Yaakov, 11
Djurnal Yisraelita, 58, 92–93
dogs, xxx, xxxvi, 9, 41–42
door, secret. *See* secret door
doors, hidden, xxxiv
drought, 100
drunkenness, 20, 42–43, 118

earthquake, 32
Edhem *Pasha*, 133
education, xxix-xxx. *See also* schools
Egypt, 40
Egyptian Market, 69
El Avenir, 112
Eldad a-Dani, 37
elementary school, 35
Emanuel ben Rubi, 66
embarrassment, 63
emissaries from Palestine, 100
enforcement. *See* power relations, and enforcement; punishments
England, 131
epidemics, 42; cholera, 52–53; dysentery, 61; plague (bubonic), 38–43
Es Hayyim printing press, 112
Es Hayyim quarter, 47
Eshref *Pasha*, 125, 126
ethnic diversity (in Salonica), xxxiii-xxxiv
Europe, 66, 119, 127, 128, 130, 131
European intervention, 23
European quarter, xxxi, 9, 47–48, 66
euthanasia (smothering), 43
excommunication, xxxviii-xxxix, 13, 56; exhaustion of, 111; by *Rav* Shaul Molho, xx, 11, 14–15, 19, 22, 24, 27–29, 34; of Sa'adi, xiv, xix, 27–29, 40, 99–101, 107. See also *herem*
extortion, 30, 48
Ezrati, Moshe, 41
Ezrati, Yusef, 37

falaka, 23, 36–37, 43
Faradji, Danielucho, 30, 83–86
Faradji, Hayyim, 107
Faradji, Menahem, 33
fasting, bridal, 51, 116
fear, liii, 13, 19, 41–42, 101, 141, 142; of fanaticism, 10–16. *See also* frightened to death
feasts. *See* banquets; weddings, feasts after
Ferdinand, Prince, 132
Fernandes, David, 76
Fernandes, Djon, 76
Fernandes, Ortensya, 76
Fernandes, Shelomo (Salomon), xxx, 59, 68, 69, 75
Fernandes brothers, 29
financial reporting, 58, 65
fire: of 1839, 47–48; of 1890, 47, 138–39; Skilich (1856), 66–68, 120
firemen, 138

firman, 58, 60, 108, 128–29
Fisherman's Synagogue, 28
flour mills, 85
folk religion, xxx
foodstuffs: cheese, 7; cheese pie, 6–7; cherries, 7; chicken, 53; cookies, 7; eggs, 6; *enchusa*, 6; goose, 8; Jordan almonds, 50–51, 115; pumpkin seeds, 113; rice pudding, 6. *See also* banquets; coffee and coffeehouses; meals; weddings, feasts after
Frankos, xxiii-xiv, xxx, 29; relations with other Jews, 48
fraternity, mutual religious, 125
Freemasonry, 9
French, 60, 75, 78
frightened to death, 8, 11. *See also* fear
Fund for Orphans and Widows, 136
fund-raising campaign, 81
funerals, 54, 125–27

Gabbay, Yehezkel, 92, 109
Gabbay *efendi*, Jak, 135
gabela, 11
gabelle, 56–58, 92
games, 117–18
Gatenyo, *Rav* Avraam, 7, 10, 16, 39, 49, 96, 106; beginning of rabbinate and dismissal, 134–36; as community representative, 126; and *Hesed 'Olam* Fund, 59, 62, 64; as Sa'adi's benefactor, 109, 141; as wedding guest, 77
Gatenyo, Shemuel, 135
Gazeta de Viena (El *Koreo de Viena*), 108
gematria, 110
Gemiluth Hasadim commission, 88
Gemiluth Hasadim printing press, 88–90
gender norms, xxxv, xxxvi, 53
General Assembly, 60
gentiles, imitation of. *See* imitation of the gentiles
gestures: hugging, 37, 51, 68; kissing, 37, 51, 115; kissing the hand, li, 15, 50, 115; oriental salute, 74; slapping the forehead, 7
gevirim, xl-xli, 11–12, 14, 17, 49, 56; as intermediary in punishment, 20–21, 23, 27, 28, 30, 43
gevirin, 11, 29
gifts, by the sultan, 75–76
gimatriya. See *gematriya*
governor general, 76
Great *Talmud Tora*, xxxi, 13, 82; choir of, 90–91; as communal gathering place, 11, 32, 67, 99, 100; and communal notification, 122, 137; as elementary school, 35, 60, 65; prayer services at, 137; punishment and confinement in, 31, 43, 54; rabbinic court of, 43, 56, 99; renovation of, 91; and Sa'adi's education, xlviii, 35–37
Greece, 132–34
Greeks, rebellion at Kasandra, 139–40
grooms (wedding), 21, 25, 49–51, 77, 115–18
Gueron, Rabbi Yakir, 58
Gumuldjina, 22. *See also* Komotini
gunpowder, 67
guns, 39–40

hahambashi, xl
Hamit II. *See* Abdul Hamid II
handyman, 34
Hasid, Yeuda, 8
Haskalah, xliv, xlix, 78n97
haskama, 122
Haten Bank, 34
Haten, Avraam, 34
Haten, Yaakov, 41
health care for the poor, 60
Hebrew, xliv, 78–79
Hekim, Shalom, 73
herem, xx. *See also* excommunication
Hesed 'Olam Fund, 59–65
Hippodrome (Constantinople), 44
Hirsch, Clara de, Baroness, 81
Hirsch, Maurice de, Baron, 80
Hirsh. *See* Hirsch
historiography, Sephardic, xxii
hodjas, 75
holidays, 6
Holy Scriptures, 37. *See also* Bible

home furnishings, 116, 118
horses, 14–15, 46, 71–73, 75, 85
hospital, 61, 81n107, 82
hospitality, 5
hunting, 13

Ignatief[f], Count Nicholas, 128
imitation of the gentiles (prohibition), xxxix, 33
insolvency, 34
insurance, 138–39
international protests, 31
Ioannina, xxxii, 107, 133
irade, 134
Ismail *Pasha*, 73
Istanbul, 33, 34, 44, 93, 113; and chief rabbinate, 10n14, 58, 92; Sephardim in, xlvi, xlix, 12, 58, 90. *See also* Constantinople
Italya Synagogue, xxxii
Izmir, xlvi, xlix, lii, 28, 99n80. *See also* Smyrna
Izzedinoglu, Murteza, 24, 32

Janissaries, 44–45
Jerusalem, lv, lvi, 24, 31, 47. *See also* Palestine
jewelry, 6, 77–78, 113
Jewish City Council, 94
Jewry, of Salonica, xiv
Jewry, Ottoman. *See* Ottoman Jewry
Jews, relations with Turks, 45

kaddish, 25
kal hamira, 122
Kamhi, Yaakov, 90
Kandiantis (alley), 18
Kapuano, Yaakov, 93
Karmona, Behor, 13
Kasandra (Cassandra), 139–41
kashrut, 122n142
kaymakam, 138
Kazes. *See* Cazès
ketubba, 77, 115
Khedive, 40
kiddush, 25
kokonas, 29
kolel fund, 32
Kolel, 42, 134
Komotini, 22n34
kon behoth, 136
Kovo, Avraam, 9
Kovo, Hayyimucho (Hayyimachi), 77, 93, 106n133
Kovo, *Rav* Asher, 10, 17, 21, 54–56, 121; death of, 134; and *Hesed 'Olam* Fund, 59; resignation of, 58, 92; and Sa'adi's excommunication, xix, 96, 102, 104, 106; and sultan's visit, 73; as wedding guest, 77
Kovo, *Rav* Yakovachi [ben Hanania], 10, 77, 138. *See also* Kovo, Yaakov
Kovo, Yaakov, 106n133. *See also* Kovo, *Rav* Yakovachi
Kremyo. *See* Crémieux
Kupat Hesed 'Olam, xxx-xxxi. See also *Hesed 'Olam* Fund
kyurdi, 37. See also *yurdi*

labor (birthing), 40
labor (work), forced, 140
Ladino, xiv, 35–36, 37, 38, 91; influences on, xxv; learning of, role of this book in, xxv; as language of the home, xxiv; as mother tongue, xxx; on Salonica's streets, xxx; transliteration of, lvix
Lag la-'Omer, 19, 86
land values, 139
landlord-tenant regulation, 121–22
Larisa. *See* Yenishehir
lazarettos, 40
lease, 121–22
leeches (medicinal), 118–19
letter delivery. *See* mail delivery
Levy, Andrew, lx
Levy, Joaquim (né Eliakim), lx
Levy, Leon David, lvi
Levy, Sadi Silvio, lvi
Lévy, Sam, xivn1, xlvi, xlvii, l, lv, lvi
Levy, Silvio (né Behor Silvio), lix
library, lv, lvi, 25n36
license to print, 66

Lipman (Lippman), Rabbi Joseph, xxxi, 60
litigation, 54, 55
lynching, 122–124

Mahmud II, Sultan, 13, 44
mail delivery, 6–7, 63
Malta [Street], 120
martial law, 124
Marx, Maurice, 80
masá, 84–86
Masonic order, 9
Matalon, *Rav* Behor, 10, 48–49
Maks. *See* Marx
meals, 7, 8. *See also* banquets; weddings, feasts after
Mehmed Ali *Pasha* (*Khedive*), 40
Mehmet Ali *Pasha* (admiral), 69–71, 73
Mehoshkim Kesef (book), 39
memma [turban], 50
memoirs, xiii
memunnim [appointed controllers], 56–59
Menashe, *Rav* Yaakov [bar Avraam], 10
Menekshe (Christos Menexes), 141
Meoré Or (book), 5
Merkado/Merkada (name), 9
mezammer, 90
militia, 140
minyan [religious quorum], 27, 100
Mishnah, quotations from: Avoth 1:14, 38; 4:21, 91
missionaries, 38
mistresses, 120
Mizrahi, Avramucho, 104–6
Mizrahi, Moshon, 28
Mizrahi, Yaakov Moshe, 91
mob violence, 97–98, 122–24
mobility, social, xxiv
modernity, xii, xiv, xxi, xxii
Modiano, Shaul, 58, 74, 81
Modiano, Yeoshua, 16, 48
Modiano, Yishak Yeoshua, 74
Modiano, Yosef Shmuel, 5
Molho, Behor, 12
Molho, *Rav* Shaul, 10–12, 17, 23, 32, 40; aversion to Turkish music, 23–29; as community representative, xli, xlii; curses and fear of, 12, 15, 18, 19; death of, 54; and excommunications, xx, 11, 14–15, 19, 22, 24, 27–29, 34; and gentile influences, xxxix, 33; and lashes, 20–21, 23, 27, 28, 43; and *Rav* Asher Kovo, 21
Monastir, 35, 73, 124
Mordoh, Chelebon, 27–28
Mordoh, Shelomo, 140–41
Moros, 30n45
Morpurgo family, xxiv, 8
Moshe ben Veniste, 64, 73
mosques, 69, 72, 73, 123
Muhammad Ali, 40n58. *See also* Mehmed Ali *Pasha*
Mulen, Jul (Jules Moulin), 123
municipality, 139
Murat, Sultan, 128–29
murder, 43
music, xxiv, xxxix, xlvii-xlviii, 27, 33; and the sultan's visit, 70–71, 91; Turkish, 23, 24–26; at weddings, 21, 51, 115–17. *See also* singing; songs
musical instruments, xxxix; tambourines, 32, 50; violins, 33
musicians, xxxvii, xxxix, xlvii, 117; female, 52, 115
mutual aid society, 94
Mutual Welfare Fund. See *Kupat Hesed 'Olam*

Nadjara, Israel, 26, 91
Nahmias, Avramachi, 34
Nahmias, Izakucho, 34. *See also* Nahmias, Yishakucho
Nahmias, *Rav* Mair [ben Yaakov], 10, 96, 134–35, 138
Nahmias, Yishakucho, 35. *See also* Nahmias, Izakucho
Nasyonal de Konstantinopla, 108
negative commandments, 8
Nehama, David, 33
Nehama, *Rav* [Hayyim Shabetai Ben Shabetai], 10, 11, 12
Nehama, Yeuda (Judah), xxx, 78–79, 84
newspapers, xiv, xxi, xlvi, 31, 108, 112; Ladino, xxi, lv, 92–93, 137, 112;

Sa'adi's, xx, xxix, xlvi, livn12, 87, 108–9. *See also under* individual names
Nigrin, Ezra, 107
Nisan (month), 121–22
Nissim Foundation, 137
nizam soldiers, 44–47, 140

occupations: banker, xv, 12, 33–35, 58n71, 120; barber, 19; book seller, 83, 109; business broker, 55, 68; butcher, 57; caretaker for the sick, 42–43; cheese maker, 57; debt collector, 62–64; doctor (physician), 6, 9, 16n31, 20, 40–42, 41, 53, 60, 66, 129; flour sifter, 85; house painter (trade), 42; insurance agent, 138–39; miller (flour dealer), 30; porter, 95; printer, 5, 38–39, 66, 77; ritual slaughterer, 8, 57, 92, 94; schoolteacher, 35–37, 61; seamstress, 9, 17; singer, 23–24, 77; stove-maker, 86; tailor, 90; tax farmer, 33–35; town crier, 32, 44, 100, 121, 137; trousseau appraiser, 20. *See also under* various communal or government posts
Old Sicily (fishermen's) synagogue, 14
Orundjik, xxxiii, 13, 52, 69, 72, 95–96, 119–21. *See also* Urumcuk
Osman [Nuri] *Pasha*, 131
Osmanlı, xxxviii, xlvii-xlviii
Ottoman Empire, European authority in, xlii
Ottoman Jewish historiography, xxxvii
Ottoman Jewry, xv, xxi-xxii; scholarship on, xxxix, liv
Ottoman social landscape, xxxviii

Palestine, 100n125. *See also* Jerusalem
Palombo, Dr., 81
Parsakaki, Dr., 6
Passover, 6, 82, 85, 119, 122
pestilence, 39, 40. *See also* epidemics
philanthropy, 16n31, 58n71, 80–81
picnics, 6, 13
Pipano, *Rav* Shelomo, 16, 25
Pirkei Avoth: 1:14, 38; 4:21, 91
pizmonim, 90
pocket watches, 76
poems, 142–48
poor, maintenance of the, 57, 60, 65, 74–75, 81–82, 134–35
Porte, the, 20, 55, 58
poverty, xxiv, xxix
power relations, and enforcement, xli-xlii
pregnancy out of wedlock (crime), 31
Preveze, 133
primogeniture, 128
printing press, 5, 83–84, 88–90, 109, 112
prison. *See* punishments, incarceration
professions. *See* occupations
progress, xxii, xxxix
prostitution, 54–55
Protestant missionaries, 38
proverbs, 37, 84, 101, 111
Psalms, recitation of, 32
punishments (communally administered), 11; banishment, 11; beatings, 54, 94; execution, 30, 31, 125; flogging, 29, 31, 43; foot beating, 27; humiliation, 55; incarceration, 11, 30, 55, 103; lashes, 21, 23, 27, 36, 43, 55. *See also* excommunication
Purim, 87, 91, 148

quarantine, 40, 42
quarrels, 11, 84
quinine, 53

rabbi, chief. *See* chief rabbi; *hahambashi*
rabbinic jurisdiction, 55–56
rabbinic power, xxxviii-xliii, 58. *See also* punishments
rabbis, blessing by, xlii, 15
railroads, 80
rain, prayers for, 100
raki, xxxvi-xxxvii, 6, 42, 51, 53, 115; distillation of, 138; as payment, 85
ram's horn, 99. See also *shofar*
rape, 43
Rashi, 36
religious observance, levels of, 6
rent, 139
resignations, 58, 64, 65, 92–93

resorts, 13
Rika, *Musyu*, 9
ritual bath, 16
Riza *Pasha*, 70–75
robes, 14, 17, 43, 46, 50, 112–13, 114–15; judicial, 21
robissa, 17
Romano, *Rav*, 10
room size, 116
Rosh a-Shana, 47
rubi, 35
Ruschuk, 130. *See also* Ruse
Ruse, 130n148
Russia, 128–32

Sa'adi a-Levi, xii, xlviii, 5–6, 9; Ashkenazi family background, xxii-xxiii; children of, 52, 107, 141; class consciousness of, xxix, l; conspiracy against, 99, 110; as debt collector, 62–64; descendants of, xivn1, xix, xxxv, xlvi, lv-lvi; excommunication of, xiv, xix, 27–29, 40, 99–101, 107; false accusations against, 93, 94–97; knowledge of Bible, 37–38, 111; knowledge of languages, 28, 65; last request, 148; as manager of communal funds and associations, xxxi, 91; memoirs of (*see* Sa'adi a-Levi's memoir); as *Osmanlı*, xlvii-xlviii; parents of, 6–9; as printer and publisher, xlv-xlvi, 24, 28, 38–39, 66, 77, 89, 108; as public reader of notices, 122; relatives of, 5–6, 37, 41–42, 45–47, 94–97, 100; schooling of, 35–37; as singer, composer, and choir director, xlvii-xlviii, 70, 71, 76, 90, 91; theological comments of, 52, 97, 104, 107, 110–11, 120, 133, 141; travel to Constantinople, 66, 92, 109; wedding of, 49–52
Sa'adi a-Levi's memoir: xix-xxii, xlv, xlix, liii, 3; as chronicle of power struggles, xli-xlii; as depiction of Jewish life in the Ottoman Empire, xxxvii-xxxviii; epilogue of, 141–42; ethnography in, l-lii; focus of, xxviii; influence of, liv; insertions in, 68, 101; insularity of, xxxiv; manuscript history of, liii-lvii; as meditation on 19th-century Salonica, xxvii-xxxvii; representations of women in, xxxv; self-disclosure in, xlv, l-li; updating of, 82n108; as voice of reform, xx, xxxviii-xliv; ways to read, xxvii
Saatli Djami, 123
Sabbath observance, 94
Sait *Pasha*, *Vali*, 72–74, 76
sales commission, 46–47
Salonica, xiv-xv, xxii, xxiii, xxvii-xxxvii, 9, 13, 22, 34, 45, 55–56, 59, 93, 96, 121; aristocracy of, 25, 59, 77; notables of, xx, xxx, xl, 74n91, 126–27, 134, 137, 141n160; precariousness of life in, lii-liii; Sephardic populations of, xxiv, 10n13, 16n31; synagogues in, 25, 47n62; sultan Abdul Medjid's visit to, 68–76, 142–48
San Stefano, 131
Saporta, *Rav* Hanania, 10, 54
Satan, 39
Sayas family, 81
scarves, 17
schoolchildren, and sultan's visit, 69–70
schools: curriculum, 35, 60, 78–79; funding, 75; reform, 59–65; tuition, 61–64. *See also* occupations, schoolteacher
scribe, 20
seashore, 6
secret door, 41, 68
Sedes, 13
selihoth, 32
Sephardi, xxii, xxv
Sephardim, 19n33
Sephardiness, xxiii
Serbia, 130
Serres, 55–56
Seven Blessings (wedding). See *shiv'a berahoth*
Seven Honorable Citizens, 10, 14, 17, 18, 73n88, 74n89
sewer, 139
sexual intercourse with a married woman (crime), 31
shackling, 11

Shaki, Behorachi, 82
Shalem, Haim, 78
Shaltiel, Moshe, 104–6
Shaltiel, Shaul, 33
shaving, 19
Shavu'oth, 6, 7, 19, 129
sheepskin rug, 36
Sheh [*Sheyh*] *ul Islam*, 128
Sheres, 55–56
Shimon Bar Yohay, 86
Shirin, 107
shiv'a berahoth, 50
shofar, 11, 14, 35; 111. *See also* ram's horn
Shulhan Gavoa (book), 28
signature (on documents), 59, 92, 100, 115, 121, 128, 135
singing, 15, 86; at funerals, 54; paraliturgical, xlvii; Sa'adi's, xlvii, 24–27, 90–91; by schoolchildren, 35, 69, 71; in Turkish, 24, 27, 29 (*see also* Turkish music); at weddings, 50–51, 77–78, 115, 116, 118. *See also* music; songs
Skilich, 66–67
Skopje, 122, 124
slavery, 140, 141
slave-wife, 119
smoking on the Sabbath, 94
Smyrna, xxxii, 7. *See also* Izmir
social class. *See* class, social
social mobility, xxiv
Society of Good Deeds, 92, 94, 98
songs, xxxiv, 23–26, 70, 76, 142–48. *See also* singing
sons versus daughters, 53
Soriano, *Rav* Avraam, 10
sultan. *See* Abdul Aziz; Abdul Medjid; Abdul Hamit II; Mahmud II; Murat
sultana, 129
superstitions, 39
synagogues, xxxii, 6, 14, 47, 86–88, 115; and excommunication, 14, 28; Sa'adi's singing in, 90–91; and weddings, 25, 50, 77, 115

tableware, 117
talmid haham, 22–23, 40, 55, 83
Talmud Tora, former, 137. *See also* Great *Talmud Tora*
Talmud, 37
Tanzimat (Reforms), xv, xxxvii, xli, xlii, 106n134
taxes, xxx, xl, 59, 134; rabbinical control of, xv, xix, xxxix, xl. See also *gabela*; gabelle
tenants, 121–22
terror, 13
testimony, false, 95
theft, 22
Thessaly, 132, 133
Tiano family, 81
Tiano, Moshe Yishak, 73
time, European versus Turkish, 126
tobacco, xxviii, 94, 95
tombstones, 136, 140
Torre Blanka, 45n60. *See also* Bloody Tower; White Tower
torture, 31
trades. *See* occupations
turban, 46, 50–51, 112–13. See also *memma*
Turkey, international relations, 127–34
Turkish (language), xxxviii, 74
Turkish bath, 42, 114, 116
Turkish music, xlvii, 23–27, 32. *See also* singing, in Turkish
Turks, commerce with, 16

ulema, 128
Urumcuk, 13n25. *See also* Orundjik

Vahan *efendi*, 126
Vali Pasha (governor of Salonica), 14, 15, 29, 30, 126; intervention of, xlii, 12, 103, 106, 123–24; and sultan's visit, 68–69 (*see also* Sait *Pasha*). *See also* Eshref *Pasha*
Valide [Sultan's Mother], 128, 129
Varsano, Behor, 20–21
Varsano, Yaakov, 21
Viennese, 82
vizir, 73
Vlestino, 133

wars: of April 17, 1897, 132; Greek-Turkish War, 132–34; between Turkey and Russia, 127–32
wealthy, the, 12, 13, 32
weddings, 21, 23, 25, 33, 49–52, 76–78, 114; dancing, 117; feasts after, 116–18; music, 117; of rabbis, 77
weights (in commerce), 94
White Tower, 45. *See also* Bloody Tower; *Torre Blanka*
widows, 12, 53, 136
wine, 15, 20, 42, 117; *azarado*, 9–10; price of, 11; tax on, xxxix, 11–12, 57, 92
witness, false, 94
womanizing, 120
women, xxxv–xxxvi, xxxix, 20, 85, 120, 128, 140; clothing of, 16–18, 113–14; and weddings, 49–51, 116–18. *See also* daughters versus sons; *kokonas*; slave-wife

Yanina. *See* Ioannina
yarsayat, 86
yatagans, 140
Yenishehir, 113
Yeoshua, Merkado, 33
Yeshilkoy, 131
yeshiva, 11n17, 25, 56, 81n104, 81n106, 137
Yosef, David, 16, 49
Yosef dela Reyna, 37
yurdi, 16–18, See also *kyurdi*
Yusuf Izzeddin, 128, 129
Yusuf *Pasha*, 68–75

Zohar, 25n36, 83–84, 86, 87